Arthur William Crawley-Boevey

The Cartulary and Historical Notes of the Cistercian Abbey of Flaxley

Otherwise Called Dene Abbey in the County of Gloucester

Arthur William Crawley-Boevey

The Cartulary and Historical Notes of the Cistercian Abbey of Flaxley
Otherwise Called Dene Abbey in the County of Gloucester

ISBN/EAN: 9783337059743

Printed in Europe, USA, Canada, Australia, Japan

Cover: Foto ©ninafisch / pixelio.de

More available books at **www.hansebooks.com**

THE
Cartulary

AND HISTORICAL NOTES OF THE

Cistercian Abbey of Flaxley,

OTHERWISE CALLED

Dene Abbey,

IN THE

COUNTY OF GLOUCESTER.

BY

A. W. CRAWLEY-BOEVEY, ESQ., M.A.,
BOMBAY CIVIL SERVICE.

The impression is limited to 45 copies royal 4to., and 100 copies demy 4to.

All rights reserved.

EXETER:
Privately printed for the Author by
WILLIAM POLLARD AND CO., NORTH STREET.
1887.

INTRODUCTION.

In the following notes an attempt has been made to weave into a connected narrative the fcattered references which may be found in the public records relating to the Ciftercian Abbey of Flaxley in Gloucefterfhire. Founded within the limits of the royal Foreft of Dean during the reign of Stephen, this Abbey occupied in many refpects an exceptional pofition. As formally notified in the Charter of Richard I., it was confidered to be fpecially under the protection of the fovereign, and all its more important rights and privileges were derived from the favor of the crown. King John and King Edward III. appear to have paid frequent vifits to Flaxley Abbey, probably for the purpofe of hunting. The vifits of the former are recorded in the well-known "Itinerary of King John." King Edward III. has left an important record of his vifits to the Abbey in the fhape of a formal deed granting to the monks a fum of £36. 9s. 1d. from the newly reclaimed land in the Foreft, on account of injuries inflicted by the deer, and of fpecial expenfes incurred by the frequent royal vifits. The privileges granted to the monks within Foreft limits appear to have brought them into conftant collifion with the Foreft authorities, who were under the control of the Conftable of St. Briavell's Caftle, and the fovereign appears to have been conftantly invoked to protect and enforce the privileges of the Flaxley monks within Foreft limits. To this circumftance are to be attributed the numerous references to Flaxley Abbey in the Clofe Rolls, confifting chiefly of writs and orders addreffed to the Foreft authorities on behalf of the monks. The Abbot of Flaxley was fummoned to Parliament on feveral occafions in the reign of Edward I., and is noticed as being prefent at the burial, in Tewkefbury Abbey, of Gilbert de Clare, in 1230; and at the fettlement of a difpute between the Abbots of Margan and Caerleon in 1256. The only important public event with which the hiftory of Flaxley Abbey feems to have been affociated, was the infurrection of Hubert de Burgh in 1234. Several extracts from the Clofe Rolls shew that Flaxley Abbey was reforted to as an afylum by feveral of Richard, Earl Marfhal's, followers; and a hue and cry was on one occasion raised to surround the Abbey, and prevent them from escaping. The extracts referred to throw an interesting light on the social condition of the times. The picture of the Abbey surrounded by men armed with bows and arrows and other weapons, keeping watch and ward at the summons of the Sheriff; the collision between the Abbot's and the Sheriff's men; the seizure of the Abbot's horses, and the excommunication of the Constable of St. Briavell's and his men by Hugh Foliot, Bishop of Hereford; the monks' appeal to the King, and the orders received to recompense the Abbot for damage to the hedges, and the loss of his horses and equipments; all these incidents are alluded to, and make up a highly interesting and characteristic picture of the times.

With the exception of the royal visits above alluded to, and the stirring events connected with the insurrection of Hubert de Burgh, the history of Flaxley Abbey seems to have been of an uneventful kind. Of the possessions and privileges of the monks, a tolerably full account is given in the notes. Henry II. confirmed to the monks the grant of the Valley of Castiard, where the Abbey was founded, and all the donations of Roger, Earl of Hereford, besides all easements in the royal Forest—viz., common of pasture, tithes of chestnuts, a moveable iron forge, and as much wood and timber as they required. The Abbey Cartulary contains a full account of the principal private gifts and benefactions made to Flaxley Abbey until the middle of the 13th century, when the Cartulary was probably written. By Popes Celestine III. and Alexander III. the Flaxley monks were granted special immunity from tithes.

The Cartulary further abounds in information of an interesting and valuable kind. Besides furnishing an important list of private benefactors, the Cartulary contains several statements of accounts, shewing the sums paid to the monks by their tenants, their various services, etc. A statement headed "Redditus Cerae," shews all the charitable grants to the Abbey of wax; another statement furnishes a most interesting catalogue of the Abbey Library. In the Cartulary are recorded the names of a large number of witnesses, most of whom were probably persons of local influence and reputation, and of whom this Cartulary is perhaps the most important evidence now remaining. The deeds recorded shew how the various special wants of the Abbey were provided for by private munificence: how Gilbert of Monmouth and Berta, his wife, granted to the Abbey and monks of Dene 5 shillings from the proceeds of the Mill of Hope (Longhope), for the purchase of wine for the celebration of the Mass, with a stipulation that if the mill should

Introduction. v.

fall down, the sum was to be paid out of cuftoms dues of the Vill of Hope, and that any furplus might be devoted to the purpofes of the Abbey Library and the repair of books. It tells how Adam of Blakeney, and his wife, Bafilia, granted to the monks 2 shillings of annual rent, to be paid to the Sacriftan of the Abbey every year on the Feaft of St. Michael, for the purchafe of oil for the three lamps that burned before the three Altars at High Mafs. How Roger, of Pultun, and his wife, Margaret, affigned to the monks 5 fhillings of rent for the purchafe of bed-clothes for poor guefts at the Abbey; and how Ernaldus of Cutberley granted to the Abbey all his land between the two bridges of the Severn at Gloucefter, for the repair of the Abbey Hofpice.

Amongft other matters of local intereft, the burning of Neweham (Newnham) is fpecially referred to in a deed executed with the monks by Galfrid· Hugelin; the date of this deed is not fpecially recorded, but bearing in mind the period when the Cartulary appears to have been prepared, the deed referred to was probably executed about the end of the 12th century.

From the additional information collected in thefe notes, a revifed and more complete lift of Flaxley Abbots than any lift hitherto publifhed has now been prepared. Two of the earlieft Abbots of Dene are briefly alluded to in the Waverley Annals, which relates that on the occafion of the visitation of Ciftercian Abbeys in 1187, Abbot Waleran of Dene refigned, and was succeeded by Abbot Alan, formerly monk of Bordefley. The Cartulary of the Abbey has feveral references to Abbot Alan, and to Abbot Richard, neither of whom have been noticed by such eminent authorities as Browne Willis, Tanner, or Stevens. In Bifhop Cantelupe's Regifter at Hereford, Abbot William is referred to as having been inftalled circ. A.D. 1277. In the Bodleian Library there is a mutilated deed of Exchange of benefices between "—— Berkeley, Abbas de Flaxley, rector ecclefiæ parochialis de Rodmarton," and "Nicholas Rewys, vicarius ecclefiæ parochialis de Weftbury" in May, 1476; the deed is attefted by John Rolues, public notary. None of the five Abbots named have hitherto been noticed by antiquaries, and the following lift of Flaxley Abbots, though obviously ftill imperfect, is more complete than any lift hitherto publifhed :—

1. Waleran	refigned	1187	'33 Hen. II.
2. Alan	elected	1187	do.
3. Richard	,,	(circ.) 1200	1 John.
4. William	,,	Feb. 1277 (?)	5 Edw. I.
5. Nicholas	,,	1288	16 Edw. I.

6. William de Rya	,,	17 Oct. 1314	8 Edw. II.
7. Richard Peyto	,,	6 July 1372	46 Edw. III.
8. William	,,	14 April 1426	4 Hen. VI.
9. —— Berkeley	,,	1476	16 Edw. IV.
10. John	,,	16 Dec. 1509	1 Hen. VIII.
11. William Beawdley	,,	1528	19 Hen. VIII.
12. Thomas Were	,,	1532	23 Hen. VIII.

Special attention has been directed to the task of fixing as accurately as possible the dates of the foundation and suppression of the Abbey. As regards the foundation, the evidence seems to point to the latter end of Stephen's reign—between the years 1148 and 1154—as the most probable date, but it must be admitted that the evidence leaves much to be desired. One new fact of considerable interest and importance, as bearing on the probable date of the foundation of the Abbey, has, however, I think, been fairly established. It may be stated with tolerable certainty that Flaxley Abbey was founded by Roger, eldest son of Earl Milo, to commemorate the death of his father who was killed while hunting in the Forest of Dean on Christmas Eve 1143. Leland, writing shortly after the suppression of the Abbey, related the tradition that a *brother* of Roger, Earl of Hereford, had been killed with an arrow, "in the very place where the Abbey since was made." I have shewn I think in my notes strong reasons for believing that Leland's tradition has been wrongly associated with one of Earl Roger's brothers instead of with his father, Earl Milo, who is known to have met his death in the manner described by Leland. Assuming then this fact to be sufficiently proved, that Flaxley Abbey was founded by Roger to commemorate the death of Earl Milo on Christmas Eve 1143, it will follow with certainty that Flaxley Abbey was founded some time after that date. Reasons have been adduced for thinking that Gilbert Foliot was probably the Bishop of Hereford, referred to by Leland, who "holp much to the buildinge of Flexeley." Gilbert Foliot succeeded Robert de Betun as Bishop of Hereford, on the death of the latter in 1148, and if it may be assumed, on the evidence now put forward, that Gilbert Foliot was the Bishop referred to by Leland, it will follow that Flaxley Abbey was founded after 1148. The earliest charter granted to Flaxley Abbey after the foundation, purports to be granted by Henry, then Duke of Normandy, some time before his accession to the throne of England; and the foundation of the Abbey would thus apparently fall some time between

Introduction.

1148 and 1154. Although the evidence does not appear to admit of any nearer conclusion being drawn, it is satisfactory to be able to shew with tolerable certainty the approximate date of the foundation. On this point I have shewn that the local historians differ widely in opinion, but no serious attempt has, it would seem, been made to examine the evidence, or to form any probable conclusion regarding the exact date.

Of the date of the suppression, or of the events which accompanied it, no direct evidence seems to be on record. Edward Fox, ex-Provost of King's College, Cambridge, was Bishop of Hereford in 1535, and was apparently in office at the time that Flaxley Abbey was suppressed; but in his original Register at Hereford, no notice of the suppression, or of the events that accompanied the dissolution, is to be found. The Abbey was summarily suppressed amongst the lesser monasteries early in 1536, and in the following year, a grant of the Abbey and the estates was made by patent to Sir William Kingston, dated 26th March, 28 Henry VIII. (1537). This grant contains a clause that Sir William Kingston and his heirs were to hold all the premises "as fully as Thomas Were, the late Abbot, held the same on the 4th day of February, 27th Henry VIII. (1536)." The date mentioned is understood to be the actual date of the suppression of Flaxley Abbey, and Sir William Kingston was thus invested, by the terms of the grant, with all the rights, titles, privileges, etc., which were enjoyed by the last Abbot, Thomas Were, on the actual date of the dissolution.

With these few introductory remarks, the notes may be left to speak for themselves. That they contain many imperfections I am well aware, but I have, at all events, collected a large amount of very interesting materials; and in attempting to give a connected account of the various scattered references to the Cistercian Monastery of Flaxley, in Gloucestershire, have done my best to supplement the very meagre accounts of this house which are given in the County histories and in Dugdale's Monasticon.

To Sir John Maclean, F.S.A., I am especially indebted for most valuable advice and assistance in connection with the preparation of these notes. It is mainly owing to his cordial encouragement that I was first induced to undertake the present work; and without his kind assistance and support, I could scarcely have hoped to accomplish, during a brief absence from India, a somewhat formidable holiday task. My obligations to Mr. Samuel Gael and to Mr. T. Fitzroy Fenwick, of Thirlestaine House, Cheltenham, I have warmly acknowledged in the notes. The publication of the Flaxley

Cartulary makes, it is hoped, a useful addition to the exiſting materials for a new county hiſtory, and will doubtleſs attract much intereſt and attention.

Mr. H. C. Beddoe, Regiſtrar to the Biſhop of Hereford, has given me every aſſiſtance in examining the original Biſhops' Regiſters at Hereford, and his kindneſs and courteſy I am anxious to acknowledge. The Rev. R. Hall, Vicar of Flaxley (1880), has materially aſſiſted me with ſeveral intereſting notes and illuſtrations; and Mr. Edmund Oliver has alſo given me ſome valuable information and ſuggeſtions. For the illuſtrations, I am indebted to my brother, Mr. Edward B. Crawley-Boevey. I think that they will be found to add materially to the intereſt and value of the preſent notes.

A. W. C-B.

FLAXLEY ABBEY.

PART I.

THE FOUNDATION.

The Ciftercian Abbey of Flaxley or Flexeley, otherwife called Dene Abbey or the Abbey of the Bleffed Mary of Dene, was founded during the reign of King Stephen between the years 1148 and 1154 by Roger fon of Milo Fizwalter Earl of Hereford. Regarding the exact date of the foundation of the Abbey the local hiftorians appear to differ widely in opinion. Sir Robert Atkyns[1] fpeaks of the Abbey being founded temp. Henry I, and on this point he is followed by Rudder,[2] Stevens[3] and Cox.[4] In Bifhop Tanner's Notitia Monaftica[5] the foundation of the Abbey is mentioned as occurring "temp. R. Steph.," no attempt being made to fix the exact date. Tanner's note in the point, fee below, is inferted in the laft edition (1825) of Dugdale's Monafticon Anglicanum,[6] the editors apparently concurring in the view that Flaxley Abbey was founded temp. Stephen. Archdeacon Rudge[7] follows the fame authority in the account given of Flaxley in his County Hiftory publifhed in 1803.

[1] Atkyns' Hiftory of Gloucefterfhire, p. 228.
[2] Rudder's Hiftory of Gloucefterfhire, p. 449.
[3] Stevens' Supplement, Vol. ii, p. 48.
[4] A Topographical, Ecclefiaftical and Natural Hiftory of Gloucefterfhire, by Rev. Thos. Cox. 1700.
[5] Tanner's Notitia Monaftica under the head of "Gloucefterfhire xi. Flexeley or Dene." Reprinted by James Nofmith, M.A., 1787. Tanner has the following note—"Sir Robert Atkyns makes this Abbey to have been founded temp. Hen. I; but I have continued it as in the former edition, Roger not being Earl of Hereford till 9 Steph. as Dugdale's Baronage, i, 538."
[6] Dugdale's Monafticon Anglicanum (1825) Vol. v, p. 588.
[7] Rudge's Hiftory of Gloucefterfhire, Vol. ii, p. 94.

Bigland[1] gives 1140 as the approximate date of the foundation of the Abbey; and this date has alfo been accepted by Fofbroke[2] and Nicholls[3] in their notices of Flaxley Abbey. In Duncumb's Herefordfhire[4] the founding of the Abbey by Roger fecond Earl of Hereford is mentioned as having taken place after the acceffion of Henry II in 1154.

The difficulty of determining the exact date arifes, of courfe, from the very fcanty notices of this foundation which have been handed down. In fact the only direct evidence on the fubject feems to be derived from Leland, who in his Itinerary gives the following account :—

"Rogerus Erle of Hereforde founder of Flaxley in the Foreft of Deene. There was a brother of Rogers Erle of Hereforde that was kylled withe an arowe in huntynge in the very place where the Abbay fyns was made. There was a table of this matier hanggid up in the Abbay Churche of Flexeley. There was a Byfhope of Hereford that holp much to the building of Flexeley."[5]

This tradition, related by Leland, has hitherto been accepted by all the local hiftorians without comment. But the tradition as it ftands seems to

[1] Bigland's Hiftory of Gloucefterfhire, p. 582.
[2] Fofbroke's Hiftory of Gloucefterfhire, Vol. ii, p. 177.
[3] Nicholls' Foreft of Dean, p. 176.
[4] Duncumb's Herefordfhire, Vol. i, p. 126.
[5] See Leland's Itinerary by Thomas Hearne, M.A., Vol. viii, p. 36

Leland vifited Gloucefterfhire fhortly after the final diffolution of the Monafteries in 1539. His "Itinerary" contains an interefting account of the various places in Gloucefterfhire visited by him. He mentions the Priory of St. Ofwald as ftanding "north north-weft from Gloucefter Abbey upon Severne ripe." Llanthony Priory is also mentioned as ftanding "upon the left ripe of Severne a little beneath Gloucefter." Newnham, Auft Cliff, Berkeley, and Thornbury are all alluded to in turn, and the narrative is then continued by Leland as follows :—

"As soon as I paffed over the arme of Severne at the weft end of Gloucefter, I entered into the foreft of Dene, the which thence downward alonge Severne into the mouth of Wye river (where it goeth into Severne) and on the other part again from Monmouth to the poynt of Wye is divided from Wales by the left ripe of Wye river.

"The soyle of the Foreft of Dene for the moft part is more fruitful of wood and graffe than of corne, and yet there is good corne sufficient for the inhabitants of it.

"The ground is plentiful of iron mines and divers forges be there to make iron.

"Flaxley Abbey of White Monks stood in Dene foreft a 5 or 6 miles from Gloucefter.

"Mr. Bainham dwelleth at Weftbury in the Foreft of Dene 6 miles from Gloucefter."

It will be noticed that Leland fpeaks of Flaxley Abbey in the paft tenfe, fhowing that it had already been diffolved. The actual date of the diffolution of this abbey was 4th Feb., 1536. The preface to the Itinerary ftates that the book was "Begunne about 1538, 30 Hen. VIII," and was infcribed to the king as a new year's gift, 38 Henry VIII, 1546-47.

require explanation, for while nothing is known of the alleged death while hunting of any of Earl Roger's *brothers*,[1] all of whom are tolerably well known, it is related by several of the old chroniclers that Milo Earl of Hereford, father of Earl Roger, did meet his death in the way described by Leland, while hunting in the Foreſt of Dean on Chriſtmas Eve 1143.[2]

Account of Earl Milo's death by John of Hexham and Gervase of Dover.

The circumſtances of Earl Milo's death are thus deſcribed in the Hiſtory of Simeon of Durham, continued by John Prior of Hexham, Twyſden Collection : page 273, line 50.

" Obiit Milo Comes Herefordiæ in vigilia natalis Domini venatui inſiſtens, et sagitta tranſfixus."

In the chronicles of Gervaſe of Dover, Twyſden collection, page 1359, line 13, Earl Milo's death is referred to in the following terms :—

" Nam Milo Comes Herefordenſis ſpecialis ipſius conſiliariis morte preventus vitam finivit."

Again in the Geſta Stephani is given the following account :—

Page 16, " dum cervis inſidiaretur a comite pectus sagitta tranſfixus sine mora interiit." And again at page 101 :—

" Dum in sacro vigiliarum nativitatis Domini die, cervis inſidiaretur, a milite sagittam imprudenter in cervum dirigente pectus tranſforatus, ſine penitentiæ fructu miſerabiliter occubuit."

Dugdale, in his account of the Earls of Hereford at page 536, Vol. i, of the " Baronage," has quoted from Gervaſe of Dover and John of Hexham, and gives the following account of Earl Milo's death :—

" But at length being wounded by the ſhot of an arrow in hunting upon

---

[1] By his marriage with Sybill daughter of Bernard de Newmarch Earl Milo had five sons :—1. Roger, 2. Walter, 3. Mahel or Michel, 4. Henry, 5. William ; and three daughters, Margery m. Humphrey de Bohun, Berta m. Philip de Braoſe, and Lucie m. Herbert FitzHerbert. Earl Roger died, it is ſuppoſed, ſometime in 1155; and his four brothers all dying ſ.p., their three ſiſters ſucceeded to the family eſtates which were partitioned between them.

[2] As regards the exact date of Earl Milo's death I have followed the author of Annales de Theokeſberia, who gives 1143 as the date, viz.:—

" MCXLIII. Innocentius Papa obiit et Celeſtinus succeſſit obiitque cui Lucius succeſſit. Obiit que Milo comes Herefordiæ."—Annal. de Theokes. Rolls Series, p. 46.

The same date 1143 is given in Nicholas' Hiſtoric Peerage as the date of Milo's death, ſee p. 246.

Dugdale gives the date as Chriſtmas 1144, see quotation in the text below ; but there is diſtinct evidence that Roger was ſtyled " Earl of Hereford " in public inſtruments at leaſt as early as 1144— ſee page 9, note 1. 1143 ſeems therefore to be the more probable date.

Xmas eve anno 1144, 9 Steph., he departed this life and was buried in the Chapter Houfe at Llanthony."

From the paffages above quoted there would feem to be abundant evidence in fupport of, the accepted account of Earl Milo's death ; and it feems difficult to refift the conclufion that the tradition of Earl Milo's death has been wrongly affociated by Leland with one of Earl Milo's fons inftead of with Earl Milo himfelf. That Flaxley Abbey was founded by Earl Roger to commemorate the fate of his father, feems to be, under the circumftances, probable enough ; and according to Leland's tradition the fite of the Abbey marks the very fpot where Earl Milo met with his death under the circumftances above defcribed.

Earl Milo Excommunicated by the Bishop of Hereford.

Earl Milo at the time of his death is ftated to have been under fentence of excommunication pronounced on him and his followers by Robert de Betun Bifhop of Hereford for feizing the goods and lands of that See. The following account is given in the Gefta Stephani of the circumftances under which this excommunication was pronounced. Earl Milo having revolted from his allegiance, and having attached himfelf to the caufe of the Emprefs Matilda, collected large forces at Gloucefter for the purpofe of harraffing the king. For the maintenance of thefe troops he endeavoured to impofe new exactions, but met with refiftance at the hands of the Bifhop of Hereford (Robert de Betun) who boldly withftood his unlawful demands, and at laft threatened him with excommunication. This so exafperated Milo that he immediately invaded the Bifhopric and all its lands and poffeffions, whereupon the excommunication was pronounced.

Bifhop Robert de Betun, who thus withftood Earl Milo, was himfelf an ex-prior of the mother houfe of Llanthony in Monmouthfhire. It was at his interceffion that Earl Milo was induced to become the patron and founder of the new Llanthony Priory near Gloucefter. The date of the foundation as given in Abbot Frouceftre's MS. Chronicle, is the 8th of the Kalends of June (May 25) A.D. 1136.

Controversy regarding the burial of Earl Milo.

The occafion of Earl Milo's death gave rife to a controverfy[1] between the monks of St. Peter's Abbey in Gloucefter, and the Canons of the newly

[1] For an account of this controverfy fee original letters from the Gloucefter Cathedral Regifter A, printed in App. to the Introd. of Hift. Mon. S. Petri, Glouc., Vol. i, pp. lxxv. to lxxvii., and W. H. Hart's Introduction to Glouc. Cart., p. xxxiii.

founded Llanthony Priory, regarding the place of burial. The controverfy was finally clofed in favour of Llanthony, and Earl Milo's body was furrendered for burial to the Canons of Llanthony Priory on the fpecial condition that Earl Roger and his wife "and all their heirs for ever and the lord of Gloucefter Caftle whofoever he might be, fhould wherever they died be buried within the walls of St. Peter's."[1]

Flaxley Abbey having been founded by Roger Earl of Hereford to commemorate the death of his father Earl Milo, the hiftory of this foundation is feen to be intimately connected with the family hiftory of the Earls of Hereford, and it will perhaps be convenient at this place to give a brief fketch of the hiftory of this family which played a very prominent part in the hiftory of thofe times.

Dugdale (Baronage, vol. i, p. 536) relates that Walter, Conftable of England, the founder of the family, erected the Caftle of Gloucefter upon his own demefne lands, and built alfo the Caftles of Briftol and Rochefter and the Tower of London. He had the cuftody of the Caftles of Gloucefter and Hereford. He endowed the Canons of Llanthony in Wales with a moiety of his Lordfhip of Beryntone; and in his old age taking the habit of Canon Regular died in Llanthony and was buried in the Chapter Houfe.

Milo FitzWalter is ftated to have been an expert foldier, and one of the chief counfellors of Henry I, who gave to him in marriage Sybill[2] the eldeft daughter of Bernard de Newmarch, Lord of Brecknock, by his wife Nefta the daughter of Griffin ap Leweline.

On the occafion of this marriage Milo received from Henry I the Honour

---

[1] The manufcript from the Surrenden Collection printed at p. 364; Vol. iii., Trans. Brift. and Glouc. Arch. Soc., ftates that Earl Roger is buried in the Chapter Houfe of Llanthony Priory clofe by his father Earl Milo. But Leland ftates in his Itinerary that Earl Roger is buried in the Chapter Houfe of St. Peter's at Gloucefter, where there is an infcription to his memory. Leland's ftatement on the point is quoted by Rudder (p. 127 and 179). According to the ftipulation made at the time of Earl Milo's burial, Earl Roger and his wife fhould apparently have been buried at Gloucefter, and the memorial infcription in the Chapter Houfe makes it probable that Leland's account is correct. Earl Roger fhortly before his death became a monk of St. Peter's Monaftery at Gloucefter, and allufions to this circumftance will be found at pp. 88 and 331, Vol. i. of Hift. et Cart. of St. Peter's Monaftery at Gloucefter. The exact date of Earl Roger's death is involved in fome uncertainty. It is fuppofed to have occurred fome time during the year 1155.—See Editorial Notes at pp. 366 and 367, Trans. Briftol and Glouceftershire Arch. Soc., Vol iii, under paper relating to St. Briavells Caftle.

[2] The record of this marriage will be found amongft the Royal Charters of Henry I in the Duchy of Lancafter Records, see Regifter 1121, Wincheftcr. Grant to Milo de Glouc. of Sibilla daughter of Bernard de Novo Mercato in marriage, pp. 6, 7, 8. P R.O.

of Brecknock, and all the lands which his father held in capite, together with the office of Conftable of the King's Court.

Dugdale further relates that on the death of Henry I, Milo " expecting through the intereft he had with Maud the King's fole daughter and heir, to attain to the Earldom of Hereford, he fubtilly ufed all his power on her behalf and went with fome ftrength to his caftle at Glouceſter, where fhe then was, and fetched her with honour thence."

From Stephen, however, Milo obtained a reftitution in fee of the whole Honour of Glouceſter with the cuftody of the Tower and Caftle there, which he had held as his patrimony in the time of Henry I, and likewife the Barony of Brecknock with all the offices and lands whereof he was poffeffed in the time of Henry I.[1]

Notwithſtanding this, in the fourth year of Stephen's reign when Maud the Emprefs landed, Milo deferted Stephen, and repairing to her at Briftol acknowledged her for his fovereign, attended her to Glouceſter, where he received her very honourably and did homage to her.

Grant to Earl Milo of St. Briavell's Castle and Forest of Dean.

On this occafion the Emprefs Maud beftowed on him St. Briavell's Caftle in Gloucefterfhire, and the whole Foreft of Dene, which so obliged him to her that he entered into a league with Robert Earl of Glouceſter her brother to aid him in keeping his caftles and all his inheritance.[2]

Again after the capture of Stephen in the battle of Lincoln a confpiracy was formed againſt the Emprefs Maud who fled for protection to Milo.

---

[1] The record of this grant I cannot find. Amongſt the Royal Charters of King Stephen tranfcribed in the Regiſter of the Duchy of Lancaſter Records are the following :—
(a) Confirmation to Earl Milo of grant made by Hen. I to Walter the Conſtable of the land of Edric the fon of Ketel.
(b) Grant to Earl Milo of all the land which the Biſhop of Exeter held in Glouceſter and had given to Milo.

[2] No record of the alleged grant can be found in the "Regiſter of Royal Charters;" from the Duchy of Lancaſter Records, but the following grants of the Emprefs to Earl Milo are recorded :—
(a) "1141. St. Albans. Grant from the Emprefs Maud to Milo de Glouceſter of the houfe which belonged to Gregory the Sewer at Weſtminſter," pp. 19, 20.
(b) "1141. Oxford. Grant from the Emprefs Maud to Milo Earl of Hereford of the Caftle and Honor of Abergavenny," pp. 20, 21.
The Charter of the Emprefs creating Milo Earl of Hereford is the only other grant between thefe parties of which a record can be found.

Earl Milo created Earl of Hereford.

On this occasion she created him Earl of Hereford; her charter of creation bearing date at Oxford on the Feast of St. James the Apostle, giving thereby to him and his heirs the Castle of Hereford with the third penny of the rent of that county, and the third penny of the pleas of the county; the lordships of Hawerdine, Luggewardine and Wilton, all in that shire; the Haies of Hereford, and the Forest of Trivele.

This charter is printed in extenso in Rymer's Fœdera, Vol. i, p. 8; and also in Vol. v, Appendix v, to the Report on the Dignity of a Peer of the Realm. At Vol. ii, p. 140, of this Report will be found the opinion of the Lords' Committee regarding this charter of the Empress. It was considered that the grant to Milo of the dignity of an Earl was a distinct grant from the grant of the landed property given by the same instrument.

The grant of the third penny of the county, which seems to have been the ancient fee of the Saxon Earl, renders it probable, in the opinion of the Committee, that as a dignity the title of Earl after the Conquest bore some resemblance to that of the Saxon Earl, though the Saxon Earl had official duties which did not belong to an Earl at the time of the creation of Milo. From the language of the charter the Lords' Committee inferred that the dignity granted to Milo was personal.[1]

Of Earl Milo's son and successor Roger, founder of Flaxley Abbey, Dugdale relates that he *succeeded* to the Earldom of Hereford, and having married Cecilie daughter of Pain FitzJohn, one of the chief counsellors of Henry I, and then lord of Ewyas, had a confirmation[2] from King Stephen of the whole inheritance of the same Pain, and likewise of all those lands he had with his daughter in marriage, which were part of the honor of Hugh de Lacy.

---

[1] On this point Sir John Maclean, F.S.A., remarks—"This would seem to be confirmed by subsequent events. Roger was *created* Earl by Henry II. He did not succeed, and was not succeeded by his brothers."

[2] The record of this confirmation is preserved amongst the Duchy of Lancaster Records in the Register of Royal Charters, and stands as follows:—

1137—1153.—Marlborough. Grant from King Stephen to Roger the son of Milo de Gloucester and Cecily his wife, daughter of Pain FitzJohn, in fee and inheritance of all the purchases which the said Pain held on the day of his death, and the marriage portion which he gave his daughter out of the honor of Hugh de Lacy, and all his rights in that honor, and moreover all that the said Pain gave his wife Sibilla in dower: pp. 29, 30, 31. P.R.O.

Charter of Henry II to Roger Earl of Hereford.

Shortly after the acceffion of Henry Ii in 1154 a charter was granted by him to Roger Earl of Hereford reciting and confirming the various pofleffions inherited by him.

This charter is fet out at length in Vol. v, App. v, of the Lords' Report on the Dignity of a Peer of the Realm above referred to. The following are the moft important clauses:—

"Sciatis nos reddidiffe et conceffiffe Rogero Comiti Herefordiæ in feudo et hereditate fibi et heredibus fuis ad tenendum de me et de meis heredibus totum feudum Comitis Milonis patris fui, et totum feudum Bernardi de Novo Mercato ubicunque fit. Infuper etiam dedi et conceffi omnia dominica quæ rex Henricus avus meus habuit intra Sabrinam et Wayem in Gloceſtrſiſ excepto caftello de Sancto Briavello, et villa de Neweham et forefta de Dena. Hæc ſ funt illa dominia videlicet Minftredwrd et Redlen et Aura et Dymoc, cum omnibus appendiciis fuis. Et ex altera parte Sabrinæ dedi ei et conceffi Ciltebam cum omnibus appendiciis fuis pro lx*li* terræ. Preterea dedi ei et conceffi motâ Hereford cum toto Caftello, et tercium denarium redditus burgi Herefordiæ quicquid unquam reddat et tercium denarium placitorum tocius comitatus Herefordiæ unde feci eum comitem."[1]

This charter of Henry II to Roger Earl of Hereford is recited in a fubfequent charter granted by King John to Henry de Bohun. Rot. Cart. 1 Joh. p. 2, m. 6. Both the charters granted to Roger Earl of Hereford and to Henry de Bohun were difcuffed by the Lords' Committee, which expreffed the opinion that in both cafes the Earldom of Hereford was a fpecial creation, and that their dignities as Earls were not by reafon of the tenure of lands.

The words of the Lords' Committee on this point are as follows:—

"The words 'unde eum fecimus Comitem Hereford, in the Charter of John to Henry de Bohun, and the words 'unde feci cum comitem' in the Charter of Henry II to Roger son of Milo, feem to import that both Roger fon of Milo and Henry de Bohun were created Earls; and that their dignities as Earls were not by reafon of tenure of lands or of the County of Hereford as an Earldom. King Henry may have difputed the grant of his mother to Milo, and in that cafe his own grant to Roger fon of Milo, though made to Roger and his heirs, may have been confidered as an original grant confined

---

[1] From Rot. Cart. 1 Joh. p. 177 in Turr. Lond., printed at length in Vol. v, App. v, of the Lords' Report on the Dignity of a Peer.

to heirs of the body of Roger efpecially with refpect to the dignity of Earl as the brothers of Roger did not fucceed to the dignity."[1]

The ftatement made by Dugdale, that St. Briavell's Caftle in Gloucefterfhire and the whole Foreft of Dene was beftowed by the Emprefs Maud on Earl Milo, is apparently bafed on fome document in the Duchy of Lancafter Records. The reference quoted by Dugdale is taken " Ex magno Regiftro in officio ducatus Lanc." I have made a search for this document,[2] but without fuccefs; and in the abfence of the original evidence, the alleged grant to Earl Milo of the Foreft of Dene and of St. Briavell's Caftle muft be accepted for the prefent on Dugdale's fole authority.

[1] The Charter granted by Hen. II to Roger Earl of Hereford is undated; but the approximate date is fixed by Mr. Eyton as about March 1155, while the Court was ftill at Weftminfter. (Court, Houfehold and Itinerary of King Hen. II by Rev. R. W. Eyton, M.A., 1878, page 9.) The death of Milo Earl of Hereford and father of Roger occurred as before fhown, on Chriftmas Eve, 1143, according to the author of the Annals of Tewkefbury. There feems to be diftinct evidence that Roger, fon and fucceffor of Earl Milo, at once affumed the title of Earl of Hereford on his father's death, for in vol. i, p. 311 of Cart. et Hift. Mon. S. Petri, Glouc., is recorded a formal deed of exchange, executed 1144 "in præfentia domini Rogeri Comitis Herefordiæ."

In the earlieft charter granted to Flaxley Abbey of which any record remains, Henry Duke of Normandy formally confirmed the donations to the Abbey of Roger, "Earl of Hereford," who himfelf appears amongft the attefting witneffes, and is ftyled Earl of Hereford.

In another charter granted by the fame Prince Henry, before his acceffion, to Robert Fitzharding of Berkeley, Roger, "Earl of Hereford," appears amongft the attefting witneffes.

Thefe facts feem clearly to prove Roger affumed the ftyle and dignity of Earl of Hereford long before the charter of Henry II which was confidered by the Lords' Committee to amount to a formal creation of that title. There is no evidence to fhow that Roger was ever recognifed as Earl of Hereford by Stephen, though Roger appears to have affumed the title on his father's death on Chriftmas eve 1143, and to have held it until the acceffion of Henry II. The probability would feem to be that Roger afpired to fucceed to all the eftates and dignities granted to his father Milo by the Emprefs Maud, including St. Briavell's Castle and the whole Foreft of Dene. Recognition of these grants by Stephen could not have been expected; and although the grants made by Earl Roger to the Flaxley monks in foreft limits were formally confirmed by Prince Henry before his acceffion, the charter granted by Henry II to Earl Roger makes fpecial exception of St. Briavell's Caftle and the Foreft of Dene, which were by implication retained in the king's own hands. In connection with the fame fubject it may be noted that the fee and inheritance of Englifh Bicknor (Byknore) which belonged to Ulric de Dene, and is fituated within the Foreft limits, is fpecially noted as having been granted by Henry I to Milo de Gloucefter the Conftable. The record of this grant is amongft the Royal Charters in the Duchy of Lancafter records. Roger Earl of Hereford would naturally have fucceeded to this eftate irrefpective of the alleged grant of the whole Foreft of Dean to Earl Milo by the Emprefs Maud—(See p. 16, note 3).

[2] This document fhould apparently be noted in the official calendar to the Duchy of Lancafter Records known as the Great Cowchers. Thefe volumes have been fearched by me without fuccefs, although I have received the courteous affiftance of an experienced official in the Public Record Office.

C

It is important, however, to notice that in the charter of Henry II to Earl Roger shortly after his acceffion, above quoted, a fpecial exception was made of "the Caftle of St. Briavell's, the vill of Neweham, and the Foreft of Dene," all of which, it muft be inferred, were retained by Henry II in his own hands.

Flaxley Abbey was founded within the limits of the Foreft of Dene after the alleged grant of that Foreft to Earl Milo by the Emprefs Maud, and before the refumption of the Foreft under the terms of the grant made by Henry II to Earl Milo's fon and succeffor Roger.

Earl Roger appears to have made up his father's quarrel with Robert de Betun Bifhop of Hereford; and is ftated to have been a great benefactor to the See of Hereford. Amongft other grants he gave back the Hayes or woods of Rofs, which are fuppofed to have been included in the gift of Edmund Ironfide, who left to the See the valuable manor of Rofs. This reftitution is thus referred to in Bifhop Swinfield's Regifter, fol. 15 a:—

"Hayas de Ros quas ante tempus meum amiferat cum omni plenitudine et dominio venationis et aliarum rerum ecclefiæ ipfius (sc. epifcopi) reftituo."

Earl Roger was alfo a great benefactor to the Abbey of St. Peter's in Gloucefter, and to the Monks of Brecknock. For a lift of his donations to St. Peter's vide references given in Hift. et Cart. Mon., St. Peter's, Glouc., vol. iii, p. 374.

In the Regifter of Royal Charters belonging to the Duchy of Lancafter Records is fet forth the deed whereby Henry I granted, A.D. 1121, in marriage to Milo de Gloucefter Sibilla, daughter of Bernard de Novo Mercato. Below the MS. tranfcript of this charter in the P.R.O., there is the following official note which feems to throw fome light on the ftatement in the text:—

"It is conceived that this charter could not have been seen by Dugdale, who evidently alludes to fome other when he fays "The King gave to Milo in marriage Sibill the eldeft daughter of Bernard de Newmarche Lord of Brecknock, together with the Honor of Brecknock, fo likewife all his father's lands held in capite with the office of Conftable of his Court as by his Charter dated at Roan appeareth."—The reference of this charter is thus given in the Baronage "Ex Regiftro magno in Ducatu Lancaftriæ," but as neither any such book, nor the charter referred to are at the prefent day (1834) to be found in the Duchy office, this and fome other allufions to the fame Regifter feem ftrongly to favour a belief that Dugdale muft have feen a third volume, fimilar to the two called the Great Cowchers, but which fince his time has paffed into other hands. The grant quoted by Dugdale is probably of a later date than the Charter now under confideration, which feems to have been made to Milo prior to his father's deceafe, and before he succeeded to the hereditary Conftablefhip of England, as he is herein only defcribed as Milo de Gloucefter."

[1] See Abftract and Illuftrations of Bifhop Swinfield's Roll by the Rev. John Webb, page xx, printed for the Camden Society.

In the charter granted by Earl Milo to the Priory of Llanthony near Gloucefter there are one or two interefting allufions to his fon Roger.

With reference to the grant of the manor of Hethamftede the charter tranflated runs as follows:—

"This donation I and my wife Sybille and my fons Roger, Walter, and Henry did make in the church of the Canons of Gloucefter. Roger who is now married took an oath upon the altar of St. Mary and upon the four Evangelifts that he would never hereafter give them any difturbance concerning that manor."

The fame charter alfo refers to the grant of a moiety of the fifhery at Hafpool "by delivering a golden ring upon the altar in the fame church which I did in gratitude for the recovery of my fon Roger."

At the time of Earl Milo's death William de Wycombe, well-known as the biographer of Robert de Betun Bifhop of Hereford, was prior of the newly founded houfe of Llanthony near Gloucefter. After Milo's death William de Wycombe wrote a narrative entitled "The whole Tyranny and malicious proceedings of the Earl, and his excommunication from the stock of Christ." This writing was brought to the notice of Roger Earl of Hereford by the monks of Llanthony, who were anxious to get rid of William de Wycombe, and Earl Roger exafperated by the pamphlet is faid to have made William of Wycombe's pofition fo difficult that he was forced to refign his office of Prior.

Earl Roger having been, as above ftated, a great benefactor to the See of Hereford, and having made up his father's quarrel with Bifhop Robert de Betun, fome light is thrown upon the ftatement made by Leland that there was a Bifhop of Hereford "that holpe muche to the buildinge of Flexeley." Who then was this Bishop? Robert de Betun was Bifhop of Hereford at the time of Earl Milo's death on Chriftmas eve 1143; and he died at Rheims on "the 16 of the Kalends of May," 1148, according to the ftatement of his biographer William of Wycombe.

Robert de Betun was succeeded at Hereford by Gilbert Foliot, who prefided over the See of Hereford until his tranffer to the diocefe of London in 1163. The Bifhop of Hereford referred to by Leland muft then apparently have been either Robert de Betun or Gilbert Foliot; and could it be afcertained which of thefe two Bifhops of Hereford took part in the building of Flaxley, the evidence would materially affift in fixing the actual date of the foundation.

There are fome reafons for thinking that Gilbert Foliot was probably the Bifhop' referred to by Leland, for had Flaxley Abbey been built in the lifetime of that bifhop's predeceffor Robert de Betun, between Chriftmas 1143, the date of Earl Milo's death, and 1148 the date of his own death, fome notice of that event would probably have been made in William de Wycombe's life of Robert de Betun which has been already referred to.

William de Wycombe was Prior of Llanthony[1] near Gloucefter; and the foundation of a neighbouring monaftery by Earl Roger the patron of Llanthony, with the affiftance of Robert de Betun, a former prior of Llanthony, was an event which William de Wycombe would have been little likely to omit had it occurred in the lifetime of Robert de Betun.

At the time of the foundation of Flaxley Abbey the Foreft of Dean appears to have formed an ecclefiaftical diftrict of itfelf, known as the deanery of the Foreft of Dean. Until the eftablifhment of the See of Gloucefter at the time of the Diffolution the Foreft Deanery was subject to the jurifdiction of the Bifhops of Hereford. The Abbey of Flaxley being founded within this jurifdiction fell naturally under the authority of the Bifhops of Hereford; and the original Regifters of that See ftill preferved at Hereford, in the cuftody of the Bifhop's Regiftrar, contain, it is fuppofed, the only evidence ftill extant of the names and dates of the inftallation of the Flaxley Abbots. Thefe records will be noticed hereafter.

Affuming then that Flaxley Abbey was founded during the epifcopate of Gilbert Foliot, and before the acceffion of Henry II on 19 December, 1154, the date of the foundation can be fixed approximately as occurring between 1148 and 1154.

---

[1] Gervafe of Dover (Twyfden), page 1377, line 63, relates that Roger Earl of Hereford wifhing to rebel againft Henry II was brought back to his allegiance by his relation Gilbert Foliot Bifhop of Hereford.

[2] Of Llanthony Priory near Gloucefter an interefting relic has been preferved at Flaxley in the fhape of a window of painted glafs bearing the arms and device of the Priory of Llanthony. A coloured print and defcription of thefe arms will be found in a work entitled "Some account of Llanthony Priory," by the Rev. G. Roberts, late Vicar of Monmouth, reprinted from the Archæologia Cambrenfis, No. iii, and publifhed in 1847 by W. Pickering, 177, Piccadilly, London. The defcription of the arms is by the late J. D. Thos. Niblett, Efq., of Hareffield Court, Gloucefter, who ftates that the window now in Flaxley Church was originally placed in the Chapel of Old Quedgeley Court, the ancient manor houfe and country feat of the Priors of Lanthony. Some of the glafs from this chapel was fet up in the mortuary chapel at Bromefberrow, and a few of the fhields were given by Mr. H. G. Dobyns Yate to the late Sir Thos. Crawley Boevey, Bart., of Flaxley Abbey, who caufed them to be inferted in the old Flaxley Church built by Mrs. Mary Pope. On the erection of the new church, which was confecrated in 1856, the Llanthony windows were tranfferred to the new church, where they may now be feen.

General description of the Public Records relating to Flaxley Abbey.

Having then fixed as clofely as the evidence will allow, the date of this foundation, it will now be convenient before difcuffing the contents of the various charters, grants, etc., made to the Abbey, to give a brief general defcription of all the records and documentary evidence which I have been able to find relating to Flaxley Abbey.

Thefe records may be conveniently claffified as follows :—

I.—Public Records confifting of antient charters, grants, confirmation charters, patents, etc., together with inquifitions, licences to acquire land, and all mifcellaneous references on record in the Public Rolls.

II.—The Cartulary of Flaxley Abbey, containing ninety-feven original documents, confifting chiefly of grants, affignments, etc., made by various local benefactors to the Abbey and Monks. The original Roll on which thefe documents are tranfcribed was in the poffeffion of the late Sir Thomas Phillipps of Middlehill, co. Warwick, and latterly of Thirleftaine Houfe, Cheltenham.

III.—Extracts from the original Regifters of the Bifhops of Hereford relating to Flaxley Abbey. Thefe records are in the cuftody of the Bifhop's Regiftrar at Hereford.

Of the documents included under the firft head no attempt has, it is believed, ever been made to furnifh anything like a complete lift. Under the brief notice of "Flexeley" Abbey in Bifhop Tanner's "Notitia Monaftica," will be found a lift of fome of thefe documents and references to the public records; and this lift has been incorporated as it ftands in the laft (1825) edition of Dugdale's "Monafticon Anglicanum."

But Bifhop Tanner's lift of references, befides being incomplete, furnifhes no information regarding the nature or contents of the various documents adverted to; and pains have, therefore, now been taken to furnifh a more complete and accurate lift with the affiftance of the excellent calendars and indexes publifhed by the Record Commiffioners; and to give fome account of the valuable and interefting papers referred to.

For convenience of reference and to affift future enquirers, I have appended to this paper a complete lift of the references confulted. See Appendix, pt. 1.

The more important and interefting of the charters, grants, etc., hitherto unpublifhed, will be found at length in the Appendix.

The following table exhibits at a glance the chief fources of information confulted by me in the Public Record Office :—

1.—Cartae Antiquae. References to Flaxley Abbey noticed in the Calendar of Sir Jofeph Ayloffe.
2.—Clofe Rolls. As far as they have been yet (1881) printed or calendared by the authorities of the Record Office; viz., to the 57th year of Henry III.
3.—Charter Rolls. Calendared from 1 John to end of Edward IV.
4.—Patent Rolls. Calendared down to 23 Edward IV.
5.—Inquifitions post mortem, and ad quod damnum. Calendared from Henry III to Richard III.
6.—Hundred Rolls for Henry II and Edward I, printed by Record Commiffioners, and Placita de Quo Warranto.
7.—Taxation of Pope Nicholas and Valor Ecclefiafticus, printed by Record Commiffioners.
8.—Annales Monaftici, Rolls Series.
9.—Records of the Duchy of Lancafter.
10.—Placita Foreftae de Dene, 42 and 54 Henry III, 10 Edward I, 9 to 15 Edward III. Four county bags in the chief clerk's office. Chapter House.

In addition to the books and records mentioned, I have obtained some few additional references from the Indexes and Calendars to the following publications:—Pipe Roll, Oblata Rolls, Originalia Rolls; and I have confulted all the Indexes and Calendars to which my attention was directed by the officials of the Public Record Office as likely to furnifh additional information. I cannot, of courfe, fuppofe that the lift of references furnifhed by me relating to Flaxley Abbey is in any fenfe complete or exhauftive. My enquiries have been limited to thofe records and publications of which calendars and indexes have been publifhed. All the records relating to Flaxley Abbey, of which I could find any mention in thefe calendars, I have carefully examined; and reference has in all cafes been made to the original Rolls, whenever it appeared neceffary to do fo for the purpofe of afcertaining their contents.

The profecution of further enquiry at the Public Record Office without the affiftance of the publifhed calendars and indexes will obvioufly be a far more laborious and difficult tafk than that which has been attempted in thefe notes.

Cartulary of Flaxley Abbey.

Of the valuable feries of documents comprifed in the Cartulary of Flaxley Abbey a notice in some detail is given hereafter; and at this place it is only neceffary for me to note my warm acknowledgments to the Rev. J. E. A. and Mrs. Fenwick, of Thirleftaine Houfe, Cheltenham, and to Mr. Samuel Gael, of Battledown Knoll, Charlton Kings, near Cheltenham.

To Mr. and Mrs. Fenwick I feel peculiarly indebted for the cordial affiftance received in the profecution of my enquiries ; and to their kindnefs and liberality I am indebted for the prefent opportunity of publifhing this interefting and valuable collection of monaftic documents.

The exiftence of the original Flaxley Cartulary in the library of the late Sir Thos. Phillipps, Bart., is mentioned in Nichols' "Collectanea Topographica et Genealogica," vol. i,. p. 203, but no account of the whole cartulary, or of its contents, has, it is believed, been ever before made public.

Registers of the Bishops of Hereford.

The extracts from the Regifters of the Bifhops of Hereford relating to Flaxley Abbey are feven in number. Six of thefe extracts relate to the inftitution of various Abbots of Flaxley, the remaining extract being a Bull of Pope Innocent granting protection to the Abbey of Flaxley, and recorded at p. 58 of the Regifter of Thomas de Cantelupe, Bifhop of Hereford, from 1275 to 1282.

The names of the Abbots inftituted, and all the particulars relating to them on record, will be noticed in the proper place hereafter. Thefe interefting records are in the cuftody of the Bifhop's Regiftrar, Mr. H. C. Beddoe, who has given me every poffible affiftance in the profecution of my enquiries at Hereford ; and I am glad to have this opportunity of publicly acknowledging my obligation to him for his uniform kindnefs and courtefy.

I. Records relating to Flaxley Abbey extant on the Public Rolls.

The earlieft charter granted to Flaxley Abbey after the foundation purports to have been made by Prince Henry Duke of Normandy. Copies of the original Latin charter[1] will be found both in Dugdale's Monafticon, and alfo in Atkyns' Hiftory of Gloucefter. The following tranflation is from Atkyns, revifed, however, in one or two points where that tranflation is at fault.

The charter of Henry Duke of the Normans reciting the grants of the benefactors of the Abbey of. Flaxley in the County of Gloucefter and confirming the fame.

[1] Cart. Antiq., x, No. 4. P.R.O

Henry Duke of Normandy and Earl of Anjou to Archbifhops, etc., greeting. Know ye that I have granted and confirmed to God and St. Mary and to the Monks of the Ciftercian order, for the good of the fouls of my anceftors and of my own foul in perpetual alms all thofe donations which Roger Earl of Hereford gave to thofe Monks in alms according to the tenor of their charters to wit—

a certain place in the valley of Caftiard[1] called Flaxley to build an Abbey there :

and all that land called Waftadene which did belong to Walfric ;

and an iron work (fabricam ferrariam) at Edland ;

and all the land under the old Caftle of Dene[2] which remains to be affarted and that which is already affarted ;

and a certain fifhery at Redley called Newerre ;

and a meadow in Pulmede[3]

. and all eafements in the foreft of Dene ;

and all the demefnes in Dymmock and the lands belonging to Walfric, but fo that if Uthred the Clerk continues in the Abbey with the lands he exchanged to wit two yard lands, that then he fhall give no account of it to any body but the Abbot ;

Half the wood at Dymmock ;

and all the tithes of Chefnuts in Dene every year ;

and all the land of Geoffry fon of the aforefaid Walfric which the Earl of Hereford did releafe ;

and all the land of Leffric de Staura which the Earl of Hereford did likewife releafe ;

Wherefore I will, etc. We do not only confirm to them thefe aforefaid

---

[1] Six acres of land under 'Cafthard' were granted to the Abbey by William de Mineriis. This grant was confirmed and additional land given by Henry fon of William de Mineriis. Other land under 'Caftiard' was given to the Abbey by William of Dene, King's forefter. See Cartulary, Nos. 9, 10, and 16.

[2] The 'old Caftle of Dene' requires identification. An allusion may, perhaps, be made to this Caftle in No. 12 of the Cartulary in which Hugh le Petit grants to the Abbey his lands at ' Neweham,' near the ditch of the old Caftle (juxta foffam veteris Caftelli).

[3] Geoffry, fon of William of Dene, granted to the Abbey the whole of that part of the meadow in Pulmede, which he held adjoining the garden of Henry de Mineriis. See Cartulary No. 17. In the Calendar of Royal Charters in the Duchy of Lancafter Records is the Tranfcript of a Charter of Henry I to Milo de Gloucefter "the Conftable," granting him the fee and inheritance of the land of Englifh Bicknor which belonged to Ulric de Dena. This Charter is printed in extenfo in the Tranfactions of the Briftol and Glouc. Archaeol. Soc., vol. iv. p. 319.

grants, but we alfo confirm all others which the fame Roger Earl of Hereford does intend to give unto them in alms.

Witneffes Roger "Earl of Hereford,"[1] William de Crevecour,[2] Richard de Humett Conftable,[3] Philip de Columbariis.[4] Robert de Ivignm. William de Augervill. William Cumin. At Evefham.

Charter of King Henry II.

Prince Henry, after fucceeding to the throne as Henry II, appears to have confirmed and extended the original charter granted to Flaxley Abbey.

Copy of the original Latin charter[5] is given by Dugdale. The following is a correct tranflation :—

The Charter of King Henry II to the Abbey of Flaxley.

Henry by the grace of God King of England, and Duke of Normandy and Aquitaine and Earl of Anjou, to Archbifhops, etc., and to all faithful as well Englifh as Normans, both prefent and to come, greeting—

Know ye that I have given and confirmed to God and the Bleffed Mary and to the Monks of Dene which I have received into my protection for the good of my foul and of my anceftors in perpetual alms a certain place within the Foreft of Dene to wit

All the valley of Caftiard and the place called Flaxley where an Abbey is founded of the Ciftercian order in honour of the bleffed Virgin Mary for the love of God and the benefit of the foul of my grandfather King Henry, and of the foul of my father the Earl of Anjou, and of Maud the Emprefs my mother, and of the foul of all my parents and anceftors, and for the good of my own foul and of my heirs and for the profperity and peace of the Kingdom of England ;

---

[1] Roger "Earl of Hereford" appears alfo as one of the attefting witneffes to the charters granted by Henry Duke of Normandy, and by Henry II to Robert Fitzharding of Berkley.—Briftol and Gloucefter Arch. Trans., Vol. i, p. 135-36.

[2] William Crevequer (Crevecour) mentioned as an attefting witnefs in a charter granted to Nuneaton.

[3] Richard de Humett Conftable mentioned as attefting charters of Henry II to Thetford Priory and Walden Abbey (Dug.) ; alfo to Nuneaton and to Robert Fitzharding of Berkley.

[4] Philip de Columbariis appears as a witnefs in the firft charter granted by Henry Duke of Normandy to Robert Fitzharding of Berkley.

[5] Cart. Antiq. NN., n. 39, and Pat. 22 R. II, p. 3, m. 16, per infpex., and Pat. 27 Henry VI, part i, m. 6.

D

I have alfo granted to them and have confirmed all the donations which Roger Earl of Hereford gave to them in alms in the fame manner as his charters do exprefs; (ficut cartæ ejus teftantur).

Moreover I have granted and confirmed to them all eafements within my foreft of Dene to wit common of pafture for their young cattle and hogs, and for all other beafts; and wood and timber to repair their houfes and buildings and for other neceffaries without committing wafte in the foreft;

And I have given them tithes of cheftnuts out of the fame foreft; (decimæ caftanearum)

And the farm called Waftedene; (Waftedena grangia)

And one iron forge (unam forgiam ferrariam) free and quit (quietam) and with as free liberty to work as any of my forges in demefne;

And all the land under the old Caftle of Dene which remains to be affarted and that which is already affarted to wit one hundred acres;

And a fifhery at Redley called Nowere;

And a meadow at Reidley called Pulmede containing four acres;

And all the land which Leuveric de Staura gave to them in alms;

And the farm which I gave them at Wallmore out of my new ploughed grounds (de effartis meis) containing two hundred acres with the meadows and paftures and all other eafements;

And four acres of Northwood;

And all my demefnes at Dymmock and five virgates (virgatas) of land and a half befide the demefnes; and half my wood at Dymmock and half my nets (retium) which I have in my hands for the convenience of my men (propter Aifiamenta hominum meorum) becaufe I would have my Monks enjoy that part of the wood peaceably and quietly without any interfering with any other perfons; and I ftraightly command that no perfon offer to difturb them on this account.

I further give to them my new ploughed grounds (effartum quoddam[1]) under Caftiard called Vincents Land.

All thefe I give unto God and to the bleffed Mary and to my Monks devoutly ferving God to have and to hold for ever quit (foluta) and difcharged (quieta) from all regards and other fecular exactions whereof I will, etc.

---

[1] Both in this and in the earlier charter of Prince Henry are feveral allufions made to clearings in the forefts technically known in foreft law as Affarts or Effarts. The meaning of this word has been thus quaintly defcribed by Manwood:—

" Verelie when that the pleafant woods of the Forefte or thicke bufhie places meete for the fecret

Witneſſes: Richard de Humett, William de Crevecour, Philip de Columbariis, William de Augerwill. At Eveſham.

Neither of theſe charters, it will be obſerved, bears any date. It appears, however aliunde, that the charter of Henry II was teſted at Eveſham between the months of April and Auguſt 1158 (Eyton's Itin., Henry II, p. 37). The earlier charter is atteſted, it will be noticed, by Roger *Earl of Hereford* amongſt others. As Earl Roger died ſometime in 1155, and Prince Henry did not ſucceed to the throne until 19 December, 1154, the earlier charter muſt, apparently, have been granted to Flaxley Abbey before that date.

Character of the foundation Charters.

Coming now to the matter of theſe two earlier charters it will be noticed that in moſt points they are in ſubſtance identical, but that the later charter of King Henry II is fuller and more specific in its terms than the earlier charter granted by Prince Henry before his acceſſion. The language uſed in King Henry II's charter ſeems to draw a marked diſtinction between the royal grants and privileges given to the Abbey, and the *private* gifts of Roger Earl of Hereford and other benefactors. In the earlier charter no ſuch diſtinction appears to be drawn; and ſo far as the language of that charter goes, it would ſeem that all the poſſeſſions and privileges of the Abbey in the foreſt of Dean were derived from the gift of Earl Roger.

King Henry II's charter purports to ſtate that the grant of "the valley of Caſtiard and the place called Flaxley where an Abbey is founded of the Ciſtercian order in honour of the bleſſed Virgin Mary" was made by the king himſelf. The land ſo granted undoubtedly formed part of the royal Foreſt of Dean, which, it will be remembered, was expreſſly reſerved to the king in the charter granted by Henry II to Roger Earl of Hereford noticed at p. 8 above.

The marked diſtinction already adverted to between the language of the earlier and later charters may, perhaps, be accounted for to ſome extent by the doubtful poſition of the Foreſt of Dean after the death of Earl Milo in 1143, and before the reſumption of that foreſt by Henry II circa 1154. It has been already noticed that a formal grant of the Foreſt of Dean was

feeding of wilde beaſtes be cut down, deſtroyed or plucked up by the rootes, and the ſame ground be made a plaine and turned into arable land, this by the lawes of the foreſte is properly ſaid to be an Aſſart or land aſſarted."

Manwood's Treatiſe on the Foreſt Laws ſhows that Aſſarts in the foreſt were ſubject to very ſtrict rules, pp. 19 to 23, 4th edition.

made to Earl Milo by the Emprefs Maud; but it is very doubtful whether this grant was ever recognifed by Stephen. Earl Roger may have afpired to fucceed to the Foreft of Dean as part of his father's poffeffions; and in fact the foundation of Flaxley Abbey within foreft limits, and the liberal grants made to the Abbey of foreft land feems to fuggeft that Earl Roger did so afpire; but there is no evidence that this pretenfion was ever recognifed by Stephen, and any doubt that may have exifted on the fubject was removed by the diftinct refervation of the Foreft of Dean in the charter granted by Henry II to Roger Earl of Hereford.

Flaxley a Cistercian Abbey.

Flaxley Abbey was founded of the Ciftercian order, and there is a tradition which is noticed by Mackenzie Walcot,[1] that the Abbey was colonized from the Abbey of Bordefley in Worcefterfhire. The Ciftercians, as is well known, were a branch of the Benedictine Order, and the ftrict obfervance of the rule of St. Benedict was one of the chief profeffions made by all Ciftercian abbots at the time of inftallation. Ciftercians were fometimes called Bernardines, becaufe St. Bernard was a great propagator of this order. Alfo White Monks, becaufe their habit was a white caffock with a narrow fcapulary; but they fometimes wore a black gown with long fleeves when they went abroad, but not to church. Flaxley Abbey was dedicated to "the bleffed Mary of Dene." The Virgin was the tutelary faint of all Ciftercian monasteries; and frequent allufions are made in the records to the abbot and monks "of the bleffed Mary of Dene." In felecting fites for their religious houfes the monks of this order were noted for their choice of the moft picturefque and inacceffible fpots, ufually buried in wood and near water.

Walter Map, writing temp. Henry II, has thus terfely defcribed, not without fatire, the characteriftic fpots chofen by Ciftercians, in accordance with the foundation ftatutes of their order, for the eftablifhment of their monafteries:—

"Locum ad habitandum habilem eligunt, fœcundum, refponfalem frugibus, non inaptum feminibus, feptum nemoribus, fcaturientem fontibus, cornucopiam locum extra mundum,"[2] which may be thus freely rendered:—

[1] "Englifh Minfters," Vol. ii, p. 121. I fhould be glad to afcertain from what fource Mackenzie Walcot derived this information. The tradition feems probable enough, and is well worth verifying if poffible. Abbot Alan, formerly monk of Bordefley, was elected Abbot of Dene in 1187, on the refignation of Abbot Waleran. In 1335, when the Abbot of Flaxley was fufpended for mifconduct, the Abbot of Bordefley was one of the three Commiffioners appointed by the Crown.

[2] Gualterus Mapes de Nugis Curia:—Camden Society publication, p. 39. For an account of Walter

Flaxley Abbey.

"They choose a place fit for habitation, fertile, good for fruit, suitable for grain, buried in woods, abounding in springs, a horn of plenty, a place apart from the haunts of men."

The Abbeys of Tintern, Dore, and Flaxley, are all three of them typical Cistercian Abbeys, remarkable for the singular beauty of their surroundings. Tintern Abbey, in Monmouthshire, has long been celebrated for its remarkable beauty of site, "with its landscape accompaniments of meadow and wood, rock, and flowing water."

The Abbey of Dore, in Herefordshire, is not so well known, but its beauty has been celebrated in Camden's description of the Golden Vale :— "which name it may well be thought to deserve for its golden rich and pleasant fertility. For the hills that encompass it on both sides are clothed with woods; under the woods lie the corn fields on each hand; and under those fields lovely and fruitful meadows. In the middle between them glides a clear and crystal river upon which Robert Earl of Ewias erected a beautiful monastery, wherein very many of the nobility and gentry of those parts were buried."

The Abbey of Flaxley, in the Forest of Dean, is probably the least well known of the three Abbeys mentioned, but the picturesque beauty of the site is, perhaps, quite as characteristic in its own style as that of either Tintern or Dore. On the one side looking towards the forest, the green vale of Castiard winds out of sight amongst a labyrinth of well wooded hills. On the other side looking towards the Severn, the eye can rove for miles as far as the Cotswold hills, over one of the most extensive and beautiful views of the Severn valley.[1]

Map, who was a native of the Welsh border, on the confines of Gloucestershire, and who, amongst other preferments, held the living of Westbury-on-Severn in Gloucestershire, conf. Introduction to his works published by the Camden Society.

In the constitutions of the Cistercian order very clear rules were laid down for the situation and character of the church and monastic buildings. The monastery was to be in a solitary place.

"In civitatibus, in castellis aut villis nulla nostra construenda sunt cœnobia, sed in locis a conversatione hominum semotis." (Inst. Capit. Gen. Ordinis. Cisterc. 1134.)

[1] Regarding the view from the park at Flaxley, Bigland thus notes at p. 583, Hist. of Glouc. :—" In the park on the north-east is a natural terrace of considerable extent commanding a most interesting view of the cultivated vale of the Severn and the City of Gloucester, flanked by the whole chain of the Cotswold mountains, from Bredon to Sodbury Hill, a line of more than fifty miles. The frequent windings of the river in the foreground appear like so many lakes in succession, and give a highly picturesque effect to this singularly pleasing landscape."

Grant of Common of Pasture throughout the Forest.

The monks of Flaxley having received from the king the beautiful vale of Caftiard to build their monaftery were, at the fame time, liberally endowed with important rights and privileges within the foreft limits. The importance of thefe rights cannot properly be appreciated without remembering that they were granted at a time when the Norman foreft laws[1] were in full operation, and when the royal prerogative was enforced by the infliction of the moft fevere and cruel penalties.

The charter of Henry II granted to the monks of Flaxley, amongft other important rights, "all eafements within my foreft of Dean, to wit, common of pafture for their young cattle and hogs, and for all other beafts; and wood and timber to repair their houfes and buildings and for other neceffaries without committing wafte in the foreft."

The right of common of pafture throughout the royal Foreft of Dean within the extenfive boundaries[2] prefcribed by the Norman kings was clearly a right of a

---

[1] For a brief and comprehenfive account of thefe laws, fee Manwood's well-known "Treatife on the Foreft Laws." The fourth edition of this treatife, publifhed 1717, contains as an Appendix the foreft laws of Canute, the Charta de Forefta of 9 Henry III, and all the later ftatutes and rules relating to forefts. The chief effects of the Charta de Forefta were (1) to put a ftop to the arbitrary extenfions of the royal forefts and to reftore them to reafonable dimenfions; and (2) to mitigate the cruel penalties previoufly enforced againft thofe who killed the king's deer. The nature of thefe penalties may be inferred from Article 10 of the Charta de Forefta, which runs as follows:—

"No man from henceforth fhall lofe neither life nor member for killing our deer; but if any man be taken therewith and convict for taking of our venison he fhall make grievous fine if he hath anything whereof to make fine; and if he hath nothing to leefe, he fhall be imprifoned a year and a day, and after the year and a day expired (if he can find fufficient furcties) he fhall be delivered and if not he fhall abjure the realm."

Article 4 of the Charta de Forefta had a fpecial importance for the Flaxley monks on account of their refidence within foreft limits.

"All Archbifhops, Bifhops, Abbots, Priors, Earls, Barons, Knights, and other our freeholders, which have their woods in forefts, fhall have their woods as they had them at the time of the firft coronation of King Henry our grandfather, fo that they fhall be quit for ever of all Purpreftures, Waftes, and Affarts, made in thofe woods after that time until the beginning of the fecond year of our coronation. And thofe that from henceforth do make Purpreftures without our fpecial licenfe, or wafte or affart the fame, fhall anfwer unto us for the fame waftes, Purpreftures, and Affarts."

In the Placita de Forefta of 10 Edward I, membrane 18, under the head of "De novo vafto bofcorum" appear the following entries:—"Bofcus Abbatis de Flexley in Parva Dene vaftatus de novo per eundem Abbatem."

"Bofci ejufdem Abbatis de Cafteyerd, Tunberhugge et Walfebery, qui continentur sub uno co-operto vaftantur de novo per eundem Abbatem."

[2] For a popular map, fhowing the foreft boundaries at various periods, conf. Nicholl's Foreft of Dean, p. 15.

very important character. This right muſt have enabled the monks of Flaxley to maintain at little coſt to themſelves large herds of cattle, and vaſt droves of ſheep and ſwine. The maſt of the oak, beech, and cheſnut trees, technically known as "pannage,"[1] furniſhed at certain ſeaſons of the year a practically inexhauſtible ſtock of provender for their ſwine, while the luxuriant herbage and abundance of water afforded excellent paſturage for the cattle and ſheep.

The monks of Flaxley, it would ſeem, were not always allowed to exerciſe their extenſive rights unchallenged; and the records in fact clearly ſhow that theſe rights and privileges were not regarded with much favour by the royal keepers and the authorities at St. Briavell's Caſtle, with whom the Flaxley monks appear to have been in conſtant colliſion.

In the 10th year[2] of Henry III, mention is made of a royal mandate addreſſed to Hugh de Kinardeſle, Conſtable of St. Briavell's Caſtle, ordering him to allow the abbot and convent of Flaxley to have the ſame rights of common of paſture in the Foreſt of Dean as they uſed to enjoy in the reign of King John in virtue of the charter of Henry II. A ſimilar order was repeated in the 15th[3] year of the ſame reign; and again in the 16th[4] and 18th[5] years. In the 19th[6] year of Henry III, appears a notice of ſome of the abbot's cattle being diſtrained for treſpaſs in "fence month," and of replevin being granted, whereby the cattle were reſtored to the abbot pending the reſult of formal proceedings in the Foreſt Court. "Fence month," it may be ſtated, was the fawning ſeaſon, commencing fifteen days before and ending fifteen days after Midſummer. During this month the ſtricteſt regulations were enforced to prevent the deer from being diſturbed.

In the 16th[7] year of Hen. III it is related that the abbot and monks

[1] Pannage (paſnagium or pannagium) is "the maſt of ſuch trees only which bear fruit to feed hogs, or elſe the money made of ſuch maſt."—"Manwood's Foreſt Laws."
In Domeſday Survey the term pannage had a double meaning, firſt, the running and feeding of hogs in the woods, and in a ſecondary ſenſe the price or rate of their running. In one or two entries it is termed Paſtio. Diſſert. on Domeſday, App. M., Second Gen. Report from Commrs. on Public Records.
[2] Rot. Claus., 10 Hen III, m. 29.
[3] Rot. Claus., 15 Hen. III, m. 14.
[4] Rot. Claus., 16 Hen. III, m. 5.
[5] Rot. Claus., 18 Hen. III, m. 15.
[6] Rot. Claus., 19 Hen. III, m. 8.
[7] Rot. Claus., 16 Hen. III, m. 5.
The Close Rolls of the reign of Henry III contain numerous references to Flaxley Abbey. For the firſt eleven years of this reign theſe rolls have been printed in extenſo by the Record Commiſſion. For the remaining years of this reign a full and excellent calendar has been prepared which greatly facilitates enquiry.

of Flaxley were pardoned £10 6s., which they were fined in the Eyre of the Juſtices for the eſcape of their cattle in the foreſt.

Grants of Wood and Timber.

The grant of wood and timber from the royal foreſt "for the repair of the abbot's houſes and buildings, and for other neceſſaries," was another right of a very important character. The very vague and general terms in which this grant was expreſſed muſt have made it ſufceptible of great abuſe; and it is not ſurpriſing to find that the monks were unable to aſſert their rights without frequent appeals to the King.

In the ſecond year of King Henry III,[1] orders were addreſſed to John of Monmouth, Conſtable of St. Briavell's, enjoining him to allow the abbot and monks of Flaxley to have timber for their uſe (mairemium ad eſtoveria ſua) from the foreſt, according to the charters of his royal predeceſſors. In the ſixth[2] year of Henry III, the Conſtable of Briſtol was commanded by the King to allow the abbot and monks of Flaxley to have reaſonable "*eſtover*"[3] (rationabile eſtoverium) in their wood of Ermegrave and Ruggemore as they had been accuſtomed to have in the time of King John.

In the ſeventh[4] year of Henry III, orders were addreſſed to John of Monmouth, bidding him to allow the abbot of Flaxley, ſubject to the view and teſtimony of the foreſters and verderers (foreſtariorum et viridariorum) to have a reaſonable allowance of waſte wood and windfall (cableicio[5]), in the foreſt for the repair of his houſes, as he had been accuſtomed to have in the reign of King John.

In the thirteenth[6] year of Henry III the abbot of Flaxley is ſpecially

[1] Rot. Claus., 2 Hen. III, m. 15 (p. 343, printed ſeries).
[2] Rot. Claus., 6 Hen. III, m. 5 (p. 507, printed ſeries).
[3] For explanation of the term "Eſtovers" in foreſt law, ſee Manwood's treatiſe, p. 132—134. Bracton defines Eſtovers in a foreſt to ſignify generally a ſupply of neceſſary timber and firewood. In ſome manors tenants have common of eſtovers, *i.e.*, neceſſary botes or allowances out of the lord's wood, in which ſenſe the term eſtover comprehends houſe-bote, hay-bote and plow-bote, ſo that if a man have in his grant theſe general words de rationabili eſtoverio in boſeis, he may thereby claim all three.
[4] Rot. Claus., 7 Hen. III, m. 19 (p. 533, printed ſeries).
[5] The term "Cableicium" or "Cablicia" is defined by Maigne D'Arnis as follows: "Rami arborum vi ventorum aut tempeſtate vel alio caſu diſjecti." In modern times amongſt the perquiſites belonging to the foreſt woodwardſhips are, "the lop and top of all felled timber and all windfall and dotard trees" (ficca et vento proſtrata).
[6] Rot. Claus., 13 Hen. III, m. 8.

Flaxley Abbey.

allowed two oaks in the *hayes* of the foreſt of Dean for the roof of an aiſle in Flaxley Church.

In the fourteenth[1] year of the ſame reign orders were again iſſued that the abbot of Flaxley ſhould have timber, etc., in the foreſt of Dean, as he had been accuſtomed to have. In the following year[2] the abbot of Flaxley was granted ten oaks in St. Briavell's foreſt to repair the houſes and church of the abbey. This grant the abbot ſeems to have found it difficult to enforce, for in the ſame year[3] appears a ſecond order awarding to the abbot ſix oaks, the reſidue of the ten granted to the abbot for the repair of his church, and of which he could only get four. This order was again repeated in the following year.[4]

In the ſeventeenth[5] year of Henry III four additional oaks were granted to the abbot for the repair of his houſes; and in the following year[6] the conſtable of St. Briavell's was again commanded not to hinder the abbot from having timber for his houſes according to the charter of Henry II.

Special Grants for Firewood.

Beſides the grant of timber, windfall, etc., from the foreſt of Dean, ſpecial grants appear to have been made to the abbey for firewood. In the Appendix to theſe notes, No. 1, will be found an intereſting original charter of Richard I, granting to the abbey and monks of Flaxley the woods around the abbey (circa abbatiam) for firewood. The ſpecial intereſt of this charter ariſes from the fact that the antient boundaries[7] of theſe woods are clearly ſpecified, and can even now be fairly identified.

---

[1] Rot. Claus., 14 Hen. III, m. 6.
[2] Rot. Claus., 15 Hen. III, m. 14.
[3] Rot. Claus., 15 Hen. III, m. 2.
[4] Rot. Claus., 16 Hen. III, m. 5.
[5] Rot. Claus., 17 Hen. III, m. 2.
[6] Rot. Claus., 18 Hen. III, m, 15.

[7] A conſiderable part of the boundary here noted as the boundary of the Flaxley wood reappears in a perambulation of the Foreſt of Dean, made in the reign of Charles II, May 29, 1667. The following extract is here ſubjoined on account of the references to Flaxley and the local names contained. After deſcribing the foreſt boundary, as far as "Newnham's Pill," the record thus continues:—"And thence up that ſtream unto the highway leading from Newnham to Dean, aſcending that highway unto Dean's hill, and thence leaving the bounds of the manor of Rodley on the right hand and the hundred of St. Briavell's on the left hand unto the pool of Flaxley's forge, and thence to Bleſdon *alias* Blaiſdon's hedge and thence to Poulton's Hill and thence leaving the hundred of

The boundaries in queſtion are thus deſcribed :—"Scilicet in longum rivuli juxta campum monachorum prediƈti loci aſcendendo uſque Fulhiate, et a Fulhiate uſque ad magnum cheminum quod tendit de Abenhall uſque ad Parvam Denam ; et de predicto chemino a latere montis qui vocatur Walſebyrie uſque ad viam equorum quæ tendit uſque ad Abenhall, et de parvo ficheto decurrente in longum predictæ viæ uſque ad boſcum Johannis de Monemue de Hope aſcendendo et de predicto boſco per diviſam inter boſcum predicti Johannis et boſcum de Tunbrug (Tymbrugg) et Caſtiard¹ uſque ad rivulum de Hope et de predicto rivulo circuendo uſque ad campum de Boſeley, et in longum predicti campi uſque ad grangiam predictorum monachorum," which may be thus rendered :

Weſtbury on the right hand unto Brimſton's Yatt and thence including the lands of the . . . . . of Walmore to the highway leading towards Framulard and thence to the . . . . leaving the ſaid . . . . . hard round about it and ſo to a place called White . . . . . a certain place leading under the park of the Ley and from that way unto a grove called Birchingrove and from that grove unto Rareham and from thence to a place where anciently was a mill called Seymour's Mill and from that place to the brook of Bleſden *alias* Blaiſdon aſcending that brook unto Gavell's Gate (alias Gawlett's Yatt) and ſo aſcending that brook unto a little ſtream called Tinbridge Sych and ſo ſtretching up by the ſaid ſtream between the woods late of the abbot of Flaxley and the woods called Hope's woods unto Hope's ſhard (*sic*) and thence to a path called Juſty path and croſſing that path keeping ſtraight forward unto the water that leadeth from Michael Dean to Hope," etc.

The brook, referred to as Hope's brook in the charter of Richard I, paſſes by the hamlet of Gawlett (alſo written Gallyat, and clearly the ſame as Gavell's Gate or Gawlett's Yatt in the perambulation above quoted) and runs through Blaiſdon, in which pariſh it is known as "Blaiſdon brook." With the name Tunbrug in Richard I's charter, compare Tinbridge in the perambulation quoted.

¹ The name "Caſtiard," otherwiſe written Caſteyerd, as in Placita Foreſtæ de Dene of 10 Edward I, or Caſthard, no longer ſurvives. It has been ſuggeſted to me that the name is not improbably derived from Caſtanea, the Latin name of the Spaniſh Cheſnut. This derivation is to ſome extent ſupported by the fact that the Spaniſh cheſtnut was, at the time when Flaxley Abbey was founded, one of the moſt important timber trees in the foreſt. The Placita Foreſtæ de Dene of 10 Edward I, contain ſeveral references to cheſnut woods (boſci Caſtanearum), and it has been already noticed that tithes of cheſnuts (decimæ Caſtanearum) throughout the foreſt were amongſt the royal grants and privileges conferred on the Flaxley monks in the foundation charter. The Rev. C. A. Johns in his intereſting work on the 'Foreſt Trees of Britain,' has drawn from this grant the inference that in the reign of Stephen and Henry II, cheſnut timber was comparatively rare and valuable, otherwiſe the remaining timber, tithe excepted, would not have been referved by the King. Under the circumſtances noticed, it ſeems not improbable that the name 'Caſtiard' was derived from the predominant timber tree of the neighbourhood, and that the valley of Caſtiard means "the Cheſnut Valley." A well-known foreſt encloſure, now almoſt entirely devoted to the rearing of oak timber, and ſituated within a mile of Flaxley, between Flaxley and Littledean, is ſtill known as "the Cheſnuts." The celebrated old cheſnut tree at Tortworth in Glouceſterſhire is mentioned in Evelyn's Sylva as being ſo remarkable for its magnitude as to have been called even in King Stephen's time "the great Cheſnut of Tortworth," and Loudon ſuggeſts in his Arboretum (London, 1838) that this famous tree may poſſibly have been one of thoſe planted by the Romans.

Flaxley Abbey. 27

"To wit along the watercourfe by the field of the monks of the aforefaid place, afcending as far as Fulhiate, and from Fulhiate to the great road which leads from Abenhall to Littledean, and from the aforefaid road from the fide of the hill, which is called Walfebyrie to the horfe road which leads to Abenhall, and from the fmall ditch which runs down alongfide the aforefaid road as far as John of Monmouth's wood, going up from Hope, and from the aforefaid wood by a divifion between the wood of the aforefaid John and the wood of Tunbrug and Caftiard to the brook of Hope, and from the aforefaid brook winding round to the field of Bofeley, and along the aforefaid field as far as the homeftead of the aforefaid monks."

By any one familiar with the locality this defcription of the boundaries can readily be identified. The name "Fulhiate" or "Fowlyatt"[1] still exifts in connection with a barn known as "Fowliatt barn," fituated on Pudding hill, at a point where the Flaxley woods adjoin the foreft enclofure, known by the name of "the Chefnuts"; and the water courfe leading to 'Fulhiate' is ftill the boundary between the Flaxley eftate and the adjoining piece of foreft land, locally known as Hangman's hill. The fame wood is ftill bounded as at the date of the grant in Richard I's time, by the high road from Abenhall to Littledean, a very antient track, which prefents even now all the characteriftic features of a Roman road; and the name of the "hill called Walfebyrie" ftill survives in the term "Welchbury," which is the name now given to the whole wood. From the hill called "Walfebyrie," the woods granted to the Flaxley monks appear originally to have run parallel to the main road to Abenhall, by the rocky hill known as Shapridge, going from thence to John of Monmouth's wood in the parifh of Hope. To the prefent day the divifion between Hope's wood and the adjoining Flaxley wood is a mere artificial line; and Hope's brook ftill forms the Flaxley boundary from the parifh of Hope, as far as Blaifdon. The boundary of the Flaxley woods in the direction of Blaifdon is now known by the characteriftic name of "Monkhill,"[2] but at the time of the grant it would feem that the whole of the land beyond the Flaxley woods was included

[1] With the name 'Fulhiate,' otherwife fpelt 'Fowliatt' or 'Fowl yatt,' compare Gawlett, alfo written 'Gawl yatt.' The termination 'yatt' or 'gate' is fingularly appropriate, to the two points on the parifh boundary now known as Fowliatt and Gawlett. At both of thefe points a narrow defile divides the Flaxley woods, on the one fide from the Foreft enclofure known as the Chefnuts, on the other from the Blaifdon woods. With the names quoted, compare the well-known Symond's Yat in the parifh of Englifh Bicknor in the Foreft of Dean.

[2] Monkhill is now the name of a farm fituated on the border of the parifh of Blaifdon, the property of Sir Thos. H. Crawley-Boevey, Bart.

E²

within the limits of "Bofeley," an important hamlet, frequently mentioned in the early records, and belonging to the hundred of Weftbury.

Befides the charters of Richard I above referred to, other allufions to the fame fubject are found in the Clofe Rolls. In the ninth year[1] of Henry III there is on record a royal letter addreffed to Hugh de Nevill, ftating that the abbot and monks of Flaxley had petitioned the king to affign them fome fpot (placia) in the foreft near the abbey to take firewood therefrom (ad capiendum bufchum ad focum fuum). Hugh de Nevill was commanded to take fome good and lawful men of thofe parts, and meafure off a fuitable fpot.

In the fame year[2] an order was addreffed to the conftable of St. Briavell's bidding him to allow the abbot and monks to occupy peaceably the fpot fo marked off.

In the following year[3] appears an order addreffed to the sheriff of Gloucefter bidding him to prevent the abbot and monks from being molefted in refpect of the wood around the abbey granted by his lord the king.

In the following year[4] another order on the fame fubject is addreffed to Hugh de Nevill, and he is enjoined to give the abbot and monks full poffeffion of the woods around the abbey without any delay.

From thefe reiterated orders it may perhaps be inferred that the abbot and monks did not always find it eafy to enforce the rights which they acquired by the favour of the fovereign.

Tithes of Chesnuts.

The grant to Flaxley Abbey of tithes of chefnuts from the foreft of Dean points to a time when the timber of the Spanifh chefnut was in England comparatively rare and valuable. It has been already noticed at p. 26, above, in the note regarding the probable meaning of the name Caftiard, that the Spanifh chefnut appears to have been, at one time, extenfively planted in the foreft as a timber tree. The Placita de Forefta of 10 Edward I, contains feveral references to chefnut woods (bofci caftanearum); and the refervation by the Crown of all the chefnut timber, fubject to the tithe of chefnuts granted to Flaxley Abbey, fuggefts that the timber was at the time of the grant confidered to be of exceptional value. Bigland has noticed that the tithes of chefnuts formerly produced a confiderable income. He has

[1] Rot. Claus., 9 Hen. III, m. 8.
[2] Rot. Claus., 9 Hen. III, m. 11.
[3] Rot. Claus., 10 Hen. III, m. 11.
[4] Rot. Claus., 11 Hen. III, m. 18.

alfo alluded to the conftant ufe of chefnut in conftructing the roofs of antient buildings; and the fruit being much ufed by the lower rank of people as food was, he ftates, confidered to be of greater value than acorns, and confequently fubject to tithe. The Rev. C. A. Johns, in his work on the 'Foreft Trees of Britain,' has ably fummed up the arguments for and againft the theory that the Spanifh chefnut tree is indigenous to this country; and has arrived at the conclufion that it is not indigenous, but was probably introduced by the Romans. He alfo fhows fome grounds for doubting whether the timber in ancient buildings, fuppofed to be chefnut, was really chefnut at all.

Grant of an Iron Forge.

The grant to the abbey of an iron forge, with the neceffary fupply of timber from the foreft for its fupport, was perhaps, in view of the confequences it entailed, the moft important grant made to the Flaxley monks, and the repeated orders addreffed by the fovereign to the foreft authorities on the fubject clearly fhow that there was no right claimed by the monks which excited fo much oppofition on the part of the royal keepers, and which the monks on their part were more tenacious of enforcing.

The charter of Prince Henry fhows that the monks of Flaxley were granted firft of all " a certain iron work at Edland " (quandam fabricam ferrariam apud Edlandam). In the charter of King Henry II this grant appears in a fignificantly altered fhape as "one iron forge, free and quit, and with as free liberty to work as any of my forges in demefne." The words ufed in the later charter, inftead of limiting the monks to one fpecified work "at Edland," placed it in their power to fet up a forge anywhere in the foreft, and this, no doubt, was the foundation of the claim fubfequently afferted by the abbey to have a "moveable forge" (forgia errans *or* itinerans).

It is noted by Nicholls[1] that thefe moveable forges formed a regular fource of income to the Crown; and that at a juftice feat held at Gloucefter Caftle, 1282, it was found that there were upwards of feventy-two moveable forges (forgiæ itinerantes) then in exiftence; and that the fum which the Crown charged for licenfing them was at the rate of feven fhillings a year.

In the fourth year of Henry III[2] orders were addreffed to John of Monmouth, enjoining him to allow the abbot and monks of Flaxley to work

[1] Nicholl's Forest of Dean, p. 12.
[2] Rot. Claus., 4 Hen. III m. 4 (p. 430, printed series).

their forge in the Foreft of Dean according to the charter of King Richard, as they had been accuftomed to work it in the time of King John at the commencement of the war between the king and the barons; and that the monks of Flaxley were not to be obftructed becaufe the king had ordered all forges, except the royal forges, to be ftopped. (Conf. Nicholls' Foreft of Dean, p. 11.) A fimilar order was repeated to John of Monmouth in the feventh year[1] of the fame king. In the following year[2] we find two fimilar orders addreffed, the one, to Walter Afmoins, conftable of St. Briavell's, under Ralph fon of Nicholas; the other, to Roger de Clifford. For mention of thefe officers fee Royal letters of Henry III, vol. I, pp. 511 and 515. Roger Clifford is alluded to in thefe letters as having charge (ballia) of the Foreft of Dean.

In the 13th year[3] of Henry III the abbot's travelling forge in the hayes of the Foreft was again the fubject of an order addreffed to the Foreft authorities. A fimilar order was repeated to Roger de Clifford in the following year,[4] and again in the year[5] after.

In the 18th year[6] of Henry III, the conftable of St. Briavell's was twice commanded not to hinder the abbot from having his travelling forge, etc., according to the charter of Henry II.

In the 26th year[7] of Henry III, the abbot was granted permiffion to have his travelling forge in the foreft of St. Briavell's, till the king should make an exchange for it; and John, son of Geoffrey, was commanded to provide an exchange for the abbot's forge. In the 30th year[8] of Henry III, this permiffion was repeated, and again in the 34th year.[9] In the 37th year[10] of the fame;reign it is noticed that the abbot was formally granted feizin of his forge in the foreft as he had it in the time when Geoffrey de Dangel was juftice of the foreft. In the 39th year[11] of the fame reign, two dry oaks in the Foreft of Dean were granted to the abbot weekly for the fupport of his forge there, till an agreement with the king concerning the fame should be

[1] Rot. Claus., 7 Hen. III, m. 23 (p. 526, printed feries).
[2] Rot. Claus., 8 Hen. III, m. 11 and 13 (pp. 583 and 587, printed feries).
[3] Rot. Claus., 13 Hen. III, m. 2.
[4] Rot. Claus., 14 Hen. III, m. 22.
[5] Rot. Claus., 15 Hen. III, m. 2.
[6] Rot. Claus., 18 Hen. III, m. 15 and 19.
[7] Rot. Claus., 26 Hen. III, m. 13.
[8] Rot. Claus., 30 Hen. III, m. 11.
[9] Rot. Claus., 34 Hen. III, m. 15.
[10] Rot. Claus., 37 Hen. III, m. 23.
[11] Rot. Claus., 39 Hen. III, m. 14.

made. This important order was twice repeated in the following year[1] to Robert Waleran, cuftos, and James Frefel, conftable of St. Briavell's; and finally in the 42nd year[2] of Henry III, an arrangement was effected with the abbot and monks of Flaxley, whereby in lieu of their itinerant forge and two oaks a week for its fupport, they received from the king a large tract of the foreft which has ever fince been known by the name of the "Abbot's woods."[3]

Charter relating to the Grant of the "Abbot's Woods."

A tranfcript of the original Latin grant will be found in the Appendix No. II. and the following official tranflation is here appended from the record of: "A Pl'e of the Forreft of Deane att Gloucefter in eight days after St. Hilliarye in the xth year of the reigne of King Edward the Firft Anno Dom. 1281 before Lucarney of Thorney, Addun Gardun, Richard of Crepinge and Peter of Lench, juftices affigned to hear and determine the fame Plea."[4]

"The xxxi Rowle.

"A charter of King Henry the 3rd fone of King John of the exchanging of the forge of the abbot of Flaxley in the Forreft of Deane.

"Henry by the grace of God Kinge of England, Lord of Ireland, Duke of Normandye, Aquitane and Earl of Angeyawe, To all Archbifhops Bifhops Abbots Priors Earles Barrons Juftices Sherriffs Baylieffes officers and to all others his faithful Bayliffes greeting.

"Know ye that whereas our well beloved in Chrift the abbot and monks of Flaxley of the order of Sifefter (*sic*) were accuftomed to receive 2 oaks in our Fforeft of Deane every feven days for the mayntenance of their forge in the fame fforeft by the fufferance of our Sovereign Lord Henry our grand-

---

[1] Rot. Claus., 40 Hen. III, m. 12 and 19. For another reference to James Frefel, fee page 51, note 4.
[2] Rot. *Cart.*, 42 Hen. III, pars unica, m. 2. A duplicate of this grant appears amongft the Cartæ Antiquæ, QQ., No. 21.
[3] The "Abbot's woods" are fituated between Littledean, Sudeley and Cinderford. They were fold by the late Sir Thomas Crawley-Boevey, Bart., in 1830, and are now the property of E. Crawfhay, Efq., whofe father, the late W. Crawfhay, Efq., of Oaklands, near Newnham, purchafed from the Crown all the referved rights. See Act of Parliament on the fubject.
[4] The tranflation above given is taken from a copy found amongft the private papers at Flaxley Abbey.

father, and by our confirmation in perpetuall almes, and this to the great hurt of the said fforeſt and to our hindrance, we being advertized of the same hurt and hindrance at the requeſt of the said abbot and monks we have sent of our Councell our beloved and faythfull Henry of Bathon and Robert of Waldrand to enquire of that behalfe as well by the oaths of knights as by other ffree and lawful men by whom the truth of the matter may be better knowne in what part or place we may aſſign part of the fforesaid fforeſt more commodiouſely to the same abbot and monks a certayne part of wood in recompenſe of the fforesaid 2 oaks to the lefs hurt of the same fforeſt and to our leſs damage. And for that we are geaven to underſtand by the inquiſition made by the fforesaid Henry and Robert that it is to our profit and to the ſafeguard of the fforesaid fforeſt to aſſigne to the said abbot and monks in recompenſe of the aforesaid two oaks a certaine parte of wood in the said fforeſt in forme under written within the bounds and diviſions videlicet from Ardlond¹ unto the ford of Sinderford (vadum de Sinderford) on the left hand from that ford into the ford of *Suthleg*² and from thence by the valley of a river which is called Smallbrooke unto the road which is called Roughway³ (cheminum qui vocatur Rugeweye), and by the aforesaid road in length unto the land of John of Rodley on the left part, and from that land unto the aforesaid Ardland ſo far as the covering of the said wood doth ſtretch itſelf. We of our Councell have aſſigned and granted to the said abbot and monks in recompenſe of the aforesaid 2 oaks the aforesaid part of wood within the bounds and diviſions before written, to have and to hold to the same abbot and monks and to their ſucceſſors and to their church of Flaxley in perpetuall almes, quit from waſte and regard and from view of the foreſters and verderers and from all things which do belong to the foreſters and verderers and to their officers (except our hunting) ſaving to us and to our heirs the herbage of the said wood and the Ayreyes of great hawkes ffalcons and ſparrow hawkes,⁴ and mynerall works if they

¹ With the name Ardlond compare "Edland," where the monks were aſſigned an iron forge in the charter of Hen. II. See alſo Inquiſition of 15 Ed. I., No. 67, poſt.
² Suthleg the modern Sudeley.
³ The road called Ruggerweye (Rugweye, Rugwey, Ruggewey) is in the village of Brockworth. Several alluſions to this road will be found in the Glouc. Cart. *See* Index, vol. iii., p. 403.
⁴ This reſervation to the Crown of the Eyries of hawks points, of courſe, to the time when hawking was a royal paſtime. An aery (eyrie), ſays Dr. Nash, includes, not only the nest or brood, but the place destined for the breeding or training of hawks. (Collect. for Worc., vol. i. p. 151). The liberty of keeping theſe aeries, he adds, was in early times granted as a privilege

be found there—fo that the faid Abbot and Monkes may have the attachments[1] of the faid wood, and when it fhall feem expedient to them yt fhall be lawfull for them to enclofe the tenth parte of the faid wood with a hedge which may be defenfable againft all manner of cattle befides againft our wild beafts and that hedge fhall ftand for four years. The tenth part of the faid wood fhall be enclofed in divers places fo that nine parts of the fame wood may always be without the enclofures. Whereof we will, etc., as above.

Witneffes Nicholas of Molis, Elya de Rabbayne, Peter of Rivall, Robert Walerande, William de Grey, Nicholas de Turri Imbervo (?), Walter of Merton, Matthew of Mara, Ralph de Bakep', William Gerun, Robert of Stephanum (de Stephanum), and others.[2]

This important grant is entered in the Charter Rolls, and is quoted in the Calendar prepared by the Record Commiffioners, p. 87, as Cart. 42 Hen. III, Pars unica membrane 2, under the following heading:—Abbas de Flexlegh Cifterc. ordinis Dene foreft; quædam pars bofci ibidem per metas: Glouc.

A duplicate of this charter is alfo preferved amongft the Cartæ Antiquæ at the Public Record Office. In Sir Jofeph Ayloffe's Calendar this charter is entered as Q.Q., No. 21 Hen. III.

The reference already quoted to the Juftice Seat held at Gloucefter 10 Edw. I (1281), fhows that the title of the monks was challenged very foon after the grant was made. On the diffolution the Abbot's woods were granted with other poffeffions of the Abbey to Sir William Kingfton; and in 1657, when the Flaxley eftate had paffed into the poffeffion of William[3] "Boeve," a formal exemplification of this grant was made by Oliver, Lord Protector. This exemplification, with the Protector's feal attached, is preferved at Flaxley Abbey.

[1] The Court of Attachments was one of the three Courts of the foreft held for the forefters to bring in their *attachments* concerning any hurt or injury done in viridi aut venatione in the Foreft. By Art. 8 of Charta de Forefta, this Court was to be held every forty days. Manwood, pp. 23-31.

[2] The names of the witneffes here given are taken from the copy of the grant enrolled in the Charter Rolls. In the tranflation from which this tranfcript has been taken many names are omitted.

[3] Flaxley Abbey and eftates were in 1647 fold by William Kingfton, a defcendant of the original grantee, to two brothers named William and James "Boeve," whose father Andrew, a native of Coutrai (Kortrik) in Flanders, was brought to England circ. 1670 to efcape from the perfecution of Olivares Duke of Alva. Andrew Boeve had a large family, and many references to domeftic events relating to the Boeves are recorded in the regifters of the Dutch Church at Auftin Friars. The laft member of the original Boeve family who refided at Flaxley Abbey was William Bovey (Boeve) who d. there 26 Aug., 1692. His widow the well known Mrs. Catherine Bovey, "the perverfe widow" of Sir Roger de Coverley, remained at Flaxley Abbey till her death on 21 Jan., 1726. Flaxley Abbey and eftates then paffed by will of Will. Bovey into the poffeffion of Thomas Crawley, of Gloucefter, a diftant kinfman by marriage, from whom the prefent Baronet is directly defcended.

F

Stationary Forge at Flaxley.

Befides the itinerant forge fo frequently before alluded to, the abbot alfo poffeffed a ftationary forge. This ftatement is made by Fofbrooke (Hift. of Glouc., vol. i, p. 83), who quotes as his authority Rot. Claus. 14 Hen. III. The ftationary forge referred to appears to have been fituated in the village of Flaxley, clofe by the Abbey, where confiderable works were erected. Thefe works muft have formed at one time a very confpicuous feature in the village. Sir Robert Atkyns,[1] in his notice of Flaxley (1712), mentions the iron forges then in full work, and the Rev. Thomas Rudge,[2] in his notice of Flaxley (1802), fpeaks of the manufacture of iron being ftill carried on, the iron being efteemed peculiarly good. "Its goodnefs does not arife from any extraordinary qualities in the ore, but from the practice of working the furnace and forges with charcoal wood, without any mixture of pit-coal. The quantity of charcoal required is fo confiderable, that the furnace cannot be kept in 'blow,' or working, more than nine months fucceffively. At this time, Oct. 28th, 1802, a ceffation has taken place for nearly a year. Lancashire[3] ore, which is brought to Newnham by fea, furnifhes the principal fupply, the mine found in the foreft being either too fcanty to anfwer the expenfe of raifing it, or when raifed too difficult of fufion and confequently too confumptive of fuel to allow the common ufe of it. A ton of Lancafhire ore in the furnace requires fifteen or fixteen facks of charcoal. When the furnace is at work, about twenty tons a week are reduced to pig iron, and in this ftate it is carried to the forges, where about eight tons a week are hammered out into bars, ploughfhares, etc., ready for the fmith."

The wheels which worked the bellows and hammers were turned by a powerful ftream of water which rifes at *St. Anthony's Well*.[4] The Rev. H.

---

[1] Sir Robert Atkyns writing of Mrs. Catherine Bovey, owner of Flaxley Abbey from 1692 to 1726, fays "She hath an handfome houfe and pleafant gardens and a great eftate, a furnace for cafting iron, and three forges."

[2] Rudge's Hiftory of Glouceflerfhire, vol. ii. p. 96.

[3] In connection with the ufe of Lancafhire ore and the whole fubject of iron works in the Foreft, fee paper entitled "Obfervations on Iron Cinders," by George Wyrall, Efq. of Bicknor Court, publifhed at p. 216-234 of the Trans. Brift. and Glouc. Arch. Soc., vol. ii.

[4] The name of St. Anthony's well is doubtlefs a relic of the monaftic period. The fpring which rifes at this well feeds the ftream which defcends the Flaxley valley; and on this ftream the proprietors of the Abbey were entirely dependent for the water power required to drive their machinery. This ftream was formerly celebrated for the excellent quality of the trout which it produced, which grew to a confiderable

G. Nicholls, after quoting Rudge's defcription of the Flaxley iron works, ftates that the aged people of the neighbourhood[1] well remember when the Flaxley furnaces were in blaft, and tell of the ancient cinders and pickings of the old mine holes being taken down to them. The iron works at Flaxley have long fince been difcontinued, and with the removal of the furnace buildings, and of the pools in which the water accumulated for driving the machinery, the whole appearance of the Flaxley valley has been changed, and changed it need fcarcely be added for the better. The memory of the Flaxley iron forge ftill, however, lingers in one or two of the local names, fuch as "Furnace Yard" and "Mill Field," but otherwife there would be little to recall the time when the Flaxley furnaces were in blaft.

Grants of Fisheries to the Flaxley Monks.

Both of the charters under notice make prominent mention of the grant to the Flaxley monks of a certain fifhery at Reidley called "Newere." Fofbroke[2] quoting from the Harleian MS., 60 and 79, ftates that Roger fon of Milo Earl of Hereford granted to Roger fon of Manaffes de Minfterworth to hold two half virgates, and the fifheries "of Dunye and Newere." Reidley is probably the fame as the modern Rodley in the parifh of Weftbury, and muft not be confounded with "Ruddle," another manor fituated in Newnham, which formerly belonged to the Abbey of Gloucefter.

In the 54th year of Henry III[3] a notice occurs in the Patent Rolls of another Severn fifhery being granted to the Abbey of Flaxley known as

fize in the various pools where the water was allowed to accumulate. Of late years however the fifh have been entirely deftroyed by the ufe of noxious chemicals at the paper manufactory fituated in Guns mills at the head of the ftream. This manufacture has now been difcontinued fince about 1879. The water rifing from the fpring at St. Anthony's well has a great local reputation for its efficacy in curing cutaneous difeafes. The abundance of iron in the foil fufficiently accounts for a reputation which is well founded. As a "wifhing well" the fame fpring is in great requeft amongft the humbler claffes; but its reputation in this refpect feems to reft on a fomewhat hazy footing. For a fketch of the well and of the beech tree formerly overfhading it, fee Nicholl's Foreft of Dean, p. 182. In connection with the Saint in whofe honour the well is named, Bollandus gives an account of many miracles wrought by St. Anthony's interceffion, particularly in what manner the diftemper called the 'Sacred fire', fince that time 'St. Anthony's fire,' miraculoufly ceafed through the mediation of that Saint, when it raged violently in many parts of Europe in the eleventh century (Alban Butler).

[1] Nicholl's Foreft of Dean, p. 190.
[2] Fofbroke's Hiftory of Gloucefter, vol. ii, p. 172, 180 and 201. Rudge's Hiftory of Gloucefter, vol. ii, p. 388 note.
[3] Rot. Pat., 54 Hen. III, m. 9.

Hynewere or Hinewere. This grant was confirmed 30 Edw. III[1] on payment to the king of an annual acknowledgement of 12 pence.

In the Flaxley cartulary it is noticed that William de Parco granted to the Flaxley monks all his fhare of the fifhery of Bollewere.[2] And in the confirmation charter of 11 Henry III[3] Hugh Chearke (Charke) is noticed as having granted to the monks fix "Pnches" in the Severn oppofite Hanecombe; and Matilda Giffard all her land under the fifhery of Befpwike.

Befides the Severn fifheries above referred to the monks of Flaxley doubtlefs made abundant ufe of the trout for which the Flaxley ftream rifing at St. Anthony's Well is faid to have been long famous. This ftream was formerly dammed up at feveral points in the valley, and extenfive pools or refervoirs were thus formed, fome of which were in exiftence down to a very recent period. In thefe ponds the fifh could grow to a confiderable fize, and were doubtlefs largely ufed by the monks as a home preferve. It is noticed in the cartulary that Roger de Bofco[4] remitted to the monks all his claims regarding the refervoirs, ditches, and fifh ponds (de ftagnis foffatis et vivariis), and agreed to remove his dam from the monks' bridge and put it where it would do no harm. Galfrid de Dene[5] is noticed as having compromifed with the monks a difpute relating to the mill dam of Roger de Bofco.

In the grant to Sir William Kingfton of the Flaxley Abbey eftates after the fuppreffion in 1536 fpecial allufion is made to the "liberas warrenas, aquas, ftagna, vivaria, pifcarias, etc.," amongft the other poffeffions of the Flaxley monks.

Miscellaneous Grants in Charter of Henry II.

The remaining grants to Flaxley Abbey in the charter of Henry II call only for brief remark. The farm called Waftedene (Waftedene grangia) ftill has to be identified. The grant of land under "the Old Caftle of Dene" is again referred to, according to Fofbroke, in the Charter Rolls[6] of 7 Edward II. The Rev. H. G. Nicholls has expreffed the opinion that the "Old Caftle of Dene" may be identical with a circular ditch and bank about 50 yards in diameter on Camp Hill between Flaxley and Little Dean. The grounds upon which this opinion was expreffed are not ftated; and the fuggeftion feems to be little more than a conjecture unfupported by evidence. No. 12 of the

---

[1] Rot. Pat., 30 Edw. III, Tertia pars, m. 19.
[2] See Cartulary No. 38, 39, poft.
[3] Rot. Cart., 11 Hen. III, pars sec. m. 8.
[4] See Cart. No. 44.
[5] See Cart. No. 18.
[6] Rot. Cart. 7 Edw. II, pars unica m. 31.

Flaxley Abbey.

Flaxley cartulary is the grant to the monks by Hugh le Petit of all his land in Neweham held by Seftan Knif, near the ditch "of the Old Caftle." The "Old Caftle" referred to in this grant may poffibly be the fame as that referred to in the charter of Henry II.

The grant of a meadow in Reidley, called "Pulmede," is referred to in No. 17 of the Flaxley Cartulary[1] which gives alfo the name of the donor, viz: Galfrid, fon of William de Dene. This meadow can, it is believed, even now be identified. A large meadow of that name the property of Maynard Wemyfs-Colchefter, Efq., fituated between the Church and the bend of the river Severn, near Garden Cliff, is ftill pointed out in the parifh of Weftbury; and the name Pulmede—the meadow on the Pill—being comparatively uncommon, it feems not improbable that this was the fame meadow that was originally granted to the Flaxley monks.

The land at Walmore is again referred to in the Clofe Rolls[2] of 13 Henry III when the abbot and monks of Flaxley were granted by the king "two acres of meadow in Walemore for the increafe of their park there." Lands were alfo granted at Northwood, which as well as Walmore and Rodley, was fituated in the hundred of Weftbury. At Dimmoc[3], in the hundred of Botloe, the monks were granted by Henry II, (1) the whole of the royal demefne (totum dominicum meum de Dimmoc); (2) Half the royal wood (dimidium nemus meum de Dimmoc); (3) Half the nets "which I have in my hands for the conveniences of my men" (dimidium retium in manu mea propter aifiamenta hominum meorum). The grant to the Flaxley monks of half the nets, employed prefumably for the capture of game in the Dimmoc woods, is an interefting fact, on which the information given in the note feems to throw fome light.

[1] Flaxley Cartulary No. 12, post.
[2] Rot. Claus. 13 Hen. III. m. 8.
[3] A place at Dymock is, I am informed, ftill called 'Hay traps.' Haiæ frequently alluded to in Domefday were enclofures for the capture of game. Spelman's Gloffary, edit. fol. Lond. 1687, p. 272 has the following: "Vallatum fuit et inclaufatum foffato haia et palatio. Hinc extenfius illud Rete quo e campis redeuntes cuniculos intercipiunt *an Haye* dicitur; eofque fic intercipere et predari *to Haye* a Gall. haier i.e. fepire."

To the exiftence of thefe Haiæ is attributed the frequent occurrence of the term 'Hay'—fpelled in various ways, as a local name. The feat of Ruffell J. Kerr, Efq., near Newnham, formerly called Hay Hill is now known as The Haie. Hayes for the capture of game were no doubt of common occurrence while the Norman foreft laws were in operation. Mention is made in thefe notes of the Hayes of Rofs, Hereford, and the Foreft of Dean. See alfo "Deer and Deer Parks" by Evelyn Shirley, (1867) pp. 10, 12, 153, 199, for further information on the subject of Hayes.

The grant of a certain clearing (effartum quoddam) under Caftiard called Vincent's land is not referred to in the earlier charter of Prince Henry. The place in queftion can no longer be identified.

Protection Charter of Richard I to Flaxley Abbey.

Having now given fome account of the various rights and privileges conferred on Flaxley Abbey by the foundation charter of Henry II, and having fhown how thofe rights and privileges were conftantly challenged by the foreft authorities, and were the fubject of reiterated orders by the sovereign, it remains to notice firft, a fpecial charter of protection granted to the abbey by Richard I, and fecondly, the various confirmation charters granted to the abbey from time to time by the sovereign of the day.

The protection charter of Richard I is enrolled amongft the Cartæ Antiquæ, and is numbered X 5 in the "Calendar of Antient Charters" publifhed by Sir Jofeph Ayloffe in 1774. In the Appendix will be found a copy of this charter, numbered III. This copy has been taken from the MS. volume at the Public Record Office, in which the Cartæ Antiquæ are tranfcribed. This charter declares that the Abbey of Dene and the Ciftercian monks belonging to it with all their lands, poffeffions, etc., were under the fpecial protection of the king; and all the authorities were charged to protect and defend the abbey as though it were the king's own, fo that no violence, infult, injury or vexation be caufed or fuffered to the abbey and monks. The charter further provided that fuits againft the abbey in refpect of any land given or fold to them of which they held the charter were only to be heard before the king himfelf or his chief iuftice.

Confirmation Charters granted to Flaxley Abbey.

From the defcription already given of the fpecial rights and privileges granted to Flaxley Abbey within foreft limits it will readily be underftood that the monks of Flaxley ftood in fpecial need of the royal protection and fupport; and accordingly it excites no furprife to find that the abbey feized every opportunity of procuring from each fovereign in turn a formal confirmation of all the rights and privileges conferred on them by Henry II and fubfequent kings. The following is a lift of all the confirmation charters which I have been able to find relating to this foundation.

Flaxley Abbey. 39

1. Charter of Prince Henry Duke of Normandy.
2. Charter of Henry II.
3. Charter of Richard I.
4. Charter of Henry III.
5. Charter of Edward II.
6. Charter of Edward III.
7. Charter of Richard II.
8. Charter of Henry VI.

Of thefe the firft three are tranfcribed amongft the Cartæ Antiquæ, vide Ayloffe's Calendar. No. 4 is enrolled in the Charter Rolls, Rot. Cart. 11 Henry III, pars prima m. 27. No. 5 is alfo on the Charter Rolls, Rot. Cart. 7 Ed. II, pars unica m. 31. No. 6 is in the Charter Rolls, Rot. Cart. 4 Edw. III, pars unica m. 23. No. 7 is on the Patent Rolls, Rot. Pat. tertia et ultima patent, 22 Ric. II, m. 16. No. 7 is alfo on the Patent Rolls, Rot. Pat. prima patent, 27 Hen. VI, m. 6.

The original Rolls on which thefe charters are engroffed have been examined by me. The charters themfelves contain as a rule no new matter, and confift entirely of formal recitations of the charters, grants, &c., confirmed to the monks by previous fovereigns. An exception muft, however, be made of the confirmation charter granted by Richard I. This charter recites the previous charter of Henry II, and adds fome important rights and privileges which require notice. The additions referred to are quoted in extenfo in the Appendix I, No. iv., and are to the following effect :

It was declared to be the king's pleafure and command that the monks were to have and hold all their lands and poffeffions with all rights pertaining thereto free and quit from all exactions in pure alms, with fac and foc,[1] tol, theam and infangenethef, and were to be free from county fuits, hundred laws and fheriff's aids. All perfons were at the fame time prohibited by the king from vexing or difturbing the monks or their men or poffeffions on pain of forfeiting ten pounds.

[1] Sac—Jurifdiction in matters of difpute. Soc—" Interpellatio majoris audientiae," a liberty, privilege or franchife granted by the king to a fubject; alfo the area within which that franchife is exercifed. Tol— Duty on imports. Theam—The right of compelling the perfon in whofe hands ftolen or loft property was found to vouch to warranty, that is, to name the perfon from whom he received it. Infangentheof— Jurifdiction over a thief caught within the limit of the eftate to which the right belonged. Stubb's Gloffary, Doc. illuft. of Englifh Hiftory.

The right of Infangenthef is thus defcribed by Bracton "et dicitur Infangenthef latro captus in terra alicujus de hominibus fuis proprio feifitus latrocimo. Outfangthefe vero dicitur latro extraneus veniens aliunde de terra aliena et qui captus fuit in terra ipfius qui tales habet libertates."

The foundation charter of Henry II and fubfequent kings contain, it will be noticed, very few names of private benefactors. Special mention only is made of Roger Earl of Hereford, Leuveric or Leffric de Staura, Walfric of Dymoc, and Geoffry fon of Walfric. The chief fource of information relative to private benefactors of the abbey is, of courfe, the Cartulary, of which a notice in detail will be given hereafter. A large number of the private grants mentioned in the Cartulary were, however, formally confirmed to the abbey by Henry III. A record of this confirmation is preferved in the Charter Rolls of 11 Henry III,[1] and the genuinenefs of the Cartulary feems to be ftrongly fupported by the independent teftimony derived from this fource. The charter referred to, being under these circumftances one of fpecial importance, will be found fet out at length in Appendix No. v; to facilitate enquiry full references will be found in the notes relating to the Cartulary given below.

Miscellaneous Grants to Flaxey Abbey.

In addition to the grants, privileges, &c., conferred on Flaxley Abbey as noticed above, under other heads there are a few additional grants and orders relating to Flaxley to which allufion is made in the Public Records.

In the fifth year of Henry III[2] a royal order was addreffed to John of Monmouth, Conftable of St. Briavell's, commanding him to allow the abbot of Flaxley to hold in peace "the hermitage of Erdlond"[3] as he had been accuftomed to hold it in the time of King John.

In the fifth year of Henry III record is made of a royal letter[4] addreffed to John of Monmouth, ftating that the king had given permiffion to the abbot and monks of Flaxley to have a fheep cot (berkeria) in Ruardean and Northden

---

[1] Rot. Cart., 11 Hen. III, pars sec. m. 8.
[2] Rot. Claus., 5 Hen. III, m. 20. (p. 441, printed feries).
[3] The eftablifhment of this hermitage, and the appointment of William the Hermit, are related in No. 25 of the Flaxley Cartulary. The Rev. E. L. Cutts ftates that hermitages or anchorages fometimes depended on a monaftery, and were not neceffarily occupied by brethren of the monaftery, but by any defiring to embrace this mode of life whom the convent might choofe. The hermit however probably wore the habit of the Order.
A hermitage in the Taynton wood, subject to St. Peter's at Gloucefter, is noticed in the Gloucefter Cartulary. There was alfo a hermitage at St. Briavells, fubject to the monaftery of Grace Dieu in Monmouthfhire, fee Cartæ Antiquæ, Q.Q. 27, and Rot. Claus. 11 Hen. III. p. 170, printed feries, noticed in Nicholl's Perfonalities, Foreft of Dean, p. 1.
[4] Rot. Claus., 6 Hen. III, m. 13. (p. 490, printed feries).

(intra Ruwarthin et Northden) for the fpace of the king's life. Given at Monmouth on the 9th day of March.

In the fifteenth year of Henry III the fheriff of Gloucefter was commanded with the conftable of St. Briavell's and others to affign to the abbot of Flaxley the two acres of moor in Rademoor which the king had granted to him.[1]

In the twenty-feventh year of Edward III (1353) there appears on the Patent Rolls[2] the record of a fpecial grant to the abbey of Flaxley of the sum of £36 9s. 1d. from the rents of the newly affarted lands of the king in the foreft of Dean in confideration of the great loffes which the abbot and convent had fuftained from the deer and other wild beafts of the foreft, and alfo from the various and conftant vifits of the king[3] (varios et frequentes acceffus noftros). In the enforcement of this claim the abbot and convent were allowed the fame power of diftraint which the king himfelf enjoyed. This grant, which is one of fome importance, will be found in extenfo in the Appendix, No. vi.

Public Inquifitions and Licences to assign Land to Flaxley Abbey.

In the fifty-fecond year of Henry III an inquifition was held to afcertain whether it would be to the injury of the king to allow the grant of a certain fifhery in the Severn to be made to the abbots of Flaxley and Perfhore. The jurors expreffed the opinion that the grant would be injurious.[4]

In the fifty-fourth year of Henry III another inquifition was held to afcertain whether it would be to the injury of the king that a grant be made of the fifhery of Hynewere in the Severn to the abbots of Flaxley and Perfhore.[5] The jurors having decided that the king would not be injured by the faid grant, a licence was iffued in the fame year which is entered on the Patent Rolls.[6]

The original inquifitions and licence on the Patent Rolls have been carefully examined by me; but I have been unable to identify the Hynewere fifhery referred to.

In the fixth year of Edward I an inquifition poft mortem was held on the death of Alexander Bleyght, forefter in fee of the foreft of Dene, who died in the

[1] Rot. Claus., 15 Hen. III, m. 9
[2] Rot. Pat. 25, 26, 27 Edw. III, infimul No. 7.
[3] Of the vifits of Edward III to Flaxley' abbey this is the only notice that I can find. The vifits of King John will be noticed hereafter.
[4] Inq. 52 Hen. III, n. 22. (See Roberts' Cal. Gen., Hen. III and Edw. I, page 131.)
[5] Inq. 54 Hen. III. No. 68. (Roberts' Cal. Gen., p. 145.)
[6] Rot. Pat., 54 Hen. III, m. 9.

preceding reign. John Bleyght, alias Byeyt, is declared to be the fon and heir of the deceafed, who held a bailiwick in the foreft of Dean, called Bleytyefbayllye, from the time of the Conqueft, and held it on the day of his death. After his death John, fon and heir of the aforefaid Alexander, remained in the charge of the king, becaufe he was under age. And being thus in the king's charge King Henry gave to the abbot and convent of Flaxley in exchange for one forge two parts of the bailiwick aforefaid, whereby the faid John Bleyght fuftained lofs to the amount of two marks a year for fourteen years, or twenty-eight marks in all.¹

In the feventh year of Edward I an inquifition was taken to enquire if Richard Talbot and his anceftors had hitherto from times paft been accuftomed to have common of pafture in the wood of the abbot of Flaxley within the bounds of the foreft as belonging to his own free land in Longhope. The jurors did not know.²

In the fifteenth year of Edward I an inquifition poft mortem was held on the death of John of Penrys. The jurors fay that the aforefaid John, and Rofa his firft wife, formerly acquired the whole of the aforefaid tenement in Dimmoc from Robert Malet, and the aforefaid tenement in Bromefberie from William de la Hulle, to be held by the faid John and Rofa and the heirs of their bodies; and that Agnes, the wife of Ivo of Clintone, the daughter of the aforefaid John and Rofa and their heir, being then of the age of fourteen years, entered upon the aforefaid tenement, and made oath of fealty to the abbot of Flaxley, and gave for her relief ten fhillings, after the death of the faid John, who died in the eleventh year of our lord the king, about the time of the feaft of the Afcenfion of our Lord.³

In the fame year (15 Edward I) an inquifition was held by Grimbald Pauncefot and William Hatheway, keepers of the foreft, regarding a complaint of the abbot of Flaxley. It was found that while Thomas de Clare was keeper of the foreft, there came a certain William de Abbenbale, Walter Page, and Elys Page all miners, and digging in the land of the abbot of Flaxley at Ardlonde, found a mine there; whereupon the abbot difcovering what they were about immediately removed them and filled up the pit with ftones and earth.⁴

¹ Inq. p.m. 6 Edw. I, No. 88. (Roberts' Cal. Gen., p. 274).
² Inq. 7 Edw. I, No. 40. (Roberts' Cal. Gen., p. 285). Gilbert Talbot appears amongft the benefactors of Flaxley Abbey, Cart. No. 13.
³ Inq. p.m. 15 Edw. I, No. 19 (Roberts' Cal. Gen., p. 378).
⁴ Inq. 15 Edw. I, No. 67 (Roberts' Cal. Gen., p. 384).

In the twentieth year of Edward I, licence was granted to Robert de Berkele and others to affign to the abbot and convent of Flaxley, a certain meffuage and the rents thereof in Erlingham.[1]

In the fecond year of Edward III an inquifition was held to afcertain whether it was to the king's injury to grant licence to John le Botiler of Lamultyt and Beatrice his wife, to give five marks of rent per annum from the manor of Bruerne to the abbey of Flaxley, being held of the king in capite by twelve pence per annum paid to the fheriff and fuit at King's Barton.[2] The jurors having found that the said grant was not to the king's injury, licenfe was formally granted by the king to John le Botiller of Lanultyt, to affign the faid rent to the abbey of Flaxley in perpetuity in return for fupplying a monk to do daily fervice for the fouls of him and his anceftors.[3]

In the thirty-fecond year of Edward III an inquifition was held on the application of Geoffry le Marchal Chaplain and John Arham for permiffion to affign four meffuages, two tofts, one mill, two carucates of land, four acres of mead and two of wood, fix marks of rent, and a moiety of the advowfon of Blechefdon (Blaifdon) to the abbey of Flaxley; the premifes aforefaid being fituate in the parifhes of Elneton, Newenham, Erlyngham, Longhope and Weftbury.[4] No injury to the king being fhown, the required permiffion was granted by a formal order in the fame year. This order is enrolled in the Patent Rolls.[5]

In the thirty-eighth year of Edward III an inquifition appears to have been

---

[1] Rot. Pat. 20 Edw. I, m. 18. Roger Berkeley, knight, is named as a benefactor of the monaftery of Flaxley in Valor Ecclesiafticus of Hen. VIII, fee p. 486. This Flaxley Manor in the parifh of Arlingham is thus alluded to in "Smyth's Berkeley MSS." Hundred of Berkeley, vol. iii, page 61.

"In this parifh alfo, the abbot of the Monaftery of ffiaxley had a little Manor, raifed like as the former by the guifts at feverall times of the lord Berkeleys and other ffreeholders, which likewife cominge to the Crowne by the diffolucion of that Monaftery in 31 H. 8. was forthwith after given by that kinge to Sir Anthony Kingfton, (at that time one of the knights of this Shire for that parliament, and then high Steward of Berkeley hundred), and his heires. By whofe death in the firft of Qu: Mary, it came to Edmond Kingfton, father of Anthony, father of William Kingfton of ffiaxley that nowe is, who is faid to have lately either fold the fee or to have made longe Leafes equivalent therto, to Robert Longney, Henry Wintle, Richard ffryer of Hockerhill, Walter Carter, and . · . . . . . . The tenure whereof is of the king by knight fervice in Capite; And for the moft part, or altogeather lye in the hamblet called Sloo, in the furtheft part northward of the parifh."

[2] Inq. 2 Edw. III, fecond numbers, No. 128.
[3] Rot. Pat., Prima pars 3 Edw. III, m. 16.
[4] Inq. 32 Edw. III, second numbers, No. 87.
[5] Rot. Pat., Secunda pars 32 Edw. III. No. 28.

held on an application to grant to the abbey of Flaxley a certain mill and meadow, with the rents thereof, in Northwode and the vill of St. Briavell's. No injury to the king being fhown, the required permiffion was given by a formal order paffed in the fame year. This order is enrolled on the Patent Rolls.[1]

In the forty-fixth year of Edward III an inquifition is faid by Tanner to have been made on a propofal to affign to the abbey of Flaxley half a knight's fee in Blecheden.[2] I cannot find the record of this inquifition, or of any licence iffued thereupon.

In the tenth year of Richard II John Sabyn Chaplain and Thomas Snodhull applied for licence to give one meffuage, one toft, one carucate of land and twenty-eight acres of mead all lying in Leye, Bofeleye and Rodeleye, together with one meffuage, fixty acres of land and meadow, and four pounds rent from Longhope and Huntley to the abbey of Flaxley.[3] No injury to the king being fhown, licence was formally granted as ufual. This licence is enrolled on the Patent Rolls.[4]

In the inquifition poft mortem of William Waryn taken in, the feventh year of Henry V, it was noticed that the eftate of Soilewell, or Sulley, in the hundred of St. Briavell's, was held by the deceafed from the abbot of Flaxley.[5]

Similarly in the inquifition poft mortem of Robert Greyndour, Arm., it was found that one meffuage and one carucate of land in Hurft were held by the deceafed from the abbey of Flaxley at the nominal rent of one red rofe.[6]

Notices of Flaxley Abbey in the Hundred Rolls of Edward I.

The Hundred Rolls, as is well known, have been printed by order of the Record Commiffioners in two volumes folio. These records contain the following references to Flaxley:

Page 176, vol. i. " Sc'us [fanctus] Brivallus. Item Abbas de Habeal tenet manerium de Habeal' de domino Rege in capite cum balliva, et abbas de Flaxel' ño habet magnam partem ballivæ, nefciunt qual'."

[1] Rot. Pat., Prima pars, 38 Edw. III. No. 38.
[2] Inq. 46 Edw. III, No. 10 is Tanner's reference.
[3] Inq. 10 Ric. II, No. 107.
[4] Rot. Pat., Prima pars, 11 Ric. II, m. 28.
[5] Inq. p.m., 7 Hen. V, No. 52 Will'us Waryn.
[6] Inq. p.m., 22 Hen. VI, No. 34, Robertus Greyndour, Arm.

Flaxley Abbey.

This entry is noticed by Nicholls[1] who has expreſſed the opinion that "Habeal" may be the ſame as " Abbenhall." The correctneſs of this opinion appears to me to be very doubtful; but I am unable to offer any more ſatiſfactory interpretation myſelf. I have carefully examined the original roll on the chance that the word might have been wrongly printed ; but the word in the original is undoubtedly "Habeal," and it remains for experts to ſay who the 'Abbas de Habeal' was, and where was ſituated the manor of that name, with the bailiwick, of which the abbot of Flaxley is ſaid to have had a great part, though on what title the jurors did not know.

In the ſame Hundred it was ſtated that John Bleyght holds one virgate of land from the king in chief, with the bailiwick appurtenant, and that the abbot of Flaxley holds the greater part of the bailiwick, though on what title was unknown.

Alſo Thomas of Blakeney held from the king one virgate of land with the bailiwick, which laſt was in the poſſeſſion of the abbot of Flaxley.

In the ſame rolls appears the following reference to Flaxley under the head of Weſtbury[2]:—

"The jurors ſay that Roger Cadel gave five acres of land out of the manor of Rodley to the abbot of Flaxley in pure alms, whereby his lord the king has loſt the tallage, etc., belonging to him."

"The aforeſaid abbot holds two meſſuages and his two tenants two acres of land out of the tenement of Walter of Chexhull in the manor aforeſaid,[3] and three acres out of the tenement of Henry of Humelmore[4] in the ſame manor, and two acres from the fee of Garne,[5] whereby their lord the king has loſt tallage."

Under the head of Botlowe appears the following[6] :—

"The jurors ſay that the abbot of Flaxley holds the tenement which belonged to Haylof who was a ceorl ('Sokemannus'[7]) of the king in Dimmoc, and half a virgate of land through William Gamages who was enfeoffed of half a knight's fee in the ſame manor by King Richard."

[1] Perſonalities of the Foreſt of Dean, by the Rev. H. G. Nicholls, p. 16.
[2] Hundred of Weſtbury, p. 180.
[3] For grants of Henry of Cheakeſhill fee Cart. No. 22 and 61, alſo Rot. Cart. 11 Hen. III, pars. ſec. m. 8.
[4] Philip of Humelmore appears amongſt the benefactors to the Flaxley monks in Rot. Cart. 11 Hen. III. pars. ſec. m. 8.
[5] For references to Hugh of Gerne (Garne) fee notes under "Additional Benefactors " poſt.
[6] Hundred of Botlowe, p. 183.
[7] Sokemannus, Sochemannus—A ceorl, a free landowner not noble. Stubb's Gloſs., 528.

"The abbot of Flaxley holds of the land which belonged to Robert Mufchet[1] two virgates of land and two acres of meadow. The fame abbot was enfeoffed of thirteen acres of land and one meffuage by William de Byfeleye."

Perambulation of Forest of Dean.

Bigland in his Hiftory of Glouceſterſhire[2] notes that the early records of the foreſt of Dean abound in accounts of perambulation. In 1225 (9 Hen. III) one was made on the petition of the monks of Flaxley, including the additions made in former reigns, which in 1300 (28 Ed. I) were difafforeſted, and called Purlieus. This fettlement was confirmed by Parliament in 1326, 1 Ed. III.

Taxation of Pope Nicholas.

The eccleſiaſtical valuations known as the Taxation of Pope Nicholas, 1292 (20 Edw. I), and the Valor Eccleſiaſticus of Henry VIII, furniſh fome intereſting information relating to Flaxley abbey. Both of thefe valuations have been printed by the Record Commiſſioners, and are well known to all hiſtorical enquirers.

In the taxation of Pope Nicholas, under the head of Hereford Temporalities, the goods of the abbey of Flaxley are thus enumerated at p. 171.

Bona temporalia Abbatis de Flaxle.

		£	s	d
Idem habet in manerio fuo de Walemore quatuor carucatas terræ precium carucatæ	- - -	0	8	0
De redditibus affiſæ per annum	- -	0	7	0
Item 20 plauſtratas feni precium cujufdam libræ	- -	0	1	0
Item idem habet tres carucatas terræ in grangia juxta Abbatiam precium carucatæ	- - -	0	8	0
De redditibus affiſæ	- - -	1	6	8
Item unum molendinum foler. ibidem precium per ann.	-	0	10	0
De uno molendino aquatico ibidem per annum	- -	0	6	8
Item apud Novam Terram duas carucatas terræ per centum carucatas		0	6	8
De redditibus affiſæ ibidem	- -	0	3	0
Item apud Dene tres carucatas terræ per centum carucatas	-	0	7	0
De redditibus affiſæ	- - -	0	5	0

[1] Robert Mufchet appears amongſt the benefactors of Flaxley Abbey in Cart. No. 31 and 32.
[2] Bigland's Hiſtory of Glouceſterſhire, p. 457, under "Foreſt of Dean."

Flaxley Abbey. 47

Item 10 plauftratas feni per cent plauftrates	-	-	0	1	0
Item apud Dymmok quinque carucatas terræ per centum carucatas		0	8	0
De redditibus affifæ per annum	-	-	0	11	0
Decem plauftratas feni per cent. cujufdam lib.	-	-	0	1	0
Item unum molendinum aquaticum p.c. per annum	-	-	0	6	8
Item apud Seddeftowe duas caruc. terræ p.c. cuj. lib.	-	-	0	6	8
De medietate unius gurgitis	-	-	-	0	10	0
De aliis pifcariis	-	-	-	0	10	0
Item in villa de Monem. de redd. afs.	-	-	-	0	1	5
Summa	-	-	-	14	0	1
Decime	-	-	-	1	8	0

At page 174 is the following:—
   Abbas de Flaxle.

Habet 35 vaccas exit. omn.	-	-	-	-	2	12	6
De multonibus 100. Exit. omn.	-	-	-	1	13	4
Item de ovibus mat'cib' 140 exit. omn.	-	-	-	3	10	0
Summa	-	-	-	7	15	0
Decime	-	-	-	0	15	7

At page 204—6, under Bath and Wells.
   Archidiaconatus Wellen. Decanatus de Axebrugg.
Abbas de Flexlegh   -   -   - 11 0 0   Blakfdon.
At page 221. Wygorn' Dioc.
   In Decanat. de Stonhoufe.

Preter hoc porcio Abbatis de Flaxle in dec. ret'. Taxatio	-	1	5	0
Decime	-	-	-	-	0	2	6

At page 238. Same diocefe. Archidiaconatus Glouceftr'.
Abbas de Flexl. habet apud Climperwell tres carucatas terræ et valet caruc. viginti folid. Item apud Erlingham unam carucatam terræ et valet viginti folidos. Item de exit. ftaur. quadraginta folidos   -   -   -   - 6 0 0
      Decime   -   -   -   - 0 12 0

Valor Ecclesiasticus of Henry VIII.

By an Act paffed in the twenty-fixth year of King Henry VIII (A.D. 1534) it was finally fettled that the Church fhould render to the king the firft fruits of all benefices and dignities, and the tenth of their annual revenues. The Act was entitled "An Acte concerninge the paiment of Firfte Fruites of all dignities, benefices and promocyons fpirituall, and alfo concerninge one annuell pencyon of the tenthe part of all the poffeffions of the Churche fpirituall and temporall granted to the Kings Highnefs and his heires."

It was to carry into effect the provifions of this Act that the Valor was formed. The only exifting Valor of the ecclefiaftical property of the kingdom was the furvey made in the time of King Edward I by Pope Nicholas IV. A new furvey was neceffary on account of the change in the value, eftimated in money, of the various dignities and benefices; (2) a great change had taken place in their relative values; (3) in the interval fince the laft valuation had arifen innumerable foundations of the fpecies denominated Chantries, from which a large revenue was about to be derived. Hence it was enacted that fuch a furvey fhall be taken by commiffioners fent in the king's name in every part of the kingdom, whofe duty it fhould be to enquire out all promotions and to return an exact account of all the temporalities and fpiritualities with which they were endowed.

The Valor Ecclefiafticus of King Henry VIII is the return into the exchequer which thefe commiffioners made.

The poffeffions of the monaftery of Flaxley within the foreft of Dean are thus enumerated under the head of the various manors in which the abbey owned lands or other revenue.[1]

Flaxley Monafterium infra Foreftam de Deane in Com. Glouceftr'.

Manerium de Bleyfdon.

Valet clare in reddit' et firm' unacû al' cafual ib'm p' annû il.
pro reddit' refolut' año regi et 13s. 4d. pro vad' Adam
Phelpis collect' reddit' ib'm. - - - 6l. 6s. 9d.

Man'ium de Walmoure cu' Membr'.

Valet clare in reddit' et firm' unacû al' cafual ib'm p' annû ultra
1s. 3½d. pro reddit. refolut'. dño regi 10s. vicar choral'
eccl'ie cath'is Hereford 2s. ad hundred' dñi regis de Weftbury et 1l. 16s. 8d. pro vad. Adam Philpis collect' reddit'
ib'm. - - - - - 26l. 3s. 9d.

Div's Terr' et Tent' in Newneham Polton villa Glouc'.
Howle et Goodrych.

Valent clare in redd' et firm' ib'm p' annû ultra 6s. 8d. folut'
pro vad Thome Boxe collect' reddit' ib'm, et 10s. pro
capit'i re*. abb'ti et convent' de Tyntharn' - - 5l. 2s. 5d.

---

[1] Dugdale's Mon. Angl., Ed. 1825, Vol. V, pp. 590, Valor Ecclefiafticus temp. Hen. VIII. (Tranfcript of Return 26 Hen. VIII. Firft Fruits Office.)

Rochellefbury.

Valet clare in reddit' et firm' unacū aħ cafual' ibm per annū ultra 7s. folut' dño Regi pro capit'li reddit' 13s. 4d. priori Sēi Joħis J'rem in Anglia pro capit'li re' 2s. aƀƀti et convent' de Keyſhem pro capit'li redđu 13s. 4d. pro vad' Thome North collect' reddit' ibm et 20ˢ pro feod' Riči Wermecombe fen^u ibm. - - - 20l. 4s. 4d.

Newland Colford et Staunton.

Valent clare in redd' affis' ibm per annū ultra 43s. 4d. pro capit'li reddit' folut' ad caftrum dūi Regis de Sčo Briavello et 13s. 4d. pro vad'. Riči Baret collect' redd' ibm. - 17l. 3s. 6d.

P'va Deane.

Valet clare in redd' et firm' unacū aħ cafual' ibm per annū ultra 20ˢ folut' pro vad' Will'i Tanner[1] collect. redd. ibm. - 10l. 17s. 2d.

Dymmocke.

Valet clare in redd' et firm' unacū al' cafual' ibm per annū ultra 10s. folut' pro vad' Joħnis Wynyet collect' reddit' ibm et 20d. pro feod' Thome Lane fen^u ibm. - 12l. 12s. od.

Arlyngham et Clymperwell.

Valent clare in redd' et firm' ibm per annū ultra 3s. 6d. folut' Waltero Yate pro capit'li redd' 20d. pro pane ann^{ti} diftribut' apud Barkeley et Slymbrydge div's pauperib⁹ pro āia Rogeri Berkeley[2] militis unius benefactor' monafterii predči et 6s. 8d. pro vad' Witti Longley collect' redd' ibm. 5l. 9s. 10d

Flaxley.

Valet clare in redd' et firm' unacū al' cafual' ibm per annū ultra 53s. 4d., folut' pro feod' Joħis Arnold armigeri capit'li fen^u oīni' terr' et teñt' predčo monafterio pertin' 6s. 8d. pro vad' Witti Fowle collect' redd' ibm et 20ˢ pro elemos' diftribut' div's paupib3 in cena dñi - - 8l. 3s. 4d.

S^{ma} clar' valor' Monafterii predči - - 112l. 3s. 1d.

Xme inde - - - - 11l. 4s. 3¾d.

---

[1] An original deed dated 21 April, 26 Hen. VIII. (1535) executed between Thomas Were, abbot of Flaxley, and William Tanner, is ftill preserved at Flaxley abbey. (See Part III, post.)

[2] Robert de Berkeley received a licenfe 20 Ed. I. to affign to the abbot and convent of Flaxley a meffuage and the rents thereof in Erlingham. (See p. 43.)

Writs of Summons to Parliament.

In Dugdale's Monasticon Anglicanum, vol. viii, App. iii, Ed. 1825, is furnished an alphabetical title of all the abbots, mafters, and priors of religious orders to whom any particular writs of fummons to Parliament iffued from anno 49 Hen. III to 23 Edward IV extant in the Clofe Rolls, and lift of fummons in the Tower of London with the feveral years of each king's reign wherein they were fummoned.

This table fhows that writs of fummons[1] to Parliament were on feveral occafions iffued to the abbot of Flaxley in the reign of Edward I, viz.—

22 Ed. I. - - - 1293-94.
23 „ - - - 1294-95.
24 „ - - - 1295-96.
28 „ - - - 1299-1300.
32 „ - - - 1302-3.

During the reigns of Edward I and Edward II it appears that the number of abbots fummoned to Parliament was fluctuating and uncertain. The lift of Parliamentary abbots was not formally fettled till the time of Edward III, when the number was fixed at 26, exclufive of two abbots and one prior which are doubtful, viz., the abbots of Leicefter and St. James, Northampton, and the prior of Coventry.

Miscellaneous references to Flaxley Abbey.

The remaining few references to Flaxley abbey which I have been able to difcover in the public records are of inferior importance.

In the Great Roll of the Pipe for the 1ft year of Richard I, 1189-1190, printed by the Record Commiffioners, the following entry occurs at p. 163 :—

Rot. 10, memb. 1. " Et Monach. de Flexeleya vi li. nūo in Dimmoc."

---

[1] In Lords' Reports on the Dignity of a Peer, vol. ii, p. 449, in the Index Summonitionum of Edw. I are the following references :—Flaxele Abbas de, 22, 23 ter., 24, 28 bis., 32.

All thefe references to the abbot of Flaxley are writs of fummons to Parliament taken from the Clofe and other Rolls, and set forth at length in Appendix i, part i, of the Lord's Report on the Dignity of a Peer. The original rolls from which the references are taken are as follows :—22 Ed. I., Rot. Vafcon., m. 4, dors; Close Rolls, 6 references, all in dorfo, viz., 23 Ed. I, m. 4; 23 Ed. I, m. 2; 24 Ed. I, m. 7; 28 Ed. I, m. 16; 28 Ed. I, m. 3; 32 Ed. I, m. 2.

Flaxley Abbey.

A reference in fimilar terms appears at page 34 of "Rotulus Cancellarii vel Antigraphum Magni Rotuli Pipæ de tertio anno regni regis Johannis," alfo publifhed by the Record Commiffioners.

In the Oblata Rolls publifhed by the fame authorities under the title "Rotuli de Oblatis et Finibus in Turri Londonenfi affervati temp. Regis Johannis," occurs the following entry at p. 546 :—

"Abbas de Flaxley dat. tertiam partem viii m[arcarum] pro habendo brevi de debito illo. Habuit brevem. Mandatum eft vicecomiti quod capiat fecuritatem de primis illis denariis de tertia parte predictarum viii m[arcarum]."

In the 11th year of Henry III the following entry appears on the Clofe Rolls :—

"Abbas de Flexl. attorn. Regin. fil. Walteri circa Johannam fil. Johannis pet. de x mare."[1]

In the fame year appears the following entry :—

"It is commanded to Richard of Efton, William of Dene, and Richard of Weftbirie, that out of the money which has accrued from the forges of their Lord the King in Dene and is in their poffeffion at Flaxley, they fhould caufe William de Patot, fheriff of Gloucefterfhire, to have xx pounds by way of loan up to the feaft of St. Michael."[2]

In the 40th year of Henry III, Clofe Rolls, appears the following entry :—

Will. de Fontibus } Acquittance of Common
    Abbot of Flaxle } Summons in Co. Somerfet.[3]

In the fame year the conftable of St. Briavell's was commanded with the advice of James Frefel and the abbot of Flaxley to fell wood in the foreft of Dene to the amount of 1,000 marks to be paid into the wardrobe.[4]

In the abftracts of the "Originalia" printed by the Record Commiffioners, vol. ii, p. 33, occurs the following :—

"Johannes le Botiller de Lanultyt finem fecit per decem marcas per licentiam habendi dandi quinque marcatas annui redditus Abbatiæ et Conventui bonæ Mariæ de Flaxleye percipiendi de manerio de Breuerne ad inveniendum quendam capellanum in Abbatia predicta ftend."—Rot. 22.

In the notice of Inquifitions connected with Flaxley abbey it is mentioned that licence was granted to John le Botiller to affign certain rents to the abbey

---

[1] Rot. Claus., 11 Hen. III, m. 10. (Vol. ii, p. 210, printed feries.)
[2] Rot. Claus., 11 Hen. III, m. 5. (Vol. ii, p. 196, printed feries.)
[3] Rot. Claus., 40 Hen. III, m. 19, dorfo.
[4] Rot. Claus., 40 Hen. III, m. 10, dorfo. Compare Note 4, p. 31, for reference to James Frefel

of Flaxley in perpetuity in return for fupplying a monk to do daily fervice for the fouls of him and his anceftors.

In Rymer's Fœdera occur feveral references to the abbot of Flaxley taken from the Clofe Rolls, viz. :—

1294, 22 Edw. I, under the head of Mandatum Regis Arcbiepifcopo Eborum et Epifcopis Angliæ de facto Vafconiæ, a Rege Franciæ fraudulenter obtentæ et nequiter detentæ.[1]

1305, 33 Edw. I. De Exequiis Johannæ Reginæ Franciæ celebrandis.[2]

1315, 8 Edw. II. Pro L marcis in menfe Pafchæ.[3]

1333, 7 Edw. III. Super memorato fubfido, de excufationibus non admittendis.[4]

1347, 21 Edw. III. De uno facco lanæ in Octabis nativitatis Beatæ Mariæ Virginis.

All the writs and orders quoted were of the nature of circulars addreffed to a large number of ecclefiaftics and others, amongft whom mention is made of the abbot of Flaxley.

Under the head of Clerical Subfidies (Exchequer) Diocefe of Gloucefter and Hereford, Ed. I to Hen. VIII in vol. viii, P.R.O., appears the following :—

"Numerus de capitibus omnium beneficiatorum et non beneficiatorum in decanat. de forefta Rofs, Irchenfeld, Heref. dioc. Tranfmiffus Abbati de Flaxley pro fubsidio levando."—2 mems.

Public events connected with Flaxley Abbey noticed in Ancient Chronicles and Public Records.

The firft important public event connected with Flaxley abbey of which I have been able to find notice is the vifitation of the Ciftercian abbeys which took place in 1187, that is, within forty years after the abbey was founded.

A reference to this vifitation will be found in the Waverley Annals (Rolls feries, vol. ii, p. 245) and is chiefly important for the prefent purpofe as bringing to light the names of two additional Flaxley abbots hitherto unnoticed by Browne Willis, Stevens, or others.

---

[1] Rymer's Fœdera, vol. i, part 2, p. 809. [2] Ibid, p. 971.
[3] Ibid, vol. ii, part 1, p. 264. [4] Ibid, p. 852.

The paſſage referred to is as follows :—

(1187) " Hoc anno defcenderunt in Angliam vifitatores miffi a capitulo Ciſtercienſi in quorum vifitatione dimiferunt Abbatias fuas Willielmus de Tinterna (ex fucceſſit Vido Abbas de Kingefwoda eique fucceſſit in Kingefwoda Willielmus prior ejufdem loci) et Willielmus Abbas de Bordefleia dimifit Abbatiam fuam, fucceſſit Ricardus fup-prior ejufdem loci. Hoc idem fecit Walerannus Abbas de Dene, et fucceſſit Alanus Monachus de Bordefleia."

'In this year came down to England vifitors fent from the Ciſtercian chapter ; at whofe vifitation William of Tintern refigned his abbacy and was succeeded by Vido, abbot of Kingfwood, who was himfelf fucceeded at Kingfwood by William, prior of the fame place ; and William, abbot of Bordesley refigned his abbacy, and was fucceeded by Richard, fub-prior of the fame place. The fame was done by Waleran, abbot of Dene, and Alan,[1] monk of Bordefley fucceeded him.'

Visit of King John to Flaxley Abbey, 1207-1214.

King John has left in hiſtory a bad reputation for his ill treatment of the Ciſtercian order of monks, an account of which is given in the Annales Monaſtici. In the year 1210 this order was fubjected to a ferious perfecution. Ranfom was extracted from them and they were forbidden to leave England. In 1212 was publiſhed a letter of King John to the fheriffs forbidding any mandate of the Pope againſt him to be received or executed, and in the fame year falfe letters were extorted from the Ciſtercians and others, whereby they profeffed to refign their property to the king. Flaxley being a Ciſtercian abbey probably bore its own fhare of the perfecution. The Itinerary[2] of King John fhews that he vifited Flaxley on. feveral occafions between 1207 and 1214, probably for the purpofe of hunting.[3]

---

[1] No. 69 and 70 of the Chartulary relate to grants made by abbot Alan (Alanus dictus Abbas de Dene) to Jordan, fon of Ralph, and to Godefrid Mog refpectively.

[2] The Itinerary here given is taken from the introduction to the Patent Rolls by Sir T. Duffus Hardy, printed by the Record Commiſſioners.

[3] Besides King John, Edward III appears to have paid frequent vifits to the abbey, probably alfo for the purpose of hunting. A fpecial grant was made to the abbey by Edward III in confequence of the loſſes fuſtained by the monks, fee notes, p. 41 ante.

A.D. 1207 at Gloucester	Nov.	14	Wednesday.
St. Briavell's	,,	15	Thursday.
,,	,,	16	Friday morning.
Flaxley	,,	16	,, evening.
St. Briavell's	,,	17	Saturday.
Hereford	,,	18	Sunday.
1212 at Flaxley	,,	8	Thursday.
,,	,,	9	Friday.
St. Briavell's	,,	10	Saturday.
,,	,,	11	Sunday.
,,	,,	12	Monday.
Flaxley	,,	12	Monday evening.
1213 at St. Briavell's	,,	28	Thursday.
,,	,,	29	Friday.
Monmouth	,,	29	Friday evening.
,,	,,	30	Saturday.
St. Briavell's	,,	30	,,
Flaxley	,,	30	,,
Gloucester	,,	30	,,
1214 at Braden's Coke	Dec.	11	Thursday.
Ashton	,,	11	,,
Flaxley	,,	11	,,

Burial of Gilbert de Clare at Tewkesbury, 1230.

In the year 1230, October 25, occurred the death of Gilbert de Clare[1] at Penros, in Brittany. His body was brought to Plymouth, and thence to Tewkesbury where he was buried, 11 November, in the presence of the abbots of Tewkesbury, Tintern, Flexley, Keynesham, Tureford and others. This event is alluded to in the Annals of Tewkesbury, (Rolls Series, vol. i, p. 76) in the following terms:—

"Venit tum corpus ad nos sabbato ante festum Sancti Martini, quievit autem in sepulcro Dominica sequenti. Sepultus vero est ante majus altare astantibus Abbatibas de Theokesberie, de Tynterue, de Flexleye, de Key-

---

[1] Several members of the De Clare family were buried in Tewkesbury Abbey. See Mr. A. Hartshorne's paper on "Monumental Effigies near Cheltenham," Trans. Glouc. and Bristol Arch. Soc., vol. iv, p. 231.

nefham, de Tureford et aliis viris religionis innumeris diversorum ordinum populisque innumeris utriufque Sexus."
'There came then the body to us on the Sabbath before the feaft of St. Martin, and was placed in the tomb on the following Lord's day. He was buried indeed before the greater altar, in the presence of the abbots of Tewkefbury, Tyntern, Flexley, Keynefham, Tureford, and a countlefs number of holy men of different orders and a multitude of both fexes.'

Connection of Flaxley Abbey with Richard Earl Marshall, 1234.

In the eighteenth year of Henry III 1233-34, ferious difturbances took place in connection with the infurrection of Hubert de Burgh and Richard Earl Marshall. After the king's quarrel with Hubert de Burgh in 1232, the latter was confined firft in the Tower and afterwards in the Caftle of Devizes. The king then made Des Roches, bifhop of Winchefter, his chief counfellor, and by his advice difmiffed the officers of his court, and garrifoned his caftle with Poiƈtevins and other foreigners.

Richard Earl Marfhall and other nobles remonftrated with the king, but obtaining no redrefs they took fteps to drive out the foreigners. Hoftages were then demanded from them by the king, but the Earl Marfhall apprehending treachery fled to Wales and made a league with Llewelyn, whereupon he was proclaimed as a traitor.

Hubert de Burgh efcaped from prifon Oƈtober 12, and joined the infurreƈtion againft the king.

The Clofe Rolls of 18 Henry VIII contain feveral allufions to this infurreƈtion, and fhow that the followers of the Earl Marfhall amongft other places fled to Flaxley Abbey, where the Conftable of St. Briavell's, the Sheriff of Gloucefter, and other officials were fent to take them.

The firft reference on this subjeƈt is dated 6 March, 18 Henry III,[1] and is as follows:—

'The fheriff of Gloucefter is commanded to take with him the conftable of St. Briavell's and the king's coroners of the county and go to the abbey of Flaxley and offer to perfons there who are againft the king that they fhall come out to ftand their trial or elfe abjure the kingdom.'

[1] Rot. Claus., 18 Hen. III., m. 28.

On the 15 March occurs the following entry :—

'The sheriff of Gloucester is commanded to permit the men armed with bows, arrows, and hatchets who came to the abbey to keep watch, because some of Richard Earl Marshall's men fled thither, to return to their parts and to retain the others for the said watch.'

This extract from the Close Rolls is printed in extensio in vol. i of Royal Letters, Hen. III, 1216-1235, edited by the Rev. Walter Shirley, app. iv, No. 7, under documents relating to fall of Hubert de Burgh as follows :—

"Mandatum est vice Comiti Glocestriæ quod omnes homines de comitatu suo juratos ad arcus et sagittas et hachias quos venire fecit usque Flexleiam ad vigilias faciendas ibidem occasione quorumdam servientium de gente comitis Ricardi Marescalli qui ad Abbatiam de Flexleia fugerunt ad partes suas sine impedimento redire permittat ad terras suas excolendas. Ceteros vero juratos ad loricas, perpunctos, et hauberinos quos ibidem ad hoc venire fecit faciat ibidem morari ad vigilias faciendas ita quod quidam unius patriæ et alii patriæ succeffint vigilias illas faciant. Teste Rege apud Wadestok decimo quinto die Martii per episcopum Wintoniensem et justiciarium."[1]

On the 20 March the following entry occurs :—

The constable of St. Briavell's is commanded to deliver up to the abbot the horses, etc., which were taken within the enclosure of the abbey, and on account of which the Bishop of Hereford excommunicated the constable and others. The Bishop is commanded to take off the excommunication.[2]

The Bishop of Hereford at this date was Hugh Folliot, confecrated 1219, died 1234. The oldest Register of the see of Hereford still in existence commences with Thomas de Cantelupe, 1275, 3 Ed. I, so that no reference to the events described is obtainable from those records.

On the 28 March the following entry appears :—

The constable of St. Briavells is commanded not to permit anything to be

[1] Rot. Claus., 18 Hen. III, m. 28, dorso. The insurrection of Hubert de Burgh took place in 18 Hen. III, 1233-34, and the extracts quoted from the Close Rolls refer to the writs for assembling the 'jurati adarma' dated A.D. 1231. The following extract from this writ, taken from Stubb's Documents illustrative of English history, is important as throwing light on the meaning of the entries in the Close Rolls relating to this insurrection :—

"Mandatum est vicecomiti Glouceftriæ quod, non obstante mandato regis ei facto de hominibus juratis ad arma et securibus veniendis ad exercitum regis venire faciat tamen homines juratos ad ferrum, videlicet loricas et haubiones et perpunctos ; faciat revenire ad eundem exercitum ducentos homines cum ducentis securibus et cum victualibus suis quadraginta dierum, quæ eis vicecomes faciat inveniri per homines comitatus sui juratos ad alia minuta arma, quos rex vult remanere in partibus suis." etc., p. 350.

[2] Rot. Claus., 18 Hen. III, m. 27.

taken in the wood of the abbot for eftovers of the keepers of the fervants of Richard Marfhall who fled to the monaftery; but to caufe him to be recompenfed for his hedges which have been burnt; and alfo reftitution of his horfes, arms and harnefs to be made. The aforefaid conftable and the fheriffs of Gloucefterfhire are commanded not to permit the aforefaid keepers to remain within the gates of the abbey or monaftery, but to perform their cuftody outfide the gates.[1]

The entries from the Clofe Rolls above referred to, I have carefully examined in the original Roll in the hope of finding fome additional particulars, befides thofe furnifhed in the excellent Index prepared by the authorities of the Public Record Office. I find, however, that the whole of the particulars mentioned in the Roll have been most carefully and accurately stated, and no additional matter of importance was obtained by me from the Roll itfelf.

Settlement of dispute between Abbots of Margan and Carlyon, 10 Aug. 1256.

The abbot of Flaxley appears in 1256 as one of the witneffes to the final fettlement of a difpute between the abbots of Margan, co. Glamorgan, and Carlyon (Carleon upon Ufke) co. Monmouth, regarding the affignment and boundaries of 100 acres of land. The original document is defcribed in the Seal Catalogue of the MSS. room of the Britifh Mufeum (75, A, 37)—

"Litteræ quibus narratur finalis compofitio controverfiæ inter abbatias de Margan co. Glamorgan, et de Karlyon (Carleon upon Ufk) co. Monmouth, fuper affignatione et limitatione centum acrarum terræ.

"Tefte abbatibus de Flexley co. Glouc., de Tinterna co. Monm., de Neth. (Neath.) co. Glamorgan : de Alba Domo co. Montgomery; et de Strata Florida co. Cardigan. Facta in Octavo S. Laurentii, 10 Aug. 1256, cum fig."

The feal of the abbot of Flaxley and of the other abbots named is or was appended to this document; but the Flaxley feal cannot now be identified. I have, however, been able to fecure from the Doubleday collection fatiffactory impreffions of the abbey feal, an account of which will be given hereafter.

Suspension of the Abbot of Flaxley for misconduct, 1335.

The laft public occurrence which I have to notice is the formal fufpenfion of the abbot of Flaxley for mifconduct in the ninth year of Edward III,

[1] Rot. Claus.,' 18 Hen. III, m. 27. N.B.—Both of thefe entries, which are of different dates, are engroffed on the fame membrane.

the charge of the abbey being meanwhile entrufted by the king to the abbots of Dore and Bordefley and to the prior of Flaxley. The record of this occurrence will be found in the Patent Rolls[1] of ninth Edward III. It relates that on account of the negligence (incuriam) and bad rule (malum regimen) of the abbots of Flaxley, the property of the abbey had been ferioufly wafted and confumed, and that the abbot and convent were deeply in debt. Under thefe circumftances it was declared that the king took the abbey and all its poffeffions into his own charge, and delivered the abbacy into the cuftody of the abbots of Dore, Bordefley,[2] and the prior of Flaxley to hold as long as the king fhall think fit. All perfons were forbidden to take away anything from the manors, granges, and other poffeffions of the abbey without the fpecial permiffion of the Commiffioners above-named. The reference in queftion, which is one of fpecial intereft, will be found in extenfo in Appendix 1, No. vii. How long the abbot was under fufpenfion is not known, but in the twenty-feventh year of Edward III. (1353) a fpecial grant to the abbey of £36 9s. 1d. was made by the king as before related, fee p. 41.

---

[1] Rot. Pat. 9 Edw. III., pars fecunda, m. 16.
[2] The Ciftercian abbey of Dore is in Herefordfhire. Bordefley is in Worcefterfhire. At the time of this fufpenfion Thomas Chorlton was Bifhop of Hereford (1327 to 1334).

PART II.

CARTULARY OF FLAXLEY ABBEY.

The following account of this Cartulary has been communicated to me by Mr. Samuel Gael of Battledown Knoll, Charlton Kings, Cheltenham. The original Roll on which the various documents relating to Flaxley abbey are engroffed was the property of Thomas Wyniatt, Efq., of Staunton in Gloucefterfhire. In 1825 it was lent by Mr Wyniatt to the late Sir Thomas Phillipps, Bart. of Middlehill, Warwickfhire, who made clear with his own hand a tranfcript of the contents of the whole Roll, which is now at Thirleftaine Houfe, Cheltenham. On the death of Mr. Wyniatt the original Roll paffed into the poffeffion of the late Sir Thomas Phillipps, and was included by him in the catalogue of his well-known library at Middlehill. In 1866 a portion of the Flaxley Cartulary, together with a table of the whole contents, was printed by the late Sir Thomas Phillipps at his private prefs at Middlehill. The print then made concludes with the following note.

" Finis Cartularii de Flaxley tranfcripti per T. Phillipps Anno Dni 1825, " et impreffi Marc. 1866.

" N.B. As the original Roll has been miflaid, the above could not be " collated with it therefore there may be a few errors. T. P."

The original Roll of the Cartulary, though known to have been in the poffeffion of the late Sir Thomas Phillipps, is unfortunately ftill miffing ; but the tranfcript of the Roll made by Sir Thomas Phillipps himfelf is in the Phillipps Library. Through the kindnefs of the Rev. Mr. and Mrs. Fenwick of Thirleftaine Houfe I received fpecial permiffion to procure a copy of this tranfcript for publication with thefe notes on Flaxley abbey ; and for this purpofe I was fortunate enough to fecure the valuable fervices of Mr. Fitzroy Fenwick to whom I am much indebted.

The Cartulary copied by Mr. Fitzroy Fenwick contained all the abbreviations and contractions fhown in Sir Thomas Phillipps' tranfcript. Thefe abbreviations have been extended in accordance with the principle adopted by the editors of the Rolls feries; and the text of the Cartulary as thus extended has been carefully revifed by a competent expert, and has been compared by Mr. Fenwick with the original tranfcript.

Although, therefore, under the circumftances explained, fome errors may poffibly have crept into the text owing to the impoffibility of collating the copy with the original Roll, it will be admitted, I hope, that pains have been taken to fecure as much accuracy as poffible. Sir Thomas Phillipps is well known to have been a very learned and fkilful antiquary; and the tranfcript made with his own hand may, it would feem, be fafely accepted as a faithful copy of the original Flaxley Abbey Cartulary.

The genuinenefs of the documents contained in the Cartulary feems to be ftrongly attefted by internal evidence. Many of the names of benefactors and witneffes correfpond with the names mentioned in other public documents; and the Cartulary as a whole prefents all the appearance of a valuable collection of original monaftic deeds. But fortunately the genuinenefs of the Flaxley Cartulary does not depend upon internal evidence alone. I have difcovered amongft the Charter Rolls of Henry III a document which contains a formal confirmation of a large number of the private gifts and benefactions recorded in the Cartulary. The document referred to is of fome length, and is quoted as follows in the printed Calendar of Charter Rolls publifhed by the Record Commiffioners: Rot. Cart. 11 Henry III, pars fecunda, m. 8.

In the abfence of the original Cartulary Roll the independent corroboration derived from this confirmation charter of Henry III feems highly important. The charter referred to has been fet out at length in Appendix, Part I No v, and fpecial notice of its contents will be given hereafter.

Amongft the contents of this Cartulary, (Cart. No. 80[1]) will be found to be a catalogue of the library of the Flaxley monks, entitled "Catalogus librorum." This catalogue feems, from a note in Sir Thomas Phillipps' handwriting, to have been printed by the Royal Society of Literature under the following heading, which contains a few additional particulars of intereft:—

> "Excerpta ex Cartulario Abbatiæ de Dene alias Flaxley agro Gloceftriæ penes Thomas Wyniatt Armigerum de Staunton in eodem Comitatu. A.D. 1825.
>
> Hoc cartularium fcriptum eft in Rotulum Pergameneum (cujus initium lacerum eft) in faeculo 13mo

---

[1] The numbers quoted refer to the numbers in the Latin Table of Contents which precedes the Cartulary, see Appendix Part II, post.

Flaxley Abbey.

Incipit in fronte Redditus de Dimmoc. In dorfo "Carta Henrici aliquando." In dorfo etiam continet Catalogus Librorum in Bibliotheca qui fequitur
"Numerus librorum noftrorum
Bibliotheca in tribus voluminibus."
Here follows a lift of books commencing with "Auguftinus fuper 'Beatus eft Vir'."

I am not aware of the grounds upon which the ftatement is made that the Cartulary was written on a parchment roll in the 13th century; and the abfence of the original Roll makes it difficult to form any opinion on the fubject. The date of many of the documents recorded in the Cartulary appears on the face of the documents themfelves. All thefe documents feem to have been executed within the firft fixty years after the foundation of the abbey: viz., before 1210.

Of the ninety-feven documents of which the Cartulary is compofed, one is a catalogue of the abbey library; one contains the letters addreffed by William, Bifhop of Hereford, to all the chaplains of the diocefe; two are Papal Rolls of privilege, one by Pope Celeftine III, the other by Pope Alexander III; four are ftatements of account; and the remaining documents, eighty-nine in number, confift (*a*) of grants of land or privileges made to the abbey by various private benefactors; (*b*) of leafes, mortgages, agreements, &c., made by the monks with private perfons in the ordinary courfe of bufinefs.

The Cartulary, with revifed Table of Contents, will be found in extenfo in Appendix, Part II.

Names of Private Benefactors.

Amongft the private benefactors enumerated in the Flaxley Cartulary the following are, perhaps, the moft important—1, Gilbert de Monmouth; 2, William de Braofe, Lord of Brechen; 3, William de la Mara; 4, William and Henry de Mineriis; 5, William de Dene; 6, Richard de Erlingham; 7, Robert Mufchet; 8, Robert and Walter de Maus; 9, William de Sancto Leodegario; 10, Walter and Robert de Ragel co. Somerfet; 11, Hugh Hofate.

Gilbert de Monmouth.

No. 6 of the Flaxley Cartulary is a grant by Gilbert de Monmouth and Berta his wife to the abbey and monks of Dene of a fum of 5s. from the proceeds of the mill of Ope¹ (Hope) for the purchafe of wine for the celebration of the facrament, with a ftipulation that if the faid mill fhould fall down, the fum aforefaid was to be paid out of the cuftoms dues (gabulo) of the faid vill of Ope. Provifion having been made for the object ftated, the fum might be applied, with the confent of the whole chapter, to the repair of books. This grant muft have been an important provifion for the fupport of the abbey library. In Cart. No. 80 will be found a catalogue of this library as it exifted in the 13th century. Gilbert de Monmouth was probably a defcendant of William Fitz Baderon of Monmouth,¹ who is noted as holding at the time of the great furvey lands in Tibberton, Huntley, Hope, Weftbury, &c.

No. 7 of the Flaxley Cartulary is another grant to the abbey by the fame Gilbert de Monmouth of freedom from tolls (quietanciam de theloneo), licence to crofs the fea, in this cafe doubtlefs the Severn (paffagio), and all cuftomary dues throughout all the land of the grantor.

William de Braose.

No. 8 is a fimilar grant of freedom from tolls and the privilege of crofling the fea as above to the monks and Holy Church of "Mary of Flaxeleya" by William de Braofe Lord of Brechen² as a propitiatory offering for himfelf,

¹ The village of Hope or Long Hope is fituated between the villages of Micheldean and Blaisdon, about two miles from Flaxley.

² For particulars relating to this family fee Mr. Alfred S. Ellis's paper on the "Domefday Tenants of Glouceflerfhire."—Trans. Briflol and Gloucefthire Arch. Soc., vol. iv, p. 130·

³ The following table, compiled from Banks, fhows the pedigree of William de Brnose—

William de Braofe.⊤

Philip de Braofe.⊤Berta dau. of Milo, Earl of Hereford.

William de Braofe d. in Paris, 1212.⊤Matilda de St. Valery, d. 1210.

William de Braofe d. 1210.   Philip.   Giles, Bp. of Hereford.

The Flaxley benefactor was William, fon of Philip de Braofe. His wife, Matilda de St. Valery, and his two fons William and Philip, are named in the deed granted to the Flaxley monks; and the following additional particulars are related by Banks: William de Braofe being called upon to pay an old debt, flew out into rebellion and was banifhed the kingdom with his family. His wife Maud was taken, brought back, and being confined in Windfor caftle was with her eldeft fon William flarved to death by order of King John in 1210. William de Braofe the elder died in Paris two years later. They had another fon Giles who was Bifhop of Hereford. Maude de St. Valery is defcribed as Lady of Haye. For additional information relating to the family of De Braofe fee articles by Sir Wm. Drake and Mr. Elwys in the "Genealogift" 1880, 1881, 1882. For the information furnifhed in this note I am indebted to Sir John Maclean, F.S.A.

his wife Matilda de St. Valery, his family, &c. Among the witneſſes to this deed are William and Philip, ſons of William de Braoſe.

William de la Mara.

No. 95 is the grant of William de la Mara[1] to "God and the Bleſſed Mary and monks of Flaxley" of all his[2] meadow at Tukeley on payment of four ſhillings at the feaſt of St. Kenelm the martyr, and of "unas botas rubeas" on the feaſt of All Saints. Among the witneſſes to this deed are William de Berkeley and Bertram de la Mare.

William and Henry De Mineriis.

No. 9 is the grant of William de Mineriis to the abbey aſſigning in perpetual alms ſix acres of land under Caſthard,[3] and one acre of meadow between the ſaid land and the adjoining ſtream. No. 10 is the grant to the abbey by Henry, ſon of William de Mineriis, of the land lying between the land given to the abbey by William de Dene[4] and the wood above. No. 20 is the confirmation to the abbey by Henry de Mineriis, as lord of the manor, of all the grants made to the abbey by [5]Adam ſon of Fulco. The confirmation charter of 11 Hen. III[6] does not allude to the grants above mentioned, but refers to the gift by Henry de Mineriis of all his portion of Hinewere[7] with all liberties.

---

[1] William de la Mara was a firſt couſin of Earl Milo: for pedigree ſee Table in Trans. Briſtol and Glouceſtſhire Arch. Soc., vol. iv., p. 162, "Domeſday Tenants of Gloucſterſhire," by Mr. A. S. Ellis.
[2] Confirmed by royal charter of 11 Hen. III. Rot. Cart., 11 Henry III, pars. ſec. m. 8.
[3] Caſthard, otherwiſe written Caſtiard or Caſteyerde, was the name of the valley where the abbey of Flaxley was founded. See notes at p. 26.
[4] For the grant of William de Dene, see Cart., No. 16.
[5] For the grants of Adam, ſon of Fulco, ſee Cart. No. 19, 63, 64. The name is alſo referred to in Rot. Cart., 11 Hen. III., pars ſec., m. 8.
[6] Rot. Cart., 11 Hen. III., pars secunda, m. 8.
[7] A Severn fiſhery, known as Hynewere or Hinewere, was granted to the abbey in the 54th year of Henry III. Rot. Pat., 54 Hen. III., m. 9. This grant was confirmed in the 30th year of Edward III, in payment to the king of an annual acknowledgement of twelve pence. Rot. Pat., 30 Edw. III, tertia pars pat., m. 19.

William and Geoffrey de Dene.

No. 16 is the grant to the abbey by William de Dene[1] 'King's Forester,' of all his land under Caftiard. In return the grantor and his heirs were to enjoy the perpetual right of nominating to the abbey one monk, who was required to be acceptable to the convent. No. 17 is the grant to the abbey by Geoffrey, fon of William de Dene, of his meadow in Pulmede,[2] adjoining the garden of Henry de Mineriis. No. 18 is the record of a compromife entered into between Geoffrey de Dene, and the monks of Flaxley, regarding a difpute relating to the mill dam of Roger de Bofco. In Cart. No. 44, Roger de Bofco agreed to remove his dam from the monk's bridge and put it where it would do no harm. See poft.

William and Richard de Erlingeham.

Nos. 30 and 50 are grants of land in Erlingeham (Arlingham) made to the abbey of Flaxley by William, fon of Gilbert, fon of Milo of Erlingham.[3] Nos. 28 and 29 are other grants of land to the abbey by Richard, fon of William de Erlingeham. Both William and Richard de Erlingeham appear to have made

---

[1] Sir Thomas Phillipps has noted in his tranfcript of the Cartulary, that from the grants above quoted (No. 16 and 17) the following pedigree is obtained:

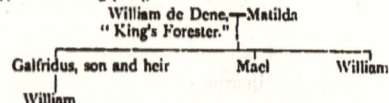

It feems probable that William de Dene was a defcendant of William Fitz Norman, keeper of the Foreft of Dene in 1080. See Mr. Alfred S. Ellis' Paper on " Domefday Tenants of Gloucefterfhire," Trans. Briftol and Gloucefterfhire Arch. Soc., vol. iv., p. 134; alfo "The Hiftory of the Manors of Dene Magna and Abenhale and their Lords," by Sir John Maclean in the fame publication, vol. vi., p. 123. The fee and inheritance of Englifh Bicknor, which belonged to Ulric de Dene, was granted by Henry I to Milo de Gloucefter, see Cal. Royal Charters, Duchy of Lanc. Records, (page 9, note 1 and page 16, note 3), and printed by Sir John Maclean in Trans. Briftol and Gloucefterfhire Arch. Soc., vol. iv, p. 319.

[2] The grant to the abbey of a meadow in Pulmede is alluded to in the Confirmation Charters of Roger Earl of Hereford, and of Henry II, see p. 16, 18, 37.

[3] From Cart. No. 50 Sir Thomas Phillipps has extracted the following pedigree—

Milo de Erlingeham
|
Gilbert
|
William—Hel...
|
Richard, o.s.p.—Matilda   Editha, d. and heir.

agreements with the abbey to be buried at Flaxley, doubtlefs in the abbey church. One of Richard's grants recites that he and his wife Matilda had given themfelves alive and dead to the abbey, and had chofen their place of burial there. The parifh of Erlingham or Arlingham is fituated oppofite to Newnham from which it is divided by the river Severn, and is about four miles diftant from Flaxley.

Robert Muschet.

Nos. 31 and 32 are the grants to the abbey by Robert Mufchet[1] of land near Walemor, and land in Linley, &c. The former grant recites that the monks have paid to Robert Mufchet three marks of filver for the grant, and that he had received from "Abbot Alan"[2] twenty fhillings.

Gilbert de Dimoc, William de Parcho, Walter de Maus.

Nos. 33a, 34, and 35, are grants made by Robert and Walter de Maus to Gilbert de Dimoc, who is defcribed as being in the fervice of Henry Kais, Reeve (prepofitus) of Gloucefter.[3] No. 36 is a grant to the abbey and monks of Dene, by Gilbert de Dimoc, of land in Briuwerna in perpetual alms, the grant in queftion being a portion of the land received by Gilbert from Robert and Walter de Maus. No. 37 is the formal confirmation of this grant to the abbey by Walter de Maus, who ftates that in return for this grant the monks had given him ten fhillings and one tunic. No. 38 is the affignment to the monks by William de Parcho, of all his rights in the land formerly held by Gilbert de Dimoc in Briuwern. The fame grant further recites that William de Parcho, moved by divine piety, grants to the monks in perpetual alms all his fhare of the fifhery of Bollewere, and a fite for building a windmill. No. 39 is the confirmation of this grant by Walter de Maus.

William de Sancto Leodegario.

No. 81 is the grant of Philip de Burci to William de Sancto Leodegario of the whole eftate of Ragel with appurtenances, and the record of the formal

---

[1] Robert Mufchet was referred to in the Hundred Rolls as owner of land in Botlowe held by the abbot of Flaxley, fee vol. i., p. 183.

[2] For other references to Abbot Alan, fee Cart., No. 69, 70, and Annales de Waverleia, Ann. Mon. Vol. ii., p. 245.

[3] Confirmed by royal charter of 11 Hen. III. Rot. Cart., 11 Hen. III., pars secunda, m. 8.

K

induction of the latter with all the feudal incidents pertaining to the tenure. The grant appears to have been made in settlement of a debt contracted by Philip de Burci, with Manaffer, Jew of Briftol, and paid by William de Sancto Leodegario. The date of the grant is the feaft of St. Michael, 1193 (5 Ric. I).

No. 82 is between the fame parties, ftipulating for an annual quit rent of two fhillings or one bizantium (2 fol. vel 1 bizant.) for all eafements belonging to Philip de Burci or his heirs, in refpect of the faid land, for a period of 31 years; the date of this grant alfo is 1193 (5 Ric. I).

No. 83 is the confirmation of grant No. 82, by the fuperior lord, who is defcribed as "William fon of Robert fon of Martin."

No. 84[1] is the affignment of the aforefaid land by William de Sancto Leodegario to the church and monks of the Holy Mary of Dene in perpetual alms, fubject to a quit rent of two fhillings payable annually at the feaft of St. Michael, and the fervice due to the fuperior lord; the deed further recites that when this affignment was made, twenty filver marks were paid by the monks to William·de Sancto Leodegario, and it feems that when the latter paid the debts of Philip de Burci, to Manaffer, Jew of Briftol, as above ftated, he did fo by means of money advanced by the monks of Dene (ex denariis ipforum monachorum); William de Sancto Leodegario and his heirs received at the fame time the perpetual right of prefenting one monk to the eftablifhment of monks at the abbey; and he and his heirs were received both in life and death into all the benefits of the church.

No. 85[2] is the formal confirmation of this grant by the fuperior lord William fon of Robert, fon of Martin, as in No. 83.

Walter and Robert de Ragel.

No. 86 is a grant by Walter, fon of Walter de Ragel, to the monks and church of the Bleffed Mary of Dene of a certain croft in Ragelbury, near

---

[1] This grant was formally confirmed to the abbey by royal charter of 11 Hen. III. Rot. Cart. 11 Hen. III., pars secunda, m. 8.

[2] From Cart. No. 85, Sir Thomas Phillipps gives the following pedigree—

Martinus (qu. if Martin de Tours, fee Pole's Devon)
    |
Robert. filius Martini
    |
William — Angaret
    |
Robert, eldest   William.

St. Andrew's fountain, and between the garden which ufed to belong to Philip de Burci and the houfe of Ofward.

No. 87 is the confirmation of this grant by Robert, brother of the aforefaid Walter, fon of Walter de Ragel. In this confirmation grant the name Ragelbury appears as Rachelbury.

No. 88 is the grant by Walter, fon of Walter Sprot, of Ragel, of two acres of land towards the fouth, lying between two acres of Emnet, and the croft which belonged to Ailward le Seigneur, and half an acre of meadow lying adjacent to the aforefaid two acres in Duddemed.

No. 89 is the confirmation of the preceding grant by Robert, brother of Walter Sprot, of Ragel.

No. 90[1] is another grant to the monks by Walter Sprot, of Ragel, of the whole of his portion of certain land in the hills, reckoned about four and a half acres: alfo common of pafture, both in the hills and fields.

Hugh Hosate.

No. 91 is the grant of Hugh Hofate to the church and monks of the Bleffed Mary of Dene of two acres of land in Ragelbury,[2] lying near the

[1] Confirmed to the abbey by royal charter, Rot. Cart., 11 Hen. III, pars fecunda, m. 8.
[2] Ragelbury or Regilbury, otherwife written "Rachelburi," as in Cart. No. 87, appears to be the fame as "Rochellefbury" of Valor Ecclefiafticus, vol. ii, p. 486, and "Rochelbury" in the grants made to Sir William and Sir Anthony Kingston when Flaxley Abbey was fuppreffed. The name Ragel is doubtlefs the fame as Ragiol of Domefday Survey, which is identified by the Rev. R. W. Eyton, with Ridge Hill in Winford, (Domefday Studies of Somerfet, 2 vols. 1880).

In Dugdale's Monafticon Ang., Ed. 1825, vol. v, p. 589, appears the following note:—

"Regill on Broadwell Down, fix miles from Briftol, in Nemnot parifh, in the county of Somerfet, was a cell to Flexeley Abbey, and as fuch in the 36 Hen. VIII was granted to Sir Anthony Kingfton."

Collinfon (Hiftory of Somerfet, vol. ii, p. 319) has the following:—

"The village of Nemnet is not mentioned in the Conqueror's Survey. It was always heretofore an appanage to the manor of Regilbury in this parifh, and held by the families of Martin and Perceval for feveral generations of the abbot of Flaxley, chief lord of that manor. After the diffolution of monasteries, that manor with lands and appurtenances in Nemnet, Blagdon, Winford, Butcombe and Regilbury was granted by King Henry VIII, in the thirty-fourth year of his reign, to Sir Anthony Kingfton, whofe fon Edward Kingfton, 7 Eliz., fold it to Edward Barnard, Efq., and he the year following conveyed the fame to Edward Baber, Efq., Sergeant at Law, and his heirs. From him defcended Edward Baber, Efq., who lived in the beginning of the prefent century, and tranfmitted this with other eftates to Sir Halfwell Tynte, his next heir, from whom it defcended to the late Sir Charles Kemys Tynte, Bart., and his heirs."

road towards the fouth, between the houfe of Ailward le Seigneur, and the houfe of Galfrid Tripel.

No. 92 is apparently another affignment of the fame land, in confideration of which the monks of Dene paid to Hugh Hofate a fum of fix fhillings. The grants of Hugh Hofate were confirmed to the abbey by royal charter of 11 Henry III.[1]

Of the remaining private benefactors mentioned in the Cartulary, brief notice only is required.

John Pichard[2] granted to the monks all his rights in the land of Walemor held by them; and in return the grantor received the perpetual right of prefenting one monk to the church of Flaxley. Cart., No. 11.

Hugh le Petit granted to the abbey all his land in Neweham held by Seftan Knif, near the ditch of the Old Caftle[3] (juxta foffam Veteris Caftelli), Cart., No. 12.

Gilbert Talbot granted to the abbey twelve pence annually from the mill of Ruddekefhale. Cart., No. 13.

Adam, of Blakeney, confirmed to the monks the gift of one "folda"[4] in Neweham made to them by his brother Jordan. Cart., No. 14. He and his wife Bafilia alfo granted to the monks two fhillings of annual rent to be paid to the facriftan of the abbey every year on the feaft of St. Michael for the purchafe of wheat for the Hoft, and for the purchafe of oil for the three lamps that burned before the three altars at High Mass. Cart., No. 15.

Regarding the manor of Regil or Ragel in Winford, the following additional particulars are given by Collinfon, vol. ii, p. 121.

"A very confiderable part of this place was given to the Ciftercian abbey of Flaxley, in Gloucefterfhire, founded by Roger, Earl of Hereford, in the time of King Henry I, and thus this place became a cell to that monaftery. In the time of Edward III the abbot thereof held the fourth part of a knight's fee in Regil; and the heir of Herbert de St. Quintin the moiety of a fee in the fame village of Hugh le Difpenser. The convent appears afterwards to have accumulated large poffeffions in the parifhes of Winford, Nemnet, Butcombe, and Stoke, and to have held moft of them in demefne."

Flax Bourton derives its name, according to Collinfon, from the fact that the abbot of Flaxley in Gloucefterfhire antiently held the principal eftate in this parifh, having exchanged for it certain of their demefnes at Regil in the parifh of Winford. (Hift. of Somerfet, vol. iii, p. 161.)

[1] Rot. Cart., 11 Henry III, pars fecunda, m. 8.

[2] John Pichard appears amongft the witneffes in Cart., No. 8, by which William de Braofe grants to the Flaxley monks freedom from paffenger tax, &c., throughout his dominions.

[3] For notice of the "Old Caftle of Dene," fee Note 2 at p. 16, ante.

[4] Solda idem q. Selda. Taberna Mercatoria.—Du Cange.

Adam, fon of Fulco, of Chekefhill, fon of Anketil,[1] granted to the monks three acres of his demefne of Chekefhill; fix felions of Bunewei; and all his meadow at . . . . fwell. Cart., No. 19. By another deed dated 1201 he granted to the monks all his demefne of Chekefhill for three years in return for a payment of three marks. Cart., No. 63. By another deed, alfo dated 1201, he made to the monks a fimilar grant for five years. Cart., No. 64.

Philip de Dunia[2] granted to the monks two acres of land in Wadleie. Cart., No. 21. By another deed dated 1195 he mortgaged to the monks all his land in the fmall marfh (in parvo marifco); all his furlong (forlongum) of Welipulle; all Cubewordin; one acre of land near the hill and eight felions in the hill of Walemore; and all his land in Wadleie, with the meadow which he held there. Cart., No. 54. The deed, No. 21 above, is attefted by William, father of Philip de Dunia, Johanna his wife, and Edith his mother.

Henry de Chekefhill[3] confirmed to the monks all the meadow which his brother Roger had given them in Littlemore, Cart., No. 22. By another deed he mortgaged to the monks all his meadow called Cumbesmedewe, for a period of five years from 1199, "the year in which king John was crowned." Cart., No. 61.

Robert Tholi[4] granted to the monks his land which lay between the land of Thomas de Monmouth, and the land held by Richard Prieft of Chirchefdun, which belonged to the fee of John de Evreus. He alfo by the fame deed gave them his land before the gate of the caftle, fituated between the gate

---

[1] From Cart. No. 19, Sir Thos. Phillipps gives the following pedigree—

       Anketil
      Fulco de Chekeshill=Edith.
  Adam=Isabella Durand Walter.

[2] In the confirmation charter of 11 Hen. III the grants of Philip de Dunia are not noticed; but the following gifts of William de Dune are confirmed, viz., two acres of land which lie above Walmorefhall' and all his land in Stangarft; alfo fourteen feliones of arable land in Wodley (Wadleie), and one acre of land at Ulnegate. Cart., No. 21, furnifhes the following pedigree—

    William de Dun=Edith.
     Philip=Johanna.

[3] Henry de Cheakefhull is noticed in the confirmation charter of 11 Hen. III, as giving to the monks all that croft which Edward held called Alinvecroft, with the meadow called Alinveplot, and all his land in Ruding, and all that croft which William Cuverer and Muriel held. Rot. Cart., 11 Hen. III, pars fec. m. 8.

[4] Robert Tholi (Toli), of Gloucefter, appears amongft the witneffes to the following grants, etc., found in the Cartulary, Nos. 12, 31, 32, 36, 37, 38, 39, 42, 70, 75.

of the invalids of St. Sepulchre's hofpital of Gloucefter,[1] and his other adjoining land belonging to the fee of the monks of St. Dionyfius. Cart., No. 23.

William Nexe granted to the monks his . . (foldam) in Newebam in return for eighteen fhillings paid by the monks. Cart., No. 24.

Roger,[2] fon of Ralph de Pulton, granted to the monks for the foul of Earl William of Warwick (Warrewic) and Countefs Margaret de Oilli, and for his own falvation and that of his wife Margaret, five fhillings of annual rent from the land held by Gilbert de Felda and Godwin de Pultun before him. The grantor ftates that thefe five fhillings were fpecially affigned for the purchafe of bed clothes for poor guefts (ad emendos pannos ad lectos pauperum hofpitum). Roger and his wife Margaret gave themfelves living and dead to the church of Dene, and their bodies for burial wherever they might die. Cart., No. 26.

Hugh Charke[3] granted to the monks the whole of his land called Eilfifcroft, and in his deed he ftates that the monks had received him and his into all the benefits of the church, both in death and in life, as a brother of the convent. He further ftates that, at his requeft, they undertook to receive his body for burial and that of his fon fhould he fo wifh, Cart., No. 27. Hugh Charke (Cherke) alfo granted to the monks, common of pafture throughout his whole land for their cattle; and he was to have common of pafture for his cattle with thofe of the monks, Cart., No. 33. By another deed, Hugh Charke mortgaged to the monks all his land called Wudelond, all Eilfifcroft, all Torfthalle, except three acres, and except the land which Luveric holds, and all the land of Hide held by Ernaldus, the carpenter, except three acres, for a

[1] With the allufion made in Cart. No. 23, of the Flaxley Cartulary to St. Sepulchre's hofpital at Gloucefter, compare No. lxxix of the Cartulary of St. Peter's monaftery at Gloucefter, edited by Mr. W. H. Hart, vol. i, p. 189. By this deed Thomas, abbot of St. Peter's, granted to the fick brethren of St. Sepulchre's hofpital, (fratribus infirmis hofpitalis Sancti Sepulcri) one acre of land for the increafe of their garden.

[2] Roger, fon of Ralph de Pultun, is noticed in the confirmation charter of 11 Henry III as having given to the abbey three virgates of land in Pultun with appurtenances. 'Rot. Cart., 11 Hen. III, pars. fec. m. 8.

[3] Hugh Chearke is noticed in the confirmation charter of 11 Hen. III, as giving to the monks that part of the meadow of Hide near the Severn, with Hayes (Haitiis) belonging to that land. He is further noticed as giving to the monks fix "Puches" in the Severn oppofite Hanecombe. Rot. Cart., 11 Hen. III, pars fec., m. 8. A "Puche" or "Puchin" is a falmon trap made of ofier, open at one end and clofed at the other. The trap is attached to flakes in the river, and refembles a long funnel fhaped bafket, feveral of which are placed one above another. The word "puche" is noticed in the Gloffary attached to the Gloucefter Cartulary, but is not explained.

period of 12 years, commencing 1195, at the feaft of St. Michael, Cart., No. 53. This deed feems to have been renewed for a period of fix years from 1201, between the fame parties, Cart., No. 65.

Roger de Bofco records that after the agreement made between him and the monks of Dene in the time of Abbot A.[1] he held from them the three acres which his father had given them in alms between his houfe and Efhul, and the monks held from him the land of Alefword in fee farm paying fix pence a year. Of this payment he remitted to Abbot Richard[2] five pence for the falvation of himfelf and his family, and in confideration of one cow and calf which the monks gave him. The monks were to hold from him in perpetuity the land of Alefword on payment of one penny. Roger de Bofco alfo remitted to the monks all his claims regarding the refervoirs, ditches, and fifh ponds (de ftagnis, foffatis, et vivariis), and agreed to remove his dam from the monks' bridge and put it where it would do no harm. He alfo granted to the monks their eafements (aifias) in his quarry (quarreria) of Efhul. Cart., No. 44.

Roger de Bofco alfo leafed to the monks for twenty years one acre of land in Cleilega, another in Whitelega, a third under Eilefhulle, a fourth in Eifhfeld, a fifth in Longlands, and a fixth at the top of the field near the ftream, commencing from the feaft of St. Michael, 1201. Cart., No. 55. Another deed to the fame effect is recorded in Cart., No. 67.

William Turc mortgaged to the monks of Dene his virgate of land formerly held by Eilwinus le Mercer, and after him by Henry Calvus, for ten years commencing from the feaft of St. Michael, 1196. Cart., No. 56.

Moyfes de Redley[3] mortgaged to the monks three acres of land in Ruding, for fix years, commencing from the feaft of St. John Baptift next after the coronation of King John. Cart., No. 57.

Nigel, fon of William Hathewi,[4] mortgaged to the monks his meadow in the marfh for five years, commencing from the feaft of St. Michael next after the coronation of King John. Cart., No. 58.

[1] Abbot A. is probably Abbot Alan who fucceeded Abbot Waleran in 1187. Annales de Waverleia. Ann. Mon., Vol. ii, p. 245. Two grants by Abbot Alan are recorded in the Cartulary, Nos. 69 and 70, which will be noticed below. He is also referred to in Cart., No. 31.
[2] For grants of Abbot Richard, fee Cart., Nos. 40, 41, 42, 43, 48, 49, 51, 52, 75.
[3] Moyfes or Moyfe of Redley is noticed amongft the witneffes in Cart., Nos. 12, 22, 54, 60, 61.
[4] William Hapewi or Hathewi was one of the keepers of Dean foreft. He is mentioned in Inq., 15 Ed. I, No. 67, in connection with a complaint of the abbot of Flaxley, fee p. 42, ante. The name alfo appears as Foreftarius de feodo in an inquifition held at Mitcheldean, 30 Nov., 1338, Glouc. Cart., Vol. iii, p. 235.

Geoffrey Hugelin mortgaged to the monks all his land of Walmore for six years; the deed states that this agreement was made at the feast of St. Michael, at the second change of the moon, and after that festival Neweham was burned[1] (et post idem festum cremata est Neweham). Cart., No. 59.

William de Minsterworth[2] leased to the monks for eight years all his meadow between Gerne and the church of Westbury from the feast of St. John, 1197, to the same festival 1204. Cart., No. 60.

Ralph Crupard[3] leased to the monks his two crofts called Hamcroft and Hulpescroft for four harvests, viz., two of wheat and two of barley, the first crop to be taken in the year 1200. Cart., No. 62.

Roger de Leinch leased to[4] the monks one virgate of land in Middletun for seven years from 1202 at Hokeday.[5] Cart., No. 66.

Master Jocelin described as clerk (clericus) of William Marshall, gave himself alive and dead to God and the Blessed Mary of Dene in the presence of Abbot Richard[6] and the convent, and chose his place of burial at the abbey wherever he might die. Cart., No. 74. Master Jocelin appears to have made a grant to Alice de Gloucester of all his land in London de Cheringa given to him by lord William Marshall; and this grant was confirmed by William Marshall. Cart., No. 72 and 73.

Walter of Budicombe[7] gave to the monks in alms, seven acres of land lying between the messuage of Stephen Aldewiche, in the hills and between the roads going to Eiffele and Kingberge, in return for one pound of cinamon (cinimi) to be paid yearly at the feast of St. Michael. He also gave the monks tithes of his two hundred sheep. Cart., No. 93.

Ernaldus de Cutberleye son of Ernaldus Dunning,[8] granted to the Blessed

---

[1] The burning of Neweham must have been an event of some local importance to have been specially recorded by the Flaxley monks.

[2] Walter, son of William de Munstrewithe, is noticed in the confirmation charter of 11 Hen. III, as giving to the monks all his land in Walemore, called Charkefeld, as Roger de Munstrewithe held it in his demesne. Rot. Cart., 11 Hen. III, pars sec. m. 8.

[3] Ralph Crupard is noticed in the confirmation charter of 11 Hen. III, as giving to the monks two crofts, to wit, Halpescroft and Hamecroft. Rot. Cart., 11 Hen. III, pars sec. m. 8.

[4] Roger de Leinch (Lench) appears as a witness in Cart., Nos. 28, 29, 50.

[5] Hokeday the second Tuesday after Easter. See Cart., No. 23.

[6] For notices of Abbot Richard, see Cart., Nos. 25, 39, and note 2, p. 71.

[7] Walter de Budicumbe appears as a witness in Cart., Nos. 84, 86, 87, 88, 89, 90, 91, 92, 94; and Gilbert de Budicumbe is also mentioned in all the deeds above noticed, except Nos. 84 and 90.

[8] Arnoldus son of Arnaldus Dunning is noticed in the confirmation charter of 11 Hen. III, as giving to the monks all the land between the two bridges over the Severn at Gloucester. Rot. Cart., 11 Hen. III, pars sec. m. 8.

Mary of Flaxley for the repair of the hofpice,[1] all his land between the two bridges of the Severn at Gloucefter, which formerly belonged to Robert, fon of Feremon, and was latterly held by Gaufrid le Lorimer. Cart., No. 96.

By another deed "Brother R. called Abbot of Flaxley" and the convent agreed to pay to Ernaldus de Cutberleg five fhillings a year for life to be paid every year on the feaft of St. Ethelbert the Martyr. Cart., No. 97.

Additional Benefactors mentioned in the Confirmation Charter of 11 Henry III.

It has been noticed above that a confiderable number of the private grants made to Flaxley abbey, and recorded in the Cartulary, were formally confirmed in the eleventh year of Henry III. It will be convenient, however, at this place to notice briefly the additional grants, alienations, &c., fpecified in this confirmation charter, of which no record is found in the Cartulary.

Roger de Heidun[2] fold to the monks nine acres of land lying between the land of Redley and the great road; two acres in the marfh lying between Heilith and John de Wodeham's land, and one acre of meadow in Holemede. He alfo gave to the monks ten acres of land as fpecified in Redley. Both the fale and gift were formally confirmed.

Margarete, daughter of Gaufrid, fon of William, gave to the monks all the land of Northwood which her father had given her.

Hugh de Gerne[3] gave all his land in the croft at Chekefhull.

Ofmund K . . . gave all his land lying between the land of Richard "Draperii," and the land of Warinus "Sellarii." Alfo all the land which lay between the land which belonged to Wace the cook, and the land which belonged to Gilbert, fon of Ralph, in Gloucefter.

Henry, fon of Odon, gave to the monks all his land in Rudinge with as full rights as his father enjoyed.

Roger de Ardern[4] gave to the monks all his land of Otleg at Cheakefhull.

[1] See Mr. Middleton's plan fhowing probable arrangement of the monaftic buildings, Plate vi.
[2] Roger de Heidun appears amongft the witneffes in Cart., No. 57.
[3] Hugo de Gerne appears amongft the witneffes in Cart., Nos. 54, 62. He is again noticed in the confirmation charter of 11 Hen. III in connection with a grant to the Flaxley monks by Matilda Giffard of certain land belonging to the tenement of Hugh de Gerne near the fifhery of Befpwike.
[4] Roger de Ardern appears amongft the witneffes in Cart., Nos. 9, 10, 11, 12, 16, 17, 18, 19, 20, 22, 31, 32, 33, 44, 53, 54, 55, 57, 60, 61, 63, 64, 65, 67.

Philip de Humelmore[1] fold to the monks four acres of land which he held in fee of William de Dune (Dene ?).

Ralph de Redley gave to the monks all his land in Redley with appurtenances lying under Heilith, and all the tenement of Walter Hendi in the meadow of Smalham.

Peter de Salso Marifo[2] (Salt Marfh) gave to the monks all his land in Tribnell with all appurtenances.

Thomas, fon of William de Harpetr, gave to the monks all the land which belonged to Henry Scepefhefed, with all the appurtenances and common of pafture for one hundred fheep in the fame vill. Alfo half virgate of land held by Ofbert the Reeve; and from the wood which belonged to the Henry aforefaid, as much timber as he required by the view of his forefter.

Richard of Blechedun[3] gave to the monks two acres of mead which Edric his fon held, and half an acre of mead adjoining.

John Ruk, fon of Ada(m), gave to the monks all his arable land in Bruern, to wit, ten feilliones in Revenefhokefeld with appurtenances.

Helie Giffard[4] gave to the monks all his demefne in Habewoldefham in his manor of Brumeffeld with pafturage for eight oxen, and fharing common of pafture with the men of the faid manor, and everywhere along with the cattle of the lord of the manor of Brumeffeld in the paftures outfide the park of Brumeffeld, and with pafturage for two hundred and forty fheep in the common paftures both of Brumeffeld and Croneham.

William de Budifeld gave to the monks lands in Budifeld as fpecified, with pafture for two hundred fheep in the common of Budifeld.

Gaufrid de Longo Capo gave to the monks all the lands which Thomas Baterick held of him in Levepeley.

John 'Difpenfator'[5] gave to the monks all his land in the croft called

---

[1] Henry de Humelmore referred to in the Hundred Rolls as owner of land held by the abbot of Flaxley, p. 45, and note 4.

[2] Dominus Johannes de Salfo Marifco referred to as a witnefs to an agreement executed between the Abbots of Gloucefter and Briftol. Glouc. Cart., Vol. ii, p. 92.

[3] Richard de Blecheden appears amongft the witneffes in Cart, No. 17. Baderun de Blecheden is noticed in Cart, Nos. 9, 10, 16, 17, 19, 27, 33, 54, 60.

[4] Helie Giffard is mentioned as a witnefs in Cart, No. 5. Three perfons of this name are alluded to in the Index to the Gloucefter Cartulary, edited by W. H. Hart, Esq. The Helias Giffard referred to in the Flaxley Cartulary appears to have been Helias Giffard of Brimpffield or Brumeffeld. For a notice of this family, fee Mr. Alfred Ellis's paper "On the Domefday Tenants of Gloucesterfhire," Trans. Bristol and Glouc. Archaeol. Soc., Vol. iv., p. 159.

[5] Geoffry and Richard le Defpenfer (Difpenfator) are referred to in the Gloucefter Cartulary, fee Vol. i, 111, 378; Vol. ii, 116, 216.

"Buveveie," which lies between the land which Adam, fon of Fulco,[1] gave to thofe monks, and the meffuage which belonged to Robert Surdus.

Amis de Tukeley[2] gave to the monks two acres of mead in Bruerne in the meadow called Wrugebat.

Matilda Giffard[3] gave to the monks all her land under the fifhery of Befpwike, to wit, twenty-four feilliones, belonging to the tenement of Hugh de Gerne.

Helie Giffard alfo gave to the monks all that half virgate of land in his manor of Brumeffeld with appurtenances which William le Cras held, and all that half virgate of land with appurtenances which Robert de Climperwell held, and all the land lying between the fifhpond of Climperwell and the land of the monks which they hold from the church of Lanthony.

Roger de . . . gave to the monks all that half virgate of land which Jordan, fon of John, held from him in Erlingham.

Grants to Flaxley Abbey by Ecclesiastics.

No. 4 of the Flaxley Cartulary is a grant to the monks of Dene by Abbot A. . . . of Vallis Dore[4] of one virgate of land in Climperwell which had been received from the prior and convent of Lanthony. No. 5 is the original grant of this land by Roger, prior of Lanthony, to the monks of Dore. This original grant was made over to the monks of Flaxley as fpecially noted in the deed of Abbot A.

No. 45 is the record of an agreement made between Ernaldus clerk of Dimoc and the monks of Dene, granting to the latter the tithes of the land cultivated by the monks in the parifh of Dimoc in return for two fhillings payable annually on the feaft of St. Michael. This convention appears to have been renewed and confirmed by William Kais[6] who fucceeded Ernaldus in the vicarage of Dimoc. Cart., No. 46.

No. 94 is the record of an agreement made between the monks of Dene

---

[1] For grants of Adam, fon of Fulco, fee Cart., Nos. 19, 63, 64.

[2] Amis de Tukeley mentioned in Cart., No. 95, as the owner of land held by the monks of Flaxley at Tukeley.

[3] Matilda Giffard, who was fhe, and what relation if any to Helias Giffard before referred to?

[4] Vallis Dore—the Golden Vale—was the feat of the Ciftercian abbey of Dore in Herefordfhire. For notice of this abbey fee pp. 21 and 58.

[5] There feems to have been a ferious difpute on the fubject of thefe tithes between William Kais and the Flaxley monks; and Abbots H. of Gloucefter and A. of Tewkefbury (Theokefbir) were deputed by Pope Clement III to fettle it. Cart., No. 47, is the record of the agreement arrived at viz., that the monks fhould pay to William Kais two fhillings a year as above ftated in Cart., No. 45.

and the church of Budicumbe with the wiſh and conſent of Gilbert parſon of Budicumbe, ſignifying that the monks were to pay each year to the church of Budicumbe two ſhillings on the feaſt of St. Michael in lieu of all tithes from the ſeven acres of land which Walter de Budicumbe[1] gave to the monks in alms.

Grants by Abbot Alan on behalf of the Convent.

No. 69 is the deed of Abbot Alan[2] granting to Jordan, ſon of Ralph, all that freehold land in Saliſbury (Saleſbiri), near that which is in the fee of the abbeſs of Rumſey, which the monks held by the will of Henry Knis. The ſaid land was to be held on payment of eleven ſhillings and an obolus in four inſtalments.

No. 70 is the deed of Abbot Alan granting to Godfrid Mog and his heirs the land which is between the land of the canons (canonicorum) and the land of Walter Crucche in the ſmith's hamlet on payment of three ſhillings annually.

Grants by Abbot Richard on behalf of the Convent.

Beſides Abbot Alan the only other Flaxley abbot referred to in the Flaxley Cartulary is Abbot Richard,[3] and ten of the documents recorded in the Cartulary appear to have been executed by him on behalf of the convent.

No. 40 is the deed of Abbot Richard granting to Robert the chaplain, ſon of Oſmond of Newcham, that " ſoldagium " in Newcham which Oſmond gave to the church in alms, on payment of twelve pence annually.

No. 41 is the grant of Abbot Richard to John le Irmongere of the land in Newcham received by the monks from Ernaldus the forefter, on payment of two ſhillings per annum.

No 42 is the grant of Abbot Richard to John, ſon of Aidanus, of half the land which belonged to Agnes, on payment of twenty-one pence per annum.

[1] For grants of Walter de Budicumbe ſee p. 72, ante.

[2] For notices of Abbot Alan, ſee Notes, p. 65 and 71 ante. It is noticed in the Waverley Annals that Alan, formerly monk of Bordeſley, ſucceeded Abbot Wakeman at Flaxley in 1187, on the occaſion of the general viſitation of the Ciſtercian abbeys.

[3] The Abbot Richard of the Flaxley Cartulary is not apparently mentioned anywhere elſe. His approximate date ſeems to have been about A.D. 1200 The earlieſt regiſter of the biſhops of Hereford ſtill extant, is that of Thomas de Cantelupe, commencing A.D. 1275. Abbot Richard of Flaxley was certainly inſtalled before that date, probably about the year 1200, as it appears that all his grants in which the date is mentioned were executed about that time.

No. 43 is the grant of Abbot Richard to Roger de Paris, of the land in Gloucefter held by the monks by the deed of Henry Kais, on payment of two fhillings a year.

No. 48 is the grant of Abbot Richard to Richard de Bofco of four acres of land in Dimmoc from their newly reclaimed lands (effartis) on payment of eight pence per annum.

No. 49 is the grant of Abbot Richard of Flaxley to William de Monafterio of Dimmoc, of that "menfuram" which lay between the burial ground and the water, with the adjoining croft and meadow, on payment of two fhillings and fix pence per annum.

No. 51 is the grant of Abbot Richard to John, fon of Leweric, brother of Faremon, of the land which Faremon gave to the abbey in alms on payment of twelve pence a year.

No. 52 is the grant of Abbot Richard to Walter de la Barra of the meffuage in Newcham which Roger de Boyville gave to the abbey in perpetual alms, on payment of two fhillings a year.

No. 75 is the grant of Abbot Richard to Ofbern, fon of Walter de Wich, of all the land which belonged to Brother Alured, formerly in the fervice of Margaret, wife of Herbert, fon of Ernaldus, son of Cutelb, which Margaret gave to Alured for his fervice, and which is fituated between the land of Ernaldus and Walter le Hore in the fmith's place, on payment of three fhillings a year.

No. 97 is the deed of "Brother R. called Abbot of Flaxley," affigning to Ernaldus de Cutberleg five fhillings a year for his life. It is probable that "Brother R." is the fame Abbot Richard whofe grants have been juft noticed. In nearly all the above grants fpecial provifion againft alienation is inferted, and in three of the grants, Nos. 40, 52 and 75, Abbot Richard fpecially records that the abbey feal was not put to the deeds becaufe of the perfidy of the Jews (proper perfidiam Judeorum).[1]

---

[1] On this fubject Sir Thomas Phillipps calls attention to Inquifitio de perfidia Judeorum in Harl. MSS., No. 79. Manaffer, Jew of Briftol, is prominently noticed in Cart., Nos. 81, 82, 84. On the fubject of debts to Jewifh money lenders, temp. Richard I and John, fee Capitula de Judaeis, A.D. 1194, in the Proceedings on the Judicial Vifitation, and articles 10 and 11 of the Great Charter of Liberties commonly called Magna Charta, A.D. 1215.—(Stubb's "Documents illuftrative of Englifh Hiftory" pp 254 and 290.

Agreement between Abbot Richard and William the Hermit.

No 25 is the record of the agreement made between Abbot Richard on behalf of the convent of Flaxley and William the hermit, ſtating that at the many prayers of many perſons he, Abbot Richard, had undertaken the charge of the chapel of Hardlande and the ſupport of William the hermit of that place, who was to receive from the abbey all things neceſſary for his food and clothing. This deed was witneſſed by Lord William Biſhop of Hereford, at whoſe advice and in whoſe preſence the deed was executed, and who atteſted the deed with his epiſcopal ſeal. The deed was alſo witneſſed by Richard the Dean, and by the chapter of Flaxley. It has been already noticed at p. 40 ante that a royal order was addreſſed to John de Monmouth, conſtable of St. Briavell's, in the fifth year of Henry III,[1] commanding him to allow the abbot of Flaxley to hold in peace the "hermitage of Erdlond" as he had been accuſtomed to hold it in the time of King John. Hardlande and Erdlond are no doubt the ſame. In the fifteenth year of Edward I an inquiſition was held regarding a complaint of the abbot of Flaxley who alleged that certain miners had diſcovered a mine in his land at "Ardlonde." The abbot is ſtated to have removed the miners and to have filled up the pit with earth and ſtones.[2]

Witneſſes.

The voluminous liſt of perſons who are named as witneſſes in the Flaxley Cartulary is of much intereſt as ſhowing who were the perſons of chief local importance at the time when the various deeds, grants, &c., were executed. The following names which appear over and over again ſuggeſt that the owners muſt have been on very intimate terms with the Flaxley monks, Roger de Weſtbury, Roger de Ardern, Baderun de Blechedun (Blaiſdon), Henry de Mineriis, Galfrid de Dene, Leweric Reeve of Newcham, Robert Tholi of Glouceſter, Walter Clerk of Aure, William de Heliun, Adam ſon of Fulco Gilbert and Walter de Budicum, Maſter Galfrid le Bel, and Godfrey Chaplain of Emnet.

Of theſe Henry de Mineriis and Galfrid de Dene have already been noticed amongſt the benefactors. They both aſſigned to the monks in perpetual alms ſome of their own land in Caſtiard, and appear to have been very near

[1] Rot. Clau., 5 Hen. III, m. 20. (Index, p. 441, Printed Cloſe Rolls.)
[2] See p. 42, ante.

Flaxley Abbey. 79

neighbours. The name of Walter Map appears as a witnefs in Charters, Nos. 10 and 54, and the date of the latter deed is given as A.D. 1195. Query—Can this Walter Map be identified with the well known author of the De nugis Curialibus, who is known to have held among other preferments the vicarage of Weftbury-on-Severn in Gloucefterfhire? At Weftbury-on-Severn Walter Map muft have been a near neighbour of the Flaxley monks, and the appearance of his name amongft the witneffes would be fatiffactorily accounted for; but I am doubtful whether this hypothefis can be reconciled with the date quoted, A.D. 1195.[1]

Several members of the Berkley family are noticed amongft the witneffes. Alfo William and Philip, fons of William de Braofe, Bertram de la Mara, Helias Giffard, Berta and James de Monmouth (Monemuta), Philip de Burci and his fons, befides many others of whom a complete lift will be found in the Index.

Papal Bulls of Privilege.

The Cartulary contains two Papal bulls of privilege, Nos. 77 and 79, the former by Pope Celeftine III, dated 1192, the latter by Pope Alexander III. It is mentioned in a note on the laft named inftrument that Flaxley abbey poffeffed two other bulls of privilege granted by Pope Alexander III, befides one by Pope Eugenius, which three were not infcribed on the Cartulary roll. The total number of Papal bulls of privilege granted to Flaxley abbey is fpecially ftated to have been five. I have found, however, at page 58 of Bifhop Cantelupe's regifter at Hereford one additional bull of protection granted by Pope Innocent; and as Bifhop Cantelupe's regifter commences in A.D. 1275, it feems probable that the Cartulary was written before that date.

Both of the bulls granted to the Flaxley monks by Pope Celeftine III and Pope Alexander III, provide for fpecial immunity from tithes. The former bull regulated the relations that were to exift between the abbey and the Bifhop of Hereford, in whofe diocefe the abbey was fituated, and feems to have been mainly intended to provide againft undue epifcopal interference or exactions. The bull of Pope Alexander III relates almoft entirely to the fubject of tithes, pains and penalties being threatened againft any one who fhould prefume to levy tithes from the monks of Flaxley.

Catalogue of Books.

It has been noticed at page 60 above that this catalogue of books has already

---

[1] See page 20, note 2.

been publifhed, having apparently been communicated by the late Sir Thomas Phillipps to the Royal Society of Literature about 1825. Provifion for the fupport of the abbey library was made from the grant of Gilbert de Monmouth, who affigned to the monks of Flaxley five fhillings from the proceeds of the mill of Ope (Hope) for the purchafe of wine for the facrament, with a provifion that any furplus might be devoted, with the confent of the whole chapter, to the repair of books. The catalogue of books is an interefting monaftic relic. Of the books themfelves no trace is known to remain. They were probably difperfed and perhaps deftroyed when the abbey was fuppreffed, in 1536, and granted to Sir William Kingfton. As might be expected, all the books appear from the catalogue to be of a devotional character, and to confift of fermons, homilies, and reflections on facred fubjects.

PART III.

EXTRACTS FROM THE REGISTERS OF THE BISHOPS OF HEREFORD, STATE PAPERS, &c.

It has been already ſtated at page 15 above, that theſe extracts are ſeven in number, ſix of which relate to the inſtitution of the various Abbots named below, and the remaining extract being a bull of Pope Innocent granting ſpecial protection to Flaxley abbey.

The oldeſt regiſter of the ſee of Hereford ſtill extant is that of Thomas de Cantelupe commencing A.D. 1275,[1] 3 Edward I. This date, it will be obſerved, is about one hundred and twenty-five years after the foundation of Flaxley abbey. The abſence of the earlier regiſters deprives us of our chief ſource of information regarding the names and dates of the earlier Flaxley abbots, and ſufficiently accounts for the imperfect liſt of abbots hitherto handed down by Browne Willis and others.

Register of Bishop Cantelupe, 1275—1282.

In the original regiſter of Thomas de Cantelupe are two references to Flaxley abbey at pages 44 and 58. The extract at page 44 is the profeſſion of William abbot of Flaxley to Biſhop Cantelupe, dated February, 1277,[2] promiſing according to the cuſtomary form " ſubjection, reverence and obedience appointed by the holy fathers according to the rule of St. Benedict to thee, Lord Father, Biſhop Thomas and to thy ſucceſſors canonically inſtituted, and to the holy ſee of Hereford."

The extract at page 58 of Biſhop Cantelupe's regiſter is referred to in the Index as a bull of protection. It purports to be made in the name of Pope

---
[1] A letter of John le Bretun, Biſhop of Hereford, dated "decimo Kalendas Aprilis" 1271, addreſſed to the abbot and convent of St. Peter's at Gloucester, written at Flaxley, is printed in Hiſt. et Cart. Mon. St. Petri, Glouc. Vol. ii, p. 222.

[2] There appears to be no date given on the extract in queſtion, but the date quoted is that of the preceding extract.

M

Innocent and is dated in the fixth year of his reign. The MS. confifts of twenty-feven and a-half lines written in a clear and diftinct character, but I regret that I have not had the opportunity of making a tranfcript.[1]

Among the ancient charters in the Harleian collection is one marked 43 A. 39. Innocentii Papæ Epiftola Epifcopo Hereford[enfi] fcripta pro capella ante portum monafterii de Flaxleye anno pontificat. xi°.

Register of Bishop Swinfield, 1282—1316.

Thomas de Cantelupe was fucceeded as Bifhop of Hereford by Richard Swinfield, during whofe epifcopate two abbots were formally inftalled at Flaxley abbey.

At page 53 of Bifhop Swinfield's regifter is the " profeffion of brother Nicholas abbot of Flaxley which he made to Lord Richard by the grace of God Bifhop of Hereford in his chapel of Bofbury on the Lord's day next before the feaft of St. Margaret, Virgin and Martyr, to wit the 15th of the Kalends of Auguft in the year of our Lord 1288.

"I brother Nicholas abbot of Flaxley promife, faving our order, that I will conftantly fhow the fubjection, reverence, and obedience appointed by the holy fathers according to the rule of St. Benedict, to thee Lord Father, Bifhop Richard, and to thy fucceffors canonically inftituted, and to the fee of Hereford."[2]

At page 189 of the fame bifhop's regifter we find a fhort entry dated

---

[1] The two references noted to Bifhop Cantelupe's regifter apparently efcaped the notice of Rudder who has furnifhed a lift of some of the references to Flaxley abbey in the epifcopal regifters at Hereford. The omiffion is important, as one of the references relates to the inftitution of an abbot of Flaxley hitherto unnoticed by antiquaries. The bull of Pope Innocent has been noticed above at page 81 in connection with the other Papal bulls relating to Flaxley abbey. In Dugdale's Mon. Angl. (Ed. 1825), Vol. v, pp. 228 to 236, will be found the text of feventeen Papal bulls granting various privileges to the Ciftercian order of monks. Five of thefe bulls were granted by Pope Innocent IV.

[2] This extract from Bifhop Swinfield's regifter is quoted by the Rev. John Webb in his "Abftract and Illuftrations of Bifhop Swinfield's Houfehold Roll," printed by the Camden Society in 1853-4. In this charming work an interefting defcription is given of one of Bifhop Swinfield's vifitation tours. Amongft other places he vifited Flaxley, which is thus defcribed, p. cxxxviii:—" A fhort turn brought them to Flaxley, March 8 (1289) where they lodged in the Ciftercian abbey of that name, feated according to the fafhion of that order in the bofom of a woody vale. It was fubject to the bifhop, and in the fuperior of that houfe he met with one to whom he had given his paftoral benediction on election and confirmation a few months before. The form of this ceremony on the part of the abbot, here tranflated from the original, is preferved as if by way of precedent in the regifter of the fee." For the account of Bifhop Swinfield's houfehold expenfes at Flaxley, fee page 61 of printed roll.

17th October, 1314, stating that William de Rya was installed as abbot of Flaxley in the Bishop's chapel of Bosbury, the bishop celebrating the mass.
The following extract from Leland (Itin. viii, p. 70) shows that Bishop Swinfield died at Bosbury, A.D. 1316, and was buried in his own cathedral at Hereford :—
"Richard Swinefield obiit Anno Dom. 1316 die 5. Gregorii Pont. Ro. apud Bosburie. Sedit annis 34. Sepultus est pompa max. in Herefordensi ecclesia."

Register of Bishop Courteney, 1360—1375.

No reference to Flaxley appears in the register of the four following Bishops of Hereford who succeeded Richard Swinfield, viz., Adam de Orleton (1317-1327), Thomas Chorlton (1327-1344), John de Trilleck (1344-1361), Ludovic Charlton (1361-1369) ; but in the register of the following Bishop William Courtenay (1369-1375) I find another reference to Flaxley at page 11. This entry relates to the installation of Richard Peyto (Payto) and is to the following effect :—
"6 July, 1372. At Sugwas Lord Richard Payto was elected abbot of the monastery of Flaxley in the diocese of Hereford. He was blessed by the Lord Bishop at a solemn mass and made profession in writing in form of words as follows :—I Richard, abbot elect of his church of the monastery of Flaxley in the diocese of Hereford, profess to the holy church of Hereford, and to thee father William, Bishop of the said Church, and to thy successors canonically instituted, canonical obedience and subjection in all things. And the same abbot afterwards subscribed the figure of the cross as follows ✠ adding $_\text{salvo ordine}^\text{nostro}$ the words, saving the rights of our order In the presence of our lords $^\text{jure}$ (dominis) Tho. Peyto, Thomas de Breynton and Hugh Frene Vicars Choral of the Cathedral Church of Hereford and others."[1].

---

[1] The original extract of which the above is a translation has been printed by Rudder, p. 449 and is here reproduced as a specimen. The other extracts relating to the installation of the Flaxley abbots being of an exactly similar character, it has been thought unnecessary to print in extenso. "6 Julii, 1372. Apud Sugwas D'nus Richardus Payto monasterii de Flaxley Hereford. Dioces. electus abbas. Fuit per d'num intra missarum solemnia benedictus et professionem in scriptis fecit sub hac forma verborum. Ego Richardus ecclesiæ suæ monasterii de Flaxley Heref. diocef. electus abbas profiteor sanctæ Hereford. ecclesiæ tibique Patri Willi'mo ejusdemque ecclesiæ episcopo tuisque successoribus in ea canonice substituendis canonicam in omnibus obedientiam et subjectionem. Et idem abbas subsequenter crucem subscripsit talem ✠ additis in verbis, salvo jure ordine nostro. Presentibus dominis Tho. Peyto. Thoma de Breynton et Hugone Frene vicariis chori ecclesiæ cathedralis Hereford. et aliis."

Register of Thomas Spofford, 1422-1448.

After William Courtenay no entry occurs in the regifter of any of the following bifhops : John Gilbert (1375-1389), John Trefnant (1389-1404), Robert Mafcall (1404-1417), Edmund Lacey (1417-1420), Thomas Polton (1420-1422), but in the regifter of the following Bifhop Thomas Spofford (1422-1448) at page 107[1] I find the following entry : "14 April, 1426. In the monaftery of Flaxley before the high altar brother William, monk of the faid Monaftery, was confecrated as Abbot, who made his profeffion of obedience in form of words following : I brother William, monk of the monaftery of Flaxley, ordained Abbot, promife before God fidelity, fubjection, obedience, reverence to thee, Bifhop of Hereford and to thy fucceffors canonically inftituted, faving the rights of our order."

Register of Richard Mayhew, 1504-1539.

After Thomas Spofford no entry occurs in the regifter of Richard Beauchamp (1448-1452), John Stanbury (1452-1474), and Thomas Mylling (1474-1504); but in the regifter of Richard Mayhew (1504-1539) at page 45 occurs the following :—

"16 December, 1509, the Lord Bifhop conferred his benediction on the Abbot of Flaxley who promifed reverence and fubjection and obedience in form of words following :—I brother John, Abbot of Flaxley, of the Ciftercian order, promife to thee Lord Father, Bifhop of Hereford, and to thy fucceffors canonically inftituted, and to the holy See of Hereford, fubjection, reverence and obedience appointed by the holy fathers according to the rule of St. Benedict, faving the rights of our order."

This is the laft entry relating to Flaxley abbey which is noted in the index to the original regifters of the diocefe of Hereford. Two other Flaxley abbots are known to have been inftalled before the diffolution, viz., William Beaudley in 1528 during the epifcopate of Charles Booth, and Thomas Were or Ware, the laft abbot in 1532.; but no reference to either of thefe abbots can be found in the original regifters at Hereford. Their names are mentioned

[1] The correct reference to the page of Thomas Spofford's regifter is that given in Arabic characters, thus 107. The fame page is alfo numbered in Roman numerals as cxiiii. This fhould be noted in verifying the original extract.

by Browne Willis[1] and Stevens,[2] and a few additional particulars relating to them are given at p. 87, note 1 below. No notice of the fuppreffion of Flaxley abbey, or of the events that accompanied the diffolution, could be found in the epifcopal regifters at Hereford.[3]

Berkeley, Abbot of Flaxley.

In addition to the Flaxley abbots noted above from the regifters of the Bifhops of Hereford my attention has been recently called to the name of another Flaxley abbot which appears in a mutilated deed in the Bodleian Library at Oxford. The deed in queftion "MS. Bodl. 88" relates to an exchange of livings between "— Berkeley Abbas de Flaxley rector ecclefiæ parochialis de Rodmarton" and Nicholas Rewys "vicarius ecclefiæ parochialis de Weftbury" in May 1476. The deed is attefted by John Rolues public notary.[4]

Revised List of Flaxley Abbots.

From the materials furnifhed in thefe notes the following revifed lift of Flaxley abbots is now fubmitted, with the authority for each name.

1. Waleran, refigned 1187. See Annales de Waverleia, Ann. Mon., Vol. ii., p. 245.

2. Alan, formerly monk of Bordefley, elected Abbot of Dene 1187 on the refignation of Abbot Waleran. See Annales de Waverleia, Ann. Mon., Vol ii., p. 245. See alfo Flaxley Cartulary, Nos. 31,' 44, 69, 70.

3. Richard, Abbot, circ. 1200. Flaxley Cartulary, Nos. 40, 41, 42, 43, 48, 49, 51, 52, 75.

    The Cartulary No. 97 alfo alludes to "Frater R. dictus Abbas de Flaxley." "Frater R." is probably the Abbot Richard above referred to.

4. William, Abbot, Feb., 1277 (?). Regifter Bifhop Cantelupe, p. 44.

5. Nicholas, Abbot, 1288. Regifter Bifhop Swinfield, p. 53.

6. William de Rya, Abbot, 1314. Regifter Bifhop Swinfield, p. 189.

[1] Mitred Abbeys, Vol. ii, p. 85.
[2] Supplement to Notitia Monaftica, Vol. ii, p. 48.
[3] All the references to Flaxley abbey noticed in the index to the Bifhop's regifters at Hereford have now been quoted. There may poffibly be other references to the abbey entered under other heads, but I have had neither the time nor the opportunity for making fuch a fearch.
[4] For this information I am indebted to an interefting note by Mr. Falconer Madan, publifhed at page 347, Vol. ii. of Glouc. Notes and Queries, No. dcclxxi.

7. Richard Payto (Peyto), Abbot, 1372. Regifter Bifhop Courtenay, p. 11.
8. William, Abbot, 1426. Regifter Bifhop Spofford, p. 107.
9. — Berkeley, Abbot, 1476. MS. Bodl. 88.
10. John, Abbot, 1509. Regifter Bishop Mayhew, p. 45.
11. William Beawdley, Abbot, 1528. Wood's Fafti, quoted by Browne Willis and Stevens.
12. Thomas Were (Ware), Abbot, 1532. Laft Abbot of Flaxley: turned out at the fuppreffion of the Abbey in 1536, died at Afton Rowant, near Thame, in Oxfordfhire, 1546. Wood's Fafti, Browne Willis "Mitred Abbeys," and Stevens' "Notitia Monaftica."

This lift is more complete than any which has been hitherto publifhed, but there are, obvioufly, many omiffions. The firft four Abbots of Flaxley named above, and Abbot Berkeley No. 9, have hitherto efcaped notice, and are not mentioned by Browne Willis, Stevens, or Bifhop Tanner.

Printed State Papers.

It remains to notice briefly the few additional references to Flaxley Abbey which are recorded in the printed State Papers of the reigns of Henry VII and Henry VIII.

At vol. i, p. 200, of the State Papers, entitled "Materials for the Hiftory of Henry VII," we have the following entry—

"1485, 6 Dec. Grant for life to Thomas Cvn' of the office of one of the fergeants of the caftle of St. Briavell within the foreft of Dean, co. Glouc., and (as a falary in the fame office) a yearly rent of 13s 4d which the abbot of the monaftery of St. Mary of Flaxley is bound to pay the king at the faid caftle at Michaelmas for a certain water mill called le New myll within the faid foreft, and all wages, fees, etc., such as Robert Hyett heretofore had. Also grant for life of the office of Clerk of the Court of St. Briavells with wages, etc., fuch as the faid Robert heretofore had.' 5 Dec. P.S. No. 549, Pat. p. 2, m. 17 (9).

At page 1047, vol. iii, part 2 (1519 to 1523), of Letters and Papers, Foreign and Domeftic, Henry VIII, feƈtion 2483, occurs the following entry—

1522. "An annual grant to be made by the Spiritualty for the king's perfonal expenfes in France for the recovery of the crown of the fame."

Among the lift of Abbots appears an entry of "Flaxlee 40l," fhewing the annual grant made by the Abbot of Flaxley.

On 7 Nov., 1514, a royal writ was addreffed to the Abbot of St. Peter's Monaftery, at Gloucefter, commanding him to receive the oath of William Kingfton, Knight, who was appointed Sheriff of the county of Gloucefter. The original writ is printed in extenfo at p. 288, vol. iii, of Hift. et Cart. Mon., S. Peter, Glouc. Edited Mr. W. H. Hart.

In Letters and Papers, Foreign and Domeftic, Hen. VII, 1519 to 1523, occurs the following entry under the head of grants in April, 1522—

"Sir Wm. Kyngifton, knight for the body and Th. ap Gwilliam, ufher of the chamber, to be conftables of the caftle of St. Briavel in Dene Foreft, Glouc. during pleafure, with fees from the faid foreft and the lordfhip of Newlond S.B."

Thefe entries are important as furnifhing fome explanation of the reafon why, at the fuppreffion of the leffer monafteries in 1536, the abbey and eftates of Flaxley were granted by the crown to Sir William Kingfton, who, both as fheriff for the county and as conftable of the caftle of St. Briavells, had held high office under the crown in the county of Gloucefter.

In the same publication, vol. iv, part 2, 1526-1528, fection 4096, page 1811, occurs the following entry—

"March 25, 1528, Circular addreffed to the Abbot of Flaxley and other abbots ftating that for her own better education and for the confolation of the King and Queen it has been ordered that the princefs fhould refide near the King's perfon. As the Council of the Marches would be encumbered by having to move a great houfehold from place to place in her abfence, her officers and fervants have been allowed to go home. But as feveral of them are deftitute of houfes or friends to refort to, the Abbot is requefted to take ...... of them in the meantime into your (sic) convenient finding."

In the fame publication, vol. iv, part 2, 1526-1528, fection 6047, page 2701, occurs the following—

"1529. Lift of perfons fummoned to the convocation of the province of Canterbury arranged in diocefes :

"Hereford dioc. ...... Will., Abbot of Flaxley, p. and by Abbot of Graces."

The abbot referred to muft have been William Beawdley, who was inftalled as abbot of Flaxley in 1528.

In 1532 William[1] Beawdley was fucceeded by Thomas[1] Were (Ware), laft

---

[1] For notices of William Beawdley and Thomas Were (Ware), fee Wood's Fafti, vol. i, p. 672 and 677, viz.—vol. i, p. 677, "1528, June 28, Father William Beawdley Abbot of Flaxley of the Ciftercian order, opponent in divinity." Vol. i, p. 672, "Thomas Ware a monk of the Ciftercian order and fometime a ftudent of St. Bernard's College in Oxon. He afterwards became the laft Abbot of Flaxley in Gloucefterfhire in the place of W. Beaudley, and living to fee his houfe diffolved

Abbot of Flaxley. In 1536 was paſſed the Act for diſſolving all the leſſer monaſteries and nunneries, namely, ſuch as poſſeſſed leſs than £200 per annum; and on 4 Feb., 1536, Flaxley Abbey was diſſolved, being granted in the following year to Sir William Kingſton, who has been already noticed as conſtable of St. Briavells in 1522, and is well known as conſtable of the Tower of London.

Sir William Kingston, first grantee of Flaxley Abbey, 1537.

The grant to Sir William Kingſton was made by patent dated 26 March, 28 Hen. VIII (1537), a copy of which is given in Appendix I, No. viii. The grant, it will be obſerved, contains a clauſe that Sir William Kingſton and his heirs were to hold all the premiſes "as fully as Thomas Were the late Abbot held the ſame on the 4th day of February, 27 Hen. VIII (1536)." Theſe words appear to import that Flaxley Abbey was diſſolved on the date mentioned, 4th February, 1536; and this is the conſtruction which has been placed on the words by Henry Hewlett, Eſq., Q.C., who has had occaſion, profeſſionally, to examine the original grant.

The patent grants to Sir William Kingſton the houſe and ſite of the late abbey or monaſtery of Flaxley, in the county of Glouceſter, ſuppreſſed by authority of the Parliament, and all the church, bell tower, and burial ground (Eccleſiam, campanile et cemiterium) of the ſaid monaſtery, with all the abbey buildings and premiſes, and the following demeſnes, manors, etc.,— Flaxley "howſe," Goodriche, Clymperwell, Walmore, Blecheden, Arlingham le Monken, Rewarden, Newland, Parva Dene, Newenham, Pulton, Dymmoc, county Glouc., and the manor of Rochelbury in county Somerſet, together with all manorial and other rights pertaining thereto, in as full, entire, and complete a manner as Thomas Were, late abbot of the ſaid abbey, enjoyed the ſame on the 4th day of February, 27 Hen. VIII (1536), "adeo plene et integre ac in tam amplo modo et formâ prout quidam Thomas Were nuper Abbas ejuſdem nuper Abbatiae ...... quarto die Februarii anno regni noſtro viceſimo ſeptimo aut antea ...... habuit."

Regarding the particulars of the ſuppreſſion very little is known. No acknowledgment of the royal ſupremacy in 1534 or formal notice of the

and himſelf and his brethren turned out thence, he retired to Aſton Rowant near Thame in Oxon where, ſpending the remaining part of his days in devotion and retiredneſs, he gave way at length to fate in a good old age, anno 1546, whereupon his body was buried in the yard belonging to the Church there."

diffolution is on record ; and even regarding the date of the fuppreffion there is no information except what may be deduced from the language of the grant to Sir William Kingfton. It is ftated, but on what authority is unknown, that at the time of the diffolution there were nine monks refident in Flaxley abbey. The monaftery was then valued according to Dugdale at £112 13s. 1d., and according to Speed at £112 3s. 1d. From the note below it will be feen that Flaxley was the firft Gloucefterfhire abbey diffolved. Being a leffer monaftery within the meaning of the Act of 1536, its revenues being under £200 a year, Flaxley abbey was one of the firft foundations to difappear. The other Gloucefterfhire abbeys named below[1] had a brief refpite till 1539. Fofbrooke,[2] quoting from Rolls, Britifh Mufeum J. 14, notes that at the diffolution the abbey was charged with a corrody of £4 6s. 8d. per annum to Agnes Smith for life.

Sir William Kingfton died 13th May, 1540, as appears from the infcription placed on his tomb in Painfwick church, Gloucefterfhire, where he was buried. This infcription is ftated by Anthony Wood to have been torn off from the tomb by foldiers in 1644, and to have fallen into the poffeffion of a defcendant of Sir William Kingfton's family from whom Anthony Wood obtained his information.

The patent granted to Sir William Kingfton was, on his death, furrendered to the crown by his fon[3] and fucceffor Anthony, who is well known as Sir Anthony Kingfton, the Provoft Marfhal notorious for his cruelty in the

---

[1] The following dates of the diffolution of the various monafteries in Gloucefterfhire are taken from Brown Willis' " Mitred Abbeys "—

Cirencefter	19 Dec. 1539 (Vol. i, p. 64.)
St. Peter's, Gloucefter	2 Dec. 1539 (Vol. i, p. 117.)
St. Auguftine's, Briftol	9 Dec. 1539 (Vol. i, p. 229.)
Hayles	24 Dec. 1539 (Vol. ii, p. 86.)
Kingswood	1 Feb. 1539 (Vol. ii, p. 86.) (1539-40. ?)
Lanthony	10 May 1539 (Vol. ii, p. 87.)
Tewkefbury	9 Jan. 1539 (Vol. i, p. 186.) (1539-40. ?)
Winchcombe	3 Dec. 1539 (Vol. i, p. 213.)

The following penfions are noted by Browne Willis as paid to incumbents of Chantries, A.D. 1553— *Little Dean*, Will. Pomfrey, Incumbent of Trinity Chantry, £4. *Michel Dean*, Henry Hooper, Incumbent of Trinity Chantry, £4. *Newland*, George Wadham, Incumbent of St. Mary's Chantry, £4, and to Edward Service and Edward Fryor, £4. *Westbury*, John Shawe, Incumbent of St. Mary's Chantry, £3 6s. 8d.

[2] Fofbrooke, Hift. of Glouc., Vol. ii, p. 177.

[3] For the Kingfton pedigree fee paper on the Flaxley Grange in Littledean by Mr. W. C. Heane, printed in vol. vi, part 2, of the Tranfactions of the Briftol and Gloucefterfhire Archæological Society.

insurrection of 1549. He was one of the commissioners appointed by the crown to superintend the execution, by burning, of Bishop Hooper, at Gloucester, in 1555.¹ A new patent of the Flaxley estates was granted to Sir Anthony Kingston 11 Feb., 34 Hen. VIII (1543). This patent also was surrendered on the ground, apparently, of some informality or change required to be inserted; and a new patent, dated 22 May, 36 Hen. VIII (1544), was finally granted to Sir Anthony Kingston and his heirs. In form, and in nearly all the material particulars, it closely resembles the grant made to Sir William Kingston; and, under these circumstances, it has not been considered necessary to furnish a copy in extenso.²

Account of all existing Monastic remains at Flaxley.

With the grant to Sir William Kingston the monastic history of Flaxley abbey comes to an end, and it only remains to notice briefly the few existing remains that recall the former character of the building.

Bigland, writing 1791, gives the following description of the abbey—"Early in the present century that part of this venerable pile which had been inhabited by the abbot and monks remained nearly perfect. It was a low structure of great length, containing in front the refectory sixty feet long, twenty-five wide, but fourteen only in height; the whole arched with stone, with plain and massive ribs intersecting the vault. The first floor consisted of a very long gallery with which the dormitory or cells were connected, and at the south end a very spacious apartment which is conjectured to have been the abbot's chief room, or used for the assembling of the convent. These are certainly parts of the original structure, much of which was destroyed by fire in 1777."

This description has been adopted both by Archdeacon Rudge (History of Gloucestershire) and by the Rev. H. T. Nicholls in his notice of Flaxley abbey in his work on the "Forest of Dean." In the last-named work will be found

---

¹ For an account of the burning of Bishop Hooper at Gloucester, see paper by Mr. John Bellows of Gloucester, regarding the discovery of the original stake near the spot where the Hooper memorial now stands, published at p. 23, vol. vii of the Proc. Cottefwold Nat. Field Club.

² In the Treasurer's Remembrancer's Office in the Exchequer are the following documents—

(a) Flaxley. De Edwardo Kyngeston arm. et uxore occasionat. ad ostendendum quo titulo tenent domum et situm nuper monasterii de Flaxley. Hil. Rec., 1 Eliz., rot. 48.

(b) Flaxley. De manibus regis amovendis de situ Mon. de Flaxley in Com. Glouc. et Antonio Kingston liberando. Hil. Rec. 3, Jac. I, rot. 110.

CLOISTERED ROOM.

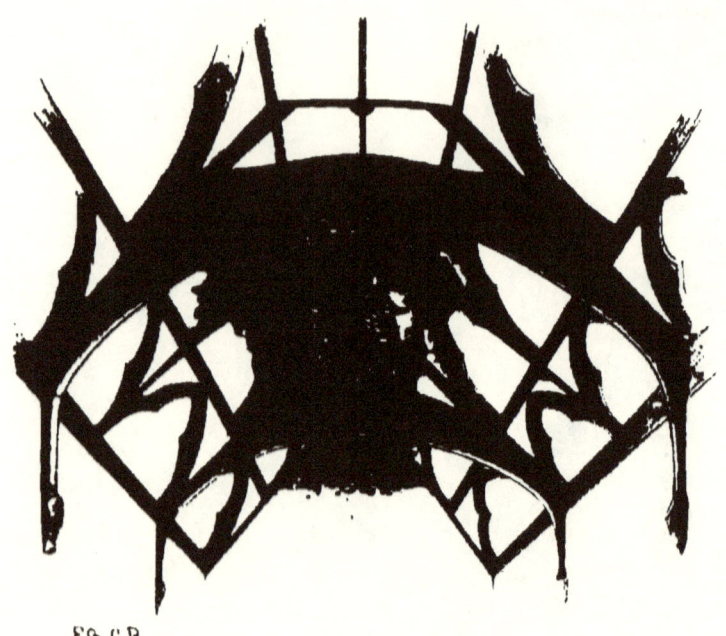

ROOF OF ABBOT'S ROOM.

at p. 181 wood-cuts reprefenting the arched vaulting of the fo-called refectory, and the open timber roof of the fpacious apartment alluded to by Bigland, which is generally known as the "Abbot's room." The wood cut reprefenting what is fuppofed to be the refectory of the abbey is not confidered to be a very succefsful reprefentation, the arches of the vaulting being more obtufe and flattened than as fhown in the fketch. The roof of the "Abbot's room" is as fhown in the accompanying Plate No. III.

The vaulted chamber, fixty feet in length by twenty-five in width, has fince Bigland's time been ordinarily accepted as the ancient refectory of the abbey; but the authority for this opinion is not apparent. It is undoubtedly a part of the original monaftery and a building of great intereft, the architecture of which is of characteriftic Ciftercian ftyle, plain and maffive, with folid circular vaulting, refting on plain capitals. The building in queftion faces the weft, on which fide was the main road leading to the abbey. It feems doubtful from the ordinary ftandard arrangement of Ciftercian buildings as defcribed by Sharpe[1] and other authorities whether this weft chamber was really the abbey refectory as fuggefted by Bigland. There is fome reafon for thinking that it was more probably the domus converforum, or quarters of the lay brethren, which in Ciftercian houfes ufually occupied a portion at leaft of the buildings on the weft fide of the cloifter court. It is probable that over this original chamber was the dormitory of the converfi or lay brethren leading into the fine room alluded to as the "Abbot's room."

The walls of the vaulted chamber above defcribed, now ufed as the abbey kitchen and fervants' offices, are of enormous thicknefs; and the cellars adjoining, alfo a portion of the original abbey buildings, are of great intereft from their maffive conftruction and characteriftic architectural details. A good idea of the chamber referred to is obtained from the accompanying picture, Plate I., made from a careful drawing by Mr. E. B. Crawley-Boevey. The architecture clofely refembles that of the Domus converforum in the abbey of Fountains as fhown in Mr. Sharpe's Plate VI., in Part I of his work on Ciftercian architecture.

Discovery of Monastic remains in 1788.

With the exception of buildings referred to, the remainder of the prefent houfe is of modern conftruction, and no trace remains of the fite of the abbey church, or of any other portion of the original ftructure. Bigland, however,

---

[1] Conf. The Architecture of the Ciftercians, by Edmund Sharpe, M.A. E.F.N. Spon., London, 1874.

states "that in 1788 the fite and floor of the *chapter house* were difcovered at a fmall depth in the garden, extending about forty-five feet, and twenty-four wide ; at the upper end a circular ftone bench, and in the centre the carved bafe of a pillar. Seven coffin lids of ftone were then found fculptured with ornamented croffes ; but upon one a right hand and arm holding a crofier, which circumftance imports it to have been the memorial of one of the abbots, as their office had not the privilege, as that of bifhops, of conferring benediction."

Bigland's account muft have been written not long after the alleged difcovery was made ; and a plan of the remains, fhewing the circular ftone bench referred to by Bigland, together with the feven coffin lids and other carved ftone work, is ftill preferved at Flaxley Abbey. It is, however, much to be regretted that thefe moft interefting remains are no longer in fitu, having been removed in the courfe of certain alterations that were carried out about fifty years ago. The fite, however, of this difcovery is ftill marked by a fmall enclofure, ftones being placed on the furface to reprefent, approximately, the fize and fhape of the remains difcovered feveral feet beneath the furface. Three out of the feven ftone coffin lids are placed in this enclofure, together with other carved ftones, bafes of pillars, etc., that were difcovered about the fame time when the excavation was made. The remaining four ftone coffin lids have difappeared ; but meafurements and drawings of them ftill remain.

The accompanying plates Nos. IV. and V. fhow the fhape and general defcription of the remains, difcovered in 1788, as related above by Bigland. The carved bafe of the pillar, difcovered amongft the remains at Flaxley, appears to be identical in fhape and pattern with the ruined pillars ftill exifting in the chapter houfe of Tintern Abbey.[1]

Since the preceding remarks were written, an interefting paper has been prepared by Mr. J. Henry Middleton, F.S.A., on the exifting remains of Flaxley

[1] In connection with the remains difcovered at Flaxley Abbey, in 1788, I find a note recorded in the handwriting of the late Sir Thomas Crawley-Boevey, 1st Baronet, of Flaxley Abbey, to the following effect—" Underneath this fpot lie the bones of Nicholas, the firft abbot of Flaxley, and fix monks buried anno domini 1288." The authority for this entry I have been unable to difcover. There was an abbot of Flaxley named Nicholas, inftalled 1288, but he was certainly not the firft abbot. Affuming that the coffin lids difcovered in 1788 were in fitu, it is not improbable that they belonged to various Flaxley abbots who alone had the privilege of interment in the chapter houfe of the monaftery. Monks and lay brethren were ufually buried in the cloifter garth; while no one under the rank of a bifhop might properly be buried in the abbey church. Conf. Monafticon Ciftercienfe, printed in Sharpe's Architecture of the Ciftercians. See however on this point Mr. Middleton, F.S.A., below.

PLATE IV.

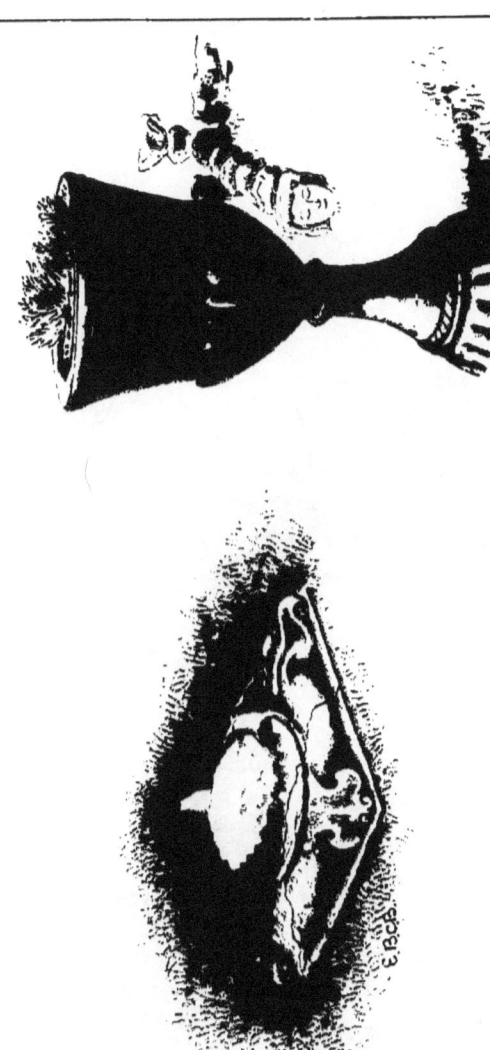

REMAINS FOUND IN RUINS OF CHAPTER HOUSE.

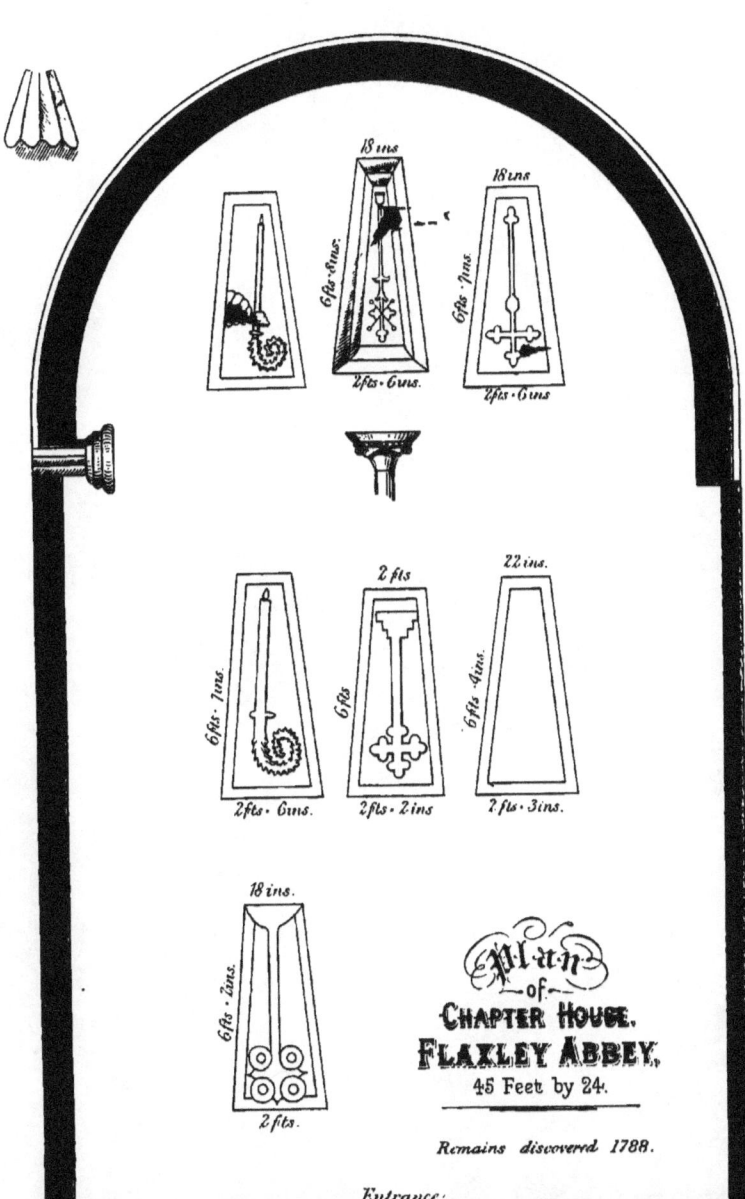

ARCH INTO WEST CLOISTER.

Flaxley Abbey. 93

abbey, in which it will be seen, he confirms the opinion expreffed above that the fine hall, now ufed as the kitchen and fervants' offices, and facing weft, cannot be the abbey refectory, which according to the ufual Ciftercian plan, occupied with the buttery, kitchen, &c., the premifes adjoining the fouth walk of the cloifter. It is quite poffible, he thinks, that the fine room called by tradition the "Abbot's room" was in reality the refectory of the hofpitium or gueft's dining hall.

Mr. Middleton's valuable paper, together with the accompanying plan fhowing the probable arrangement of the monaftic buildings, has been, by permiffion, extracted from the "Tranfactions of the Briftol and Gloucefter Archæological Society,"[1] and is given below. The accompanying plates Nos. I. and III. fhowing the fine hall referred to above, and the roof of the Abbot's room are from fketches made by my brother, Mr. E. B. Crawley-Boevey.

"There are no remains whatever of the abbey church above ground, though the foundations probably ftill exift.

"Of the monaftic buildings, one block (or part of a block) only is ftill ftanding. This confifts of a fine hall, about fixty-five feet long by twenty-five feet wide, vaulted in five bays with fimple chamfered groin-ribs, fpringing from corbels, about five feet above the floor. The whole is very folid and plain, after the ufual Ciftercian fafhion, and appears to have been built about A.D. 1200. This room (see Plan, Plate VI.) runs north and fouth. The windows, one in each bay, on the weft fide are much modernifed, but feem to be in the places of the original ones. At the fouth end of this hall there are two narrow parallel rooms, with plain barrel vaults.[2]

"On the eaft fide[3] of the large hall there is a fine richly-moulded archway of Tranfitional character, and another fmaller doorway, further fouth. All other openings appear modern, and are not fhown on the plan.

"It will be at once evident to any one who is acquainted with the Ciftercian plan that this fine hall cannot be the monks' refectory, or frater, as mediæval writers called it (see *Rites of Durham*, cap. xxxix.[4]) The Ciftercian refectorium opened out of the middle of the fouth cloifter walk, and was flanked on the eaft by the kitchen, and on the weft by the buttery. It was fet at

---

[1] Vol. vi, part 2.
[2] A good idea of this hall is obtained from plate No. III. which faces page 91.
[3] See plate No. II. facing p. 93.
[4] Some confufion has been made by certain modern writers, who have called the Common-Houfe the Frater, without any authority whatever; in Ciftercian writings the common-houfe is called the calefactorium.

right angles to this cloifter walk, and not parallel to it, as was the cafe with the refectories of other orders, the fide of which generally occupies nearly the whole length of the cloifter from eaft to weft.

" In a Ciftercian monaftery the cooking was done by the monks themfelves, who took this duty in turns : and not by regular paid cooks, as in moft other monaftic orders. For this reafon, probably, the refectorium was turned round, fo as to allow room on each fide of it for the kitchen and buttery, clofe up againft the main cloifter, which formed the living room of the monks.

" It is, I think, quite clear that the exifting hall, with its range of windows on the weft, and its doors on the eaft, was part of that great weftern range of buildings which formed fo important a part of every Ciftercian monaftery.

" This range has been called by Mr. Sharpe the domus converforum, but it would be better I think to keep to the old nomenclature, and call it, as the Ciftercians themfelves did, the cellarium.

" The cellarium was not one building, but a whole range of buildings, and was fo called becaufe it was under the fpecial fupervifion of the cellararius, who, next to the abbot, was the moft important man in a Ciftercian houfe. He managed all the worldly affairs of the abbey, received all money, and bought the neceffary fupplies of food. Under his charge were all the converfi, or working lay brothers, and he was alfo the fupervifor of all arrangements for the reception of guefts.

" The hofpitium, in fact, was part (i.e., the fouthern part) of the cellarium, while the converfi, and the cellararius himfelf, with his officers, occupied the northern part—the divifion, that is, neareft to the church.

" Of this great range the exifting hall at Flaxley is certainly a part, but what its fpecial use was it is now impoffible to fay ; it may have been a refectorium for the converfi, or poffibly a place where fome of their indoor labours were carried on.

" The narrow rooms at the fouth end of the hall are probably a neceffarium ; the drain with a ftream of water being carried through the narrower two divifions. This precife arrangement may be feen in almoft every exifting Ciftercian abbey. It fhould be noticed that the eaft wall of the hall is of the enormous thicknefs of eight feet, while that on the weft is only about fix feet thick. The reafon for this evidently was that, as the weft walk of the cloifter came againft the eaft wall of this hall, it was impoffible to have projecting buttreffes. While the oppofite wall was free, and fo could have a thinner wall with a buttrefs to each bay.

" Over the hall itfelf there appears to be no early work remaining, but over

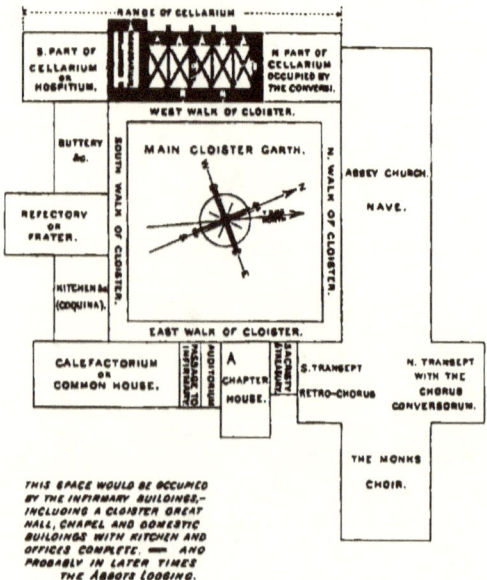

the neceffarium there is a very fine room, about forty feet by fixteen feet, with a handfome open roof of late fourteenth century work. This roof, which is very well preferved, has arched and moulded principals, with braces curved and cufped, and wall pieces coming down on to fmall ftone corbels.[1]

"There is a good cornice about fixteen feet above the floor. At the weft end of the room there is a large pointed window, which has loft all its tracery, and been much modernifed. Tradition calls this the "Abbot's room;" but it is much more probable that it was the refectory of the hofpitium, or gueft's dining hall. It is now fitted up as a library. In early times, that is during the twelfth and thirteenth centuries, while the ftrictnefs of the Ciftercian rule remained in full force, the abbot had no fpecial rooms. He flept in the common dortor with all his monks, and dined with the better clafs of guefts in the refectory of the hofpitium. In later times, when Ciftercian abbots began to have fpecial apartments fet apart for them, the place chofen for the abbot's lodgings feems to have been far away to the eaft of the monaftic buildings.

"With the Ciftercians, juft as with the Benedictines, the infirmary buildings were a very large and important range, including a cloifter, large infirmary hall and a chapel. Confiderable remains of this range exift at Rievaulx, Fountains, and many other Ciftercian abbeys. There feems no doubt that the later abbots occupied part of the infirmary buildings, which are always to the eaft of the main cloifter, and are reached from it by the paffage which adjoins the auditorium (fee Plan, Plate No. VI.)

"In the prefent garden there are three fine ftone coffin-lids of thirteenth or fourteenth century work; two of them are carved with abbots' croziers. Thefe and a quantity of vaulting fhafts are faid to have been found at, or near, the fpot where they now lie—marked A on the plan—and this is traditionally the fite of the Chapter houfe; which it very well may be. It was the Ciftercian cuftom to bury their abbots in the Chapter houfe—no one under the rank of a bifhop being allowed to be buried in the church. The monks were interred—never in the cloifter garth, as fome writers have afferted—but in their own cemetery to the eaft of the church.[2]

"I fhould wifh to record my thanks to Sir Thomas and Lady Crawley-Boevey for their kindnefs in allowing me to examine thoroughly their houfe in my fearch for the remains of the abbey buildings."

---

[1] See plate No. III. facing page 91 above.
[2] See note (1) on page 92 above.

Original deeds of Thomas Were, last abbot of Flaxley.

With the exception of the buildings still in situ, above described, the only remaining relics of the monastic period are two original deeds, both executed by Thomas Were, the last abbot of Flaxley, and the abbey seal, of which some account must be given.

The first of these original deeds is dated 8th December, 25 Hen. VIII (1534), and purports to be made between Thomas Were, abbot of the monastery of Flaxley, and John Hayll, of Borsley, relating to the reversion of a tenement called the Wake mill, and other premises, lands, etc., belonging to the abbey of Flaxley.

The second deed is dated 21st April, 26 Hen. VIII (1535), between Thomas Were, abbot, on the part of the convent of Flaxley, and William Tanner,[1] otherwise called William Mors, relating to the reversion of a tenement with garden, in Little Dean, on payment of a sum of twelve pence on the feast of the Annunciation and St. Michael the Archangel.

Both of the deeds are of an ordinary character. Their date shows that they were both of them executed just before the dissolution of the abbey and the grant to Sir William Kingston. Both deeds are in good preservation, and to the first is still attached the abbot's original seal. From the second deed the seal has disappeared.

Flaxley Abbey Seal.

Besides the original seal just referred to belonging to the owner of Flaxley Abbey, two seals of Flaxley abbots have been found in the Public Record Office; and another Flaxley seal is said to be attached to the document in the British Museum, noticed at p. 57 above ; and is entered in the Seal Catalogue of the Museum as 75 A. 37.

The original seal at Flaxley abbey is attached to the deed of 8th December, 1534, executed between Abbot Thomas Were and John Hayll of Borsley. It represents two figures seated side by side under a canopy. The legend is no longer legible ; and portions of the seal have altogether disappeared.

Of the two seals relating to Flaxley Abbey now in the Public Record Office, one from the Westminster Chapter House Records is entered in the Seal catalogue under the following heading :—

[1] A person of the name of William Tanner is referred to in Valor Ecclesiasticus under the head of Parva Deane, p. 49.

1.
Box 16, 42.
"Flaxley (Glouc.), Abbot of, A remife of Land by Wm. Abbot of Flaxley to Hugo Defpenfer and his heirs. 10 Ed. 2. (1316-17.) Seal of red wax, perfect."

The other feal is attached to a document from the Duchy of Lancafter Records, and is thus referred to at page 34 of the thirty-fifth Annual Report of the Deputy Keeper of the Public Records dated 2nd March, 1874, in an Index to Clafs X (Grants in Boxes) of the Duchy of Lancafter Records.

"No. 367. A.D. 1315. Obligation from the abbot and convent of Flaxleye in Gloucefterfhire, to the Lord Henry de Lancaftre, to receive two clerks on the prefentation of the fame Henry and his heirs, for the perpetual celebration for the fouls of Edmund, fon of King Henry and Blanche, his wife, fometime Queen of Navarre. Flaxleye on Friday next before the feaft of St. Laurence the Martyr (8th Auguft), 9 Edw. II. (1315-16)—part of feal."

This deed purports to be executed by "Frater Willelmus dei gratia Abbas de Flaxleye;" and the portion of the feal ftill attaching to the deed, exactly refembles the perfect feal ftill attaching to the document from the Weftminfter Chapter Houfe records. Both deeds were apparently executed by the fame Flaxley Abbot—William de Rya, one in the ninth and one in the tenth year of King Edward II, viz. 1315 and 1316.

The deed of 10 Ed. II, from the Weftminfter Chapter Houfe, runs as follows :

"Omnibus Chrifti fidelibus prefens fcriptum vifuris et audituris frater Willelmus Abbas de Flaxleye et ejusdem loci conventus falutem in domino fempiternam. Noverit univerfitas veftra nos unanimi affenfu et voluntate pro nobis et fuccefforibus noftris remififfe et quietum clamaffe domino Hugoni Defpenfer et heredibus fuis totam terram et communam omnimodam quam habuimus infra parcum dicti Domini Hugonis infra bofcum de Calveleye quod eft infra parcum de Lamufardere fine ullo retenemento noftro et fuccefforum noftrorum in perpetuum. Ita quod nos nec fucceffores noftri aliquid juris vel clamii in predicta terra communam quamcunque de cetero exigere potuimus in perpetuum fed per prefentes undique fumus exclufi. In cujus rei teftimonium prefenti fcripto figillum noftrum commune eft appenfum. Hiis teftibus Domino Willelmo Tracy milite, Johanne Jorge, Galfrido de Wefton et multis aliis. Datum in cápitulo noftro de Flaxleye die exaltationis fanctæ crucis Anno Regni Regis Edwardi filii Regis Edwardi decimo.

The feal attached to this deed is as defcribed in the official catalogue in perfect condition. It reprefents an abbot ftanding erect under a canopy, flightly ornamented, with a paftoral ftaff in his right hand, and holding with his left a book on his breaft furrounded, by the legend S. ABBATIS DE FLAXLE.

The counter feal is a hand with a paftoral ftaff and other ornaments, viz., a fleur-de-lis, &c., furrounded by the words CONTRA SIGILL ABBATIS DE FLAXLE.[1]

Reprefentations of the feal and counter feal are here fhown from cafts taken by Mr. W. Ready of the Britifh Mufeum.

In addition to the three original Flaxley feals defcribed above, a fourth feal is faid to be attached to an original document in the Britifh Mufeum, and the feal is mentioned in the Seal Catalogue of the Mufeum as 75 A, 37. The Abbot of Flaxley appears as one of the attefting witneffes to the deed of reconciliation briefly defcribed at page 57 above, and the abbot's feal, together with feveral others, is faid to be appended to the original deed. The feal in queftion I have endeavoured with the affiftance of the Mufeum authorities to identify, but without fuccess. Moft of the feals are fo much injured as to be illegible. In another department of the Britifh Mufeum I was fucceffful in obtaining from the Doubleday collection of Mr. Robert Ready two excellent impreffions of feals alleged to relate to Flaxley abbey.

1. Seal of a Flaxley abbot (1338) alleged to have been taken from a charter in the Duchy of Lancafter records. This feal appears to correfpond exactly with the feal defcribed above, of which a reprefentation has been given. It

[1] This feal is defcribed in almoft identical terms at p. 179 of Nichol's "Foreft of Dean." It is alfo referred to in a work entitled "Collectanea Gloceftrienfia, being a catalogue of Books, tracts, prints, coins, &c., relating to the county of Gloucefter in the poffeffion of John Delafield Phelps, Efq., of Chevenage Houfe." At page 167 of this work, reference is made to two Flaxley feals, one from the Chapter Houfe of Weftminfter Records, and one from the records of the Duchy of Lancafter. The latter is doubtlefs the fame as the imperfect feal alluded to above, which is attached to the deed of 9 Edw. II, from the Duchy of Lancafter records.

was doubtlefs taken from the fame charter which has been already defcribed; but there is a difcrepancy about the date which fhould apparently be 1316-17, inftead of 1338.

2. Seal of the abbey of St. Mary of Dene reprefenting the Virgin ftanding erect with the infant Saviour in her arms under an ornamental canopy with the legend S. ABBATISSE SCE MARIE DEANNE.

It feems to be very doubtful whether this fecond feal belongs to Flaxley at all. Sir John Maclean, F.S.A., who has been good enough to examine a caft of the feal, has expreffed a decided opinion that it does not. The legend, fo far as it can be deciphered, feems to difclofe clearly the word ABBATISSE, but the concluding word is doubtful. The feal is apparently that of fome abbess, and has, I think, no connection whatever with Flaxley abbey.

Rank and Status of Abbots of Flaxley.

Allufion has already been made to the fact that Flaxley abbey was under the jurifdiction of the Bifhops of Hereford, and was included amongft the leffer monafteries whofe revenues were lefs than £200 per annum. Under thefe circumftances it is not altogether eafy to underftand why Sir Robert Atkyns, Rudder, and others, have expreffed the opinion that Flaxley was a "Mitred abbey," a term of much fignificance in ecclefiaftical nomenclature. Sir Robert Atkyns thus writes at p. 4, of the "Hiftory of Gloucefterfhire."

"All abbeys which had mitres, had them by grant from the Pope; but they held their baronies folely and immediately of the King. There were fix mitred abbeys in this county, Gloucefter, Cirencefter, Tewkefbury, Winchcomb, Hailes and Flaxley, three of which Gloucefter, Cirencefter and Winchcomb were peeral, and held place in Parliament until their diffolution, and even the abbots of the other monafteries were fometimes anciently fummoned to Parliament, as the abbot of Flaxley in the reign of Edward I, the abbot of Hailes in the reigns of Edward I and II, and the abbot of Tewkefbury in the reigns of Henry III, Edward I and II."

Unlefs it can be fhown that Flaxley abbey received from the Pope the grant of a mitre, it is not apparent why Flaxley is included by Atkyns amongft the mitred abbeys of Gloucefterfhire. No fuch grant is on record in the Cartulary, nor is there, fo far as I am aware, any evidence in fupport of the ftatement that Flaxley was a mitred abbey.

The term "mitred abbey," as ordinarily ufed by ecclefiaftical hiftorians, feems to have involved two important rights, firft, the right of exemption from epifcopal jurifdiction, and fecondly, the right of the abbot to fit in Parliament. Cowel fays of abbots, "Such as were mitred were exempted from the jurifdiction of the diocefan, having themfelves epifcopal authority within the fame limits." Godolphin, in Report Eccl., writes to the fame effect. In another place Cowel in alluding to mitred abbots, thus writes— "Thefe abbots were not called to Parliament becaufe they were mitred, but becaufe they received their temporals from the king."

In Fuller's "Church Hiftory," where a fpecial fection is devoted to the fubject, "of fuch abbots who attained to be Parliamentary Barons," the term "mitred abbot" is limited to thofe abbeys in which the abbot enjoyed the right of fitting in Parliament, and of exemption from epifcopal fupervifion (fee pp. 292 to 296). Such abbots were called abbots general or abbots fovereign, as acknowledging no fuperior. Bifhop Tanner in the preface to his "Notitia Monaftica," p. xvi, note v, ftates that exemption from their diocefan, being honoured with the mitre, and called to Parliament, certainly depended upon different royal grants, for feveral abbots are known to have enjoyed one privilege without the other.

The fact that the abbot of Flaxley was feveral times fummoned to Parliament[1] in the reign of Edward I is not apparently, taken by itfelf, conclufive evidence that Flaxley was a mitred abbey as afferted. Fuller has fhown that in the forty-ninth year of Henry III (1264) no lefs than fixty-four abbots and thirty-fix priors, as he quaintly terms it "a jolly number," together with the Mafter of the Temple "were voluntarily out of the king's free will and pleafure (no right that they could claim themfelves) fummoned to Parliament."

Fuller alfo relates how in the reigns of Edward I and II, the number of abbots fummoned was fluctuating and uncertain, *e.g.*, forty in the twenty-feventh year of Edward I ; feventy-five in the twenty-eighth year of the fame king ; fifty-fix in the firft year of Edward II, and fifteen in the fecond year of the fame reign. In the reign of Edward III, the lift of Parliamentary abbots was for the firft time formally fettled, and their number fixed at twenty-fix, exclufive of two abbots and one prior which are doubtful, viz., the abbots of Leicefter, and St. James, Northampton, and the prior of Coventry. To thefe twenty-fix Parliamentary abbots one more was added by Henry VIII, viz : the abbot of Taviftock ; and the abbot of Tewkefbury alfo appears on the Parliamentary Rolls, making up a total of twenty-eight Parliamentary abbots, who alone are ordinarily recognized in ecclefiaftical hiftory as mitred. The twenty-eight mitred abbeys

[1] See page 50 above.

are all that are noticed by Fuller, Tanner, or Browne-Willis, and no mention is made of Flaxley by any of the ecclefiaftical hiftorians who have given a lift of mitred abbeys.

The following curious extract from Fuller's "Church Hiftory" may be quoted in oppofition to the paffage from Atkyns given above.

"Of all counties in England, Gloucefterfhire was moft peftered with monks, having four mitred abbeys, befides St. Auftine's in Briftol (who fometimes paffed for a Baron) within the compaffe thereof, viz: Gloucefter, Tewkefbury, Cirencefter and Wevelfcomb, hence the topical wicked proverb deferving to be banifhed out of that country, being the prophane child of fuperftitious parents—'as fure as God is in Gloucefterfhire'—as if fo many convents had certainly faftened His Gracious Prefence to that place."—p. 296. Flaxley is here by implication pointedly excluded from the mitred abbeys of Gloucefterfhire.

All the mitred abbeys had confiderable revenues, and were included amongft the greater monafteries, *i.e.*, thofe poffeffed of £200 annual revenue. Flaxley was one of the leffer monafteries with a comparatively infignificant revenue. Again the mitred abbeys, with the exception of St. John's of Jerufalem, were Benedictine; Flaxley was Ciftercian.

The grant of a mitre denoted ecclefiaftical independence. It has been above noticed that Flaxley abbey was fupervifed by the Bifhop of Hereford, who inftituted the abbots and exercifed epifcopal jurifdiction over the abbey and furrounding churches in the Deanery of Hereford.[1]

From a review of all thefe facts above ftated, it would feem fufficiently clear that the Ciftercian abbey of Flaxley has no lawful pretenfion to be confidered a mitred abbey within the ordinary meaning of ecclefiaftical nomenclature.

---

[1] See on this point "Abftracts and Illuftrations of Bifhop Swinfield's Houfehold Roll," edited by the Rev. John Webb, and printed by the Camden Society. As regards the legal relation of the monaftery of Flaxley to the Bifhopric of Hereford, fee Bull of Pope Celeftine III, Cartulary, No. 77.

APPENDIX. PART I.

EXTRACTS FROM THE PUBLIC RECORDS RELATING TO
FLAXLEY ABBEY, CO. GLOUC.

Classified List of References in the Public Records to Flaxley Abbey, Co. Glouc.

I. *Cartæ Antiquæ* (Calendar of Sir Jofeph Ayloffe).

1. R. No. 19. 2. X. No. 4. 3. N.N. No. 39. 4. Q.Q. No. 23. Being all tranfcripts of the confirmation charter of Henry II to Flaxley Abbey.

5. X. No. 5. Protection charter of Richard I.

6. P.P. No. 50. 7. Q.Q. No. 29.

Tranfcripts of charter of Richard I, granting to the abbots the woods around the abbey for firewood.

8. Q.Q. No. 28. Confirmation charter of Richard I.

9. Q.Q. No. 21. Grant of the Abbot's Woods by Henry III.

II. *Close Rolls.*

No.			No.		
1	Rot Claus.	1 Hen. III, m. 26[1]	15	Rot Claus.	10 Hen. III, m. 11
2	do.	2 Hen. III, m. 15	16	do.	do. m. 29
3	do.	4 Hen. III, m. 4	17	do.	11 Hen. III, m. 5
4	do.	5 Hen. III, m. 20	18	do.	do. m. 10
5	do.	6 Hen. III, m. 5	19	do.	do. m. 18
6	do.	do. m. 13	20	do.	13 Hen. III, m. 8[4]
7	do.	7 Hen. III, m. 19	21	do.	do. m. 8[5]
8	do.	do. m. 23	22	do.	do. m. 12
9	do.	8 Hen. III, m. 11	23	do.	14 Hen. III, m. 6
10	do.	do. m. 13	24	do.	do. m. 22
11	do.	do. m. 25[2]	25	do.	15 Hen. III, m. 2
12	do.	9 Hen. III, m. 8	26	do.	do. m. 2[6]
13	do.	do. m. 11	27	do.	do. m. 9
14	do.	do. m. 18[3]	28	do.	do. m. 14

[1] Quoted by Tanner; not mentioned in the Clofe Rolls, printed by Record Commiffion.
[2] Quoted by Tanner; not mentioned in printed feries.
[3] Quoted by Tanner; not mentioned in printed feries.
[4] Tanner's references to the Clofe Rolls, end with 13 Hen. III, membrane 8.
[5] Second reference on the fame membrane.
[6] Second reference on the fame membrane.

Flaxley Abbey.

29	Rot. Claus.	16 Hen. III, m. 5	39	Rot. Claus.	30 Hen. III, m. 11
30	do.	17 Hen. III, m. 2	40	do.	32 Hen. III, m. 9
31	do.	18 Hen. III, m. 15	41	do.	34 Hen. III, m. 15
32	do.	do. m. 19	42	do.	37 Hen. III, m. 23
33	do.	do. m. 27	43	do.	39 Hen. III, m. 14
34	do.	do. m. 27[1]	44	do.	40 Hen. III, m. 10 *dorso*
35	do.	do. m. 28	45	do.	do. m. 12
36	do.	do. m. 28 *dorso*	46	do.	do. m. 19
37	do.	19 Hen. III, m. 8	47	do.	do. m. 19 *dorso*[2]
38	do.	26 Hen. III, m. 13			

III. *Charter Rolls.*

1. Rot. Cart. 11 Hen. III, *pars prima* m. 22[3]
2. Rot. Cart. 11 Hen. III, *pars prima* m. 27.
3. Rot. Cart. 11 Hen. III, *pars secunda* m. 8.
4. Rot. Cart. 14 Hen. III, m. 6.[4]
5. Rot. Cart. 42 Hen. III, m. 2.
6. Rot. Cart. 7 Edw. II, m. 31 *pars unica.*
7. Rot. Cart. 4 Edw. III, m. 23 *pars unica.*
8. Rot. Cart. 7 Edw. III, m. 31.[5]
9. Rot. Cart. 25 Edw. III, No. 7.

IV. *Patent Rolls.*

1. Rot. Pat. 54 Hen. III, m. 9, vel. 19 De medietate gurgitis in aqua Sabrinæ vocati Hynewere 34.
2. Rot. Pat. 3 Ed. I, m. 33 *dorso.*[6]
3. Rot. Pat. 20 Ed. I, m. 18.
4. Ditto 3 Ed. III, p. 1 vel. 3 m. 19.[7]

---

[1] Second reference on the fame membrane.
[2] The indexes to the Clofe Rolls, continue to the 57 year of Hen. III, but no reference to Flaxley Abbey appears after those quoted above.
NOTE. Both in this and in the following lifts, feveral of the references given by Tanner appear to be mifquoted. They are mentioned in thefe lifts to fhow that they have not been overlooked.
[3] Quoted by Tanner only. [4] Quoted by Tanner only. [5] Quoted by Tanner only.
The references to the Charter Rolls quoted by Tanner only are not mentioned in the Calendar of the Record Commiffioners, and appear to be wrongly quoted.
[6] Quoted by Tanner only. [7] Quoted by Tanner only.

5. Rot. Pat. 3 Ed. III, *prima pars.* m. 16.
6. Rot. Pat. 9 Ed. III, *Sec. pars.* m. 16.
7. Rot. Pat. 30 Ed. III, p. 3 m. 18 vel. 19.[1]
8. Rot. Pat. 32 Ed. III, *Sec. pars.* m. 28.
9. Rot. Pat. 32 Ed. III, *Sec. pars.* m. 22 and 27.[2]
10. Rot. Pat. 38 Ed. III, p. 1 m. 38.
11. Ditto 11 Ric. II, p. 1 m. 28.
12. Ditto 22 Ric. II, p. 3 m. 16 *tertia et ultima pars.*
13. Ditto 27 Hen. VI, m. 6 *prima pars.*

V. Inquisitions.

A. Ad quod damnum.

1. Inq. 52 Hen. III, No. 22
2. do. 54 do. No. 68
3. do. 7 Edw. I, No. 40
4. do. 15 do. No. 67
5. Inq. 2 Edw. III, secd. num. No. 128
6. do. 32 do. secd. num. No. 87
7. do. 46 do. No. 10[3]
8. do. 10 Ric. II, No. 107

B. Post mortem

1 Inq. 6 Edw. I, No. 88 p.m. Alexander Bleyght.
2 Inq. 15 Edw. I, No. 19 p.m. John of Penrys.
3 Inq. 7 Hen. V, No. 52 p.m. William Waryn.
4 Inq. 22 Hen. VI, No. 34 p.m. Robert Greyndour, Arm.

---

[1] Quoted by Tanner only.
[2] Quoted by Tanner only.
The references to the Patent Rolls quoted by Tanner only are not mentioned in the Calendar of the Record Commissioners, and appear to be wrongly quoted.
[3] Quoted by Tanner only.

Index to the Charters and other Documents given in this Appendix.

1. Grant to Flaxley Abbey of the woods around the Abbey for firewood.
2. Grant to Flaxley Abbey by Henry III of the woods, called the Abbot's Woods.
3. Charter of protection to Flaxley Abbey by Richard I.
4. Confirmation charter of Richard I to Flaxley Abbey, reciting charter of Henry II with additions.
5. Confirmation charter of Henry III to Flaxley Abbey, reciting gifts and donations of private benefactors, 1227.
6. Grant of Edward III to Flaxley Abbey of £36 9s. 1d. per annum, from the rents and profits of the kings newly affarted lands in the foreft of Dean, 1353.
7. Notification of Edward III, that on account of the bad rule of the Abbots of Flaxley, he had refumed charge of the Abbey and had entrufted it to the Abbots of Dore, Bordefley and the Prior of Flaxley till further notice, 1335.
8. Grant of Flaxley Abbey with all its appurtenances to Sir William Kingfton by King Henry VIII, 27 March, 1537.

APPENDIX No. I.

Grant to Flaxley Abbey of the woods around the Abbey for firewood. Cart. Antiq. Q.Q. No. 29 from transcript in P.R.O.

Cartæ Antiquæ. Q.Q. 29 :—Henricus Dei gratia etc. Sciatis nos intuitu Dei et pro falute animæ noftræ et antecefforum et heredum noftrorum dediffe conceffiffe et hac carta noftra confirmaffe Deo et ecclefiæ Beatæ Mariæ de Dena et abbati et monachis Ciftercienfis ordinis Deo ibidem fervientibus et fuccefforibus fuis in liberam puram et perpetuam eleemofynam totum bofcum circa prædictam abbatiam ad focum fuum per metas fubfcriptas fcilicet in longum rivuli juxta campum monachorum prædicti loci afcendendo ufque Fulhiate et a Fulhiate ufque ad magnum cheminum quod tendit de Abbenhale ufque ad Parvam Dene, et de predicto chemino a latere montis qui vocatur Walfebyre ufque ad viam equorum quæ tendit ufque ad Abbenhale et de parvo ficheto decurrente in longum prædictæ viæ ufque ad bofcum Johannis de Munemuta de Hope afcendendo et de prædicto bofco per divifam inter bofcum predicti Johannis et bofcum de Tymbrigge et Caftiarde usque ad rivulum de Hope et de prædicto rivulo circuendo ufque ad campum de Rofeley et in longum prædicti campi ufque ad grangiam prædictorum monachorum quæ eft juxta prædictam abbatiam, claudendum baffa haia et parvo foffato : ita quod feræ intrare et exire poffint.

Et fciendum quod prædictus abbas et fuceffores ipfius et monachi ejufdem loci nihil capient vel capere poffunt in forefta noftra de Dene de cætero ad focum fuum fine licentia noftra vel heredum noftrorum ficut in ea capere confueverunt ante donacionem et conceffionem iftam per cartam Henrici regis avi noftri quam inde habent. Volumus etiam quod totus prædictus bofcus circa prædictam abbatiam infra metas prædictas quietus fit in perpetuum de regardo et vafto et de omnibus quæ ad foreftarium vel viridarium vel eorum miniftros pertinent excepta venatione noftra. Quare volumus et firmiter præcipimus quod prædicti abbas et monachi prædictæ ecclefiæ Beatæ Mariæ de Dena habeant et teneant totum prædictum bofcum per metas prædictas in liberam puram et perpetuam eleemofynam bene et in pace libere, quiete, integre, plenarie cum omnibus pertinentiis libertatibus et liberis confuetudinibus fuis in omnibus locis et rebus, quietum in perpetuum de regardo et vafto et de omnibus quæ ad foreſtarium vel viridarium vel eorum miniſtros pertinent et ab omni feculari fervitio et exactione, excepta venatione noſtra ſicut prædictum eſt. Hiis teſtibus etc. Datum apud Weſtmonaſterium xi° die Februarii anno regni noſtri undecimo.

N.B. A duplicate of the firſt half of this charter down to the words "exire poſſint" is given in Cart. Antiq. P.P. No. 50.

APPENDIX No. II.

Grant to Flaxley Abbey by Henry III of the woods, called the Abbot's Woods. 42 Henry III Cart. Antiq. Q.Q. No. 21.

Henricus Rex Angliæ etc.

Sciatis quod cum dilecti nobis in Chriſto Abbas et conventus de Flixlege Ciſtertienſis ordinis percipere confueverint duas quercus in foreſta noſtra de Dena ſingulis ſeptimanis ad ſuſtentacionem unius forgiæ ſuæ in eadem foreſta ex collatione domini Henrici avi noſtri et confirmatione noſtrâ, in perpetuam eleemoſynam, et hoc ad magnum detrimentum dictæ foreſtæ et ad damnum noſtrum.

Nos detrimentum ibidem et damnum advertentes ad inſtantiam dictorum Abbatis et monachorum miſimus de conſilio noſtro dilectos et fideles noſtros Henricum de Bathonia [et Robertum] Waleraund ad partes illas ad inquirendum per ſacramentum tam militum quam aliorum liberorum et legalium hominum, per quos rei veritas melius ſciri poſſet in hac parte predictæ foreſtæ commodius aſſignare poſſemus eiſdem Abbati et monachis quandam partem boſci in recompenſationem prædictarum duarum quercuum ad minus detrimentum ejuſdem foreſtæ et minus damnum noſtrum.

Quia vero accepimus per inquiſitionem factam per prædictos Henricum et Robertum quod eſt ad commodum noſtrum et ſalvationem prædictæ foreſtæ aſſignare dictis Abbati et Monachis in recompenſationem prædictarum duarum quercuum quandam partem boſci in eadem foreſta in forma ſubſcripta infra has bundas ac in diviſas videlicet :—de Ardlonde uſque ad vadum in Sinderforde in ſiniſtra parte et de vado illo uſque ad vadum de Suthlege et abinde per vallem rivuli qui vocatur Smalebroke uſque ad cheminum qui vocatur Rugeweye et per prædictum cheminum in longitudine uſque ad terram

Johannis de Rodleye in finiftra parte et a terra illa ufque ad prædictum Ardlande ficut coopertum dicti bofci fe extendit.

Nos de confilio noftro affignavimus et conceffimus eifdem Abbati et monachis in recompenfationem prædictarum duarum quercuum prædictam partem bofci infra bundas et divifas præfcriptas habendam et tenendam eisdem Abbati et monachis et eorum fucceffioribus et ecclefiæ fuæ de Flexlege in perpetuam eleemofynam quietam de vafto et regardo et de vifu foreftarii et viridarii et de omnibus quæ ad foreftarium et viridarium vel eorum miniftros pertinent excepta venatione noftra.

Salvis nobis et heredibus noftris herbagio dicti bofci et aeriis aufturcorum, falconum, et fparvariorum, et mineria fi inveniatur ibidem. Ita etiam quod ipfi Abbas et monachi habeant attachiamenta dicti bofci et fi fibi viderit expedire liceat decimam partem dicti bofci claudere fepe quæ fit defenfabilis contra omnia animalia præterquam contra feras noftras et ftet fepes illa per quadrennium tantum et tunc. diruatur et alibi claudatur decima pars per quadrennium et fic de quadrennio in quadrennium claudatur decima pars dicti bofci in diverfis locis ita quod novem partes ejusdem bofci semper fint extra claufturam.

Quare volumus et firmiter præcipimus pro nobis et heredibus noftris quod prædicti Abbas et Monachi et eorum succeffores et ecclefia fua de Flexlege habeant et teneant in recompenfationem prædictarum duarum quercuum prædictam partem bofci infra bundas et divifas præfcriptas in perpetuam eleemofynam, quietam de vafto et regardo et de vifu foreftarii et viridarii et de omnibus quæ ad foreftarium vel viridarium vel eorum miniftros pertinent excepta venatione noftra. Salvis nobis et heredibus noftris herbagio dicti bofci et aeriis aufturcorum, falconum, et fparvariorum, et mineria fi inveniatur ibidem.

Ita etiam quod prædicti Abbas et monachi habeant attachiamenta· dicti bofci et fi viderit fibi expedire liceat eis decimam partem dicti bofci claudere fepe quæ fit defenfabilis contra omnia animalia præterquam contra feras noftras, et ftet fepes illa per quadrennium tantum et tunc diruatur, et alibi claudatur decima pars per quadrennium, et fic de quadrennio in quadrennium claudatur pars decima dicti bofci in diverfis locis ita quod novem partes ejufdem bofci femper fint extra claufturam ficut prædictum eft.

Hiis teftibus etc. Datum apud Clarendon xxviii° die Maii anno regni noftri quadragefimo fecundo.

N.B. A duplicate of this grant is entered on the Charter. (Rolls Rot. Cart. 42 Hen. III, pars unica m. 2.)

In the tranfcript from which this Copy has been taken the names of the witneffes are omitted. In the Englifh tranflation given in the text the names have been added from the copy of this grant enrolled in the Charter Rolls.

APPENDIX No. III.

Charter of Protection to Flaxley Abbey by Richard I. Cart. Antiq. X., No 5. Copied from Volume of Transcripts in P.R.O.

Ric. Dei gratia Rex Angliæ Dux Normanniæ, Aquitaniæ, Comes Andegaviæ Archiepifcopis Epifcopis Abbatibus Archidiaconis decanis comitibus baronibus jufticiariis vicecomitibus et omnibus miniftris et fidelibus fuis falutem.

Sciatis quod Abbatia de Dene et monachi ordinis Ciftercienfis ibidem Deo fervientes et omnes terræ et redditus et poffeffiones fuæ funt in manu et cuftodia et protectione noftrâ et ideo præcipimus quod ipfam Abbatiam et monachos et terras et redditus et omnes res et poffeffiones fuas cuftodiatis et manu teneatis et protegatis ficut noftras dominicas ita quod nullam violentiam vel contumeliam vel injuriam aut gravamen eis faciatis nec fieri permittatis plufquam noftris dominicis rebus vel poffeffionibus. Et fi quis eis fuper hoc in aliquo foriffacere præfumpferit. plenariam eis fine dilatione inde jufticiam faciatis; et prohibemus ne pontantur in placitum de ullo tenemento fuo unde habent cartas dominorum vel donatorum vel venditorum fuorum nisi coram nobis ipfis vel capitali juftitia (*sic*) noftra. T.W. Comite de Mandeville vi° die Septembris apud Weftmonafterium.

APPENDIX No. IV.

Confirmation Charter of Richard I to Flaxley Abbey, reciting Charter of Henry II, with additions. Cart. Antiq. QQ. No. 28.

Ricardus dei gratia, etc. Sciatis nos conceffiffe et præfenti carta noftra confirmaffe Deo et Sanctæ Mariæ et monachis de Flexleye de ordine Ciftercienfi ibidem Deo fervientibus pro falute noftra et anteceflorum noftrorum in perpetuam eleemofinam omnes illas donationes quas Rogerus Comes Herfordiæ . . . (and fo on as in Cart. of Henry II, Dugd. Mon.) Quare volumus et firmiter præcipimus quod prædicti monachi omnia ista prædicta cum ceteris pertinentiis et omnes terras et homines et poffeffiones fuas habeant et teneant libere et quiete integre et plenarie in liberam eleemofynam et quæcunque alia in futuro pia devotione fidelium vel conventione venditorum illis de cujuscunque feodo fuerint rationabiliter collata cum omnibus pertinentiis et libertatibus et liberis confuetudinibus in terris et in efcambiis terrarum et emptionibus, in marifcis, in grangiis et virgultis, in civitatibus et villis, ftagnis, pifcariis, in bofco et plano, in pratis et pafcuis, in aquis et molendinis, in viis et femitis, et in omnibus aliis locis et rebus, cum faca et foca tol et theam et infangenethef foluta et libera ab omni feculari fervitio, falvis conventionibus erga univerfos fecundum rationabiles cartas vel chirographa fua, et quieti fint de fectis comitatus, lez hundreds et auxiliis vicecomitis et omnium miniftralium eorum et de omnibus ad eos pertinentibus. Prohibemus etiam quod nullus eos aut poffeffiones aut homines aut res fuas vexet vel difturbet contra libertates cartarum fuarum fuper decem librarum foriffacturam. Datum apud Dumfronte xxi° die Decembris anno regni noftri decimo.

APPENDIX No. V.

Confirmation charter of Henry III to Flaxley Abbey, dated 1227, reciting gifts and donations of private benefactors.

Charter Roll 11. Henry III. Part 2.—Membrane 8.

Pro Abbate de Flaxl[eya].

Henricus Rex etc. Salutem. Sciatis nos intuitu Dei conceffiffe et hac carta noftra confirmaffe Deo et Ecclefiæ beatæ Mariæ de Dena et abbati et monachis ibidem Deo fervientibus omnes donationes, conceffiones et venditiones fubfcriptas eifdem abbati et monachis racionabiliter factas videlicet De venditione Rogeri de Heidune novem acras terræ quæ jacent inter fabulum de Redlege et magnum cheminum, et duas acras in marifco quæ jacent inter Heilithe et tres feilliones Johannis de Wodeham et unam acram prati in Holemede. Item de dono ejufdem Rogeri decem acras terræ fuæ de Redlege, fcilicet totam terram fuam ad occidentem meffuagii Reginaldi de Heidune, et ex altera parte chemini totam terram fuam arabilem quæ jacet inter pullam quæ venit de Wildemore et tres feilliones Johannis de Wodeham cum pertinentiis et cum Walla et tribus parvis feillionibus quæ jacent extra prædictam vallam. De dono Margaretæ filiæ Gaufridi filii Willelmi totam terram fuam de Northwode quam pater fuus ei dedit. De dono Willelmi de Dune duas acras terræ quæ jacent fuper Walemorefhulle et totam terram fuam in Stangarft. Item de dono ejufdem Willelmi quatuordecim feilliones terræ arabilis in Wodlege cum prato ejufdem latitudinis quod jacet ad caput eorundem feillionum verfus terram de Lege cum forerda quæ eft ad aliud caput eorundem feillionum cum pertinentiis et unam acram terræ ad Wlnegate fupra cheminum. De dono Rogeri filii Radulphi tres virgatas terræ in Pultune cum pertinentiis. De dono Gileberti de Dimmoc totam terram fuam de Bruerne quam habuit de domino fuo Roberto de Mauns. De dono Henrici de Cheakefhull totam croftam illam quam Edwardus Hoc tenuit quæ fcilicet appellatur Alinvecroft cum prato quod tenuit fcilicet Alinveplot et totam terram fuam in Rudinge et croftam illam quam Willelmus Cuverur et Muriel tenuerunt. De dono Hugonis de Gerne totam terram fuam in crofta apud Cheakefhulle. De dono Ofmundi H . . . . totam terram fuam quæ jacet inter terram Ricardi Draperii et terram Warini Sellarii omnes etiam terras quæ jacent inter terram quæ fuit Waci Coci et terram quæ fuit Gileberti filii Radulphi in Glouceftria. De dono Arnaldi filii Arnaldi Dunninge totam terram inter duos pontes Savernæ apud Glouceftriam. De dono Henrici filii Henrici Kais totum jus quod habuit in duabus terris in Glouceftria quas de eo tenuit Ricardus filius Willelmi Burgeis. De dono Radulphi Crupard duas croftas videlicet Hulpefcroft et Hamecroft. De dono Henrici filii Odonis totam terram fuam in Ruding ficut unquam pater suus plenius eam tenuit. De dono Rogeri de Arderne totam terram fuam de Otlege apud Cheakefhulle. De venditione Philippi de Humelemore quatuor acras terræ fuæ quas tenuit de feudo Willelmi de Dune. De dono Radulphi de Redlege totam terram fuam in fabulo de Redlege cum pertinentiis fuis quæ fcilicet jacet fubtus Heilithe et totum tenementum quod Walterus Hendi tenuit de eo in prato de Smalham cum omni jure et fervitio quod ad ipfum vel ad heredes fuos inde pertinuit vel pertinere potuit. De dono Petri de Salto Marifco totam terram fuam in villa de Tribnelle cum omnibus pertinentiis fuis. De dono Hugonis Chearke illam partem campi qui dicitur de Hide quæ eft proximior Sabrinæ cum Haitiis ad eandem terram pertinentibus. De dono Willelmi de Sancto Leodegario totam terram fuam de Ragel quæ fuit Philippi de Burci cum pertinentiis fuis. De dono Thomæ filii Willelmi de Harpetre totam terram fuam quæ fuit Henrici Scepefhefed cum omnibus pertinentiis fuis et unam dimidiam virgatam terræ quam Olbertus præpofitus tenuit cum omnibus pertinentiis fuis et communem pafturam centum ovibus in eadem villa et communem pafturam animalibus fuis quantum pertinet ad unam virgatam terræ et de bofco qui fuit prædicti Henrici quantum meremium opus fuerit per vifum foreftarii fui. De dono Ricardi de Blechedune duas acras prati quas Edricus Ris tenuit et dimidiam acram prati quæ jacet proxima prædictis duabus acris. De dono Johannis Rufi filii Adæ totam terram fuam arabilem in Bruerne fcilicet decem feilliones in Revenefhokefelde cum pertinentiis præter pratum. De dono Heliæ Giffarde totum dominicum fuum in Habewoldefham in manerio fuo de Brummeffelde cum paftura octo boum et in communi paftura cum hominibus prædicti manerii et ubique fimul cum bobus domini de Brummeffelde in paftura extra parcum de Brummeffelde et cum paftura duodecies viginti bidentium in communi paftura tam de Brummeffelde quam de Croneham. De dono Willelmi de Budifelde illam partem terræ fuæ in Budifeld apud Feneftegate quæ jacet a rivo qui defcendit de Climperwelle per femitam de Tatemounefpflade et inde directe per medium Wodecroftarum ufque Thikegrove. Illam partem terræ fuæ quæ jacet a Stielweie per rivum prædictum ufque Wlfledefwelle et ducentas bidentes in perpetuum in communi paftura de Budifeld. De dono Gaufridi de Longo campo totam terram quam Thomas Baterich tenuit de eo in Levepeley fcilicet duos lundiers cum omnibus pertinentiis fuis. De dono Henrici de Mineriis totam partem fuam de Hinewere cum omnibus libertatibus fuis. De dono Willelmi de la Mara totum pratum fuum apud Tukel quod fcilicet jacet in longum fubtus campum Abbatis de Glouceftria. De dono Roberti filii Walteri Sprot totam partem fuam illarum acrarum quæ funt in montibus quæ funt inter dominum fuum Rogerum de Winterburne et prædictum Robertum quæ computantur pro quatuor acris et dimidia et communam etiam tam in montibus quam in campis. De dono Johannis difpenfatoris totam terram fuam quæ eft in crofta quæ dicitur Buveveie quæ jacet inter terram quam Adam filius Fulconis dedit eisdem monachis et meffuagium quod fuit Roberti Surdi.

De dono Amifii de Tukelege duas acras prati in Bruerne in prato quod appellatur Wrugehat quæ jacent inter pratum Radulphi de Wilintune et pratum Abbatis de Glouceftria et illam goram prati quæ jacet ad caput prædictarum acrarum et viginti tres feilliones et duas goras cum forerda fubtus jacentes proxime juxta le merher quod dividit inter terram Abbatis Glouceftriæ et suam tenendas pro tribus acris cum haicio quantum prædictæ tres acræ durant et etiam duas acras unam juxta Feldedich et aliam quæ appellatur Gordrodaker. De dono Walteri filii Willelmi de Munftrewurthe totam terram suam in Walemore quae appellatur Charkefelde ficut Rogerus de Munftrewurthe eam tenuit in fuo dominico. De dono Willelmi filii Willlelmi de Budifelde totam medietatem W[o]decroftarum in Budifelde et totum pendentem de Fifbechefegge, scilicet de Becoltefegge in longum rivuli usque ad Stielwie cum pertinentiis suis. De dono Hugonis Charke fex puchas in Sabrina contra Hanecombre. De dono Matildis Giffarde totam terram fuam fubtus pifcariam de Bifpwike fcilicet viginti quatuor feilliones cum omnibus pertinentiis quæ funt de tenemento Hugonis de Gerne. De dono Heliæ Giffarde totam illam dimidiam virgatam terræ in manerio fuo de Brummesfelde cum pertinentiis quam Willelmus le Cras tenuit: et totam illam dimidiam virgatam terræ cum pertinentiis quam Robertus de Climperwelle tenuit: et totam terram illam quæ jacet inter vivarium de Climperwelle et terram prædictorum monachorum quam tenent de Ecclesia de La[n]tonia. De dono Hugonis Hosati totam terram fuam de Emneia cum pertinentiis fuis. De dono Rogeri de . . . . totam illam dimidiam virgatam terræ quam Jordanus filius Johannis tenuit de eo in Erlingham. Quare volumus et firmiter præcipimus quod prædicti Abbas et Monachi habeant et teneant omnes terras et tenementa prædicta bene et in pace libere et quiete et integre cum omnibus pertinentiis fuis in perpetunm ficut cartæ donatorum et venditorum prædictorum quas inde habent rationabiliter teftantur. Hiis teftibus venerabilibus patribus Euftachio Londonienfi, Jocelino Bathonienfi, et Ricardo Sarefberienfi Epifcopis; H[ubertò] de Burgo Comite Kantiæ Jufticiario noftro; Willelmo de Sancto Johanne, Hugone de Neville, Mauritio de Gaunt, Hugone de Mortuo Mari, Ofberto Giffarde, Godefrido de Craucumbe Senefcallis noftris, Henrico de Capella et aliis. Datum per manum venerabilis patris Radulphi Ciceftrenfis Epifcopi Cancellarii noftri apud Weftmonafterium. Nono die Julii Anno regni noftri undecimo (1227).

APPENDIX No. VI.

Grant of Edward III to Flaxley Abbey of £36 19s. 1d. per annum, from the rents and profits of the King's newly assarted lands in the Forest of Dean, A.D. 1353.

CHARTER ROLL, 25, 26, 27, EDW. III, No. 7, 27TH YEAR.

Pro Abbati et Conventu de Flaxleye.

Rex Archiepiscopis, Episcopis, Ducibus, Comitibus, Baronibus, Justiciariis, Vicecomitibus, Præpositis, Ministris, et omnibus ballivis et fidelibus suis salutem. Sciatis quod intuitu caritatis ac pro dampnis gravibus quæ dilecti nobis in Christo Abbas et Conventus de Flaxleye tam per feras forestæ nostræ de Dene quam per varios et frequentes accessus nostros ibidem ante hæc tempora sunt perpessi, volentes eosdem Abbatem et conventum in auxilium sustentationis suæ et ut ipsi et successores sui pro salute nostra dum vixerimus et anima nostra cum subtracti fuerimus ab hac luce ac animabus antecessorum et heredum nostrorum divina perpetuo celebrent respicere gratiose dedimus et concessimus pro nobis et heredibus nostris et hac carta nostra confirmavimus præfatis Abbati et Conventui quod ipsi et successores sui in perpetuum habeant et percipiant triginta et sex libras, decem et novem solidos, et unum denarium singulis annis de exitibus terrarum nostrarum in dicta foresta de novo assartatarum per manus tenentium terrarum earundem. Ita quod quotiescunque dictus redditus vel aliqua parcella ejusdem ad aliquem terminum solutionis redditus illius a retro fuerit liccat prædictis Abbati et Conventui pro eodem redditu vel parcella sic a retro existente distringere et districtiones retinere quousque sibi de eo quod sic a retro fuerit plene fuerit satisfactum prout nos distringere possemus si dictus redditus ad nos pertineret statuto de terris et tenementis ad manum mortuam non ponendis edito non obstante. Quare volumus et firmiter præcipimus quod prædicti Abbas et conventus et successores sui in perpetuum habeant et percipiant triginta et sex libras decem et novem solidos et unum denarium singulis annis de exitibus terrarum nostrarum in dicta foresta de novo assartatarum per manus tenencium terrarum earundem Ita quod quotiescunque dictus redditus vel aliqua parcella ejufdem ad aliquem terminum folutionis redditus illius a retro fuerit liceat præfatis Abbati et Conventui pro eodem redditu vel parcella fic a retro exiftente diftringere, et diftrictiones retinere quoufque fibi de eo quod fic a retro fuerit plene fuerit fatiffactum, prout nos diftrinque poffemus fi dictus redditus ad nos pertineret dicto ftatuto non obftante ficut prædictum est. Hiis teftibus venerabilibus patribus S. Cantuarenfi Archiepifcopo tocius Angliæ Primato J. Eboracenfi Archiepifcopo Angliæ Primate Cancellario noftro Willelmo Wyntonienfi Epifcopo Thefaurario noftro, Henrico Duce Lancaftriæ Willelmo de Bohun Norhamtoniæ, Ricardo Arundelliæ Comitibus, Henrico de Percy, Radulpho de Nevyll, Johanne de Grey de Retherfelde, fenefcallo hofpicii noftri et aliis. Datum per manum noftram apud Weftmonafterium xx° die Septembris (1353) per breve de privato sigillo.

Et mandatum eft tenentibus terrarum prædictarum quod eifdem Abbati et conventui de prædictis triginta et fex libris decem et novem folidis et uno denario fingulis annis prout moris eft intendentes fint et refpondentes, Tefte Rege apud Weftmonafterium xi° die octobris [1353.]

Per idem breve.

APPENDIX No. VII.

Notification of Edward III, that, on account of the negligence and bad rule of the Abbots of Flaxley, he had resumed charge of the Abbey, and had entrusted it to the Abbots of Dore, Bordesley and the Prior of Flaxley till further notice, 1335.

PATENT ROLL OF 9 EDW. III, PART 2, MEMBRANE 16.

De cuftodia Abbatiæ de Flaxleye propter incuriam Abbatis certis cuftodibus commiffa ad voluntatem Regis.

Rex omnibus ad quos, &c., falutem. Sciatis quod cum Abbatia de Flaxleye quæ de progenitorum noftrorum quondam Regum Angliæ fundatione noftroque patronatu exiftit tam per incuriam et malum regimen Abbatum loci illius quam aliis adverfitatibus et infortuniis variis his diebus tam miferabiliter deprimatur et bona Abbatiæ illius confumantur et diverfimode diffipentur quod exitus et proficua dictæ domus ad fuftentationem Monachorum et fervientium domus illius et folutionem debitorum in quibus Abbas et Conventus dicti loci diverfis creditoribus obligantur, necnon ad pietatis opera ibidem ordinata manutenenda non sufficiunt per quod de ftatus dictæ domus defolatione et monachorum divina ibidem pro animabus dictorum progenitorum noftrorum et aliorum defunctorum fidelium celebrantium difpoerfione ac eleemofynarum et aliorum piorum operum fubtractione verisimiliter formidatur nifi remedium per nos fuper hoc celerius apponatur Nos ftatui Abbatiæ predictæ compatientes et ejufdem relevationi volentes prout ad nos attinet providere Abbatiam illam cum terris, tenementis, rebus, redditibus, et omnibus poffeffionibus ad eandem Abbatiam fpectantibus cepimus in protectionem et defenfionem nostram fpecialem et cuftodiam Abbatiæ illius cum terris tenementis rebus redditibus et omnibus poffeffionibus prædictis commifimus dilectis nobis in Chrifto . . Abbati de Dore, Abbati de Bordefleye et Priori dictæ domus de Flaxleye de quorum fidelitate et circumfpectione fiduciam reportamus Habendam quamdiu nostræ placuerit voluntati. Ita quod omnes exitus redditus et proventus terrarum, tenementorum et poffeffionum prædictarum falva rationabili fuftentatione Abbatis Prioris et Conventus dicti loci et miniftrorum fuorum fine quibus Abbatia illa commode regi non poterit ad exonerationem debitorum fuorum prædictorum et relevationem ftatus ejufdem Abbatiæ maneriorum et locorum ad eam fpectantium referventur et eifdem relevationi et exonerationi per vifum adjutorium et confilium aliquorum de majoribus et difcretioribus dictæ domus prout fibi melius expedire videbitur applicentur. Et nolumus quod aliquis vicecomes, ballivus, feu minifter nofter aut alius quicumque in Abbatia prædicta, maneriis, grangiis aut locis ad eam fpectantibus hofpitetur, nec de bladis fœnis, equis, carectis, cariagiis, victualibus aut aliis bonis ejufdem Abbatiæ quicquam capiat feu afportet fine licentia dictorum Abbatum de Dore et Bordefleye, ac Prioris prædictorum durante cuftodia fupradicta In cujus etc. Tefte Rege apud Berewicum fuper Twedam xiiii° die Octobris [1335].

APPENDIX No. VIII.

Grant of Flaxley Abbey with all its appurtenances to Sir William Kingston, by King Henry VIII, 27 March 1537.

PATENT ROLL, 28 HEN. VIII, PART 5, MEMBRANE 19.

De conceffione Willelmo Kyngefton.

Rex omnibus ad quos, etc., Salutem. Sciatis quod nos in confideratione boni veri et fidelis fervitii per dilectum fervientem noftrum Willelmum Kyngefton Militem ante hæc tempora nobis facti de gratia noftra fpeciali ac ex certa fcientia et mero motu noftris dedimus et conceffimus ac per præfentes damus et concedimus eidem Willelmo Kyngefton domum et fitum nuper Abbatiæ five Monafterii de Flaxley in comitatu noftro Glouceftriæ auctoritate parliamenti suppreffi et diffoluti, ac totam ecclefiam, campanile, et cœmeterium ejufdem nuper Monafterii necnon omnia domos ædificia, grangias horrea ftabula, columbaria, hortos, pomaria, gardina, ftagna, vivaria terram fundum et folum noftra infra fitum, ambitum, circuitum et præcinctum dictæ nuper Abbatiæ five Monafterii exiftentia et eidem adjacentia. Ac etiam dominia, maneria, et grangias noftra de Flaxley howfe, Goodriche, Clymperwell, Walmore, Blechedene, Arlyngham le Monkyn, Rewardene, Newland, Parva Dean, Newenham, Pulton et Dymmok cum pertinentiis in comitatu prædicto ac dominium et manerium noftrum de Rochelbury cum pertinentiis in comitatu noftro Somerfetenfi dictæ nuper Abbatiæ five monafterio fpectantia et pertinentia Necnon omnia maneria grangias, meffuagia, cotagia, terras, tenementa, molendina, prata, pascuas, pafturas, bofcos, fubbofcos, redditus, reverfiones, fervitia redditus et firmas tenentium, et firmariorum annuitates, feodi firmas, feoda militis, wardas, maritagia, efcaetas, relevia, curias letas, vifum franci plegii, ac omnia quæ ad vifum franci plegii pertinent, perquifitiones, et proficua curiæ, warrennas, aquas, ftagna, vivaria, communias, pifcarias, libertates, jurifdictiones, advocationes, præfentationes, donationes et jura patronatus ecclefiarum, rectoriarum, vicariarum et capellarum quarumcunque, ac alia jura poffeffiones rectorias appropriatas, et hereditamenta noftra quæcumque tam fpiritualia quam temporalia cujufcumque fint generis, naturæ vel fpeciei et quibuſcumque nominibus cenfeantur feu cognofcantur in villis, campis, hamelettis et parochiis de Flaxley bowfe, Claxhill, Cleve, Holle, Goodriche, Wefton Clymperwell, Walmore, Northwood, Adcette, Elvyngton, Burfley, Denny, Mynfterworthe, Glouceftria, Blechedene, Arlyngton le Monken, Rewarden, Newland, Parva Dean, Newenham, Pultun et Dymmoke ac alibi ubicunque tam in dicto comitatu noftro Glouceftrenfi quam in comitatu noftro villæ noftræ Glouceftriæ ac in Rochelbury et alibi ubicunque in dicto comitatu Somerfetenfi prædictæ nuper Abbatiæ five Monafterii in jure ejufdem nuper Abbatiæ five Monafterii fpectantia et pertinentia adeo plene et integre ac in tam amplis modo et forma prout quidem Thomas Were nuper Abbas ejufdem nuper Abbatiæ five Monafterii in jure nuper Abbatiæ five Monafterii illius quarto die Februarii anno regni noftri vicefimo feptimo aut antea omnia et fingula præmiffa cum fuis juribus, pertinentiis, et commoditatibus habuit tenuit vel gavifus fuit et adeo plene et integre prout ea omnia et fingula ad manus noftras ratione et pretextu cujufdam Actus de quibufdam Monafteriis Abbatiis, prioratibus et domibus religiofis diffolvendis in parliamento noftro apud London tertio die novembris anno regni noftri vicefimo primo inchoato et deinde ufque Weftmonafterium adjornato et per diverfas prorogationes ufque ad et in quartum diem Februarii anno regni noftri vicefimo feptimo continuato et tunc ibidem tento inter alia edita et provifa devenere et devenire debuere et deberent ac in manibus noftris jam exiftentibus et exiftere debent et deberent. Quæ quidem fitus ecclefia, campanile, cœmeterium, dominia, maneria, terræ tenementa, et cætera omnia et fingula præmiffa, fuperius per præfentes conceffa, cum pertinentiis funt clari valoris centum quadraginta quinque librarum, quatuordecim folidorum et unius denarii et non ultra per annum. Habendum tenendum et gaudendum fitum, ecclefiam, campanile, et cœmeterium prædicta, ac omnia et fingula prædicta dominia, maneria, grangias, terras, tenementa, molendina, prata, pafcuas, redditus, reverfiones, fervitia, poffeffiones, hereditamenta, curias letas, vifum franci plegii, et cætera omnia et fingula præmiffa fuperius conceffa, expreffa, et fpecificata cum fuis juribus pertinentiis et commoditatibus quibufcumque, præfato Willelmo Kyngefton et heredibus de corpore fuo legitime procreatis, tenendum de nobis heredibus et fucceffbribus noftris, in capite, per fervitium militare videlicet per decimam partem fervitii unius feodi militis ac per annuum redditum feptuaginta feptem librarum et octo denariorum ad curiam augmentationum reventionum coronæ noftræ ad feftum fancti Michaelis Archangeli omnino folvendum pro omnibus aliis fervitiis exactionibus et demandis quibufcumque proinde nobis heredibus et fucceſſoribus noſtris quovis modo reddendo folvendo vel faciendo et ulterius de uberiori gratia noſtra damus ac per præfentes concedimus præfato Willelmo exitus reventiones et proficua prædicti ſitus ac omnium et ſingulorum prædictorum dominiorum maneriorum terrarum, tenementorum et cæterorum præmiſſorum omnium et ſingulorum cum pertinentiis a feſto Annuntiationis beatæ Mariæ Virginis anno regni noſtri viceſimo ſeptimo hujuſque provenientia ſive creſcentia Habenda eidem Willelmo ex dono noſtro abſque compoto ſeu aliquo alio proinde nobis heredibus vel fucceſſoribus noſtris quoquo modo reddendo ſolvendo vel faciendo et alterius volumus ac pro nobis heredibus et fucceſſoribus noſtris per præſentea concedimus præfato Willelmo Kyngeſton et heredibus ſuis prædictis quod nos heredes et fucceſſores noſtri eundem Willemum et heredes ſuos prædictos verſus quandam Agnetem Smyth de quodam corrodio eidem Agneti pro termino vitæ ſuæ per ſcriptum ſub ſigillo conventuali dicti nuper monaſterii dato et conceſſo de tempore in tempus exonerabimus acquietabimus et defendemus per præſentes eo quod expreſſa mentio &c. In cujus rei &c. Teſte Rege apud Weſtmonaſterium xxvij° die Marcii (1537) Per breve de privato ſigillo et de data etc.

In the margin :

 Vacat Irrotulamentum harum literarum patentium pro eo quod Antonius Kyngeſton miles, filius et heres Willelmi Kyngeſton Militis defuncti decimo die Februarii Anno regni Regis infraſcripto xxxiij° coram eodem Domino Rege in Cancellaria ſua perſonaliter conſtitutus ſurſum reddidit has literas patentes in manus ipſius Domini Regis ibidem cancellandas ea intentione quod idem Dominus Rex alias literas patentes de omnibus et ſingulis maneriis et cæteris præmiſſis infraſcriptis eidem Antonio Kyngeſton et heredibus ſuis ſub alia forma concedere dignaretur. Ideo irrotulamentum prædictum una cum literis patentibus prædictis cancellatur et dampnatur.

APPENDIX. Part II.
CARTULARY OF FLAXLEY ABBEY, CO. GLOUC.

INDEX[1]

CARTULARIUM DE FLAXLEY.

CONTENTA ROTULI INCIPIENTE A FRONTE SUNT.

1. Redditus de Dimmoc.
2. Redditus folvendi a Monachis de Dene.
3. Redditus debiti Monachis de Dene.
4. Carta A... Abbatis Vallis Dose de terra de Climperwell.
5. Carta Rogeri Prioris Lanthoniæ de eadem terra.
6. Carta Gileberti de Monemuta de terra in Ope (Hope).
7. Carta Gileberti de quietancia.
8. Carta Willelmi de Braofe Domini de Brechen de quietancia.
9. Carta Willelmi de Mineriis de decem acris terræ in Cafthard.
10. Carta Henrici de Mineriis de alia terra in Cafthard.
11. Carta Joannis Pichard de terra in Walemor.
12. Carta Hugonis le Petit de terra in Neweham.
13. Carta Gilberti Talbot de molendino in Ruddekefhale.
14. Carta Adæ de Blakeneia de terra in Neweham.
15. Carta Adæ de Blakeneia de redditu.
16. Cartæ Willelmi de Dena Regis Foreftarii de terra in Caftiard.
17. Carta Galfridi filii ejus de terra in Pulmeda.
18. Carta Galfridi de Dena de exclufa molendini Rogeri de Bofco.
19. Carta Adæ filii Fulconis de terra in Chekefhill.
20. Confirmatio Henrici de Mineriis de terra in Chekefhill.
21. Carta Philippi de Dunia de terra in Wadleie.
22. Carta Henrici de Chekefhill de terra in Littlemore.
23. Carta Roberti Tholi de terris in ......

[1] This Table correfponds fubftantially with the Index prepared by the late Sir Thomas Phillipps, which was privately printed by him, together with extracts from the Cartulary. But the abbreviations have been extended, and a few corrections have been introduced where it feemed neceffary.

24. Carta Willelmi Nexe de terra in Neweham.
25. Conventio inter Abbatem de Dene et Willelmum Heremitam de Herdelande.
26. Carta Rogeri filii Radulphi de Pultun de redditu.
27. Carta Hugonis Charke de terra quæ vocatur Eilfifcroft.
28. Carta Ricardi filii de Willelmi de Erlingeham de terris in Cupleforerd.
29. Carta Ricardi de Erlingeham de terra in Erlingeham.
30. Confirmatio Willelmi patris Ricardi de Erlingeham de terris.
31. Carta Roberti Mufchet de terra in Walemor.
32. Carta Roberti Mufchet de terra in Linleg.
33. Carta Hugonis Cherke (Charke) de communa pafturæ.
33A. Carta Roberti de Maus quam fecit Gileberto de Dimmoc.
34. Carta Roberti de Maus quam fecit Gileberto de Dimmoc de terra in Bruerne.
35. Confirmatio Walteri filii Roberti de Maus quam fecit Gileberto de terra in Bruerne.
36. Carta Gileberti de Dimoc de terra in Bruerne.
37. Confirmatio Walteri de Maus de terra in Bruerne.
38. Carta Willelmi de Parcho de terra in Bruerne.
39. Confirmatio Walteri de Maus de terra in Bruerne.
40. Chirographum Roberti Capellani de terra in Neweham.
41. Chirographum Joannis le Tremongere de terra in Neweham.
42. Chirographum Joannis Aidani de terra.
43. Chirographum Rogeri Paris de terra in Glouceftria.
44. Chirographum Rogeri de Bofco de Aldeworde.
45. Chirographum Ernaldi Clerici de Dimmoc.
46. Chirographum Willelmi Kais Perfonæ de Dimmoc.
47. Confirmatio Abbatum H. de Glouceftria et A. de Theokefburi.
48. Chirographum Ricardi de Bofco de terra in Dimmoc.
49. Chirographum Willelmi de Monafterio de terra in eadem.
50. Carta Willelmi filii Gilberti de Erlingeham de terra in Erlingeham.
51. Chirographum Joannis filii Luveric.
52. Carta Walteri de la Barra de meffuagio in Neweham.
53. Carta Hugonis Charke de terris A.D. 1195.
54. Chirograph m Philippi de Dunie A.D. 1195.
55. Chirographum Rogeri de Bofco de terris A.D. 1201.

33 and 33A. In Sir Thomas Phillipps' printed Index thefe two grants which are feperate, are included in one, apparently by a miftake of the printer.

56. Chirographum Willelmi Turc A.D. 1196.
57. Carta Moyfi de Redleia de terra in Ruding A.D. 1199.
58. Carta Nigelli filii Willelmi Hathewi de terris A.D. 1199.
59. Chirographum Galfridi Hugelin de terra in Walemor.
60. Carta Willelmi de Munfterword de terra in Gern et Weftbury.
61. Chirographum Henrici de Chakehill de terra quæ vocatur Cumbefinedewe A.D. 1199.
62. Chirographum Radulphi Crupard A.D. 1200.
63. Carta Adæ filii Fulconis de terra in Chekefhill A.D. 1201.
64. Carta Adæ filii Fulconis de terra in Chekefhill A.D. 1201.
65. Carta Hugonis Charke de terra quæ vocatur Wudelond A.D. 1201.
66. Carta Rogeri de Leinch de terra in Mideltun A.D. 1202.
67. Chirographum Rogeri de Bofco de terris A.D. 1201.

In dorso Rotuli continentur.

68. Redditus Ceræ.
69. Carta Jordani filii Radulphi de terra in Com. Wilton.
70. Carta Godefridi Mog.
71. Chirographum Rogeri Paris.
72. Carta Jofcelini Clerici de terra in London vocata Cheringa.
73. Confirmatio Willelmi Marefcalli.
74. Carta Magiftri Jocelini.
75. Carta Ofberni filii Walteri de Wich.
76. Redditus de Dimmoc.
77. Privilegium Papæ Celeftini III de libertatibus Abbatiæ S. Mariæ de Dene, 1192.
78. Literae W. Herefordenfis Epifcopi univerfis Epifcopatus Capellanis.
79. Privilegium Alexandri III Papæ de decimis pro Abbatia de Flexleche.
80. Catalogus librorum.
81. Carta Philippi de Burci de terra in Ragel.
82. Carta Philippi de Burci de terra in Ragel.
83. Confirmatio Willelmi filii Roberti filii Martini.
84. Carta Willelmi de Sanéto Leodegario de terra in Ragel.
85. Confirmatio Willelmi filii Roberti filii Martini.
86. Carta Walteri filii Walteri de Ragel de terra in Ragel.
87. Confirmatio Roberti filii Walteri de Ragel.
88. Carta Walteri filii Walteri Sprot de Ragel.
89. Confirmatio Roberti filii Walteri Sprot de Ragel.

90. Carta Walteri Sprot de Ragel.
91. Carta Hugonis Hoſate de terra in Ragelburi.
92. Carta Hugonis Hoſate de terra in Ragelburi.
93. Carta Walteri Budicumbe.
94. Chirographum inter Monachos de Dene et Eccleſiam de Budicumbe.
95. Carta Willelmi de la Mara de terra apud Tukeliam.
96. Carta Ernaldi de Cutberleye de terra inter duos pontes Savernæ apud Glouceſtriam.
97. Carta R. Abbatis de Flexley ad Ernaldum de Cutberley.

No. 1.

REDDITUS DE DIMMOC.

Radus de Hulla viiis. iid.
Wills. de Dunhampton viiis. et de opere in falc. et in mefs.
.... iiis. iiid. in autumpno.
Wills. de Soppegrave xixd. et pro parco de Haia debet ipfum claudere et iiiid. debet in aut.
Terram quæ fuit Lefredi tenet Hugo Lamb, qui redd. iis., fed quietus eft quie fecit ferramenta.
Elwredus Wevereth xxd. et iiid. in autumpno.
Mabilia xiid.
Walt. Malcuvenant ad. S. Mich. iiid.
Gerardus iiiis. et iiid. in aut.
Galfridus Perfon vid.
Wills. de Cemiterio vs.
Haraldus viiid. et iiiid. in aut.
Adam Sale xxxiiid.
.... Godchep vid. et ii dies in aut.
.... vid. et iii dies in aut.
Alured in the Velde xiiid. et i dies in aut. et poft obitum fuum terra revertetur ad nos.
Ricardus Lefredi xxviid. et i... dies in aut.
Ernaldus Clec xxxiiid. et iii dies in aut.
.... Bofco viiiid. et ii dies in aut.
.... iid. et ii dies in aut.
.... Willi de Thalamo iiid. ad Scm. Mich.
Elured de Chadburn xxid.
.... iiid. et iiii dies.
Walt. Hacheth i libram cimini ad fest. S. Ephelberti[1] (*sic*).

    Summa redditus nri. de Dimmoc lviiis. iid.

'N.B. All the above feem to have been partly erafed and the following names and rents written by the fide of them in a later hand, viz.,

[1] All the notes above are by Sir Thos. Phillipps.

Galfridus in Mora xviii*d*.
Robt. Withorn viii*s*.
Wmi. Tape Muftre¹ (*sic*) v*s*.
Radulfus Wallenfis ii*s*. et vi*d*.
Hug. Fal ....
Adam Fab. xvi*s*.
Symon Millecrofte xii*d*.
Symon Sutor viii*d*.
Roger Longus v*s*.
Roger le Forefter v*s*.
Roger Roi ii*s*. et viii*d*.
Robt. Cipping xii*d*.
Robt. Dives xiii*d*.
Will. Roches xii*d*.
Walt. le Charbuner xxi*d*.
L . . . iii*s*.
Godes ii*s*.
Galfridus Propofitus² v*s*. and v*d*.
     Redditus in Walemor.

Walt. le Hunte xxviii*d*.
Roger North iiii*d*.
Anneis xii*d*.
    Redditus Novæ Terræ.

Afehart iiii*d*.
.... filius ejus viii*d*.

No. 2.

[REDDITUS SOLVENDI A MONACHIS DE DENE.]

  Istis debemus redditus annuatim in perpetuum.
Abbati de Chormayles, ii*s*. ad fm. Sci Michis.
Priori Lantonie, iii*s* ad fm. Sci Michis.

¹ The above note is by Sir Thos. Phillipps.   ² Præpofitus, the Reeve.

Willo. del Parc, ii*s*. vi*d*. ad fm. S. Michis.
xviii*d*. ad fm. S. Andreæ.
vi*d*. ad fm. S. Mar. Marcial.
xii*d*. ad f. Nat. J. Bapt.
Wmo. de Sto Leodegario, ii*s*.
.... Filio Philippi de Burci, i buz.
Robto. Mufchet. iiii*s*. ad S. Mar. Marciali.
ii*s*. ad f. S. Mich.
Rogero Bofcho. i*d*. ad f. Purif. S. Mariæ.
Willo. filio Milonis, vi*d*. ad f. S. Mich.
Eccliæ de Emnet, i*s*. et ii*d*. ad. f. S. Mich.
Eccliæ de Budichumbe ii*s*. ad f. S. Mich.
De terra Londoniarum, i *lib*. piperis ad f. S. Mich.
Dno. de Budichum, i *lib*. cimini ad feft. S. Mich.
Bafilæ Moniali, ad Pafch.

No. 3.

REDDITUS DEBITI MONACHIS DE DENE.

Isti debeat redditus ex elemosina.

Ex dono Gilberti de Monemuto de fuo molendino de Hope v*s*. in perpet. Unam cartam habemus ad vinum.

['*This means that the grant was made in order to find the Monks in wine.*]

Ex dono Rogeri de Pultun, v*s*. in perpet. Chartam habemus ad hofpitium.

['*This signifies, I believe, for the relief of strangers, or travellers.*]

Ex dono Adæ de Blacheneia ii*s*. in perpet. i carta habemus ad lumen, et ad hoftias.

['*This signifies to find them candles or tapers for the Altars, and to find them the host or holy wafer.*]

Notes 1, 2 and 3 above are by Sir Thos. Phillipps, Bart.

Ex dono Johis. de Munemuta, dimid. marc. de terra in Hope, ad 4 term. Chrifti Nat., Pafch., S. Johis., et S. Mich.
Wmi. Sacer. de Ruwordin xii*d*. in Affumptione.
Laurentius de Ruwordin xii*d*. in Affumptione.
Elyas de Ruwordin vi*d*. in Affumptione.
Odericus dux de Ruwordin iiii*d*. in Affumptione.
.... *or* Hawere xii*d*. ; vi*d*. in die Affumt. et vi*d*. in die O.S.
Adam filius Petri, vi*d*. in Affumptione.
Radus. frater ejus, iiii*d*. in Affumptione.
Alwredus frater ejus, iiii*d*. in Affumptione.
Thomas Spichfet iiii*d*. in Affumptione.
..........na de Caftello Godrici, vi*d*. in annuitat. et ad obitum fuum aliquam cognicionem de catallis fuis.
Wmo. de la More de Ros, vi*d* in Affumptione.
Mabilia Monialis, iii*d*.
Matildis filia Dru. iii*d*.
Robtus. Balle de Walford vi*d*. ad Pentecoft., et ad obit. fuum, unum de melioribus catallis fuis.
Alex. de Sto. Briavel, clericus, quolibet anno 6 focc. Hæc pertinent ad cantariam.
Roger Dun, et mater ejus, xii*d*. et unum cannoc. bladi.
Wmus. focius ejufdem Rogeri, iiii*d*. ad S. Michel.—Ifti manent apud Walford.
Hugo Mufchet quolibet anno i*d*. et ad obit. fuum aliquam cognicionem de catallis fuis.
Adam Foreftarius de Bikenor, fimiliter.
Ernaldus Ruffus, fimiliter.
Gilebertus Talbot xii*d*. in perpet. Cartam habemus ad lumen.
Roger de Buevile 4 cannoc. frumenti—ad hoftias.
Rogerus Carpentarius de Dimmoc ii*d*.
Hugo de la Hulle iiii*d*. ad Purif.
Ricardus Faber de Sidebire, iiii*d*. ad Purif.
Adam le Orblowere iiii*d*. in die Annunc.
Robt. Granter de Monemut pro libra ceræ unde reddere folebat vi*d*. redditus, dat. in perpet. terra de quod in Munemut ad lumen.
Wmi. de Brunefhoppe pater   mi xii*d*. quolibet anno.
Ofmundus et Gunnora uxor ejus, de Kenepet vi*d*. quolibet anno in Palmis.

No. 4.
CARTA A. ABBATIS VALLIS DORE DE TERRA DE CLIMPERWELL.

Sciant præfentes et futuri quod ego A. dictus Abbas Vallis Dore et ejufdem loci conventus communi affenfu conceffimus patribus noftris Monachis de Dene in perpetuum virgatam terræ in Climperwell tenendam de nobis in perpetuum ita libere et quiete ficut nos candem melius tenuimus de Priore et Conventu Lantoniæ. Ita tamen quod illos tres folidos quos nos annuatim reddebamus Lantboniæ Ecclefiæ prædicti Monachi de Dene loco noftro reddent fingulis annis præfato Conventui Lantboniæ pro omnibus fervitiis falvo fervitio Domini Regis. Nos autem dimittimus eis omne jus quod in prædicta terra habemus. Et cartam Prioris et Conventus Lanthoniæ eifdem Monachis reddidimus. Quod fi Priori et Conventui Lanthoniæ non place[a]t ut a Monachis de Dene folitum cenfum percipiant nobis reddetur, et ut poft eundem redditum canonicis perfolvemus. Propter dictam autem conceffionem nobis de Dene prædicti Monachi 40 folidos [dederunt].

No. 5.
CARTA ROGERI, PRIORIS LANTHONIÆ DE EADEM TERRA.

Rogerus Prior Lanthoniæ et ejus loci Conventus [univerfis] ad quos præfens carta pervenerit falutem. Notum fit vobis nos conceffiffe Monachis de Dora unam virgatam terræ in Climperwelle in perpetuum de nobis tenendam per tres folidos nobis annuatim ad feftum S. Michaelis inde nobis reddendos quam virgatam Helyas Giffard Ecclefiæ noftræ in perpetuam dedit [in puram] eleemofynam. Hanc autem dedimus et conceffimus fupradictis Monachis in perpetuum [per dictos] tres folidos de nobis tenendam liberam et quietam ab omni fervitio, excepto fervitio regis. Hiis teftibus Helya Giffard, Willelmo de Stantun, Euftachio de Will., Hugone Parmentario, Philippo Clerico, Leggi, Mauld de Lauda.

No. 6.
CARTA GILEBERTI DE MONEMUTA (HANC HABET SACRISTA).

Sciant tam præfentes quam futuri quod ego Gilebertus de Monemuta et Berta uxor mea et heredes mei donamus et concedimus finceræ pietatis affectu Deo et Beatæ Mariæ et Abbatiæ de Dene in perpetuam eleemofynam pro falute animarum noftrarum fimiliter prædeceſſorum noſtrorum quinque folidos de reditu molendini de Ope ad terminum mediæ quadragefimæ perfolvendos ad emendum vinum ad divinum officium ibidem celebrandum et fi aliquo modo prædictum molendinum, quod Deus avertat, deciderit prædicti quinque folidi perfolvantur de gabulo prædictæ villæ de Ope. Hac tamen conditione ut quinque folidi de pretio vini Monachorum ad divina officia celebranda prius affignati pari et communi affenfu totius capituli in reparatione librorum ponantur. Si quis autem in futuro hanc conventionem temerarie infringere voluerit, prædicti quinque folidi mihi vel heredibus meis revocentur [? revertentur]. Hanc autem donationem ut [in] perpetuum rata et illibata permaneat hac carta noftra munimine figilli noftri corroborata confirmavimus. Hiis teftibus Roberto tunc temporis Priore de Monemuta, Magiftro Rogero Medico de Glouceftria, Jacobo de Monemuta, Willelmo de Colevilla, Roberto filio Radulphi, Willelmo de Marifco, Willelmo de Hereford, Ada de Blakeneia tunc temporis Senefchallo, Radulpho de Wifham, Ricardo Marmiun, Stephano le Norreis, Obeſſune, Thudrico de Thibertun, et multis aliis et audientibus et videntibus.

No. 7.
ITEM CARTA GILEBERTI DE QUIETANCIA. [HÆC EST IN MANIBUS CELLERAII ET ILLA REG.]

Sciant tam præfentes quam futuri quod ego Gilebertus de Monemuta et Berta uxor mea et heredes mei donamus et concedimus Deo et Beatæ Mariæ et Abbatiæ de Dene in perpetuam eleemofynam pro redemptione animarum noftrarum et fimiliter prædeceſſorum noſtrorum quietantiam de theloneo de omnibus rebus quas Monachi de Dena ad proprios ufus fuos emerint vel vendiderint per totam terram noftram necnon de paffagio et de omni confuetudine. Prohibemus autem ne quis eos inde vexare præfumat. Hanc autem donacionem ut in perpetuum rata et illibata permaneat hac carta noftra munimine figilli noftri corroborata confirmavimus. Hiis teftibus, Roberto tunc temporis Priore, de Monemuta, Magiftro Roger Medico Gloceftria, Jacobo de Monemuta, Willelmo de Colevilla, Roberto filio Radulphi, Willelmo de Marifco, Willielmo de Hereford, Ada de Blakenea tunc temporis Senefchallo, Radulpho de Wifham, Ricardo Marmiun, Stephano le Norreis, Obeffune, Tbudrico de Thibertun, et multis aliis vel audientibus vel videntibus. In perpetuum.

No. 8.

CARTA WILLELMI DE BRAOSA DE QUIETANTIA. (HÆC EST IN MANIBUS CELLARII.)

Sciant præfentes et futuri quod ego Willelmus de Braofa Dominus de Brechen dedi et hac mea carta confirmavi Deo et ecclesiæ Sanctæ Mariæ de Flaxeleya et Monachis ibidem Deo ferventibus pro falute animæ meæ et uxoris meæ Matildis de Sancto Walerico et puerorum noftrorum et amicorum et omnium antecefforum noftrorum quietantiam de tolneto et pa(ff)agio per totam terram meam ad tenendum de me et heredibus meis in perpetuam eleemofynam. Quare omnibus ballivis meis et hominibus firmiter præcipio ne illos Monachos vel homines illorum in aliquo fuper foriffacturam meam injufte gravetis et laboretis, nec gravari et labori eosdem permittatis. Hiis teftibus Willelmo et Philippo filiis meis; Joanne Richard ; Ricardo le Hagan ; Willelmo de Waldebof ; Willelmo de Burh., Roberto de Burh., Waltero de Traveleg ; Waltero de Evreus ; Nicolao de Dammartin ; Macci [? Marco] Præpofito de Bergevenia ; Roberto Præpofito de Bergervenia.

No. 9.

CARTA WILLELMI DE MINERIIS DE ELEEMOSYNA.

Univerfis Sanctæ Ecclefiæ filiis tam præfentibus quam futuris Willelmus de Mineriis falutem. Noverit univerfitas veftra me conceffiffe et in perpetuam eleemofynam dediffe Deo et Abbatiæ Sanctæ Mariæ de Dene decem acras terræ fub Caftpard (Cafthard) et unam acram prati inter prædictam terram et proximum fluvium pro falute mea et heredum meorum et pro animabus antecefforum meorum et omnium amicorum meorum. Igitur ut Monachi prædictæ Abbatiæ hanc eleemofynam liberam et quietam ab omnibus fervitiis et confuetudine et exactione feculari a me et pofteris meis in eternum poffideant figilli mei impreffione confirmo fub teftimonio Henrici filii mei, Rogeri [de] Weftburia, Rogeri de Arden, Baderunis de Blecheden, Hugonis de Sancto Ligera, Galfridi de Albo Monafterio, Walteri clerici, Huberti clerici, Nicolai clerici. In perpetuum.

No. 10.

CARTA HENRICI FILII WILLIELMI DE MINERIIS DE ELEEMOSYNA.

Univerfis Sanctæ Matris Ecclefiæ filiis Henricus de Mineriis falutem. Sciatis me conceffiffe et hac carta mea confirmaffe Abbatiæ de Dene eleemofynam patris mei ficut ejus carta teftatur. Infuper dedi et conceffi Deo et Beatæ Mariæ et prædictæ Abbatiæ pro animabus patris mei et fratris mei et heredum meorum et pro falute mea et [antecefforum] meorum terram illam quæ eft inter terram quam Willelmus de Dene dedit prædictæ Abbatiæ et nemus defuper in perpetuam et firmam eleemofynam pro qua Sancti Monachi præfatæ Abbatiæ folebant in fingulis annis [mihi unum] bizantium perfolvere. Ut autem hæc donatio mea in pofterum rata maneat et inconcuffa, hanc cartam meam figilli mei fuppofitione confirmo et fubfcriptorum virorum teftimonio Walteri Map, Willelmi de Dene, et Galfridi, et Mael' et Willelmi filiorum ejus, Rogeri Militis, Baderonis de Blachedun, Rogeri de Herderne. In perpetuum.

No. 11.

CARTA JOHANNIS PICHARD.

Sciant tam præfentes quam futuri quod ego Joannes Pichard et heredes mei pro falute noftra et tam prædecefforum quam succefforum noftrorum in pleno comitatu Gloeceftria, Hamelino Muchegros tunc temporis Vicecomite loco Willelmi Marefcalli, remiffimus Deo et Beatæ Mariæ de Dene et Monachis ibidem Deo fervientibus quicquid juris clamavimus in terra de Walemor quam prædicti Monachi habuerunt et tenent. Prædicti vero Monachi gratia hujus remiffionis noftræ concefferunt nobis pro falute noftra et parentum et amicorum noftrorum unius Monachi fufceptionem in Ecclefiam fuam ita ut in perpetuum uno decedente alius loco ejus fubftitutatur fecundum noftram reprefentationem. Præterea fub eadem condicione et conventione præfati Monachi duodecim marcas argenti mihi dederunt et filio meo et heredi Willelmo unum bizantium. Ut hæc coventio et remiffio rata fit et inconcuffa hanc præfentem cartam figilli mei fuperpofitione et fidei interpofitione confirmo necnon et fubfcriptorum meorum [? virorum] teftimonio. Hiis [funt] teftes Willelmus Marefcallus, Henricus de Mineriis, Willelmus de Sancti Leodegario, Ricardus de Muchelgros, Nicolaus Avenel, Reinaldus de Gofintun, Milo Pichard, Willelmus heres ejus, Willelmus Poer, Radulphus Avenel, Rogerus nepos ejus, Ricardus clericus, Walterus de Aura, Robertus de Shlocterus [?], Galfridus de Littletuna, Rogerus de Arderne, Galfridus filius Willelmi de Dene, cum multis aliis.

No. 12.[1]

CARTA HUGONIS LE PETIT DE ELEEMOSYNA.

Sciant præfentes et futuri quod ego Hugo le Petit dedi Deo et Beatæ Mariæ de Dene et monachis ibidem Deo fervientibus in perpetuam puram et liberam eleemofynam pro falute mea et tam antecefforum quam heredum meorum terram meam in Neweham illam, fcilicet, totam quam Seftan Knif de me aliquando tenuit et eft juxta foffam Veteris Caftelli : et ut hæc mea donatio in perpetuum prædictis monachis ratæ permaneat præfentem cartam figilli mei impreffione confirmavi. Hiis teftibus Milone fratre meo ; Waltero de Aura tunc temporis Ballivo de Neweham ; Luverico tunc Præpofito ; Rogero de Herderne ; Roberto Toli de Gloceftria ; Moyfe de Redleia, et multis aliis. In perpetuum.

[1] Cartæ No. 12 to No. 80 inclufive were not included in the extracts printed by the late Sir Thos. Phillipps at his private prefs. With the exception of No. 80, which is a catalogue of books belonging to the Flaxley Monks, and which appears to have been printed by the Royal Society of Literature, all the other documents, No. 12 to No. 79 inclufive, are now printed for the firft time. The text is from the Tranfcript of the Flaxley Cartulary made by the late Sir Thomas Phillipps himfelf. A copy of this tranfcript was made for the author by Mr. T. Fitz Roy Fenwick of Thirleftaine Houfe, Cheltenham.

No. 13.
CARTA GILBERTI TALEBOT DE ELEEMOSYNA. (HANC HABET SACRISTA.)

Sciant præfentes et futuri quod ego Gilebertus Talebot dedi et conceffi Deo et Beatæ Mariæ de Dene et Monachis ibidem Deo fervientibus pro falute animæ meæ et uxoris meæ Adelinæ et puerorum meorum et antecefforum meorum in perpetuam et liberam et quietam eleemofynam duodecim denarios annuatim de molendino de Ruddekefhall reddendos per ipfum in cujus manu molendinum fuerit ad feftum Sancti Michaelis Ita quod prædicti Monachi nihil aliud poffint exigere de me vel heredibus meis vel de illo qui molendinum tenuerit præter prædictos duodecim denarios. Ut vero hæc donatio rata fit et perpetua de me et de heredibus meis, eis præfenti fcripto et figilli mei appofitione confirmavi. His teftibus, Drugone tunc temporis Vice Archidiacono, Johanne Capellano meo, Willelmo filio Hingani, Galfrido de Dene Ricardo de Capella, Ada de Felileia, Ada de la Forda et multis aliis. In perpetuum.

No. 14.
CARTA ADÆ DE BLAKENEIA DE ELEEMOSYNA.

Sciant præfentes et futuri quod ego Adam de Blakeneia heres patris mei Jordani de Blakeneia devoto [corde] concedo Deo et Beatæ Mariæ de Dena et Monachis ibidem Deo fervientibus eandem donationem foldæ unius in Neweham quam prædictus Jordanus fecit prædictis Monachis. Solda autem illa eft inter foldam Hivetenon et fabricam Johannis Fabri in Macello contra oftium Clementis. Et quia volo ut hæc donatio in perpetuum rata fit præfentem cartam figilli mei appofitione confirmo. His teftibus Waltero Perfona de Aura, et alio Waltero de Aura Clerico, Hugone de Blipeflau (Blitheflau), Luverico de Neweham, Geri [?Geraldo] de Neweham, Rogero filio Hugonis et multis aliis. In perpetuum.

T

No. 15.

ITEM CARTA ADÆ DE BLAKENEIA DE ELEEMOSYNA.
(HANC HABET SACRISTA.)

Sciant præfentes et futuri quod ego Adam de Blakeneia et Bafilia uxor mea pro falute noftra et heredum noftrorum et prædeceſſorum noftrorum dedimus et conceſſimus Deo et Beatæ Mariæ de Dena et Monachis ibidem Deo fervientibus in puram et perpetuam eleemofynam duodecim denarios quos meſſuagium Willielmi W[o]decoc nobis et prædeceſſoribus noftris folebat reddere et duodecim denarios quos mafnagium Galfridi Carbonarii nobis et prædeceſſoribus noftris folebat reddere. Ita fingulis annis quicunque tenuerint prædicta mafnagia ad feftum Sancti Michaelis reddent Sacriftæ predictæ Abbatiæ duos folidos ad emendum frumentum ad hoftias faciendas et ad emendum oleum ad tres lampades ardentes coram tribus Altaribus ad omnes miſſas ibidem cantandas. Prædicti vero monachi nobis refignaverunt mafnagium noftrum de Neweham quod illis prius dederamus et cartam noftram nobis reddiderunt. Si vero prædicta mafnagia aliquo modo, (quod Deus avertat) deciderint, nos vel heredes noftri duos folidos annuatim prædicto Sacriftæ ad prædictum terminum five de Forgiis five de aliis redditibus noftris reftituemus. Et ut hæc donatio rata et firma in perpetuum permaneat præfenti carta figilli noftri impreſſione corroborata confirmavimus. His teftibus, Willielmo de Dene, et Galfrido filio ejus, Willelmo filio Hingan, Waltero Clerico de Aura, Hugone de Blitheflawe, Luverico de Neweham, Geri [?] de Neweham et multis aliis. In perpetuum.

No. 16.

CARTA WILLELMI DE DENA.

Sciant tam præfentes quam futuri quod ego Willelmus de Dena Regis Foreftarius, dedi et conceſſi Abbatiæ de Dene et Monachis ibidem Deo fervientibus totam terram meam fub Caftiard pro amore Dei et falute animæ meæ et prædeceſſorum meorum necnon et uxoris meæ et heredum meorum. Hoc idem conceſſerunt uxor mea Mathildis et heredes mei. Conventus vero prædicti loci conceſſit mihi et heredibus meis quod caritative retinebit monachum unum acceptabilem et per me vel per heredes meos præsentandum pro salute mea et [heredum] meorum in perpetuum. Ita ut uno decedente alius acceptabilis per me vel per heredes meos præsentandus loco ejus suscipiatur. Ut hæc conventio rata sit et inconcussa hanc presentem cartam sigilli mei suppositione confirmo et subscriptorum virorum testimonio. Hi sunt testes. Gaufridus filius et heres meus, Michael Sacerdos de Blechedun, et Baderun de Blechedun, Rogerus de Erdern, Rogerus et Willelmus de Chekeshille. In perpetuum.

No. 17.

CARTA GALFRIDI DE DENE, FILII EJUS.

Sciant præsentes et futuri quod ego Galfridus de Dene dedi et concessi Deo et Beatæ Mariæ et Monachis de Dene in perpetuam liberam et puram eleemosynam totam illam partem prati quam habeo in Pulmeda proximam gardino Henrici de Mineriis sicut ego et antecessores mei plenius et liberius eam tenuimus, tenendam et habendam de me et heredibus meis pro salute mea et tam antecessorum quam heredum meorum et præcipue pro animabus patris et matris meæ. Ut autem hæc donatio rata sit in perpetuum præsentem cartam sigillo meo confirmavi. His testibus, Henrico de Mineriis, Baderune, de Blechedun, Ricardo de Blechedun, Rogero de Erderne, Maelo et Willelmo fratribus meis, Willelmo filio meo, Alexandro de Dene, Ricardo filio Ranewin, et multis aliis. In perpetuum.

No. 18.

ITEM CARTA GALFRIDI DE DENE SUPER EXCLUSAM ROGERI DE BOSCHO.

Sciant præsentes et futuri quod loquela quæ fuit inter Monachos de Dene et Galfridum de Dene super Exclusam molendini quod tenuit Rogerus de Boscho ex consensu utriusque partis terminata est in hunc modum, scilicet, quod ego Galfridus de Dene vel heredes mei vel aliquis alius qui de nobis tenuerit molendinum prædictum in perpetuum non removebimus Exclusam illam de quâ lis fuit propius ponti Monachorum quam modo fita eft, fcilicet, xx^{ti} perticis longe a ponte Monachorum ad menfuram perticæ regis. Pro hac autem conceffione et conventione prædicti Monachi focerint de propriis fumptibus fuperiorem exclufam quæ eft propter inundationes facta [de novo] iterum eam reficient ex debito. Et quum nolo ut Monachi iterum graventur fuper hoc per me vel heredes meos vel per alium de nobis tenentem præfenti chirographo et figillo meo prædictam conventionem confirmavi. His teftibus, Henrico de Mineriis, Waltero de Aura, Rogero de Ardern, Willelmo de Heliun, et multis aliis. In perpetuum.

No. 19.

CARTA ADÆ FILII FULCONIS DE ELEEMOSYNA.

Sciant præfentes et futuri quod ego Adam filius Fulconis de Chekefhill filii Anketil cum bona voluntate et admonitione Ifabellæ uxoris meæ dedi et conceffi Deo et Beatæ Mariæ et Monachis de Dene pro anima patris mei Fulconis et matris meæ Edithæ et animabus antecefforum noftrorum et pro falute mea et uxoris meæ et fratrum meorum Durandi et Walteri in perpetuam puram et liberam eleemofynam tenendas de me et heredibus meis tres acras de dominicatu meo de Chekefhill videlicet Bune Wei juxta fepem tredecim feillones et unam Goram et duas forerdas quantum eadem terra extenditur et omnes hæc nominatæ terræ funt pro una acra et dimidia. Et fuper aulam Marmiun et in Cubeworde quatuor feillones pro dimidia acra. Dedi etiam eifdem Monachis fex feillones Bunewei juxta dominicatum meum qui fuerunt de terra Ernuldi Fals (qu. Fabri) qui fcilicet juxta terram Johannis Difpenfatoris cum forerdis adeo longis. Dedi etiam eis illam partem meam prati apud .... fwell ad finem haicii fpinei Joannis Difpenfatoris qui habet ex parte de Weft pratum Henrici Marmiun, et ex altera parte .... hominum meorum. Hæc omnia dedi prædictis Monachis habenda et tenenda libera et quieta ab omni fervitio et confuetudine et exactione et loquela. Ut hæc donatio mea firma fit in perpetuum præfentem cartam figilli mei impreffione confirmavi. His teftibus, Rogero de Weftbiri, Baderune de Blechedun, Gaufrido de Dene, Ricardo filio Baderonis, Rogero de Arderne, Johanne le Defpenfer, et multis aliis. In perpetuum.

No. 20.
CONFIRMATIO HENRICI DE MINERIIS SUPER SUPERIOREM CARTAM.

Sciant præsentes et futuri quod ego Henricus de Mineriis pro salute mea et tam antecessorum quam heredum meorum concessi et hac mea carta confirmavi Deo et Beatæ Mariæ de Dene et Monachis ibidem Deo servientibus totam terram et omnem donationem quam Adam filius Fulconis eisdem Monachis dedit tenendam et habendam in perpetuum in omnibus libere et quiete et plenarie in perpetuam et puram eleemosynam, sicut carta quam præfatus Adam prædictis Monachis fecit, testatur. His testibus, Galfrido de Abenhale, Rogero de Westbire, Willelmo de Heliun, Rogero de Arderne, et multis aliis. In perpetuum.

No. 21.
CARTA PHILIPPI DE DUNIA DE ELEEMOSYNA.

Sciant præsentes et futuri quod ego Philippus de Dunia dedi Deo et Beatæ Mariæ de Dene et Monachis ibidem Deo servientibus pro salute mea et tam antecessorum quam heredum meorum in perpetuam puram et liberam eleemosynam duas acras in prato et in terra arabili quas habeo in Wadleie liberas et quietas ab omni servitio et consuetudine ita quod ego et heredes mei adquietabimus prædictas duas acras tam de regali servitio quam de omni alio et eas contra omnes homines warrantizabimus et quia volo ut hæc mea donatio et concessio rata maneat in perpetuum præsentem cartam sigilli mei impressione confirmo. His testibus, Magistro Reginaldo, Decano de Hamme, Roberto Capellano de Munsterworth, Willelmo fratre meo, Johanna uxore mea, Editha matre mea. In perpetuum.

No. 22.
CARTA HENRICI DE CHEKESHILL.

Sciant præsentes et futuri quod ego Henricus de Chekeshill concessi et præsenti carta confirmavi Deo et Beatæ Mariæ de Dena et Monachis ibidem Deo servientibus totum pratum illud quod Rogerus frater meus dedit illis in Littlemore in eleemosynam perpetuam tenendum de me et heredibus meis ita libere et quiete et plenarie ficut tenuerunt illud tempore Rogeri fratris mei, fcilicet, fecundum latitudinem terræ Radulphi filii Eilwi ficut divifum eft a prato meo per foffatum. Pro hac autem conceffione et confirmatione dederunt mihi Monachi fex folidos. Hanc confirmationem fideliter obfervandam manu mea affidavi et præfenti cartæ figillum meum appofui. His teftibus, Rogero de Weftbire, Rogero de Arderne, Moyfe de Redleia, Willelmo de Heliun, Radulpho Venatore, Henrico de Walemor, Rogero de Bofco, et multis aliis. In perpetuum.

No. 23.

CARTA ROBERTI TOLI DE ELEEMOSYNA POST EJUS DECESSUM.

Sciant præfentes et futuri quod ego Robertus Toli pro falute mea et meorum dedi Deo et Beatæ Mariæ de Dene et Monachis ibidem Deo fervientibus in perpetuam et liberam et puram eleemofynam terram illam quæ eft inter terram Thomæ de Monemuto et terram quæ fuit Ricardi Sacerdotis de Chirchefdun et eft de feodo Johannis de Evreus ut eam habeant et teneant plenarie poft dies meos per redditum tunc capitali Domino in die Sancti Ofwaldi duorum denariorum et oboli et ad Hoccedei Abbati Sancti Petri de Gloeceftria quod et quarantena pro orto. Et ego in vita mea dabo de recognitione de eadem terra fingulis annis Ecclefiæ de Dene unam libram ceræ in Affumptione. Præterea dedi eis terram meam ante Portam Caftelli quæ eft inter portam infirmorum Sancti Sepulcri Gloeceftriæ et aliam terram meam quæ proxima eft et eft de feodo monachorum Sancti Dionyfii, ut eam habeant tam in vita mea quam poft in perpetuam et liberam eleemofynam reddendo prædictis capitalibus dominis fingulis annis quatuor denarios et obolum in Rogationibus. Ut hæc mea donatio in perpetuum firma fit et ftabilis præfentem cartam figillo meo confirmavi. His teftibus Willelmo Burgeis, Ricardo Rufo, Ricardo filio ejus, Roberto Calvo, Ricardo filio Jordani, et aliis multis. In perpetuum.

No. 24.

CARTA WILLELMI NEXE.

Sciant præfentes et futuri quod ego Willelmus Nexe affenfu filiæ et heredis meæ et Ernaldi generi mei dedi Deo et Beatæ Mariæ et Monachis de Dene in perpetuam et quietam eleemofynam foldam meam in Neweham duodecim pedum in latitudine et duodecim in longitudine intra parietes et eſt contra ſoldam Luverici quam habet de Domo Hoſpitalis Jeruſalem juxta ſoldam quam prædicti monachi habent ex dono Jordani de Blakeneia. Prædicti vero monachi ex gratia ſua pro paupertate mea caritative mihi dederunt decem et octo ſolidos. Hanc autem donationem præſenti carta et ſigillo meo confirmavi et infra appoſitum eſt ſigillum Walteri de Aura tunc temporis Baillivi de Neweham in teſtimonio. His teſtibus, Luverico de Neweham tunc præpoſito, Willelmo de Staura, Ivone le Palmer, Geri ..., Ernaldo Fabro, et multis aliis in hundredo de Neweham. In perpetuum.

No. 25.

CONVENTIO INTER ABBATIAM DE DENE ET WILLELMUM HEREMITAM.

Omnibus Sanctæ Matris Eccleſiæ filiis notum ſit quod ego Ricardus dictus Abbas de Dene et ejuſdem loci Conventus multis multorum petitionibus ſuſcepi curam Capellæ de Herdlande in divino officio ſuſtinendo in perpetuum curam etiam omnium rerum et poſſeſſionum et laborum Willelmi ejuſdem loci Heremitæ, ad ejuſdem Willelmi ſuſtentationem et eorum quos ſecum habet nolentes per nos impediri bonum ejus propoſitum. Quo propoſuit ſe in arctiori vita ſcilicet anachooritica ibidem includere pro ſtabilitate et pace regni et pro anima Regis Henrici a quo locum ſuſcepit, pro ſalute etiam Ricardi Regis et pacificorum [? benefactorum] ſuorum Ita ut præfato Willelmo omnibus diebus vitæ ipſius neceſſaria miniſtremus in victu, ſcilicet, et in veſtitu quantum pertinet ad Religionem Incluſi. Quod ſi idem Willielmus prædicta omnia in manibus noſtras manutenere non poterit quantum per licentiam Epiſcopi ſui poterit ut ea nobis defendat curam adhibebit ſicut pro rebus ſuis, et non interim ei neceſſaria miniſtrabimus. Si autem nullatenus potuerit in manus noſtras [curam] prædictam revocare nos a prædictis conventionibus et permiſſionibus liberi erimus. Et ne per nos vel per ſucceſſores noſtros in poſterum divinum officium in prædicta capella vel aliqua præſcriptarum conventionum ducatur in irritum præſens chirographum ſigillo noſtro communimus. Teſtibus Domino Willelmo Herefordenſi Epiſcopo cujus conſilio et in cujus præſentia hæc facta ſunt, et ſigillo teſtificata. Teſte etiam ejuſdem eccleſiæ Ricardo Decano et Capitulo. In perpetuum.

No. 26.

CARTA ROGERI FILII RADULFI DE PULTUN.

Sciant præsentes et futuri quod ego Rogerus filius Radulphi de Pultun dedi Deo et Beatæ Mariæ et Monachis de Dene pro anima Comitis Willelmi de Warrewic et pro anima Comitiffæ Margaretæ de Oilli et pro falute heredum eorum et pro falute mea et uxoris meæ Margaretæ et antecefforum et heredum meorum in perpetuam et puram eleemofynam quinque folidos de redditu de terra quam Gilebertus de Felda tenuit et Goduwinus de Pultun ante eum reddendos annuatim in quatuor terminis, fcilicet, ad feftum Sancti Michaelis quindecim denarios, ad feftum S. Andreæ totidem, ad feftum Sanctæ Mariæ in Martio totidem, in nativitate Sancti Johannis Baptiftæ totidem, et de hoc redditu quinque folidorum eis fideliter reddendo in prædictis terminis præfatus Gilbertus eis fecit fecuritatem et quicunque prædictam terram tenuerit poft eum faciet eis eandem fecuritatem juramento. Prædictam vero donationem ego et heredes mei contra omnes homines warrantizabimus. Quod fi ego vel heredes mei de prædicta terra aliud facere voluerimus prædictis monachis alibi dabimus plenam valentiam antequam fint diffaifiati ne aliquid impedimentum vel damnum habeant de redditu quinque folidorum. Et hos quinque affignavi nominatim ad emendos pannos ad lectos pauperum hofpitum. Propterea ego et Margareta uxor mea reddidimus nos vivos et mortuos prædictæ ecclefiæ de Dene, et corpora noftra ad fepulturam ubicunque obierimus. Et ut hæc mea donatio ftabilis fit et perpetua de me et heredibus meis præfentem cartam figilli impreffione confirmavi. His teftibus, Richerio filio Radulfi, Johanne Lupo, Waltero de Aura, Waltero perfona de Aura, Roberto de Baioo, Waltero de Coleftun, Hugone de Blipeflawe, Nicolao de Pultun, Rogero Pichot, et multis aliis. In perpetuum.

No. 27.

CARTA HUGONIS CHARKE DE ELEEMOSYNA.

Sciant præfentes et futuri quod ego Hugo Cherke cum affenfu et bona voluntate Hugonis filii et heredis mei et Johannæ uxoris meæ dedi et conceffi Deo et Beatæ Mariæ de Dene et Monachis ibidem Deo fervientibus pro falute mea et tam antecefforum quam heredum meorum totam terram meam quæ appellatur Eilfifcroft cum illa forerda quæ proxima eft a parte de North quam fcilicet Luverithus de Neweham tenuit ficut aqua eam dividit, tenendam de me et heredibus meis in perpetuum et puram et liberam eleemofynam Ita fcilicet quod ego et heredes mei in perpetuam warrantizabimus et adquietabimus prædictam terram ab omni fervitio et confuetudine ficut puram eleemofynam noftram. Prædicti vero monachis receperunt me et meos in omnibus beneficiis ecclefiæ fuæ tam in morte quam in vita ficut fratrem ejufdem loci et ad petitionem meam receperunt corpus meum in fepulturam et corpus filii mei fi voluerit. Ita quod audito obitu meo venient propter me cum ecclefia parochiæ meæ habuerit fua jura de me. Pro hac autem donacione concedenda prædicti monachi dederunt filio meo Hugoni duos folidos et unam juvencam et ego et filius meus prædictus pariter affidavimus de omnibus prædictis donationibus fine dolo tenendis et ego præfentem cartam figillo meo confirmavi. His teftibus Baderune de Blehchefdun, Rogero de Weftbiri, Galfrido de Dene, Willelmo de Boxa, et Ricardo fratre ejus, Arnulpho de Blakeneia, Luverico de Neweham, Ricardo filio Willelmi, et multis aliis. In perpetuum.

No. 28.

CARTA RICARDI FILII WILLELMI DE ERLINGEHAM.

Sciant præfentes et futuri quod ego Ricardus filius Willelmi filii Gileberti filii Milonis de Erlingham conceffi et liberavi Deo et Beatæ Mariæ et Monachis de Dene duodecim feillones de terra mea, viz., quinque feillones in Cupleforerde et tres contra Maladeriam de Niweham extra Wallam et duos qui merchiant prato de Weftmere et duos qui merchiant fupra forerdam Petri de Wike ex una parte et ex altera parte fupra Weft Walle Tenendos et habendos de me et heredibus meis in perpetuum in feodi firmâ liberos [et] quietos ab omni fervitio et confuetudine et exactione Reddendo fingulis annis mihi vel heredibus meis fex denarios pro omni fervitio ad feftum S. Michaelis. Ego vero et heredes mei prædictam terram præfatis Monachis contra omnes homines warrantizabimus et adquietabimus et pro hac confentione tenenda dederunt præfati Monachi mihi viginti folidos et unum bovem juvenem et unum pullum mafculum trium annorum et agnos crifpos xxxviiii de introitu. Et ut hoc ratum et firmum permaneat dextera mea affidavi et præsenti carta sigillo meo impressa confirmavi. Et pro hac pactione concedenda dederunt præfati Monachi Willelmo patri meo quatuor solidos et duodecim denarios ad suas botas emendas. His testibus, Rogero de Buivile, Willelmo filio Milonis, Rogero de Leinch, Roberto filio Bertrami, Ricardo filio Aeluredi, Hugone Cherke, Luverico de Neweham, Gerhi, et multis aliis. In perpetuum.

No. 29.

ITEM ALIA CARTA EJUSDEM RICARDI.

Sciant præsentes et futuri quod ego Ricardus filius Willelmi filius Gilberti filius Milonis de Herlingham concessi et dedi Deo et Beatæ Mariæ de Dene et Monachis ibidem Deo servientibus pro salute mea et Mathildis uxoris meæ et prædecessorum meorum in perpetuam et puram eleemosynam illum seillionem de terra mea in Herlingham qui merchiat prato de Westmere, et unum seillionem de Grandi Acra quam habeo in Glesinero, in middel surlong qui proximior (*sic*) est Herlingeham et totam superiorem partem croftæ meæ divisam autem a superiori angulo grangiæ meæ per medium usque ad gardinum Roberti Knivet totam usque ad viam superiorem. Similiter concessi eis introitum et exitum per inferiorem partem præfatæ croftæ absque omni impedimento vel contradictione sicut eis opus fuerit. Et hæc prædicta habebit et tenebit in perpetuum libera et quieta ab omni servitio et omni consuetudine et exactione et ego et heredes mei warrantizabimus et acquietabimus hæc predicta contra omnes homines sicut puram eleemosynam meam. Ego etiam Ricardus et Mathildis uxor mea dedimus nosmet ipsos vivos et mortuos Deo et Beatæ Mariæ de Dene ibique locum sepulturæ nobis elegimus. Et quia volui hanc donationem meam ratam in perpetuum permanere eam præsenti carta sigillo meo impressa confirmavi. His testibus Rogero de Buivilla, Willelmo filio Milonis, Rogero de Leinch, Roberto filio Bertrami, Ricardo filio Aluredi, Lewerico de Neweham, Geri, et multis aliis. In perpetuum.

No. 30.

CONFIRMATIO WILLELMI PATRIS EJUSDEM RICARDI.

Sciant præsentes et futuri quod ego Willelmus filius Gileberti filius Milonis pro salute mea et uxoris meæ Helenæ et tam antecessorum quam heredum meorum dedi Deo et Beatæ Mariæ de Dena et Monachis ibidem Deo servientibus in perpetuam et puram eleemosynam duos seilliones de terra mea in Herlingham, quorum unus eft fub Berdun quartus in Crofta a parte auftrali, alter eft in Weftmere in Sidefurlung inter feillionem Jacobi filii Dolfin et forerdam Rogeri filii Andreæ, liberos et quietos ab omni fervitio et confuetudine. Ita quod ego et heredes mei prædictos feilliones præfatis monachis warrantizabimus et contra omnes homines acquietabimus ficut puram eleemofynam. Dedi etiam corpus meum ad eundem locum in fepulturam Conceffi etiam et confirmavi eis omnes conventiones et donationes quas Ricardus filius meus eis fecit. Ut autem hæc mea donatio et conceffiones meæ ratæ maneant in perpetuum eafdem tenendæ manu mea affidavi et præfentem cartam figillo meo confirmavi. His teftibus Rogero de Buivill, Rogero filio Ricardi, Roberto filio Bertrami, Gilberto filio Ernaldi, Lewerico de Neweham, Ricardo filio Aeluredi, Geri, Rogero filio Roberti, et Jordano fratre ejus, et multis aliis. In perpetuum.

No. 31.

CARTA ROBERTI MUSCHET DE CONVENTIONE.

Sciant præfentes et futuri quod ego Robertus Mufchet cum affenfu et voluntate Helenæ uxoris meæ et Roberti filii mei dedi et conceffi et hac carta mea confirmavi Deo et Beatæ Mariæ de Dene et monachis ibidem Deo fervientibus quinque acras terræ meæ quas dudum dederam eis quarum tres et dimidia jacent per fe et furlungum meum vertitur fupra illas ; et una et dimidia ficut inter terram meam et pratum meum juxta Walemor quod Ernaldus de Chekefhill olim tenuit et eft inter pratum Henrici de Chekefhill et pratum meum. Præterea conceffi eis tenendam de me et heredibus meis totam terram quam Ricardus Prefbyter tenuit de me tam in Linleg quam fupra vineam de Walemor Reddendo annuatim mihi vel heredibus meis quatuor folidos pro omni fervitio falvo fervitiis Domini Regis cum evenerit in terra quæ fuit prædicti Ricardi ficut prædictus Ricardus folebat, fcilicet, de redditu duos folidos ad feftum Sancti Michaelis et duos folidos ad Sanctam Mariam in Martio. Præterea remifi prædictis Monachis totum jus quod clamavi in quatuor acris eorum quæ funt juxta terram prædicti Ricardi quas clamavi in illis feillionibus eorum juxta terram prædictam fupra vineam et totum jus quod clamavi in terra eorum quam tenet Walterus le Hunte. Ut hæc omnia prædicta habeant et teneant libera et quieta ab omni fervitio et confuetudine nifi quod prius quam dictam terram Ricardi [habeant] dabunt quatuor folidos et fervitium

Regis, dederunt mihi prædicti Monachis pro omnium confirmatione et concessione tres marcas argenti et recepi de Abbate Alano viginti folidos Ita quod ego vel heredes mei prædictam terram vel pratum Monachis warrantizare per aliquam violentiam non poterimus rationabile efcambium eis faciemus vel prædictam fummam denariorum eis reddemus. Omnes prædictas donationes et remiffiones et conventiones firmiter tenendas et defendendas ego et uxor mea H. et filius meus Robertus pariter affidavimus et ego præfentem cartam figillo meo confirmavi. His teftibus Domino Willelmo Abbate de Bordefley, Adam Cappellano de Hehhamftud Ricardo facer[dote] qui fupradictam terram tenuit, Roberto Tholi, Willelmo de Heliun, Rogero de Erderne, Hugo Wither, Rogero Wither. In perpetuum.

No. 32.

ITEM ALIA EJUSDEM ROBERTI MUSCHET DE ELEEMOSYNA.

Sciant præfentes et futuri quod ego Robertus Mufchet cum affenfu et bona voluntate Helenæ uxoris meæ et Roberti filii mei pro falute noftra et antecefforum et heredum noftrorum dedi et conceffi et hac carta confirmavi Deo et Beatæ Mariæ de Dena et Monachis ibidem Deo fervientibus totam terram quam Ricardus Prefbyter tenuit de me tam in Linleg quam fupra vineam de Walemor ficut eam plenius tenuit Tenendam de me et heredibus meis in perpetuam eleemofynam, et liberam ab omni fervitio et confuetudine nifi quod annuatim reddent mihi vel heredibus meis eundum redditum quem predictus Ricardus folebat reddere, fcilicet, duos folidos ad feftum Sancti Michaelis et duos folidos ad Sanctam Mariam in Martio. Præterea confirmavi eis illas quinque acras quas dudum dederam eis Tenendas in puram et perpetuam eleemofynam quam tres et dimidia per fe jacent et furlungum meum vertitur fuper illas et una et dimidia inter terram meam. Item confirmavi eis in eleemofynam puram pratum illud juxta Walemor quod Ernaldus de Chekefhill olim tenuit et eft inter pratum meum et pratum Henrici de Chekefhill. Remifi etiam prædictis Monachis totum jus quod clamavi in terra eorum quam tenuit Walterus le Hunte. Omnia prædicta dedi eis habenda et tenenda in perpetuam eleemofynam et quietam ab omni fervitio præterquam quod dabunt pro fupradicta terra Ricardi Prefbyteri quatuor folidos et prædictas donationes firmiter tenendas et ficut proprias terras noftras pro poffe noftro defendendas. Ego et uxor mea Helena et filius meus Robertus pariter affidavimus ; et ego præfentem cartam figillo meo confirmavi, Ita tamen ut Monachi refpondeant pro fervitio Domini Regis. His teftibus Ada Capellano de Hehhamftude, Ricardo Sacerdote qui fupradictam terram tenuit, Roberto Tholi, Willelmo de Heliun, Rogero de Erderne, Hugone Wither, Rogero Wither.

No. 33.
ITEM ALIA CARTA HUGONIS CHERKE DE ELEEMOSYNA.

Sciant præfentes et futuri quod ego Hugo Cherke dedi et concefli Deo et Beatæ Mariæ de Dene et Monachis ibidem Deo fervientibus in perpetuam et puram eleemofynam communem pafturam totius terræ meæ averiis fuis ficut meis propriis averiis et bobus fuis cum bobus meis. Similiter idem monachi conceflerunt mihi et heredibus meis communam fuam averiis meis cum averiis fuis. Hanc autem eleemofynam warrantizabimus ego et heredes mei in perpetuum prædictis monachis contra omnes homines et ut hæc donatio rata et firma permaneat præfenti carta figillo meo impreffa confirmavi. His teftibus, Galfrido de Dene, Rogero de Weftburi, Rogero de Erderne, et Petro filio ejus, Raderune de Blechesdun, et Ricardo filio ejus, et aliis multis.

No. 33. A.[1]
CARTA ROBERTI DE MAUS QUAM FECIT GILBERTO DE DIMMOC.

Sciant præfentes et futuri quod ego Robertus de Maus confenfu uxoris meæ Salernæ et confenfu Walteri heredis mei concefli et dedi Gilberto fervienti Henrici Kais pro amicitia et fuo magno fervitio quod mihi fecit quatuordecim acras terræ feminabilis et tres acras et dimidiam prati videlicet de meo dominio fex acras terræ feminabilis quarum tres funt in Campo de Refmes ac proximiores Tuckelega, una in Pirifeld juxta Springwellam, et duæ acræ in Campo de Rinlega juxta foffam propiorem villæ. Item dedi ei totam terram quam

---

[1] This number as it ftands is an additional number, No. 33, of the printed Index is as follows "Ditto Hugonis Cherke de communa pafturæ Roberti de Maws de terra in Tuckeleg" Carta No. 33 does not refer to Robert de Maws at all, and it is clear that two feparate grants have been mixed up together.

Ricardus Yliun tenuit cum omnibus fuis pertinentiis in bofco, in prato, viis, femitis, planis, pafturis Præterea dedi ei tres acras et dimidiam in Brademeda quas præfatus Henricus tenuit de me. Item dedi ei totum pafturam de Ombercrofte tenendam de me et heredibus meis fibi et heredibus fuis liberam [et] quietam ab omni fervitio excepto Regali fervitio videlicet pro duodecim denariis annuatim reddendis pro omni fervitio vid. ad duos anni terminos ad Sanctam Mariam Martialem fex denarios, ad S. Michaelem fex denarios. Hanc autem donationem et liberalitatem feci ei pro fuo fervitio nominatim pro duabus marcis argenti quas mihi dedit per partes, et præterea pro una tunica de perffeburneta de tribus et dimidia ulnis quam dedit Johannæ filiæ meæ et [pro] uno peplo de feia [?erico] quem dedit eidem Johannæ et pro uno gladio quem dedit Waltero heredi meo pro fuo confenfu, et quia volo eum ore fecurum de me et pofteris meis carta mea figillo meo impreffa corroboravi. His teftibus, Thoma de Sancto Nicolao, Roberto Sacerdote de Thingeworde Henrico Kais, Ede... de Bares, Herberto de Ledene, Willelmo filio Uvenat, Ernaldo de Walefword, Gocelino filio fuo, Johanni fratre fuo, Galfrido de Breuwerne Regis Pincerna, Amifio de Tuckelega, Roberto filio Swein, Helia Kelnefwombe, Johanne Clerico et toto Halimoto de Breuwerne.

No. 34.[1]

ITEM ALIA [CARTA] EJUSDEM ROBERTI GILBERTO.

Notum fit univerfis quod ego Robertus de Maus tradidi et conceffi Gileberto homini Henrici Kais et præpofito Glouceftriæ affenfu uxoris meæ Salernæ et Walteri heredis mei et omnium heredum meorum totam terram quæ fuit Wimundi in Briwerne in prato in paftura in campo in vias in femitis et in omnibus (fcilicet) pro fervitio fuo et homagio et pro una marca argenti et pro quibusdam calcaribus argenteis, Tenendam de me et heredibus meis fibi et heredibus fuis liberam et quietam pro (ab) omnibus fervitiis excepto fervitio Domini Regis quod prædictæ terræ pertinet, Reddendo fingulis annis duos folidos et fex denarios ad feftum Sancti Andreæ Apoftoli fex denarios et ad feftum Sanctæ Mariæ Martialis fex denarios, ad feftum nativitatis Sancti Joannis Baptiftæ fex denarios, ad feftum S. Egidii duodecim denarios. Quia hoc ratum et inconcuffum volo fieri hac carta mea præfenti et figillo meo

---

[1] This grant appears in the printed Index as "No. 34 ditto ditto in Brewerne."

confirmavi coram his teftibus Henrico Kais tunc Præpofito, Ede (?) de Bares, Reginaldo Capellano de Effelefworde, Ernaldo de Walefworde, Ernaldo de Effelefworde, Galfrido de Briwerne, Willelmo clerico filio Aluredi Albi, Roberto filio Swein, Amifio de Tuckelia, Waltero fratre Galfridi, Ricardo Sacrifta Abbatiæ S. Petri, Johanne Clerico filio Ricardi Draperii, et pluribus aliis. In perpetuum.

No. 35.

CONFIRMATIO WALTERI FILII ROBERTI DE MAUS QUAM FECIT GILEBERTO.

Sciant præfentes et futuri quod ego Walterus de Maus dedi et conceffi et prefenti carta mea confirmavi Gileberto fervienti Henrici Kais omnes terras quas idem Gilebertus tenuit de Roberto de Maus patre meo tenendas de me et de heredibus meis illi et heredibus fuis ita libere et quiete in bofco et plano in pratis et pafcuis in campis et viis in omnibus libertatibus et liberis confuetudinibus per idem fervicium quod Robertus de Maus pater meus prædicto Gileberto et heredibus fuis confirmaverit, et ficut ei ejufdem cartæ teftantur. Ut autem hæc mea conceffio rata et inconcuffa perfeveret præfenti carta figilli mei impreffione munita præfato Gileberto et heredibus suis corroboravi. Et præter hanc conceffionem et confirmationem dedit mihi præfatus Gilebertus duos bizantios. His teftibus Thoma Pic Capellano, Willelmo Keis, Ernaldo Ketelb, et Herberto filio ejus, Ada filio Fulconis, Galfrido de Briuwerne, Amifio de Tuckeleia, Roberto filio Swein et multis aliis. In perpetuum.

No. 36.

CARTA GILEBERTI DE DIMMOC QUAM FECIT NOBIS.

Sciant præfentes et futuri quod ego Gilebertus de Dimoc ferviens quondam Henrici Kais dedi Deo et Beatæ Mariæ de Dena et Monachis ibidem Deo fervientibus in perpetuam hereditatem et liberam eleeomfynam totam terram meam de Briuwerna quam habui et tenui de Domino meo Roberto de Maus et poftea de filio et herede ipfius Walteri de Maus, mihi et heredibus meis ficut cartæ eorum teftantur. Ita quod prædicti Monachi fingulis annis perfolvent prædicto Waltero vel heredibus fuis tres folidos et fex denarios pro omni fervitio falvo fervitio domini Regis videlicet octodecim denarios ad feftum S. Michaelis fex denarios, ad feftum S. Andreæ duodecim denarios, ad feftum S. Mariæ in Martio et fex denarios ad nativitatem S. Johannis. Ut autem hæc donacio quam prædictis Monachis ficut heredibus meis feci rata fit in perpetuum præfentem cartam figilli mei impreffione confirmavi His teftibus Willielmo Kais, Thoma Pic Capellano, Ricardo Clerico Caftelli, Roberto Tholi, Ricardo Rufo, Ricardo filio Jordani, et multis aliis. In perpetuum.

No. 37.

CONFIRMATIO WALTERI DE MAUS QUAM FECIT NOBIS SUPERIORIS CARTÆ.

Sciant præfentes et futuri quod ego Walterus de Maus conceffi et hac carta mea confirmavi Monachis de Dena totam terram illam quam Gilebertus de Dimuc ferviens quondam Henrici Kais illi dedit in perpetuam hereditatem et puram eleemofynam ficut carta ejufdem Gileberti teftatur quam fecit prædictis Monachis totam, fcilicet, quam tenuit et habuit in Brinwern primo de patre meo Roberto de Maus, poftea de me et heredibus meis fibi et heredibus fuis ut prædicti Monachi eam habeant et teneant de me et heredibus meis in perpetuum ut heredes ejufdem Gileberti ex conceffione mea, Ita liberam et quietam ab omni fervitio et confuetudine ab omnibus querelis et exactionibus ficut unquam prefatus Gilbertus eam melius tenuit et habuit et ut carta patris mei et mea eidem Gilberto teftantur pro tribus folidis et fex denariis mihi vel heredibus meis annuatim folvendis pro omni fervitio falvo fervitio Regali. Et pro hac conceffione et confirmatione prædicti Monachi dederunt mihi decem folidos et unam tunicam. Hanc autem conceffionem et confirmationem in omnibus fideliter et fine dolo tenendam manu mea affidavi. Ita quod nulla arte et ingenio præfatum Gilbertum vel ipfos monachos gravabo in omnibus prædictis et præfentem cartam figillo mea confirmavi. His teftibus Jocelino de Walefword et Milone fratre ejus; Ada filio Fulconis et Durando fratre ejus, Henrico de Bares, Ricardo Rufo de Glouceftria, Roberto Tholi, Ricardo filio Jordani, et multis aliis. In perpetuum.

No. 38.
CARTA WILLELMI DE PARCHO QUAM FECIT NOBIS.

Sciant præfentes et futuri quod ego Willelmus de Parcho totum jus quod clamavi in terra quam tenuit jure hereditario Gilbertus de Dimuc quondam ferviens Henrici Kais de Roberto Maus in Briuwern, Deo et Beatæ Mariæ de Dene et Monachis ibidem Deo fervientibus quietum clamavi ; Ita quod prædicti Monachi tenebunt terram illam de me et de heredibus meis in perpetuum liberam et quietam ab omni fervitio quod ad me et heredes meos pertinet, falvo fervitio Domini Regis, fingulis annis reddendo mihi vel heredibus meis tres folidos et fex denarios, videlicet, ad feftum S. Michaelis octodecim denarios, et ad feftum S Andreae fex denarios, et ad feftum S. Mariæ in Martio duodecim denarios, et ad nativitatem S. Johannis Baptiftæ fex denarios. Ita quod tenebunt terram illam liberam et quietam in pratis in viis in pafturis et in omnibus locis ad prædictam terram pertinentibus, ficut cartæ quas ipfe Gilebertus habuit de Roberto de Maus et Waltero de Maus teftantur. Pro hac autem conceffione mea dederunt mihi prædicti Monachi duas marcas et dimidium. Præterea divinæ pietatis intuitu dedi et conceffi Deo et Beatæ Mariæ de Dene et Monachis ibidem Deo fervientibus in perpetuam et puram eleemofynam totam partem meam gurgitis de Bollewere quem gurgitem Walterus de Maus mihi dedit et carta fua confirmavit, et iter quod ad predictum gurgitem extendit, et unam placiam ad faciendum molendinum unum ad ventum in capite de Pireforlong fupra cheminum quod vadit ad villam. Hanc autem donationem et prædictam conceffionem prædictis Monachis contra omnes homines ego et heredes mei warrantizamus, et ut hæc donatio et conceffio mea futuris temporibus rata et inconcuffa permaneat eam prefenti carta et figillo meo confirmavi. His teftibus, Rogero de Weftbiri, Roberto Achard, Waltero Wiberti, Roberto de Felda, Ada filio Fulconis, Ricardo Rufo et Ricardo filio ejus, Ricardo filio Jordani, Roberto Tholi, et multis aliis.

No. 39.
CONFIRMATIO WALTERI DE MAUS QUAM FECIT NOBIS SUPERIORIS CARTAE.

Sciant præfentes et futuri quod ego Walter Maus affignavi et conceffi quod Monachi de Dene fervitium quod pertinebat ad me et heredes meos de terra quam Gilebertus quondam ferviens Henrici Kais tenuit jure hereditario de patre meo et me et heredibus meis in Briuwern ficut carta mea et carta patris mei teftantur faciant Willelmo de Parcho cui et heredibus fuis prædictum fervitium totum dedi et conceffi pro fervitio fuo et quietum clamavi. Ita quod mihi et heredibus meis de terra illa vel de pertinentiis fuis in ullo refpondebunt Monachi prædicti. Præterea donationem et conceffionem quam idem Willelmus divinæ pietatis intuitu in puram et perpetuam elemofinam fecit prædictis Monachis de parte fua gurgitis de Bollewere et de itinere quod ad prædictum gurgitem extendit et de placia una ad faciendum molendinum ad ventum in capite de Pirefurlong fupra cheminum quod vadit ad villam ratam et gratam habeo et prefenti carta mea et figillo meo confirmavi. His teftibus Rogero de Weftburi, Roberto Achard, Waltero Wiberti, Roberto de Felda, Ada filio Fulconis, Ricardo Rufo et Ricardo filio ejus, Ricardo filio Jordani, Roberto Tholi, et multis aliis. In perpetuum.

No. 40.

CHIROGRAPHUM ROBERTI CAPELLANI.

Sciant præfentes et futuri quod ego Ricardus dictus Abbas de Dene et ejufdem loci conventus tradidimus et conceffimus Roberto Capellano filio Ofmundi de Neweham illud foldagium in Neweham quod præfatus Ofmundus dedit Ecclefiæ noftræ in eleemofynam perpetuam tenendam de Ecclefia noftra in feodi firmam fibi et heredibus fuis in perpetuum. Ita fcilicet quod heres ejus fit quemcunque ipfe defignaverit liber et quietus per duodecim denarios annuatim reddendos nobis pro omni fervitio quod ad nos pertineat in duobus terminis, fcilicet, ad feftum S. Michaelis fex denarios et ad Sanctam Mariam in Martio fex denarios. Et idem Robertus fecit nobis fecuritatem quod prædictam terram nec dabit nec vendet nec efcambiabit nec in vadium ponet nec ad alium locum religionis transferet, nec alio modo a nobis alienabit fine licentia noftra et heredes ejus cum fibi fuccedant eandem nobis facient fecuritatem. Hanc conceffionem firmiter tenendam et warrantizandam præfenti chirographo confirmavimus. Sigillum vero noftrum propter perfidiam Judæorum non appofuimus. His teftibus Waltero de Aura, Lewerico filio Sterman,' Simeone tunc temporis præpofito, Galfrido filio Radulphi de Dene, Ricardo fabro, et filio ejus Jordano, Aluredo filio Wimundi, Ivone le Palmer, et filio ejus Jordano, et Hundredo de Neweham. In perpetuum.

No. 41.

CHIROGRAPHUM JOANNIS LE IREMONGERE.

Sciant præfentes et futuri quod ego Ricardus dictus Abbas de Dene et ejufdem loci conventus dedimus et conceffimus Joanni le Irmongere et heredibus fuis terram noftram in Neweham quam habemus de Ernaldo Foreftario quam et ipfe habuit de Waltero le Mew et eft tercia terra a flumine, tenendam de nobis in feodo firmam libere et quiete pro duobus folidis annuatim reddendis, fcilicet, in Annunciatione S. Mariæ duodecim denarios, et ad feftum S. Michaelis duodecim denarios. Ita quod ipfe vel heredes fui prædictam terram nec vendent nec dabunt nec in vadimonium ponent nec efcambiabunt nec alio modo ab ecclefia noftra alienabunt fine licentia noftra. Pro hac conceffione prædictus Joannis homagium fecit Ecclefiæ noftræ cum juramento de prædicta conventione ex parte fua fideliter tenenda et duodecim denarios dedit nobis in introitu et nos ei et heredibus fuis hanc conceffionem hujus chirographi divifione confirmamus. His teftibus, Luverico tunc præpofito, Geri, Rogero filio Hugonis, Ada le Flamene et pleno Hundredo de Neweham. In perpetuum.

No. 42.

CHIROGRAPHUM JOHANNIS AIDANI.

Sciant præfentes et futuri quod ego Ricardus dictus Abbas de Dene et ejufdem loci conventus conceffimus Joanni filio Aidani tenendam de nobis fibi et heredibus fuis in feodo et hereditate medietate(m) terræ noftræ quæ fuit quondam Agnetis liberam et quietam ab omni fervitio quod ad nos pertineat per viginti et unum denarios annuatim reddendos fcilicet ad feftum S. Mariæ in Martio decem denarios et obolum et totidem ad feftum S. Michaelis. Eft autem illa medietas proximior terræ Galfridi filii Radulphi filii Galfridi. Pro hac conceffione prædictus Joannes homagium fecit ecclefiæ noftræ et fecuritatem quod terram præfatam nec dabit nec vendet nec efcambiabit nec in vadium ponet nec ad alium locum religionis transferet nec alio modo ab ecclefia noftra alienabit fine licentia noftra, et heredes [ejus cum] ei fuccedant eandem nobis facient fecuritatem. His teftibus Waltero de Aura tunc ballivo de Newebam, Luverico de Neweham, Geri, Simeone, Ivone le Palmer, et multis aliis. In perpetuum.

No. 43.

CHIROGRAPHUM ROGERI PARIS DE GLOUCESTRIA.

Sciant præfentes et futuri quod ego Ricardus Abbas de Dene et ejufdem loci conventus conceffimus Rogero de Paris et heredibus ejus terram noftram in Glouceftria quam habuimus de divifa Henrici Kais et eft inter terram Willelmi le Macecrer et terram Jordani le Saluer tenendam de nobis in feodi firmam libere et quiete pro duobus folidis pro omni fervicio annuatim reddendis in quatuor terminis, fcilicet, in Natali Domini fex denarios, ad S. Mariam in Martio fex denarios, ad Natale S. Joannis Baptiftae fex denarios, ad S. Michaelem fex denarios ita quod prædictus Rogerus vel heredes fui prædictam terram nec dabunt nec vendent nec efcambiabunt nec in vadium ponent nec alio modo ab Ecclefia noftra alienabunt fine licentia noftra. Pro hac conceffione prædictus Rogerus homagium fecit ecclefiæ noftræ cum juramento de prædicta conventione ex parte fua fideliter tenenda et redditu noftro in fuis terminis reddendo et heredes fui cum fibi fuccedant eandem nobis facient fecuritatem prædictam conventionem præfenti chirographo teftamur et confirmamus. His teftibus, Roberto Tholi, Ricardo le Rus, Roberto Calvo, Ricardo filio Jordani, Helya Præpofito de Glouceftria, Radulpho Auri-fabro, et multis aliis. In perpetuum.

No. 44.

CHIROGRAPHUM SIGILLATUM ROGERI DE BOSCO.

(Alium habemus ad terminum.)

Sciant præfentes et futuri quod ego Rogerus de Bofco poft conventionem factam inter me et Monachos de Dene tempore A. Abbatis (?per quam) ego tenebam de illis tres acras illas quas Pater meus dedit illis in eleemofynam inter domum meam et Efhul et ipfi tenebant de me terram de Alefworde in feodi firmam reddendo fingulis annis fex denarios remifi domino Ricardo Abbati et prædictis monachis de fex prædictis denariis quinque denarios pro falute animæ meæ et meorum et pro una vacca cum vitulo [quam] mihi dederunt. Ita vero in perpetuum ipfi teneant de me et heredibus meis terram de Aldefword pro tribus acris prædictis et unum denarium annuatim reddendo. Remifi etiam prædictis Monachis omnem querelam de ftagnis, foffatis et vivariis et removebo exclufam meam a ponte monachorum et fic eam locabo ut fine damno monachorum et ad voluntatem eorum componatur. Conceffi etiam eis aifias fuas in quarreria mea de Efhul fecundum .... meum et confilium meum. Hanc conventionem in omnibus fideliter tenendam ego affidavi. His teftibus Rogero de Weftbiri, Willelmo de Munfterword, Galfrido de Dena, et fratribus fuis Maiolo et Willelmo, Philippo de Dunia, Rogero de Ardern, Godfrido Cadel, et multis aliis. In perpetuum.

No. 45.

CHIROGRAPHUM ERNALDI CLERICI DE DIMMOC.

Sciant præfentes et futuri hanc effe conventionem inter Ernaldum clericum de Dimmoc et Monachos de Dene quod prædictus Ernaldus conceffit Monachis decimas fuas liberas et quietas de terris quas in parochia excoluerunt de Dimmoc propter duos folidos ad feftum S. Michaelis fingulis annis reddendos. Ut hæc conventio futuris temporibus rata habeatur legitimorum noftrorum teftimonio eam confirmamus qui propriis nominibus exprimuntur; Walterus de Keteford, Ricardus de Bofco, Hucdrædus Clericus, Svanus de Dunhantun, Hugo Albus et multi alii. In perpetuum.

No. 46.

CHIROGRAPHUM WILLELMI KAIS, PERSONÆ DE DIMMOC POST ERNALDUM.

Sciant tam prefentes quam futuri quod ego Willelmus Kais eandem conventionem quæ fuit inter Ernaldum prædecefforem meum perfonam tunc temporis ecclefiæ de Dimmoc et ecclefiam de Dene cum prædicta ecclefia firmam et inconcuffam habeo. Forma autem conventionis hæc fuit quod, scilicet, prædictus Ernaldus conceffit ecclefiæ de Dena decimas fuas liberas et quietas de terris quas Monachi in parochia de Dene excoluerunt propter duos folidos ad feftum S. Michaelis reddendos. Ut autem hæc conventio in pofterum rata maneat [et] inconcuffa eam hujus chirographi divifione et fubfcriptorum virorum teftimonio confirmo Galfridi tunc temporis Capellani de Dimmoc, Walteri filii Hugonis, Ricardi de Bofco, Ernaldi de Keteford, Joannis Burgeis, Ernifii, Thomae Pic, Roberti, Nicolai, Capellanorum de Glouceftria, et multis aliis. In perpetuum.

No. 47.

CONFIRMATIO DUORUM PRÆSCRIPTORUM CHIROGRAPHORUM DE DIMMOC.

Univerfis Sanctæ Matris ecclefiæ filiis ad quos præfens fcriptum pervenerit H. de Glouceftria et A. de Theokefbiria Dei gratia Abbates falutem in Chrifto. Fraternitati veftræ notum fieri voluimus quod cum caufa quæ vertebatur inter Monachos de Dene et Willelmum Kais perfonam de Dimoc fuper decimis terrarum quas iidem Monachi excolunt in parochia de Dimoc a Domino Papa Clemente tertio nobis commiffa eft et dicenda hoc fine conquievit: Abbas, videlicet, et Monachi de Dene perfolvent annuatim duos folidos jam dicto Willelmo pro prenominatis decimis ad feftum S. Michaelis ficut prædeceffori fuo Arnaldo folvere confueverunt. Ut autem haec conventio in pofterum rata maneat et inconcuffa eam auctoritate nobis a Summo Pontifice in hac caufa commiffa confirmamus et figillorum noftrorum appofitione communimus.

No. 48.

CHIROGRAPHUM RICARDI DE BOSCO IN DIMMOC.

Sciant prefentes et futuri quod ego Ricardus dictus Abbas de Dene et ejufdem loci conventus conceffimus Ricardo de Bofco quatuor acras de terra noftra in Dimoc de effartis noftris illas, fcilicet, quæ jacent inter terram prædicti Ricardi et bofcum noftrum contra meffuagium Beulfi ex alia parte viæ Tenendas de nobis omnibus diebus vitæ fuæ liberas et quietas ab omni fervitio et confuetudine præter fervitium Domini Regis pro octo denariis annuatim reddendis in quatuor terminis per quatuor partes et pro fidelitate confilii et auxilii quam nobis promifit in principio hujus conceffionis. Quod fi heres prædicti Ricardo tantum nobis fciverit ut nobis acceptus fit citius ei prædictam terram concedemus quam alio. Ut hæc noftra conceffio ei rata fit omnibus diebus [vitæ] ejus hanc conceffionem præfenti chirographi teftificamus et confirmamus. His teftibus Rogero de Ledentun, Henrico de Ledintun, Simone Clerico, Thurbno tunc præpofito, et multis aliis. In perpetuum.

No. 49.
CHIROGRAPHUM WILLELMI DE MONASTERIO DE DIMMOC.

Sciant præfentes et futuri quod ego Ricardus dictus Abbas de Dene et ejus loci conventus conceffimus Willelmo de Monafterio homini noftro de Dimoc illam menfuram quæ eft inter cœmeterium et aquam cum crofta adjacente et prato tenendam de nobis liberam et quietam omnibus diebus vitæ fuæ ab omni fervitio et confuetudine falvo fervitio Domini Regis Reddendo annuatim duos folidos et fex denarios pro quatuor terminis. Concedimus etiam ei fub eadem libertate acram unam in Seilesfeld pro tribus denariis. Pro hac conceffione prædictus Willelmus dedit nobis dimidiam marcam et nos eam præfenti chirographo confirmamus. His teftibus, Galfrido Capellano de Dimoc, et Simone alumno ejus, Hugone Morker, et multis aliis. In perpetuum.

No. 50.
ITEM ALIA CARTA WILLELMI FILII GILBERTI DE ERLINGHAM.

Sciant præfentes et futuri quod ego Willelmus filius Gilberti filius Milonis de Erlingham dedi et præfenti carta confirmavi Deo et Beatæ Mariæ de Dene et Monachis de Dene pro falute mea et Hyla (Hylariae qu) uxoris meae et pro anima Ricardi filii mei et tam anteceffbrum quam heredum meorum in perpetuam et puram eleemofynam duos feillones de terra mea in Herlingeham quorum unus eft fub Berdun quartus [?] in cultura a parte auftrali alter in Weftmers in Sudefurlong inter feillonem Jacobi filii Dolfini et forerdam Rogeri filii Andreæ, Dedi etiam eis dimidiam acram meam in Glefmers cum alia una parte ejufdem acrae quam Ricardus filius meus eis dedit ficut ejus carta teftatur Et item unum feillonem in Wrplefwei et necnon illum feillonem qui merchiat prato de Weftmers quem prædictus Ricardus filius meus eis dedit. Et hæc prædicta habebunt et tenebunt libera et quieta ab omni fervitio et confuetudine et exactione feculari. Concessi etiam eis et confirmavi omnes conventiones et donationes de illis terris de quibus reddebant annuatim fex denarios eidem Ricardo filio meo ficut carta ejus teftatur fcilicet de quinque feillonibus in Cuple-forerd et tres contra maladeriam de Neweham extra Wallam et duos qui merchiant prato de Weftmers et duos qui merchiant fuper forer dam Petri de Wike ex una parte et ex altera parte fuper Weftwalle. Ita quod reddent eofdem fex denarios mihi vel heredibus meis ad feftum S. Michaelis fingulis annis. Et ego et heredes mei omnia prædicta warrantizabimus eis contra omnes homines et acquietabimus ab omni fervitio. Quod fi aliqua prædictarum terrarum venerit in dotem Helne uxoris meæ vel Matildis uxoris Ricardi filii mei ego vel heredes mei efcambium eis faciemus ad plenam valentiam ante quam Monachi diffaifiantur. Et pro his conceffionibus et donationibus et conventionibus et earum confirmatione prædicti Monachi dederunt mihi unum equum cum plenario hernafio et duos boves et Edithæ filiæ et heredi meæ unam juvencam pregnantem in teftimonio voluntariæ conceffionis fuæ. Ut hæc mea donatio rata fit in perpetuum præfentem cartam figillo meo confirmavi. Et ego et Editha filia mea et heres de prædictis omnibus tenendis et warantizandis affidavimus. His teftibus Rogero de Buivilla, Rogero filio Ricardi de Lench, Radulpho Walenfe, Simeone tunc præpofito de Neweham, Thuverico, Geri, Ivone le Paumer, Rogero le Venur, Rogero de Bolleia et Galfrido fratre ejus, et multis aliis. In perpetuum.

No. 51.

CHIROGRAPHUM JOANNIS FILII LUVERICH.

Sciant præfentes et futuri quod ego Ricardus dictus Abbas de Dene et conventus ejufdem loci conceffimus et tradidimus Joanni filio Luverich fratris Faremonis terram illam quam idem Faremon dedit domui noftræ in eleemofynam tenendam et habendam fibi et heredibus fuis in perpetuum Reddendo inde fingulis annis duodecim denarios ad duos terminos anni, ad S. Mariam in Martio fex denarios, ad S. Michaelem fex denarios. Et pro hac conceffione prædictus Joannes de eadem terra homagium fecit ecclefiæ noftræ et fecuritatem quod præfatam terram non dabit nec vendet nec efcambiabit nec in vadium ponet nec ad alium locum religionis transferet, nec alio modo ab ecclefia noftra alienabit fine licentia noftra, et heredes cum [ei] fuccedant eandem etiam nobis facient fecuritatem. Tamen idem Joannes vel heredes ejus hanc eandem terram tenebit liberam et quietam ab omni fervitio quod ad nos pertinet falvo Domini Regis fervitio. His teftibus, Roberto Mufchet, Ada filio Fulconis, Luverico de Neweham, Simeone tunc præpofito, Ada Flandrenfe, Ricardo filio Willelmi, Ricardo filio Aluredi, Waltero le Karl, Waltero filio Walteri Corviferii (qu. pro Cerevifarii—a brewer) et multis aliis.

No. 52.
CARTA WALTERI DE LA BARRA.

Sciant præfentes et futuri quod ego Ricardus dictus Abbas de Dene et ejufdem loci conventus conceffimus Waltero de la Barra quoddam meffuagium in Neweham illud, fcilicet, quod Rogerus de Boyville dedit ecclefiæ noftræ in perpetuam eleemofynam et eft juxta terram quæ fuit quondam Sevari Palmer, Tenendum de nobis fibi et heredibus fuis in feodo et hereditate liberum et quietum ab omni fervitio quod ad nos pertineat pro duobus folidis annuatim reddendis (fcilicet) in Annunciatione Sanctæ Mariæ duodecim denarios et ad feftum Sancti Michaelis duodecim denarios. Pro hac autem conceffione prædictus Walterus homagium fecit ecclefiæ noftræ et fecuritatem quod terram præfatam, fcilicet, meffuagium nec dabit nec vendet nec efcambiabit nec in vadimonium ponet nec ad alium locum religionis transferet nec alio modo ab ecclefia noftra alienabit fine licentia noftra et heredes cum ei fuccedant eandem nobis facient fecuritatem, et duodecim denarios nobis de introitu. Hanc conceffionem firmiter tenendam et warrantizandam præfenti chirographo confirmavimus. Sigillum vero noftrum proper perfidiam Judæorum non appofuimus. His teftibus, Waltero Clerico de Aura, Ricardo filio Willelmi, Ricardo filio Aluredi, et Jordano filio ejus, Joanne filio Aidani, Ivone Palmer, Nicolao filio ejus, et multis aliis in Hundredo de Neweham.

No. 53.
CARTA HUGONIS CHARKE PRIMA EX CONVENTIONE AD TERMINUM.
(Alias duas habemus ex eleemofyna.)

Sciant præfentes ex futuri quod ego Hugo Charke affenfu uxoris meæ Johannæ et filii et heredis mei Hugonis tradidi in vadimonium Monachis de

Dene totam terram meam quæ vocatur Wudelond cum hominibus qui in ea funt et totum Eilfifcroft et totum Torfthalle exceptis tribus acris et excepta terra quam Luvericus tenet et totam terram de hida quam Ernaldus Carpentarius tenuit exceptis tribus acris Tenendas de me et heredibus meis tam libere ficut ego eas liberius tenui et quietas ab omni fervitio excepto regali fervitio ufque ad terminum duodecim annorum fumpto initio ab anno Incarnationis Dominicæ millefimo centefimo nonagefimo quinto ad feftum S. Michaelis pro fex marcis quas mihi prædicti Monachi in principio hujus conventionis commodaverunt et præter hæc pro decem folidis quos mihi annuatim folvent ex redditu ...... duobus terminis, fcilicet, in Annunciatione S. Mariæ et in fefto S. Michaelis ita quod in fine duodecim annorum terræ ad me non revertentur antequam fex marcas eis reddiderim. Quod fi circa præcedentem Hoccedei inquifitus ab eis vel præmuniens eos ad fubfequentem ...... terminum duodecim annorum eis fex marcas reddere non potero ad illam Hoccedei terram waretabunt et fequens fructus eorum erit ... tamdiu fuo prædicta convencione et libertate et redditu decem folidorum eas tenebunt donec eis fex marcas reddiderim. Quod fi infra hunc terminum deceffero eis ipfam conventionem heres meus tenebit de eifdem terris. Vel fi aliquo cafu illas prenominatas terras warrantizare non poterit de aliis ad penam valentiam eandem conventionem antequam monachi fint diffaifiati. Ut hæc conventio rata fit et fine dolo fervata uxor mea Jo[anna] recepit a Monachis unum bizantium et filius meus H. unam tunicam in teftimonium affenfus eorum et ego manu mea affidavi et præfentem cartam figillo meo confirmavi. His teftibus Domina mea Berta de Monemuta, Ada de Blakeneia, Willelmo de Munfterworth, Galfrido de Dene, Willelmo de Bofceliva, Rogero, Ricardo et Jacobo, fratribus ejus, Willelmo de Staure, Rogero de Herderne, Helia de Rudel[eia?], Waltero Bleith, et multis aliis. (Ad terminum).

No. 54.

CHIROGRAPHUM PHILIPPI DE DUNIE SIGILLATUM.

(Et Cartam habemus ex eleemofyna.)

Anno ab Incarnatione Domini millefimo centefimo nonagefimo quinto ad feftum Sancti Michaelis facta eft hæc conventio inter Philippum de Dunie et Monachos de Dene, fcilicet, quod ego Philippus de Dunia liberavi Monachis de Dene in vadimonium totam terram meam quam habeo in parvo Marifco et totum forlongum meum de Welipulle, et totum Cubewordin, et unam acram juxta quam tenditur fuper montem et octo feillones in monte de Walemore, et totam terram meam quam habeo in Wadeleia, cum prato quod ibidem habeo, tenendas de me et heredibus meis liberas [et] quietas ab omni fervitio et confuetudine tamdiu donec prædicti Monachi de qualibet illarum terrarum perceperint octo fructus, et de prato duodecim pro quatuor marcis quas mihi dederunt prædicti Monachi in principio hujus conventionis. Ita quod quælibet terrarum illarum ad me vel heredes meos quiete revertetur cum prædicti Monachi octo fructus fuos perceperint præter pratum quod dabit eis duodecim. Et in fine duodecim annorum quatuor marcæ quas a Monachis accepi mihi quiete remanebunt. Quod fi infra prædictum terminum deceffero et aliqua illarum terrarum inciderit in dotalium uxoris meae heredes mei illam terram predictis Monachis efchambiabunt ad plenam valentiam, antequam prædicti Monachi fint diffaifiati. Hanc autem conventionem in omnibus fideliter fine dolo tenendam et contra omnes homines warrantizandam ego et heres meus Willelmus et filii mei Ricardus et Philippus affidavimus et ego præfens chirographum figillo meo confirmavi et Monachi ex parte fua fuum figillum appofuerunt. His teftibus, Baderune de Blechedune, Rogero de Weftbiri, Willelmo de Munfterword, Moyfe de Rodleia, Roberto de Baieus, Rogero de Erderne, Waltero Map, Henrico de Mineriis, Randolpho de Salewerpe, Willelmo de Heliun, Willelmo filio Ernewi, Hugone de Gerne, Ricardo filio Ranewin, et Reginaldo fratre ejus, Golefr' Cadel, Radulpho Venatore, Joanne Difpenfatore, Willelmo de Walemore, et multis aliis.

No. 55.

CHIROGRAPHUM SIGILLATUM ROGERI DE BOSCO.

(Alterum habemus ex conventione in perpetuum.)

Sciant præfentes et futuri quod ego Rogerus de Bofco confenfu Margaretæ uxoris meæ tradidi Monachis de Dene per manum fratris Ricardi de Molendino fex acras terræ feminatoriæ noftræ et totum pratum meum in medio campi qui eft juxta domum meam, videlicet, unam acram in Cleilega et alteram in Whitelega quae vertit fupra priorem acram, tertiam fub Eilefhulle in eodem campo, quartam in Eifhfeld, quintam in longa terra, fextam fupra caput prati

juxta rivum, Tenendas de me vel heredibus meis liberas et quietas ab omni
servitio et omnibus consuetudinibus usque ad terminum viginti annorum, videlicet,
pro sexdecim solidis quos ipse dederunt mihi de introitu, et præterea reddendo
singulis annis duodecim denarios de redditu pro omnibus rebus ad duos anni
terminos, ad S. Mariam in Martio sex denarios, ad S. Michaelis sex denarios,
et in fine presatorum viginti annorum ...... piam ego vel heres meus terram
meam cum prato solutam et quietam, Tali pacto quod ego vel heres meus
interim warrantizabo præsatam [terram eis]dem monachis et stabo pro eadem
terra cum prato contra omnes homines vel seminas. Et si ego infra terminum
præfatum viginti annorum ...... decessero et eadem terra vel pars illius terræ
et pratum contigerit Margaretæ uxori meæ ad partem dotis suæ heres meus
equivalentem terram ...... de suo eidem Margaretæ tradet vel finem pro se
faciet ut Monachi suam sæpedictam terram et pratum in pace teneant usque
ad terminum prædictum suum et hanc prædictam terram et pratum tradidi
eis ad festum S. Michaelis Anno Incarnationis Dominicæ millesimo ducentesimo
primo et hoc totum assidavi sine malo ingenio tenendam. Ego et Margareta
uxor mea volentes quod heredes nostri hoc idem fide sua firmiter teneant et ut
securiore sint prædicti Monachi ut super hoc non implacitentur chirographo
meo sigillo meo impresso hoc totum eis confirmavi. His testibus Galfrido de
Abbenhale, Rogero de Arderne, Hugone Cherke, Ricardo filio Hugonis militis,
et multis aliis. (Ad terminum).

No. 56.

CHIROGRAPHUM WILLELMI TURC SIGILLATUM.

Sciant præsentes et futuri quod ego Willelmus Turc assensu et voluntate
M. uxoris meæ et heredum meorum invadiavi Monachis de Dene pro catallis
quæ ab eis accepi illam virgatam terræ meæ totam quam Eilevinus le Mercer
aliquando tenuit et Henricus Calvus post eum Tenendam de me et heredibus
meis liberam et quietam ab omni servitio et consuetudine decem annis sumpto
initio ab festo S. Michaelis quod fuit anno ab Incarnatione Domini millesimo
centesimo nonagesimo sexto. Ita quod ad Hoccedei ante decimum cropum
ego vel heredes mei recipiemus warectum et prædicta terra omnino libera et
quieta post illam rasuram revertetur ad nos. Hanc conventionem in omnibus
fideliter et sine dolo tenendam ab omni servitio liberandam et contra omnes

homines warrantizandam ego et filius et heres meus et uxor mea affidavimus et ego eandem præfenti chirographo et figillo meo confirmavi. His teſtibus, Roberto de Doudfwell, Ofberto de Sciptun, Brico (qu. Henrico) de؛Hagenep, et Rogero de Hagen[ep], et aliis. (Ad terminum.)

No. 57.
CARTA MOYSIS DE REDLEIA.

Sciant præfentes et futuri quod ego Moyfes de Redleia affenfu et voluntate Margaretæ uxoris meæ et heredum meorum Henrici et Radulphi invadiavi monachis de Dene tres acras terræ in Ruding ficut funt divifæ, fcilicet, duodecim feillones qui fimul tenduntur ufque ad viam et tres alios per fe et item unum per fe Tenendas de me et heredibus meis liberas et quietas ab omnibus fervitiis pro decem folidis et fex denariis quos mihi præ manibus dederunt. Has tres acras receperunt ad feftum S. Joannis Baptiſtæ proximum poſt coronationem Joannis Regis non wareċtatas et tenebunt eas fex annis fcilicet ad quatuor cropos et reddent eas non wareċtatas. Hanc conventionem in omnibus fideliter tenendam ego manu mea affidavi et hac carta confirmavi et Margareta uxor mea et filii mei fimiliter affidaverunt quicquid de me contingat His teſtibus Michaele Capellano, Rogero de Weſtbiri, Rogero de Herderne, Willelmo de Heliun, Ricardo de Clive, Rogero de Heidun, et multis aliis. (Ad terminum.)

No. 58.
CARTA NIGELLI HAPEWI (HATHEWI).

Sciant præfentes et futuri quod ego Nigellus filius Willelmi Hapewi cum voluntate et conceffione [confenfu] Sarræ uxoris meæ invadiavi Monachis de Dene totum pratum meum quod habeo in Marifco tenendum quinque annis ut jus inde recipiant quinque falcationes et dimidium, fœnum fexti annis pro viginti folidis quos mihi præ manibus dederunt. Hanc conventionem feci cum prædiċtis monachis ad feftum S. Michaelis proximum poſt coronationem Joannis Regis et poſt illud feftum habebit prædiċtas falcationes Et cum fuum plenum habuerunt monachis pratum meum omnimo quietum ad me revertetur, Ut hæc conventio firmiter teneatur ego manu mea affidavi et præfenti fcripto figillum meum appofui. Tefte et plegio Roberto Mufchet, teftibus etiam Gileberto Capellano de St. Briavelli, Joanne le Blunt, Roberto juvene Mufchet, Willelmo .... Alexandro Clerico, Hugone Wiper (Wither), et multis aliis. (Ad terminum.)

No. 59.

CHIROGRAPHUM GALFRIDI HUGELIN.

Hæc eft conventio facta inter Galfridum Hugelin et Monachos de Dene, fcilicet, quod ego Galfridus Hugelin affenfu Bafileæ uxoris meæ et Willelmi filii mei tradidi Monachis de Dene totam terram meam de Walemor tenendam de me et heredibus meis fex annis liberam et quietam ab omni fervitio et confuetudine. Ita quod ego vel heredes mei acquietabimus eandem terram ab omni fervitio et confuetudine prædicti autem Monachi tenebunt prædictam terram primis quatuor annis omnino quietam pro decem folidis quos nobis prae manibus pacaverunt quinto autem et fexto anno reddent annuatim quatuor folidos mihi vel heredibus meis pro omni fervitio, fcilicet, duos folidos in Annunciatione Dominica, et duos ad feftum Sancti Michaelis. Hæc conventio facta fuit et incepta ad feftum S. Michaelis quando curfus lunæ fuit fecundus, et poft idem feftum cremata eft Neweham. Hanc conventionem fideliter et fine dolo tenendam et warrantizandam ego et Bafilen uxor mea et filius meus Willelmus affidavimus. His teftibus Waltero de Auro tunc ballivo de Neweham, Ada Capellano, Luverico de Neweham, Waltero Bleith, Ricardo filio Aluredi, et multis aliis. (Ad terminum.)

No. 60.

CARTA WILLELMI DE MUNSTERWORD.

Sciant præfentes et futuri quod ego Willelmus de Munfterword affenfu A. uxoris meæ et heredum meorum liberavi et tradidi Monachis de Dene totum pratum meum quod eft inter Gerne et Ecclefiam de Weftbiri Tenendum et habendum de me et heredibus meis liberum et quietum ab omnibus rebus cum opere quod ad id pratum pertinet octo annis Ita quod prædicta monachi percipient primam falcationem ad feftum S. J.(oannis) anno ab Incarnatione

Domini millesimo centesimo nonagesimo septimo et ultimam ad eundem terminum anno ab Incarnatione Domini millesimo ducentesimo et quarto. Prædicti vero monachi pacaverunt mihi præ manibus pro toto tempore prædicto quatuor marcas et duos solidos et octo denarios, scilicet, pro quolibet anno septem solidos; Quod si præfatis monachis id pratum usque ad præfatum terminum warrantizare non potero ego alterum pratum equivalens ad judicium fidelium hominum eis dabo in escambium; Quod si morte perveniente id facere non potero uxor mea et heredes mei se id facturos affidaverunt. Hanc conventionem in omnibus fideliter et sine dolo tenendam manu mea affidavi et præsenti cartæ sigillum meum apposui. His testibus Henrico de Mineriis, Baderune de Blechedune, Rogero de Westbiri, Philippo de Dune, Rogero de Erderne, Moyse de Redleia, Willelmo de Heliun, Ricardo filio Rawin (Renewin), Aulf (? Willelmo) de Munsterword et multis aliis.

No. 61.

CHIROGRAPHUM HENRICI DE CHAKESHULL SIGILLATUM.

(Et cartam habemus ex elemos.)

Sciant præsentes et futuri quod ego Henricus de Chakeshill invadiavi Monachis de Dene totum pratum meum quod dicitur Cumbesmedewe Tenendum de me et heredibus meis 5 annis ad 5 salcationes pro xv solidis quos mihi præ manibus pacaverunt. Tenebunt vero idem pratum usque ad prædictum terminum libere et quiete ab omni servicio et omni redditu. Hæc conventio facta est ad festum Omnium Sanctorum anno ab Incarnatione Domini MC nonagesimo nono, anno scilicet quo Rex Johannes coronatus. Et post prædictum festum recipient prædicti Monachi prædictas 5 falcationes. Ut hæc conventio rata sit præsenti cyrographo sigillum meum apposui. His testibus Rogero de Westbir, Rogero de Arderne, Moyse de Redleia, Willelmo de Heliun, Ricardo filio Renewin, Radulpho Venatore, Henrico de Walemore et multis aliis. (Ad terminum.)

No. 62.

CHIROGRAPHUM RADULPHI CRUPARD SIGILLATUM.

Hæc est conventio inter Radulphum Crupard et Monachos de Dene. Quod ego Radulphus tradidi prædictis monachis duas croftas meas, scilicet, Hamcroft et Hulpescroft tenendas de me et heredibus meis liberas et quietas ab omni servitio ad cropos quatuor ; duos, scilicet, de avena et duos de frumento de utraque crofta prædicta, pro sex solidis quos mihi præ manibus dederunt. Habebunt autem prædicti monachi primum cropum hujus conventionis in anno ab Incarnatione Domini millesimo ducentesimo. Ut hæc conventio firma sit præsenti chirographo sigillum meum appofui. His teftibus Henrico de Chekeshill, Hugo de Gerne, Henrico de Walemore, Willelmo de Walemore, et multis aliis. (Ad terminum)

No. 63.

CARTA ADÆ FILII FULCONIS EX PRIMA CONVENTIONE.

Sciant præfentes et futuri quod ego Adam filius Fulconis affensu Domini mei Henrici de Mineriis et conceffione Durandi fratris mei tradidi Monachis de Dene totum dominicatum meum de Chekeshill tenendum de me et heredibus meis liberum et quietum ab omni confuetudine et querela excepto regali fervitio pro tribus marcis quas mihi præ manibus dederunt tribus annis Ita quod recipient warectum ad Hokedei anno ab Incarnatione Domini millesimo ducentesimo primo ufque ad tres cropos et ego prædictam terram contra omnes homines warrantizabo vel heredes mei poft me Et si hoc facere non poterimus prædictis monachis ad plenam valentiam fatisfaciemus. Ut hæc conventio firmiter teneatur præfentem cartam figillo meo confirmavi et de ea tenenda affidavi. His teftibus Domino meo Henrico de Mineriis, Galfrido de Dene, Rogero de Weftbiri, Rogero de Erderne, Willelmo de Heliun, Joanne Difpenfatore, et multis aliis. (Ad terminum.)

No. 64.

ITEM CARTA ADÆ FILII FULCONIS EX SECUNDA CONVENTIONE.

Hæc eft conventio inter Adam filium Fulconis de Chekeshilla et Monachos de Dene, fcilicet, quod ego Adam filius Fulconis affenfu domini mei Henrici de Mineriis et conceffione Durandi fratris mei tradidi monachis de Dene totum dominicatum meum de Chekeshilla tenendum de me et heredibus meis liberum et quietum ab omni servitio et confuetudine et querela falvo fervitio Domini Regis quinque annis pro quinque marcis quas mihi præ manibus pacaverunt. Ita quod recipient warectum ad Hoccedei anno ab Incarnatione Domini millefimo ducentefimo primo et habebunt quinque cropos et ego prædictam terram ufque ad prædictum terminum contra omnes homines warrantizabo vel heredes mei poft me quod fi non poterimus, prædictis monachis fatiffaciemus ad plenam valentiam. Ut hæc conventio firma fit præfens chirographum figillo meo et fide interpofita confirmavi. His teftibus Domino meo Henrico de Mineriis, Rogero de Weftbiri, Galfrido de Dene, Rogero de Arderne, Willelmo de Heliun, et multis aliis.

No. 65.

CARTA HUGONIS CHARKE DE SECUNDA CONVENTIONE.

Sciant præfentes et futuri quod ego Hugo Charke affenfu Jo[annæ] uxoris meæ et filii et heredis mei Hugonis tradidi in vadium Monachis de Dene totam terram meam quæ vocatur Wudelond cum hominibus in ea tenentibus et totum forftal exceptis tribus acris et excepta' terra quam Luvericus tenuit in Forftal et totam terram de Hida exceptis tribus acris quas Rogerus de la Boxe tenuit et aliis tribus quas ego Hugo retinui in manu mea videlicet tenenda de me et heredibus meis tam libere ficut ego eas liberius tenui et quietas ab omni fervitio excepto regali fervitio, fcilicet, ad feftum Sancti Michaelis anno Dominicæ Incarnationis millefimo ducentefimo primo ufque ad terminum fex annorum pro octo marcis quas dicti monachi commodaverunt mihi præ manibus et præter hæc pro decem folidis et octo denariis de redditu annuatim folvendo duobus, fcilicet, anni terminis ad feftum Sanctæ Mariæ in Martio et ad feftum S. Michaelis. Ita quod in fine fex annorum dictorum præfatæ terræ ad me non revertentur antequam dictas octo marcas præfatis monachis perfolvero. Quod fi ego requifitus ab eis ad Hoccedei proximum ante ultimum terminum vel eos præmuniens ad ultimum terminum fex annorum dictas octo marcas perfolvere eis non potuero tunc ad illum Hoccedei terras warectabunt et fequens fructus illius warecti illorum erit et tamdiu fub eadem conventione et libertate et redditu decem folidorum et octo denariorum eas tenebunt donec eis octo marcas perfolvero. Quod fi infra hunc terminum ego deceffero heres meus eandem conventionem eis tenebit vel fi forte aliquo infortunio illas prædictas terras ego vel heres meus eis warrantizare non potero de aliis terris meis ad plenam valentiam eandem conventionem ego vel heres meus antequam prædicti monachi diffeifientur perficiam. Et ut hæc conventio' rata fit et fine dolo fervata uxor mea Jo[anna] pro fuo conceffu recepit a monachis unum bizantium et Hugo filius meus unam tunicam pro fuo affenfu. Hoc itaque ego Hugo pro me et pro heredibus meis affidavi fine dolo tenendum et præfenti carta figillo meo impreffa confirmavi. His teftibus Domina mea Berta de Monemuta, Galfrido de Dene, Rogero de Erderne, Willelmo de Heliun, Willelmo de Boxeliva, Rogero, Ricardo, et Jacobo fratribus ejus, Willelmo de Staure, Helya de Rudele, Waltero Bleith, Luverico de Newcham. Ad terminum.

No. 66.

CARTA ROGERI DE LEINCH.

Hæc eft conventio inter Rogerum filium Ricardi de Leinch et monachos de Dene viz. quod ego Rogerus filius Ricardi de Leinch tradidi monachis de Dene unam virgatam terræ meæ, fcilicet, totam medietatem dimidiæ hidæ meæ de Middeltun in agris et pratis et pafturis et omnibus aliis rebus tenendam de me et heredis meis feptem annis liberam et quietam ab omni fervitio et confuetudine falvo fervitio Domini Regis pro quinque marcis et quadraginta denariis quas mihi præ. manibus pacaverunt. Ita tamen quod fi in partitione prædictæ dimidiæ hidæ aliquod mafagium cum hominibus qui in [pofterum] in fortem monachorum devenerint faciam eis rationabile efcambium in terra arabili ad plenam valentiam. Prædictam vero terram receperunt prædicti monachi anno ab Incarnatione Domini milleſimo ducentefimo fecundo ad Hokedei et inbladationem avenae et fabarum quam tunc habuerit unde [hic] eft de prædicta conventione fextus annus annorum Quod fi infra hunc terminum obiero et aliqua terrarum quas Monachi tenuerint venerit in dotem uxoris meæ heredes mei facient monachis efcambium ad plenam valentiam antequam fint diffaifiati. Hanc conventionem in omnibus fideliter et fine dolo tenendam manu mea affidavi et uxor mea Marg[areta] pariter affidavit et ego præfens chirographum figillo meo confirmavi. His teftibus Domina mea A. de Berkeleia, Magiftro Petro tunc Ballivo ejus, Rogero de Buivill et Helia filio ejus, Gaufrido de Dene, et Maelo fratre ejus, Thoma de Abenhale, Roberto Kinvet, et multis aliis. (Ad terminum.)

No. 67.
CHIROGRAPHUM ROGERI DE BOSCO SIGILLATUM.

Sciant præfentes et futuri quod ego Rogerus de Bofcho tradidi Monachis de Flaxleh de terra mea fex acras, viz. unam acram in Cleilega et alteram in Witeleia quæ vertit fupra priorem acram, tertiam fub Eilefhull in eodem campo, quartam in Eihffelde, quintam in longam terram, fextam fuper caput prati juxta rivum Et totum pratum meum quod eft in medio campi juxta molendinum Tenendas de me et heredibus meis liberas et quietas ab omni fervitio et confuetudine ufque ad terminum viginti annorum viz. pro viginti tribus folidis quos mihi præ manibus integre pacaverunt ut toto tempore hujus conventionis fint quieti omnino ab omnibus rebus. Et ego et heredes mei interim omnes prædictas partes terræ warrantizabimus prædictis monachis ufque ad terminum fuum contra omnes homines et feminas. Tradidi prædictis monachis præfatam terram ad feftum S. Michaelis anno Incarnatione Domini millefimo ducentefimo et in fine præfatorum viginti annorum omnes prædictas partes terræ ad me quiete revertentur vel ad heredes meos Quod fi ego interim deceffero et aliqua prædictarum partium devenerit in dotem Margar[etæ] uxoris meæ heres meus prædictæ uxori meæ vel per aliam terram vel quomodo poterit fatiffaciet ut monachi prædicta omnia in pace et fine inquietudine teneant ufque ad terminum fuum. Hanc igitur conventionem fideliter et fine malo ingenio tenendam affidavimus in omnibus ego et Margareta uxor mea de nobis et heredibus noftris. Et quia volo eos in omnibus effe fecuros ego dictus Rogerus omnia prædicta hoc chirographo figillo meo impreffo confirmavi. His teftibus Galfrido de Dene, Ricardo de Weftbiri, Rogero de Erderne, Hugone Cherke, Galfrido fratre meo, et Henrico fratre meo, et multis aliis. Ad terminum.

No. 68.
REDDITUS CERÆ.

[1] The back of the Roll now commences, but, as a part has been formerly cut off, I can only collect the following—

---
[1] This note is by Sir Thos. Phillipps.

Carta Hervici [Hervei] aliquando..........
Carta ...... reddita eſt et fracta.
Carta prima Jordani de Glouc. quam habuit de Abbate Alano reddita eſt et fracta.
Carta Godefridi Mogge reddita eſt et fracta.
Carta ... .. (eraſed) ſancti monialis fracta eſt.

Then follows, in regular order, but damaged by being a little *rongé* at the ſides:
Debent nobis Redditus ceræ de Eleemoſyna.
...go Capellanus unam libram ceræ.
... .. Capellanus de ...... dimidiam libram ceræ. Ad Aſſumptionem.
...... Capellanus de Ledebiri dimidiam libram. Ad Aſſumptionem.
.... unam libram ceræ in Aſſumptione.
...... Alwredu le Blunt unam libram ceræ ad feſtum S. Mariæ et corpus ſuum ad ſepulturam.
...... de Glouceſtria.
... al. filius Alweredi de Neweham unam libram ceræ annuatim ad nativitatem S. Mariæ.
...... ardus de Brotheſtun unam libram ceræ ad nativitatem S. Mariæ.
...... filius Ædwardi dimidiam libram ceræ.
...... de Monemuta unam libram ceræ et Nicolaus filius ejus unam libram ceræ.
Gruinard? de Monemuta unam libram ceræ.
.... ſſur dimidiam libram ceræ.
...... filius Oſmundi unam libram ceræ ad feſtum S. Michaelis.
...... Albus de Briſtoc unam libram ceræ.
...... de Upton unam libram ceræ ad feſtum S. Michaelis.
......dus de Weſton et Hepenill unam libram in die Aſſumptionis.
.... de Kenecoſtre dimidiam libram in Aſſumptione.
......auriga unam libram ceræ.
Galfridus le Mercer unam libram ceræ.
... frater Walteri Porterel unam libram ceræ.
...... le Schereman unam libram ceræ.
...... Cherebule unam libram ceræ.
...... Faber ferarum libram ceræ.
......ltr le Deveneis unam libram ceræ.
Willelmus Vinarius dimidiam libram ceræ.
....de Waltun dimidiam libram ceræ.

Reginaldus Lob. (?) unam libram ceræ.
...... faber ferrarum unam libram ceræ.
Robertus Calvus unam libram ceræ.
Henricus Mercer unam libram ceræ in Affumptione S. Mariæ.
Hugo Job unam libram ceræ in Affumptione S. Mariæ.
Simon filius Willelmi de Bikenore unam libram.
Godefridus Bate unam dimidiam libram ceræ.
Simon le Mercer de Glouceftria, unam libram ceræ.
Ricardus filius Jordani, unam libram ceræ.
Rogerus filius Hugonis de Neweham unam libram ceræ.
Simeon de Neweham unam libram ceræ.
Herbertus de Glouceftria qui venit cum Azone fratre Abbatis unam libram ceræ.

No. 69.

CARTA JORDANI [FILII RADULPHI DE TERRAM COM. WILTON.]

Sciant præfentes et futuri quod ego Alanus dictus Abbas de Dene et ejufdem loci conventus conceffimus Jordano filio Radulphi totam terram illam quæ eft de feudo [noftro] in Salefbiri et illam juxta quæ eft de feodo Abbatiffæ de Romefie quas habuimus de teftamento Henrici Kais ficut Ofmundus pater ejus eas tenuit. Quarum prima incipit juxta terram Prioris de Lanthonia, fecunda terminatur in Scrudelone, Tenendas de domo noftra in perpetuum fibi et heredibus fuis liberas et quietas ab omnibus fervitiis exceptis fervitiis capitalium dominorum, viz. pro undecim folidis et obolo annuatim reddendis in quatuor anni terminis, primam partem in natali Domini, fecundam in Annunciatione, tertiam in natali Sancti Joannis Baptiftæ, quartam in fefto Sancti Michaelis. Et ipfe Jordanus pro hac ipfa conceffione de minifterio fuo et ut frater domus noftræ in eo quod poterit domui noftræ miniftrabit. Et ut hæc conventio firma et rata sit in perpetuum hac carta figillo noftro impreffa ei confirmavimus. His teftibus Ernifio filii Ketelb,' Ricardo Burgeis, Henrico Calvo, Roberto Calvo, et aliis.

No. 70.

CARTA GODEFRIDI MOG.

Sciant præfentes et futuri quod ego Alanus dictus Abbas de Dene et ejufdem loci conventus conceffimus Godefrido Mog et heredibus fuis terram noftram quæ eft inter terram canonicorum et terram Walteri Crucche in vico fabrorum tenendam de nobis in feodo firmam liberam et quietam ab omnibus fervitiis ad nos pertinentibus pro tribus folidis annuatim reddendis in quatuor terminis, fcilicet, in natali Domini, in Annunciatione Sanctæ Mariæ, in nativitate Sancti Joannis, in fefto Sancti Michaelis in quolibet termino novem denarios, et ipfe Godefridus juramentum præftitit quod fidelis erit ecclefiæ noftræ et quod per eum non elongabitur terra noftra a nobis aliquo modo. Ut hæc conventio rata fit et ftabilis hanc cartam figillo noftro confirmavimus. His teftibus Ricardo Rufo, Willelmo Burgeis, Roberto Tholi, Ricardo filio ben...... Ferrario.

No. 71.

(Chirographum Rogeri Paris fcriptum eft- in alia parte Rotuli inter Chirographa de Neweham).

The deed referred to is probably No. 43.

No. 72.

CARTA MAGISTRI JOCELINI QUAM FECIT ALICIÆ DE GLOUCESTRIA DE TERRA LONDONIARUM.

Sciant præfentes et futuri quod ego Magifter Jocelinus Clericus Willelmi Marefcalli dedi et conceffi Aliciæ de Glouceftria pro Dei amore in fervitio fuo totam terram meam in London de Cheringa cum omnibus pertinentiis fuis quam Dominus Willelmus Marefcallus mihi dedit pro fervitio meo ita libere et quiete habendam et tenendam de Domino meo Willelmo Marefcallo ficut carta ipfius quam ipfe Willelmus mihi dedit teftatur. Et ut hæc mea donatio rata et firma permaneat præfenti carta figilli impreffione mei corroborata confirmo. His teftibus Philippo de Sancto Matthæo London. Capellano meo, Hugone Argent, Rogero Argent, Willelmo Argent, hominibus meis ; Ofmundo filio Henrici Kes, et Henrico fratre ejus ; Ricardo capellano ; Ada filio Fulconis ; Willelmo filio Hernifii.

No. 73.

CONFIRMATIO WILLELMI MARESCALLI EIDEM ALICIÆ DE SUPRADICTA TERRA LONDONIARUM.

Willelmus Marefcallus omnibus hominibus et amicis fuis Francis et Anglis præfentibus et futuris falutem. Noveritis me dediffe et conceffiffe et hac præfenti carta mea confirmaffe ad petitionem Jocelini clerici mei Aliciæ de Glouceftria forori Willelmi T...... et heredibus fuis totam terram meam de Cheringa cum omnibus pertinentiis fuis liberam et quietam de me et heredibus meis [ab] omni fervitio pro una libra piperis ad feftum Sancti Michaelis Reddendo mihi et heredibus meis falvo hoftagio meo ad cuftum meum. His, fcilicet, teftibus, Philippo de Salefburi, Alano de Sancto Georgio, Nicolao, Avenel, Joanne Juvene Marefcallo, Hugone de Samford, Willelmo Waleran, Ricardo de Stutefcumba, Joanne filio Simonis, Roberto de Ponte, Waltero Camerario, Humfrido Marefcallo, Rogero Capellano, Michaele, Pentecofte, Willelmo, Clericis, Thoma [de] Rupe, Ada de Crendun, Rogero de Cheddeworthe, et multis aliis.

No. 74.
CARTA MAGISTRI JOCELINI DE EO QUOD SE IPSUM VIVUM ET MORTUUM DEDIT ECCLESIÆ NOSTRÆ.

Sciant præfentes et futuri ad quos præfens fcriptum pervenerit quod ego Magifter Jocelinus Clericus Willelmi Marefcalli dedi me vivum et mortuum Deo et Beatæ Mariæ de Dene in præfentia Domini Ricardi Abbatis et ejufdem loci conventus. Ibique locum fepulturæ meæ elegi ubicunque mortuus fuero, et ut hæc donatio mea rata et firma permaneat præfenti fcripto impreffione figilli mei corroborato confirmo. His teftibus Philippo de Sancto Matthæo London. Capellano meo, Ada filio Fulconis, Ofmundo filio Henrici Kes, Willelmo filio Hernifii.

No. 75.
CARTA OSBERNI FILII WALTERI DE WICH.

Sciant præfentes et futuri quod ego Ricardus dictus Abbas de Dena et ejufdem loci conventus conceffimus Ofberno filio Walteri de Wich in feodi firmam totam terram illam quæ fuit Aluredi fratris noftri quondam fervientis Margaretæ uxoris Herberti filii Arnaldi filii Cutelb' quam prædicta Margareta dedit ei pro fervitio fuo quæ fita eft inter terram prædicti Ernaldi et Walteri le Hore in placea fabrorum, fuitque Sevari filii Bernardi, tenendam et habendam de nobis liberam et quietam ab omni fervitio pro tribus folidis annuatim in quatuor terminis reddendis, fcilicet, ad feftum Sanctæ Mariæ in Martio novem denarios, ad Natale Sancti Joannis Baptiftæ novem denarios, ad feftum Sancti Michaelis novem denarios, ad natale Domini novem denarios. Hanc prædictam terram warrantizabimus contra omnes homines et [a] laudgabulo acquietabimus. Ita quod ipfe vel heredes fui prædictam terram nec vendent nec dabunt nec in vadimonium ponent nec efcambiabunt nec alio modo ab Ecclefia noftra alienabunt fine licentia noftra. Pro hac conceffione prædictus Ofbernus homagium fecit Ecclefiæ noftræ cum juramento de prædicta conventione ex parte fua fideliter tenenda et unum bizantium dedit nobis de introitu. Et nos ei et heredibus fuis hanc conceffionem hujus chirographi divifione confirmamus. Sigillum vero noftrum propter perfidiam Judæorum non appofuimus. His teftibus Ricardo filio Jordani, Ernaldo filio Cutelb', Ricardo filio Willelmi Burg[eis], Roberto Toli, Jordano filio Radulphi focero ejus, et multis aliis.

No. 76.

REDDITUS DE DIMMOC.

Willelmus de Dunhantun octo folidos ad quatuor terminos et arare tres acras et feminare de hibernagio de femine fuo et herciare equo fuo et ad trameis' arare quatuor acras et feminare de femine noftro et herciare in autumpno ad meffionem per tres dies tres homines ad cultum fuum et quarto die duos homines et ad falcationem prati unum hominem per unum diem et habebit obolum ad potum et adjuvabit ad fœnum levandum. Omnia hæc folebat facere.

  Radulphus de la Hulle tam in redditibus quam in operibus.
  Ricardus Faber xvii fol. viii*d*.
  Robertus Withorn viii fol. et ad meffionem tres homines.
  Willelmus de Abenhale viii fol.
  Mabilia de Munftre vs. vi*d*. et ad meffionem tres homines.
  Galfridus de la Mora ij*s*.
  Aldit Berde ij*s*. vj*d*. et ad meffionem tres homines.
  Dominus de Bachinesfeld folet reddere ij*s*.

---

[1] In Sir Thomas Phillipps' transcript this word is marked as doubtful, probably it should be 'terminos.'

Flaxley Abbey.

Mald Simonis xij*d*. et ad meſſionem tres homines.
Robertus Turpin ij*s*. ij*d*.
Henricus Rotarius xij*d*.
Johannes Luefred iij*s*. et ad meſſionem tres homines.
Terra quæ fuit Rogeri le Norreis v*s*. et ad meſſionem tres homines.
Willelmus Seilard iij*s*. do. do.
Rogerus Longus iij*s*. do. do.
Hugo Pauper iiij*s*. do. do.
Emma Cupping i*s*. vi*d*. do. do.
Hulle Baterich i*s*. do. do.
Alexander Cockel i*s*. do. do.
Wiraundus de Sortegrave vi*d*. do. do.
Malle de Sortegrave vi*d*. do. do.
Willelmus de Wildecote i*s*. do. do.
Radulphus Spondre i*s*. iiij*d*. do. do.
Heredes Ricardi de Bosco pro quatuor acris quæ jacent contra domum Willelmi de Abenhale viij*d*. et pro quinque feillonibus quæ jacent juxta terram Rogeri Longi et terram Ricardi Fabri juxta Haicium ad meſſionem duos homines.
Walterus Haket ij*d*. ob. ad feſtum ſanćti Æthelberti pro tribus acris quas tenet in Brocrigge in capite campi verſus orientem ad tempus vitæ ſua.
Willelmus ......ue iij*s*. vj*d*. pro dimidio Burgagio et pro una acra.
Mahel pro dimidio Burgagio ij*s*. et de hoc redditu reddendi ſunt ad Niwent iiij*s*. pro nomine decimæ et Domino Regi xv*d*. de Langablo.
Giliana Taillur i*s*. vi*d*.
Domus quam Malle de Henneberge tenuit [de] Margareta Bateric ii*s*. de Kenepel et ad meſſionem tres homines apud Dimoc.
Robertus Mainhaggere ij*s*. ad infirmitorium fecularium et ad meſſionem tres homines
Summa redditus de Dimoc iiij*li*. ix*s*. ix*d*. ob.

No. 77.

PRIVILEGIUM PAPÆ CELESTINI TERTII DE LIBERTATIBUS
[ABBATIÆ SANCTÆ MARIÆ DE DENE DATUM 1192.]

Celeftinus Epifcopus fervus fervorum Dei, dilectis filiis ... Abbati monafterii sanctæ Mariæ de Dena ejusque fratribus tam præfentibus quam futuris regularem vitam profeffis in perpetuum [falutem et Apoftolicam benedictione.] Religiofam vitam eligentibus Apoftolicum convenit adeffe præfidium ne forte cujuflibet temeritatis incurfus aut eos a propofito revocet aut robur, quod abfit, facræ religionis infringat. Ea propter dilecti in Domino filii, veftris juftis poftulationibus clementer annuimus, et præfatum Monafterium sanctæ Dei genetricis et Virginis Mariæ de Dena in quo divino mancipati eftis obfequio, fub Sancti Petri et noftra protectione fufcipimus et præfentis fcripti privilegio communimus. Inprimis fiquidem ftatuentes ut ordo monafticus qui fecundum Deum et Beati Benedicti regulam in eodem monafterio inftitutus effe dinofcitur perpetuis ibidem temporibus obfervetur. Præterea quascunque poffeffiones quæcunque jura idem monafterium in præfentiarum jufte et canonice poffidet aut in futurum conceffione Pontificum, largitione regum vel principum, oblatione fidelium feu aliis juftis modis, præftante Domino, poterit adipifci, firma vobis veftrifque fucceffibus et illibata permaneant in quibus hæc primis duximus exprimenda vocabulis : locum ipfum in quo præfatum monafterium fitum eft cum omnibus pertinentiis fuis fane laborum veftrorum quos propriis manibus aut fumptibus colitis tam de terris cultis quam incultis, five de hortis et virgultis et pifcationibus veftris vel de nutrimentis animalium veftrorum nullus a vobis decimas exigere vel extorquere præfumat. Liceat quoque vobis clericos vel laicos liberos et abfolutos e feculo fugientes ad converfionem recipere et eos abfque contradictione aliqua retinere. Prohibemus ut nulli fratrum veftrorum poft factam in veftro monafterio profeffionem fas fit abfque abbatis fui licentia de eodem loco difcedere ; difcedentem vero abfque communium litterarum cautione nullus audeat retinere. Quod fi quis forte retinere præfumpferit licitum fit vobis in ipfos monachos five converfos fententium regularem proferre. Illud diftrictius inhibentes ne terras feu quidlibet beneficium ecclefiæ veftræ collatum fit licitum perfonaliter dare five alio modo alienare abfque confenfu totius capituli vel majoris partis et fanioris. Si quæ vero donationes vel alienationes aliter quam dictum eft factæ fuerint eas irritas cenfemus. Ad hæc etiam prohibemus ne aliquis monachus sive converfus fub profeffione domus veftræ aftrictus fine cenfenfu et licentia Abbatis et majoris partis capituli pro aliquo fide jubeat vel ab aliquo pecuniam mutuo recipiat ultra pretium capituli veſtri igitur conſtitutum niſi propter manifeſtam domus veſtræ utilitatem. Quod ſi facere præſumpſerit non teneatur conventus pro his aliquatenus reſpondere. Licitum præterea ſit vobis in omnibus [cauſis] propriis ſive civilem ſive criminalem contineant quæſtionem fratrum veſtrorum teſtimoniis uti, ne pro defectu teſtium jus veſtrorum in aliquo valeat deperire. Inſuper auctoritate apoſtolica inhibemus ne ullus Epiſcopus vel quælibet alia perſona ad ſinodos vel conventus forenſes vos ire vel judicio ſeculari de veſtra propria ſubſtantia vel poſſeſſionibus veſtris ſubjicere compellat, nec ad domos veſtras cauſa ordines celebrandi cauſas tractandi vel aliquos publicos conventus provocandi venire præſumat, nec regularem electionem Abbatis veſtri impediat aut de inſtituendo vel removendo eo qui pro tempore fuerit contra Statuta Ciſtercienſis ordinis ac aliquatenus intromittat. Si vero Epiſcopus in cujus parochia domus veſtra fundata eſt cum humilitate ac devotione qua convenit requiſitus ſubſtitutum Abbatem benedicere et alia quæ ad officium Epiſcopale pertinent vobis conferre forte renuerit, licitum ſit eidem Abbati ſi tamen ſacerdos fuerit proprios novitios benedicere et alia quæ ad officium ſuum pertinent exercere, et vobis omnia ab alio Epiſcopo percipere quæ a veſtro fuerint indebite denegata. Illud adjicientes ut in recipiendis profeſſionibus quæ a benedictis vel benedicendis Abbatibus exhibentur ea ſunt epiſcopi forma ut expreſſione contenti quæ ab origine ordinis noſcitur inſtituta, ut ſcilicet Abbates ipſi ſalvo ordine ſuo profiteri debeant, et contra ſtatuta ſui ordinis nullum profeſſionem facere appellantur. Pro conſecrationibus vero altarium vel eccleſiarum ſuarum pro oleo ſancto vel quolibet eccleſiaſtico ſacramento unllus a vobis ſub oſtentu conſuetudinis vel alio modo quocumque audeat extorquere. Si hæc omnia gratis vobis Epiſcopus diœceſanus impendat alio quin liceat vobis quemcunque malueritis catholicum adire antiſtitem gratiam et communionem ſacroſanctæ Romanæ ſedis habentem qui noſtra fretus auctoritate vobis quod poſtulatur impendat. Quod ſi ſedes diœceſani epiſcopi forte vacaverit interim omnia eccleſiaſtica ſacramenta a vicinis epiſcopis accipere libere et abque contradictione poſſitis. Sic tamen ut ex hoc in poſterum propriis epiſcopis nullum prejudicium generetur. Quia vero interdum propriorum epiſcoporum copiam non habetis ſi quem epiſcopum Romanæ ſedis induximus communionem habentem et de quo plenam notitiam habeatis per vos tranſire contigerit ab illo benedictionem vaſorum et veſtium, conſecrationes altarium, ordinationes monachorum auctoritate ſedis Apoſtolicæ recipere valeatis. Porro ſi epiſcopi vel alii eccleſiarum rectores in monaſteria veſtro vel perſonas in ibi conſtitutas ſuſpenſionis et excommunicationis vel interdicti ſententiam promulgaverit ſeu etiam in mercem [... dena]rios veſtros pro eo quod decimas non ſolvitis vel aliqua occaſione eorum quæ ab apoſtolica benignitate vobis indulta ... ſeu benefactores veftros pro eo quod aliqua vobis beneficia vel obfequia ex caritate præftiterint vel ad laborandum adjuven ......in illis diebus in quibus vos laboratis et alii feriantur eandem fententiam protulerint ipfam tanquam contra fedis apoftolicæ indulta prolatam decernimus irritandum nec literæ ullæ firmitatem habeant quas tacite nomine Cifterticnfis ordinis ... contra tenorem apoftolicorum privilegiorum conftiterit impetrari. Præterea cum commune interdictum terræ fuerit liceat vobis in veftro monafterio [claufis januis] exclufis excommunicatis et interdictis nihilominus divina officia celebrare. Paci quoque et tranquillitati veftræ paterna in pofterum folicitudine providere volentes auctoritate apoftolica prohibemus ut infra claufuras locorum feu grangiarum veftrarum nullus rapinam feu furtum facere, ignem apponere, fanguinem fundere, hominem temere capere vel interficere feu [aliquam] violentiam audeat exercere. Præterea omnes libertates et immunitates et libertates a prædeceſſoribus noftris piæ recordationis Romanis Pontificibus ordini veftro conceſſas necnon libertates et exemptiones fecularium exactionum a regibus et principibus vel aliis fidelibus rationabiliter vobis indultas auctoritate apoftolica confirmamus, et præfentis fcripti privilegio communimus. Decernimus ergo ut nulli omnino hominum liceat præfatum monafterium temere perturbare, aut ejus poſſeſſiones auferre vel ablatas retinere, minuere, feu quibuflibet vexationibus fatigare, fed omnia integra conferventur eorum pro quorum gubernatione ac fuftentatione conceſſa funt ufibus omnimodis pro futura falva fedis apoftolicae auctoritate. Si qua igitur in futurum ecclefiaftica fecularifve perfona hanc veftræ conftitutionis paginam fciens, contra eam temere venire tentaverit fecundo tertiove commonita nifi reatum fuum congrua fatiſſactione correxerit, poteftatis honorifque sui dignitate careat, reamque fe Divino judicio exiftere de perpetrata iniquitate cognofcat, et a facratiſſimo corpore ac fanguine Dei et Domini Redemptoris Noftri Jefu Chrifti aliena fiat, atque in extremo examine diftrictæ ultioni fubjaceat. Cunctis autem eidem loco fua jura fervantibus fit pax Domini Noftri Jefu Chrifti quatenus hic fructum bonæ actionis percipiant et apud diftrictum Judicem præmia æternæ pacis inveniant. Amen. Amen.

Datum Romæ apud Sanctum Petrum per manum Ægidii Sancti Nicolai in carcere Tulliano Diaconi Cardinalis Idibus Junii Indictione decima, Incarnationis Dominicæ Anno MCXCII, Pontificatus vero Domini Cæleftini Papæ tertii anno fecundo.[1]

[1] The MS. gives a rough fketch of the papal feal, on the border of which occurs a verfe from Pfalm xvi—*Perfice greſſus meos in femitis tuis.* The centre of the feal bears the following infcription :—

Scs	Scs
Petrus	Paulus
Celes	tinus
pp	III

No. 78.
LITERÆ DOMINI W. HEREFORDENSIS EPISCOPI UNIVERSIS EPISCOPATUS CAPELLANIS (SIGILLATÆ).

W. Dei Gratia Herefordenfis ecclefiæ minifter humilis univerfis Epifcopatus Herefordenfis capellanis falutem et benedictionem. Ex debito poteftatis noftræ nobis incumbit Religioforum qui fub nobis funt paci et tranquillitate providere confulere et congaudere. Quod ficut debemus ita et volumus ; In his præcipue in quibus magiftram habemus Apoftolicæ sedis auctoritatem igitur pro dilectis filiis noftris monachis de Dene univerfitati veftræ præcipiendo mandamus. Quatenus cum aliquis contra ipsorum monachorum privilegia eosdem gravare vel in'eorum fratres vel res injuftam manum injicere præfumpferit eorundem monachorum voluntati acquiefcatis fuper eifdem malefactoribus fuis et excommunicationis fententia feriendis cum vobis innotuerit privilegiorum tenor et delinquentium culpa et monachorum gravamen eofque non ex peccato Archidiaconi vel diaconi concilio vel præcepto præfentium auctoritate literarum excommunicare non differatis.

No. 79.
PRIVILEGIUM DOMINI ALEXANDRI III. PAPÆ DE DECIMIS [PRO ABBATIA DE FLEXLECHE.]

Alexander Epifcopus, Servus Servorum Dei, venerabili fratri Cantuarenfi Archiepifcopo Apoftolicæ Sedis Legato et fuffraganeis ejus et dilectis filiis Archidiaconis, Decanis et Prælatis in ejus Diœcefi conftitutis, salutem et Apoftolicam benedictionem. Audivimus et audientes vehementi fumus admiratione turbati quod cum fratres de Flexleche ficut alii Cifterliencis ordinis a folutione decimarum de laboribus fuis quos propriis manibus vel fumptibus excolunt de benignitate fedis Apoftolicæ liberi fint et penitus immunes quidam clerici et laici veftræ jurifdictionis ab eis nihilominus contra indulgentiam fedis Apoftolicæ decimas exigere per violentiam non verentur interpretatione prava et finiftra Apoftolici capitium (?) privilegii pervertentes afferendo de novalibus debere intelligi ubi nofcitur de laboribus effe infcriptum. Quum igitur manifeftum et omnibus qui recte fapiunt interpretationem hujusmodi perverfam effe et intuitui fano contrariam cum fecundum capitulum illud a folutione decimarum tam de terris illis quas deduxerunt vel deducunt ad cultum quam de terris cultis quas ipsi propriis manibus vel fumptibus excolunt penitus fint immunes ne ullus habeat contra eos de cætero materiam malignandi vel ipfos quomodolibet contra jufticiam moleftandi univerfitati veftræ per Apoftolica fcripta præcipiendo mandamus quatenus univerfis veftræ poteftati fubjectis auctoritate Apoftolica diftrictius prohibere curetis ne a memoratis fratribus de Flexleche de novalibus vel etiam de aliis terris quas propriis manibus vel fumptibus excolunt feu de nutrimentis animalium fuorum ullatenus decimas exigere vel extorquere præfumat. Nam fi de novalibus tam voluiffemus intelligi ubi ponimus de laboribus de novalibus feciffemus apponi ficut in privilegiis quorundam aliorum apponimus. Quia vero periculofum eis eft ut contra privilegia fedis Apoftolicæ quoquomodo venire præfumant qui obtinere debent inviolabilem firmitatem præfentium vobis auctoritate præcipiendo mandamus quatinus fi qui de ordine ecclefiaftico vel feculari contra privilegia fedis Apoftolicæ prædictos fratres port commonitionem veftram decimarum exactione gravaverint laicos excommunicationis fententia procellatis, viros autem ecclefiafticos contradictione et appellatione ...... ceffante ab officio fufpendatis et tam excommunicationis quam fufpenfionis fententiam obfervetis et faciatis ufque ad dignam fatiffactionem inviolabiliter obfervari nifi conventio forte facta fuerit inter eos ex qua decimas aut aliquid pro eis folvere teneantur. Si vero contra memoratos fratres de Flexleche fuper decimis vel aliis quæ ordini Ciftertienfi fpecialiter Apoftolica fedes indulfit, nulla facta Ciftertienfis ordinis mentione literæ fuerint a nobis veritate tacita impetratæ nullum eis prejudicium valeant generare. Ad hoc iterum vobis præcipiendo mandamus quatenus fi quis in fratres præfcripti monafterii manus violenter injecerit, accenfis candelis excommunicatum publice nuncietis et faciatis ab omnibus ficut excommunicatum diftrictius evitari donec paffis injuriam congrue fatiffaciat et abfolvendus cum literis diœcesani Episcopi rei veritatem continentibus fi venire potuerit Apoftolico fe confpectu reprefentet.

Datum Anagniæ iii Kalendas Novembris.

Duo alia privilegia habemus a domino Papa Alexandro tertio et unum a domino Papa Eugenio quæ non funt fcripta in hoc rotulo. Omnia privilegia noftra funt quinque.

No. 80.
CATALOGUS LIBRORUM.

Numerus Librorum noftroru Bibliotheca in tribus voluminibus.
Auguftinus fuper "Beatus eft vir."
Petrus Lumbardus fuper Pfalterium in tribus voluminibus.
Petrus Lumbardus fuper Epiftolas Pauli in duobus voluminibus.
Gilbertus ... .erianus fuper Pfalterium.
Sententiæ Petri Lumbardi.
Hiftoria Scholaftica Petri Manducatoris.
Judicum et Jofuæ gloffæ in uno volumine.
Actus Apoftolorum gloffæ; Apoftoli Jacobi gloffæ in eodem.
Matthæus gloffatus.
Epiftolae canonicae glossatae.
Apocalypfis Canticum Canticorum Ecclefiafticus Glos. in uno volumine.
Parabolæ Salomonis et Tobias, Ruth in eodem loco gloffata.
Item Cantica gloffata.
Epiftolæ Decretales.
Decreta Ivonis ;—De Dedicatione Ecclesiæ in eodem.
Vitæ Patrum.
Malogranatus.
Paffionalis Liber Antiquus.
Paffionalis Liber novus ;—Vita Sancti Bernardi in eodem.
Vita Sancti Malachiæ in quaternis.
Vita Sancti Godrici.
Cronicæ Ivonis.
Miracula Sanctæ Mariæ.
Collationes decem.
Diadema Monachorum.
Auguftinus de Trinitate.
Auguftinus fuper epiftolam Johannis primam et de Penitentia et Hugo de Clericali Difciplina in eodem.
Liber Confeffionum Auguftini.
Regula Sancti Auguftini et quidam Sermones.
Hugo fuper Regulam Sancti-Auguftini et de Clericali Difciplina et quidam Sermones.

Gregorius super primam partem Job in quaterniis.
Gregorius super Ezechielem.
Paſtorale Gregorii et Canticum Canticorum expoſita et quædam alia.
Speculum de morali Gregorii
Iſidori Etymologiarum [liber]
Omeliæ Euſebii Aniceni et Sermones Cæſarii Epiſcopi "quod arbore .... ſimiliter."
Literæ et quidam ſermones et Bernardinus de dictaminibus ſimul.
Quod est tri[bul]are et quidam tractatus de Cruce et quædam alia ſimul.
De tribus principalibus protegendis et moralium dogma et Libellus Martini Epiſcopi ſimul.
Omne Caput languidum.
Hugo de Arca Nöe.
Hugo " Principium et Cauſa."
Auguſtinus [de] Abuſivis;—Benjamin de Clauſtra animæ ſimul.
Bernardi conſideratio num qua ab animali de amore Dei miſſus est contra Angelus [in] quaterniis.
Bernardi Liber apologeticus de Dei gratia et libero arbitrio; de diligendo Deo.
De gradibus humilitatis'; vos qui .... eſtis; et quædam alia simul.
Sermones Babino.
Sermones Roberti Pullani.
Speculum eccleſiæ; Sermones per annum; de tabernaculis ſimul.
Petrus Manducator de Sacramentis. Alanique Walteri et alia quædam.
Sermones Abbatis Ivonis.
Lumina Magiſtri Johannis Belet et Ricardus de Miſſa.
Abbreviatio Amalarii.
Iſidorus de officiis eccleſiaſticis. Exiit edictum et ſermones ſimul.
Auguſtinus de Sermone Domini in Monte.
Pars epiſtolarum Petri Ales et excerpta de gloſſis Evangelii.
Rationes theologicæ et Pater noſter Petri Pictavienſis.
De libero arbitrio Roberti Meludi et allegoriæ ſuper vetus Teſtamentum.
Auguſtinus contra ......nicium. Idem contra paſcentium, et idem Exameron contra Vianus (?). Beda ſuper Canticum Abacuc.
Petrus Manducator de Sacramentis et quædam alia.

Item duo volumina parva de excerptis—*in asseribus.*
Duo libri Anglici.
Gallice—Vita St. Godrici.
Gallice—Vita St. Thomæ Martyris.
Phyficus Liber, Anglice.
Paffio Sanctæ Margaretæ.
Compilationes quæ incipiunt " De decem plagis ;"
Do. .do. " Perfona eft."
Item de Sancto Vincentio Sermo et alia quædam.
De Miraculis Sancti Nicolai et alia quædam.
Ante Cham virgituam(?).
Libellus prognofticorum et alia ante.

Hic eft finis Catalogi librorum.

No. 81.

CARTA PHILIPPI DE BURCI QUAM FECIT WILLELMO DE SANCTO LEODEGARIO.

Sciant præfentes et futuri quod ego Philippus de Burci dedi et conceffi Willelmo de Sancto Leodegario totam terram meam de Ragel cum omnibus pertinentiis fuis liberam et quietam de me et heredibus meis in perpetuum tenendam reddendo mihi et heredibus meis fingulis annis unum bifantium pro duobus folidis ac de hoc redditu fatisfecit mihi præ manibus ipfe Willelmus et heredibus meis ufque ad annum Incarnationis Dominicæ millefimo ducentefimo vigefimo quarto et de illo bizantio vel de illis duobus folidis folvendis tempore illo fecuritatem fide interpofita mihi fecit et iterum faciet ipfe vel heredes fui mihi vel heredibus meis tempore prænominato. Prædictus autem Willelmus et heredes fui tenebunt fupradictam terram de Capitali Domino meo, fcilicet Willelmo filio Roberti filii Martini et heredibus ejus [de] donatione et conceffione mea, et homagium facient illi pro prædicta terra et omne fervitium quod ad prædictam terram pertinet facient illis, fcilicet, fervitium duarum partium unius militis. Ego enim Philippus adduxi prædictum Willelmum de Sancto Leodegario in curiam Domini mei de Blachedun, et ibidem prædictum Willelmum propria manu mea domino meo tradidi et homagium suum de prædicta terra ipsi domino meo facere feci et totum jus quod ad me et heredes meos pertinebat prædicto domino meo et heredibus suis in perpetuum ego et Galfridus filius meus quietum-clamavimus præter bizantium vel duos solidos post prædictum terminum mihi vel heredibus meis reddendos et præter securitatem quam de eodem bizantio tunc fecit mihi et post prædictum terminum iterum facturus est mihi vel heredibus meis ipse vel heredes sui. Hanc autem donationem et concessionem seçi prædicto Willelmo de Sancto Leodegario pro servitio suo et pro quindecim marcis argenti quas mihi dedit præ manibus et pro octoginta marcis et centum solidis de quibus me acquietavit versus Manasserum Judæum de Bristol. Et hanc donationem et concessionem firmiter et legaliter tenendam illi et heredibus suis ego pro me et heredibus meis et Galfridus filius meus pro se et heredibus suis affidavimus et hanc terram et hanc donationem warrantizabimus ego et heredes mei in perpetuum prædicto Willelmo et heredibus ejus contra omnes homines. Facta est autem prædicta donatio [anno] ab Incarnatione Domini millesimo centesimo nonagesimo tertio in festo Sancti Michaelis. Ut hoc ratum permaneat præsenti carta sigillo meo impressa prædictam donationem confirmavi. His testibus Roberto de Berkelai, Roberto Juvene, Joanne de Herleia, Willelmo de Morevilla, Willelmo Martel, Rogero de Riveria, Roberto de Sancta Cruce, Rogero de Aldewike, Ricardo Clerico de Thornberi, Daniele Russo, Joanne la Warre, et Petro fratre ejus, Willelmo Cordwanerio et multis aliis.

No. 82.

ITEM ALIA EJUSDEM QUAM FECIT EIDEM.[1]

Sciant præsentes et futuri quod ego Philippus de Burci dedi et concessi Willelmo de Sancto Leodegario et heredibus suis totam terram meam de Ragel cum omnibus pertinentiis suis tenendam in perpetuum in feodi firmam de me et heredibus meis pro quindecim marcis argenti quas mihi præ manibus et pro octoginta marcis et centum solidis quibus ipse Willelmus acquietavit me et prædictam terram de manibus Manasseri Judæi de Bristol.

---

[1] Under this grant appears the following :—" Duas alias fecit idem Philippus de Burci eidem Willelmo de Sancto Leodegario quas habemus."

Prædictus autem Willelmus vel heredes sui reddent mihi vel heredibus meis singulis annis duos solidos vel unum bizantium pro omni servitio quod ad me vel heredes meos pertineat sed de hoc redditu satisfecit prædictus Willelmus præ manibus usque ad triginta et unum annos. Quare idem Willelmus et heredes sui tenebunt et habebunt præfatam terram usque ad præfatam terminum triginta et unius annorum solutam et liberam ab omnibus servitiis et consuetudinibus et demandis quæ ad me et ad heredes meos pertinent salvo regali servitio et servitio Capitalis Domini mei quod ad prædictam terram pertinet scilicet duabus partibus servitii unius militis. Hanc autem conventionem fideliter tenendam affidavi ego Philippus de Burci pro me et heredibus meis et Galfridus filius meus pro se et heredibus suis prædicto Willelmo et heredibus suis in perpetuum. Hæc autem conventio facta fuit ad festum Sancto Michaelis [anno] ab Incarnatione Domini 1193. Et ut hoc ratum permaneat, præsenti carta sigillo meo impressa prædictam donationem confirmavi. His testibus Roberto Juvene, Joanne de Herleia, Roberto de Everci, Willelmo Martel, Baderone de . Treget, Rogero de Riveria, Joanne filio Simonis, Roberto de Ponte, Petro de Wintreburna, Ricardo Clerico de Thornbire, Joanne la Warre et Petro fratre ejus, Daniele Rufo, Willelmo Cordewanerio, et multis aliis.

No. 83.

CONFIRMATIO CAPITALIS DOMINI QUAM FECIT WILLELMUS FILIUS ROBERTI FILII MARTINI.

Sciant tam præsentes quam futuri quod ego Willelmus filius Roberti filii Martini concessi et præsenti carta mea confirmavi ad petitionem et concessionem Philippi de Burci totam terram de Ragel cum omnibus pertinentiis suis Willelmo de Sancto Leodegario et heredibus suis de me et heredibus meis tenendam, sicut carta prædicto Philippi testatur libere et quiete, scilicet, quod præfatus Willelmus debet inde facere duas partes [servitii] unius militis. Ita quod ab anno Incarnationis Domini millesimo ducentesimo vigesimo quarto debet ipse Willelmus vel heredes sui solvere unum bizantium annuatim ad festum Sancti Michaelis prædicto Philippo vel heredibus suis et inde cepi homagium sepedicti Willelmi in curia mea de Blacaduna [de] petitione prædicti Philippi qui eum illuc adduxit et propriis manibus suis prædictum Willelmum mihi tradidit. His teſtibus Aleis de Nunant, Ingareta sponſa mea, Willelmo de Morreville, Radulpho de Merri, Radulpho de Ruſſel, Ricardo de Bicaſaud, Willelmo Bodino, Roberto de Sancta Cruce, Willelmo filio ejus, Philippo de Burci, Henrico fratre ejus, Phifippo de Nerber, Henrico Mallerb, Radulpho Bloet, Andrea Arch', Willelmo Picot, Godefrido Maraſc', Moraduo, Gervaſio, et multis aliis.

No. 84.

CARTA WILLELMI DE SANCTO LEODEGARIO QUAM FECIT NOBIS DE TERRA IN RAGEL.

Omnibus Sanctæ Matris Ecclefiæ filiis præfentibus et futuris Willelmus de Sancto Leodegario falutem. Sciatis me dediſſe et conceſſiſſe et hac carta mea confirmaſſe Deo et Ecclefiæ Sanctæ Mariæ de Dena et Monachis ibidem Deo fervientibus totam terram meam de Ragel quæ fuit Philippi de Burci cum omnibus pertinentiis ſuis intra villam et extra in perpetuam et puram eleemoſynam tenendam de me et heredibus meis liberam et quietam ab omni feculari fervitio et confuetudine et exactione præter folummodo duos folidos mihi et heredibus meis annuatim reddendos ad feſtum Sancti Michaelis et præter fervitium duarum partium unius militis quod facient Domino meo Willelmo, filio Roberti filii Martini et heredibus ejus. Ita tamen quod cum venerit terminus annorum ab anno Incarnatione Domini milleſimo ducenteſimo vigefimo quarto quem præfigit carta præfati Philippi prædicti Monachi perfolvent annuatim heredibus præfati Philippi unum bizantium vel duos folidos præter duos folidos quos mihi et heredibus meis annuatim reddent. Et quando feci prædictis Monachis hanc donationem tunc ipfi dederunt mihi viginti marcas argenti. Et prædictum Philippum de Burci deliberavi de debitis quæ debuit Manaſſero Judæo de Briftolio ex denariis ipforum Monachorum. Conceſſerunt etiam mihi et heredibus meis in perpetuum habere unum monachum de noftra præfentatione in ipfa domo ita quod, eo decedente, alius per manum meam vel heredum meorum et per confilium Abbatis ejufdem loci fufcipiatur quem et domui fuæ et mihi neceſſarium judicaverit. In omnibus beneficiis fuis me et meos receperunt tam in morte quam in vita et pro me ficut pro uno monacho profeſſo facient. Hanc autem donationem in omnibus fideliter et fine dolo tenendam manu mea aſſidavi et ad plenam fecuritatem monachorum præfentem cartam figillo meo confirmavi. His teftibus, Willelmo Marefcallo, Willelmo filio Joannis, Willelmo de Morevill, Ricardo de Bikefaud, Willelmo Bodin, Roberto de Sanéta Cruce et Willelmo filio ejus, Alano de Morton, Waltero de Budicum, et Willelmo Picot, Joanne Capellano, et multis aliis.

Et alias duas cartas habemus de prima inter nos couventione.

No. 85.

CONFIRMATIO CAPITALIS DOMINI DE PRÆDICTA TERRA QUAM NOBIS FECIT.

Willelmus filius Roberti filii Martini omnibus amicis fuis et hominibus Francis et Anglis et Wallenfibus. Sciatis me conceffiffe et hac præfenti carta confirmaffe Monachis de Dena totam terram de Ragel quæ est de feudo meo cum omnibus pertinentiis fuis quam Willelmus de Sanéto Leodegario prædiétis Monachis dedit in perpetuam et puram eleemofynam ficut idem Willelmus de Sanéto Leodegario prediétis monachis carta fua confirmavit et conceffit; falvo fervitio quod prædiétus Willelmus et heredes fui mihi et heredibus meis facere debent, fcilicet, fervicium duarum partium unius militis ficut carta mea teftatur, quam diéto Willelmo feci. Confirmavi etiam prædiétis monachis et conceffi omnem donationem et conventionem quam Philippus de Burci fecit præfato Willelmo ficut carta præfati Philippi teftatur. Et pro hac confirmatione prædiéti Monachi mihi dederunt tres marcas argenti et uxori meæ Angaretæ duos bizantios et Roberto filio meo et heredi unum bizantium et Willelmo filio meo juniori duodecim denarios. Et ut hæc confirmatio inter me et heredes meos et ipfos Monachos et inter prædiétum Willelmum de Sanéti Leodegario et heredes ipfius et ipfos Monachos in perpetuum firma et ftabilis permaneat eandem prefenti carta et figilli mei appofitione confirmavi. His teftibus Willelmo de Cantiton, Roberto de Cantiton, Willelmo de Bauzan, Willelmo de Cokinton, Willelmo Norreis, Alano de Morton, Ricardo de Bikefauda, Roberto de Sancta Cruce, Rogero Capellano, Waltero de Sanéto Sepulcro, et multis aliis.

Tres cartae Philippi de Burci contra Judæos prima de novem marcis, secunda de decem marcis, tertia de duodecim marcis. Chirographum unum contra Judæos et dua ftarra Judæorum. Omnia ifta acquietavit

Willelmus de Sancto Leodegario. Duæ cartæ de terris acquietatis; una de Waltero de Wintreburn, et alia de Hugone de Gerneth, quas acquietavit Willelmus de Sancto Leodegario; et breve unam de feifina. Omnia ista habentur in fcrinio Catharino.

No. 86.

CARTA WALTERI FILII WALTERI DE RAGEL.

Sciant tam præfentes quam futuri quod ego Walterus filius Walteri de Ragel dedi et conceffi Deo et Beatæ Mariæ de Dena et Monachis ibidem Deo fervientibus in perpetuam et puram eleemofynam pro falute mea et prædeceſſorum meorum illam croftam quam habui in Ragelbiri quæ eft prope fontem Sancti Andreæ et inter gardinum quod fuit Philippi de Burci et domum Ofwardi liberam et quietam ab omni feculari fervitio et confuetudine et exactione. Et contra omnes homines ego et heredes mei prædictis monachis prædictam croftam ficut puram eleemofynam warrantizabimus. Et ego pro me et heredibus meis hoc manu mea affidavi tenendum. Et ut hæc donatio rata et firma in perpetuum permaneat præfenti carta figillo meo impreſſa eandem donationem eis confirmavi. His teftibus, Willelmo filio Willelmi filii Johannis, Willelmo Bodin, Waltero de Budicum, Magiftro Galfrido le Bel, Godefrido Capellano de Emnet, Gilberto de Budicum, Joanne de Crumhale, Galfrido Burci, et multis aliis.

No. 87.

CONFIRMATIO ROBERTI FRATRIS EJUS DE PRÆDICTA CROFTA.

Sciant tam præfentes quam futuri quod ego Robertus filius Walteri de Ragel conceffi et hac præfenti carta mea confirmavi Deo et Beatæ Mariæ de Dene et monachis ibidem Deo fervientibus pro falute mea et prædeceſſorum meorum donationem illius croftæ in Rachelburi quam Walterus frater meus dedit prædictis Monachis in perpetuam et puram eleemofynam ficut carta ipfius Walteri teftatur. Et ut hæc confirmatio in perpetuum rata et firma permaneat præfenti carta figilli mei impreſſione munita confirmavi.

His teftibus, Willelmo filio Willelmi filii Joannis, W[illelmo] Bodin, Waltero de Budicum, Magiftro Galfrido le Bel, Godefrido Capellano de Emnet, Gilberto de Budicum, Joanne de Crumhale, Galfrido de Burci, et multis aliis.

No. 88.

ITEM ALIA CARTA WALTERI FILII WALTERI SPROT DE RAGEL.

Sciant præfentes et futuri quod ego Walterus filius Walteri Sprot de Ragel dedi et concefli. Deo et Beatæ Mariæ de Dena et monachis ibidem Deo fervientibus in perpetuam et puram eleemosynam pro falute mea et prædeceforum meorum illas duas acras quas tenui in Ragelburi versus auftrum quæ funt inter duas acras de Emnet et croftam quæ fuit Alwardi le Seignor et dimidiam acram prati quæ proxima eft prædictis duabus acris in Duddemede, habendas et tenendas de me et de heredibus meis in perpetuum liberas et quietas ab omni fervitio et confuetudine et exactione. Ego vero et heredes mei prædictam donationem prædictis monachis contra omnes homines warrantizabimus et acquietabimus ficut puram eleemofynam meam. Et ut hæc donatio in perpetuum rata et firma permaneat eandem prefenti carta figillo meo imprefla confirmavi. His teftibus, Stephano Perfona de Wunford, Magiftro Galfrido Bello, Godefrido Capellano de Emnet, Gilberto Perfona de Budicum, Waltero de Budicum, Rogero de Allewike, Roberto filio Walteri Sprot de Ragel, Ricardo de Loveftreng, et multis aliis.

No. 89.

ITEM CONFIRMATIO PRÆDICTI ROBERTI FRATRI WALTERI DE DUABUS ACRIS.

Sciant præfentes et futuri quod ego Robertus filius Walteri Sprot de Ragel concefli et hac prefenti carta mea confirmavi Deo et Beatæ Mariæ de Dene et Monachis ibidem Deo fervientibus omnem donationem quam frater meus Walterus Sprot de Ragel dedit prædictis Monachis, fcilicet, illarum duarum acrarum verfus auftrum de Ragelburi quæ funt inter duas acras de Emnet et croftam quæ fuit Alwardi le Seignur, et dimidiæ acræ prati quæ proxima eft prædictis duabus acris in Duddemede ficut carta prædicti Walteri teftatur. Et ut hoc ratum permaneat præfentem cartam figillo meo confirmavi. His teftibus Stephano Perfona de Wunford, Magiftro Galfrido Bello, Godefrido Capellano de Emnet, Gilberto Perfona de Budicum, Waltero de Budicum, Rogero de Allewike, Ricardo Luverfteng, et multis aliis.

Adhuc duas cartas habemus Walteri Sprot de fupra fcripta crofta; unam de emptione (fcilicet, x sol.), et alteram de efcambio fi nobis warrantizare non poterit.

No. 90.
ITEM CARTA WALTERI SPROT DE ELEEMOSYNA.

Sciant præfentes et futuri quod ego Walterus Sprot de Ragel dedi et conceffi Deo et Beatæ Mariæ de Dene et Monachis ibidem Deo fervientibus in perpetuam et puram eleemofynam pro anima mea et uxoris meæ Yfabellæ et prædecefforum meorum totam partem meam illarum acrarum quæ funt in montibus qui funt inter dominum meum Rogerum de Winter- burna et me quæ computantur pro quatuor et dimidia acris. Adhuc etiam conceffi prædictis monachis communiam in pafcuis meis tam in montibus quam in campis. Ego vero et heredes mei prædictam donationem prædictis monachis contra omnes homines warrantizabimus et acquietabimus ficut puram eleemofynam noftram. Et ut hæc donatio rata et firma in perpetuum permaneat eandem prefenti carta figillo meo impreffa confirmavi. His teftibus, Godefrido Capellano de Emnet, Gilberto Capellano de Budicum, Ricardo Capellano de Blakedun, Hugone Capellano de Wunford, Waltero de Budicumb, Waltero Sprot, Ricardo Loveftreng, Galfrido de Burci, et multis aliis.

No. 91.
CARTA HUGONIS HOSATI DE ELEEMOSYNA.

Notum fit omnibus præfentibus et futuris quod ego Hugo Hofatus dedi et conceffi pro falute mea et prædecefforum meorum in puram et perpetuam eleemofynam Deo et Ecclefiæ Beatæ Mariæ de Dene et Monachis ibidem Deo fervientibus illas duas acras terræ in Ragelburi quæ funt juxta viam verfus auftrum inter domum Alwardi le Seignour et domum Galfridi Tripel habendas et tenendas de me et de heredibus meis in perpetuum liberas et quietas ab omni fervitio. Hanc autem donationem affidavi ego pro me et pro heredibus meis firmiter tenendam et contra omnes homines eifdem monachis warrantizabo. Et ut hæc mea donatio rata permaneat figilli mei impreffione eam confirmavi. His teftibus, Godefrido Capellano de Emnet, Magiftro Galfrido Bello, Gilberto de Budicum, Waltero de Budicum, Alexandro Avelac, Waltero de Ragel, Ricardo Lufeftreng, Rogero Hosato, Willelmo de Kainesham.

No. 92.
CARTA EJUSDEM HUGONIS HOSATI DE EMPTIONE.

Notum fit tam præfentibus quam futuris quod ego Hugo Hosatus dedi et conceffi Deo et Beatæ Mariæ de Dene et Monachis ibidem Deo fervientibus illas duas acras terræ in Ragelburi quæ funt juxta viam verfus auftrum inter domum Alwardi le Seignor et domum Galfridi Tripel, habendas et tenendas de me et heredibus meis in perpetuum liberas et quietas ab omni fervitio et in recognitione hujus donationis dederunt mihi prædicti Monachi quadraginta folidos præ manibus. Hanc donationem affidavi ego pro me et heredibus meis firmiter tenendam et contra omnes homines prædictis Monachis warrantizabo. Et ut hæc mea donatio rata permaneat figilli mei impreffione eam confirmavi. His teftibus, Godefrido Capellano de Emnet, Magiftro Gaufrido Bello, Gilberto de Budicumbe, Waltero de Budicumbe, Alexandro Avelac, Rogero Hosato, Waltero de Ragel, Ricardo Lufeftreng, Magiftro Willelmo de Keinesham.

Et breve quoddam habemus quod misit idem Hugo Hosatus per Rogerum fratrem fuum ratum et gratum habiturus, quicquid in fuo negotio faceret de prædicta emptione.

No. 93.

CARTA WALTERI DE BUDICUMBE DE ELEEMOSYNA.

Sciant præfentes et futuri quod ego Walterus de Budicumbe dedi et conceffi Deo et Beatæ Mariæ de Dene et Monachis ibidem Deo fervientibus in perpetuam et puram eleemofynam illas feptem acras quæ funt inter mafagium Stephani Aldewiche in montibus quas Edwinus tenuit et inter viam quæ tendit Eiffele et viam quæ tendit Kingberg liberas et quietas ab omni confuetudine et fervitio et exactione per unam libram cumini fingulis annis mihi vel heredibus meis reddendam ad feftum Sancti Michaelis. Concedo etiam et dono prædictis Monachis communiam ducentis ovibus fuis tam in montibus quam in campis et in omnibus locis ficut meis propriis ovibus fi tot ovibus fufficere poffit eadem communia. Dimidium vero compofitum tam domus quam faldagii mihi et heredibus meis remanebit et faldagium per certos dies dividetur et medietatem ftramenti fub ovibus inveniam et ufque ad bercheriam faciam trahere. Prædictam vero donationem et conceffionem et omnia prædicta prædictorum monachorum in omnibus locis contra omnes homines ego et heredes mei eis warrantizabimus. Ut hæc donatio rata permaneat in perpetuum eandem tenendam manu mea affidavi et præfentem cartam figilli mei impreffione confirmavi. His teftibus, Magiftro Gaufrido Bello, Godefrido Sacerdote de Emnet, Gilberto Perfona de Budicum, Willelmo de Waltun, Rogero de Aldewiche, Stephano de Aldewiche, Huberto de Leie, Roberto de Hale, et multis aliis.

No. 94.

CHIROGRAPHUM SIGILLATUM INTER NOS ET ECCLESIAM DE BUDICUMBE.

Hæc eft conventio facta inter Monachis de Dene et Ecclefiam de Budicumbe ex confenfu et voluntate Gileberti perfonæ de Budicumbe, videlicet, quod prædicti monachi fingulis annis in fefto Sancti Michaelis dabunt duos folidos Ecclefiæ de Budicumbe pro omnibus decimationibus quæ folvi confueverunt de illis feptem acris quas Walterus de Budicumbe dedit prædictis monachis in perpetuam et puram eleemofynam quæ, fcilicet, funt inter mafagium Stephani de Aldewiche in montibus quod Edwinus tenuit et inter viam quæ tendit Eiffele et viam quæ tendit Kingberg et pro omnibus decimationibus ducentorum ovium quas prædicti monachi debent habere in pafcuis de Budicumbe ita quod a perfona de Budicum[be] nil amplius exigetur nomine decimarum præter prædictos duos folidos. Ut hæc conventio firma maneat et inconcuffa eandem utriufque partis figillo confirmavimus. His teftibus, Magiftro Galfrido Bello, Godefrido Sacerdote de Emnet, Waltero de Budicum, Willelmo de Waltun, Rogero de Aldewiche, Stephano de Aldewiche, Huberto Lege, Roberto de Hale, et multis aliis.

No. 95.

CARTA WILLELMI DE LA MARA.

Sciant præsentes et futuri quod ego Willelmus de la Mara pro falute mea et uxoris meæ et tam heredum meorum quam antecefforum meorum dedi et conceffi Deo et Beatæ Mariæ et Monachis de Flaxlega totum pratum meum apud Tukeleiam quod, fcilicet, jacet in longum fubtus campum Abbatis de Gloceftre et fubtus terram prædictorum monachorum quam habent de Amifio de Tukeleia tenendum et habendum de me et heredibus meis in perpetuum liberum et quietum ab omni fervitio et confuetudine Reddendo mihi et heredibus meis annuatim quatuor folidos ad feftum Sancti Kenelmi Martyris et duas[1] botas rubeas ad feftum Sanctorum Omnium pro omni fervitio ad me et heredes meos pertinente. Et quia quod hæc mea donatio et conceffio rata fit in perpetuum præfenti carta et figilli mei impreffione eam confirmavi. His teftibus Willelmo de Berkele, Radulpho de Wilintun, Roberto de Deudefwell, Bertramo de la Mara, Hamelino de Gundeville, Henrico de Barris, et multis aliis.

No. 96.

CARTA ERNALDI DE CUTBERLEGA.

Sciant præfentes et futuri quod ego Ernaldus de Cutberlega filius Ernaldi

---

[1] In the copy made from Sir Thomas Phillipps' tranfcript, the word "duas" was, by a clerical error, written "unas," which being unintelligible, was quoted verbatim in the text at p. 63.

Dunning pro falute mea et tam anteceſſorum quam heredum memorum dedi et conceſſi Deo et Beatæ Mariæ de Flexlega ad emendationem hoſpitii totam terram meam inter duos pontes Savernæ apud Glouceſtriam illam, ſcilicet, quam Gaufridus le Lorimer tenuit de me quæ quondam fuerat Roberti filii Feremon Tenedam de me et heredibus meis libere et quiete in perpetuam et puram' elemoſynam et quietam ab omni ſervitio et conſuetudine quæ ad me vel heredes meos poſſint pertinere ſalvo Longabulo [? Landgabulo] ſcilicet uno denario quem reddent prædictus Gaufridus et heredes fui Domino Regi. Et ego et heredes mei prædictam terram prædictis monachis contra omnes homines et feminas warrantizabimus. Et quia volo quod hæc mea donatio et conceſſio in perpetuum rata fit et nota eam hac præſenti carta mea et ſigilli mei impreſſione confirmavi. His teſtibus, Ricardo Rufo de Glouceſtria, Henrico Kais, Ada le Valeis, Joanne Rufo, Thoma Toli, Rogero Paris, Joanne fratre meo, et Davide fratre meo, et multis aliis.

No. 97.

CARTA R. ABBATIS DE FLEXLEGA AD ERNALDUM DE CUTBERLEGA.

Omnibus ad quos præſens ſcriptum pervenerit Frater R. dictus Abbas de Flexlega et ejus loci Conventus in Domino Salutem. Noverit univerſitas veſtra nos debere Ernaldo de Cutberlega annuatim quinque ſolidos quamdiu idem Ernaldus vixerit reddendos eidem Ernaldo ſingulis annis ad feſtum Sancti Ethelberti Martyris. Quod ut ratum fit et notum præſenti ſcripto et ſigillo noſtri teſtimonio confirmavimus. His teſtibus, Mauricio filio Durandi de Glouceſtre, Thoma Toli, Willelmo Neirun, Rogero Paris, et multis aliis.

N.B.—*At p. 59 it is stated that a portion of the Flaxley Cartulary, together with a table of the whole contents was printed by the late Sir Thomas Phillips at his private press at Middlehill, in 1866. The portion so printed was Cart. No. 1 to 11, and No. 81 to 97 inclusive. The remainder of the Cartulary is now printed for the first time.*

INDEX TO NAMES OF PERSONS.

A. Abbot of Dene, 71.
A. Abbot of Tewkefbury, 75n, 158.
A. Abbot of Vallis Dore, 75, 132.
Abbenhall (Abenhale), Geoffry de, 141, 164.
―――――― William de, 42, 176, 177.
―――――― Thomas de, 170.
Achard, Robert, 153, 154.
Adam, fon of Fulco, 63, 69, 75, 78, 114, 140, 141, 151, 152, 153, 154, 161, 168, 174, 175.
―――― fon of Peter, 131.
―――― the fmith, 129.
―――― forefter of Bicknor, 131.
―――― the Fleming, 161.
―――― le Flamene, 155.
―――― le Valeis, 196.
―――― le Orleblowere, 131.
―――― chaplain of Hethamftede, 148, 149.
―――― chaplain, 166.
Agnes, 76, 155.
Aidanus, 76.
―――――― John, fon of, 76, 155, 161.
Ailward, le Seigneur, 67, 68, 191, 193.
Alan, Abbot of Dene, 20n. 53, 65, 71n, 76, 85, 148, 172, 173.
Aldewich (Allewike) Stephen, 72, 194, 195.
―――― Roger, 186, 191, 192, 194, 195.
Alexander III., Pope, 61, 79, 181, 182.
―――――― of St. Briavell's, clerk, 131.
―――――― the clerk, 166.
Alfred (Alured, Elured, Aclured, Alwredus)
―――― in the Velde, 128.
―――― fon of Wimund, 154,
―――― brother of Ralph, 131.
―――― brother, 77, 175.
―――― le Blunt, 172.
Alward, see Ailward.

Alva, Olivares Duke of, 33n.
Andrea, Arch., 188.
Anjou, Earl of, 16, 17.
Anketil, 69, 140.
Anneis, 129.
Arden, fee Ardern.
Ardern (Erderne, Herderne, Arden.)
―――― Roger de, 73, 78, 113, 135, 136, 139, 140, 141, 142, 148, 149, 157, 162, 163, 164, 165, 167, 168, 169, 170, 171.
―――― Peter, fon of Roger de, 149.
Argent, Hugh, 174.
―――― Roger, 174.
―――― William, 174.
Arham, John, 43.
Arnald (Arnaldus, Ernaldus), 158.
―――― forefter, 76, 155,
―――― carpenter, 70, 162.
―――― clerk of Dimmoc, 75, 148, 157, 158.
―――― fmith, 140, 143.
―――― fon of Cutelb, 77, 175, 176.
Arnold, John, armiger, 49.
Arlingham (Erlingham, Herlingham).
―――― Milo de, 64, 145, 146, 159.
―――― Gilbert de, 64, 145, 146, 159.
―――― William de, 64, 145, 146, 159.
―――― Richard de, 61, 64, 145, 146, 159.
―――― Edith de, 64n, 160.
―――― Matilda, wife of Richard de, 146, 160.
―――― Helena, wife of William de, 146.
―――― Hyla (Hylaria) wife of William de, 159.
Arundel, Richard, 117.
Afehart, 129.
Afmoins, Walter, Conftable of St. Briavell's Caftle, 30.
Atkyns, Sir Robert, 1, 15, 24, 99.

Angervill, William de, 17, 19.
Aure (Aura) Walter of, 136, 140, 143, 144, 154, 156, 166.
—— Walter of, clerk, 78, 137. 138, 161.
—— (Aura) Walter, parson of, 137, 144.
Avelae, Alexander, 193.
Avenel, Ralph, 136.
—— Roger, nephew of Ralph, 136.
—— Nicholas, 136, 175.
Ayloffe, Sir Joseph, Calendar of Cartæ Antiquæ, 14, 33, 38, 39.
Azo, 173.

Baber Edward, Serjeant-at-Law, 67n.
Bachineffeld, Dominus de, 176.
Bainham, Mr., of Weftbury on Severn, 2.
Baieus, Robert de, 163.
Baioo, Robert de, 144.
Bakep' Ralph de, 33.
Balle, Robert, 131.
Banks, 62n.
Bares, Edward de, 150, 151.
—— Henry de, 152.
Baret, Richard, 49.
Barnard, Edward, 67n.
Barra, Walter de la, 77, 161
Barris, Henry de, 195.
Bafila, 130.
Bafilia, wife of Adam of Blakeney, 68.
Bate, Godfrey, 173.
Baterick, Thomas, 74, 114.
—— Hulle, 177.
—— Margaret, 177.
Bath (Bathon), Henry of, 32, 109.
Bauzan, William de, 189
Beauchamp, Richard, Bifhop of Hereford, 84.
Beaudley (Beawdley) William, Abbot of Flaxley, 1528—84, 86, 87.
Beddoe, H. C., 15.
Bellows, John of Gloucester, 9on.
Berde, Aldit, 176
Berkeley (Berkele, Barkele).
—— Robert Fitzharding of, 9n, 17n.
—— Robert de, 43, 49n, 186.

Berkeley Roger, Knight, 43n, 49.
—— William de, 63, 195.
—— Abbot of Flaxley (1476), 85, 86.
—— A. de, 170.
Berta, wife of Philip de Braofe, 3n, 62.
—— wife of Gilbert de Monmouth, 61, 162.
Betun, Robert de, Bifhop of Hereford, 4, 10, 11, 12.
Beulph, 158.
Bicafaud, Richard de, 188, 189.
Bicknor (Bikenore), William de, 173.
Bigland, 2, 21n, 28, 46, 90, 91, 92.
Bikenore, fee Bicknor.
Blachedun, fee Blaifdon.
Blacheneia, fee Blakeney.
Blaifdon (Blachedun, Blechedun, Blechedune, Blecheden), Richard of, 74, 114, 139.
—— Edric, fon of Richard of, 74.
—— Baderun of, 74n, 78, 135, 137, 139, 140, 145, 149, 163, 167.
Blakedun, Richard, chaplain of, 192.
Blakeney (Blacheneia) Thomas of, 45.
—— Adam of, 68, 130, 133, 134, 137, 138, 162.
—— Jordan, father of Adam of, 137, 143.
—— Jordan, brother of Adam of, 68.
—— Bafilia, wife of Adam of, 68, 138.
—— Arnulf of, 145.
Blanche, Queen of Navarre, 97.
Blechedun, fee Blaifdon.
Bleith, Walter, 162, 166, 170.
Bleyght, Alexander, 41, 42.
—— John, 42, 45.
Blipeflawe, fee Blitheflawe.
Blitheflawe, Hugh de, 137, 138, 144.
Bloet, Ralph, 188.
Bodin, William, 188, 189, 190, 191.
Boeve (Bovey), William, 33.
—— James, 33n.
—— Andrew, 33n.
Bovey, Sir Thos. Crawley-, 1st Bart. of Flaxley Abbey, Co. Glouc., 12n, 31n, 92n.
—— Sir Thos. Hyde Crawley-, 5th Bart., 27n, 95.
—— E. B. Crawley-, 91, 93.

Bohun, Humphrey de, 3n.
———— Henry de, 8.
———— William de, 117
Bollandus, 35n.
Bollein, Roger de, 160.
———— Geoffry, brother of Roger de, 160.
Booth, Charles, Bifhop of Hereford, 84.
Bordefley, William, Abbot of, 53.
———— Richard, Abbot of, 53.
Bofceliva (Boxeliva), William de, 162, 170.
———— Roger de, 162, 170.
———— Richard de, 162, 170.
———— James de, 162, 170.
Bofco, Roger de, 36, 64, 71, 130, 139, 142, 156, 157, 163, 171.
———— Margaret, wife of R. de, 163.
———— Geoffry, brother of Roger de, 171.
———— Henry, brother of Roger de, 171.
———— Richard de, 77, 158, 177.
———— . . . . . 128.
Botiler, John le, 43, 51.
———— Beatrice, wife of John le, 43.
Bovey (Boeve), Mrs. Catherine, of Flaxley Abbey, Co. Glouc., 33n, 34n.
Boxa, William de, 145.
———— Richard, brother of William de, 145.
Boxe, Thomas, 48.
———— Roger de la, 169.
Boxeliva, fee Bosceliva.
Boyville, Roger de, 77, 161.
Bracton, 24n.
Bmose, Philip de, 3n, 62n, 63, 79, 134.
———— William de, 61, 62, 63, 68n, 79, 134.
———— Giles de, 62n.
Bretun, John le, Bifhop of Hereford, 81n.
Breuerne, fee Bruerne.
Breynton, Thomas de, 83.
Brifloc . . . . Albus de, 172.
Browne Willis, 52, 85, 86, 89n, 101.
Brothestun, . . . ardus de, 172.
Bruerne (Breuwerne, Briwerne) Geoffry de, King's cupbearer, 150, 151.
Brunefhoppe, William de, 131.
Budicumbe, fee Butcombe.
Budifeld, William de, 74, 114.

Budifeld, William, fon of William de, 115.
Buevile (Buivilla), Roger de, 131, 146, 147, 160, 170.
———— Helias, fon of Roger de, 170.
Burci, Philip de, 65, 66, 79, 114, 130, 185, 186, 187, 188, 189 190.
———— Geoffry, fon of Philip de, 186, 187, 190, 191, 192.
———— Henry, brother of Philip de, 188.
Burgh, Hubert de, 55, 115.
Burgeis, William, 113, 142, 174.
———— Richard, son of William, 113, 173, 176.
———— John, 158.
Burh, William de, 134.
———— Robert de, 134.
Butcombe (Budicumbe), Walter of, 72, 76, 78, 189, 190, 191, 192, 193, 194, 195.
———————————— Gilbert of, 72n, 78, 190, 191, 193.
———————————— Gilbert, parfon of, 76, 191, 192, 194.
Butler, Alban, 35n.
Byfeleye, (Byfeley?) William de, 46.

Cadel, Godfrey, 157, 163.
———— Roger, 45.
Calvus, Henry, 71, 164, 173.
———— Robert, 142, 156, 173.
Camden, "Golden Vale," 21.
Cantelupe, Thomas de, Bifhop of Hereford, 15, 56, 76n 79, 81, 82.
Cantiton, William de, 189.
———— Robert de, 189.
Carter, Walter, 43n.
Cecilie, daughter of Pain Fitzjohn, 7.
Celeftine III., Pope, 3n, 61, 79, 101n, 178.
Cemiterio, William de, 128.
Chadburn, Alfred de, 128.
Charke, fee Chearke.
Charles II., King of England, 25n.
Charlton, Ludovic, Bifhop of Hereford, 83.
Chaxhill (Chakefhull, Cheakefhill, Chekefhill, Chexhull).
———— Henry of, 45n, 69, 73, 113, 141, 147, 148, 167, 168.

Chaxhill Roger, brother of Henry of, 69, 139, 141.
——— William de, 139.
——— Fulco of, 69, 140.
——— Edith, wife of Fulco of, 69n.
——— Adam, fon of Fulco of, fee Adam.
——— Durand, fon of Fulco of, 69n.
——— Walter, fon of Fulco of, 69n.
——— Arnald of, 147, 148.
Chearke (Charke, Cherke) Hugh, 36, 70, 113, 115, 144, 149, 161, 164, 169, 170, 171.
——— Hugh, fon of Hugh, 144. 145, 169, 170.
——— Johanna, wife of Hugh, 144, 161, 169, 170.
Cheddeworthe, Roger de, 175.
Chorlton, Thomas, Bifhop of Hereford, 83.
Cipping, Robert, 129.
Clare, Thomas de, 42.
——— Gilbert de, 54.
Clement III., Pope, 75n, 158.
——— 137.
Clifford, Roger de, 30.
Climperwell, Robert de, 75, 115.
Clintone, Ivo of, 42.
——— Agnes, wife of Ivo of, 42.
Clive, Richard de, 165.
Cockel, Alexander, 177.
Cokinton, William de, 189.
Coleftun, William of, 145.
——— Walter de, 144.
Colevilla, William de, 133, 134.
Collinfon, 67n, 68n.
Columbariis, Philip de, 17, 19.
Courteney, William, Bishop of Hereford, 83, 84.
Coverley, Sir Roger de, 33n.
Cowel, 100.
Cox, Rev. Thomas, 1.
Cras, William le, 75, 115.
Craucumbe, Godfrey de, 115.
Crawley, Thomas of Gloucefter, 33n.
Crawfhay, W., of Oaklands, near Newnham, 31n.
——— E., 31n.
Crendon, Ada de, 175.
Crepinge, Richard of, 31.
Crevecour (Crevequer), William de, 17, 19.
Crucche, Walter, 76, 174.

Crumhale, John of, 190, 191.
Crupard, Ralph, 72, 113, 167.
Cumin, William, 17.
Cupping, Emma, 177.
Cutherleye (Cutberleg), Arnald de, 72, 73, 77, 195, 196.
——— John, brother of Arnald de, 196.
——— David ——————196.
Cutelb, Ernaldus, fon of, 77, 175, 176.
Cutts, Rev. E. L., 40n.
Cuverer, William, 69n, 113.
Cvn', Thomas, 86.

Dammartin, Nicholas de, 134.
Dangel, Geoffrey de, 30.
Dene, William de, "King's Forefter," 37, 51, 61, 63, 64, 135, 138.
——— Matilda, wife of William de, 138.
——— Geoffrey, fon of William de, 16n, 37, 64, 135, 136, 138, 139, 140, 149, 157, 168, 169, 170, 171.
——— Mael, fon of William de, 135, 139, 157, 170.
——— William, fon of William de, 135, 139, 157.
——— William, fon of Geoffrey de, 139.
——— Geoffrey de, 36, 78, 137, 145, 162.
——— Alexander de, 139.
Dene, Ralph de, 154.
——— Geoffrey, fon of Ralph de, 154.
——— Ulric de, 9n, 16n, 64n.
——— A., Abbot of, 71.
Defpenfer (Difpenfator) John, 74, 114, 140, 163, 168
——————————— Hugh le, 68n, 97.
——————————— Geoffrey le, 74n.
——————————— Richard le, 74n.
Deudefwell, fee Doudefwell.
Deveneis le, ...ltr, 172.
Difpenfator, fee Defpenfer.
Dolfin, James, fon of, 147, 159.
Doudfwell, Robert de, 165, 195.
Dover, Gervafe of, 3, 12n.
Drake, Sir William, 62n.
Drugo, Archdeacon, 137.
Dugdale, Mon. Angl., 1, 13, 17, 48n, 50, 67n.
——— Baronage, 1n, 3, 5, 6, 7, 9, 10n.

Dun, Roger, 131.
—— William, friend of Roger, 131.
Duncumb, Herefordshire, 2.
Dune (Dun), William de, 69n, 74, 113.
———————— Edith, wife of William de, 69n.
———————— Philip, son of William de, 69n, 167.
———————— Johanna, wife of Philip de, 69n.
Dunhantun, Svanus de, 157.
Dunhampton, William de, 128, 176.
Dunia, Philip de, 69, 141, 157, 162.
—————— William, brother of Philip de, 69, 141.
—————— Johanna, wife of Philip de, 69, 141.
—————— Edith, mother of Philip de, 69, 141.
—————— William, son of Philip de, 163.
—————— Richard, son of Philip de, 163.
—————— Philip, son of Philip de, 163.
Dunning, Arnald, 72, 113, 195.
—————— Arnald, son of Arnald, 113.
Durand, brother of Adam, son of Fulco, 140.
Durham, Simeon of, 3.
Dymmock (Dymoc, Dimoc), Gilbert de, 65, 113, 149, 151.
—————— Walfric of, 40.
—————— Geoffry, son of Walfric of, 40.

Edith, mother of Adam, son of Fulco, 140.
———— mother of Philip de Dunia, 69, 141.
———— daughter and heir of William of Arlingham, 160.
Edmund Ironside, 10.
—————— son of King Henry, 97.
Edric, son of Ketel, 6n.
—— son of Richard of Blechedun, 74.
Edward I, King of England, 14, 22n, 26n, 28, 31, 41, 42, 43, 44, 46, 48, 49n, 50, 52, 78, 81, 99.
———— II, do., do., 36, 39, 52, 97, 99.
———— III, do., do., 14, 39, 41, 43, 44, 46, 50, 52, 53n, 57, 58, 68n, 100, 116, 117.
———— IV, do, do, 14, 50.
———— 172.
Edwin, 194, 195.
Eilwinus (Eilevinus), le Mercer, 71, 164.
Eilwi, Ralph, son of, 142.

Ellis, A. S., 62, 64n, 74.
Elwys, Mr., 62n.
Emnet, Godfrey, chaplain of, 78, 190, 191, 192, 193, 194, 195.
Ernewi, William, son of, 163.
Ernisius, 158, 173.
Effelesword, Arnald of, 151.
Eston, Richard of, 51.
Eugenius, Pope, 79, 182.
Eustace, Bishop of London, 115.
—————— de Will, 132
Evelyn, Silva, 26n
Everci, Robert de, 187.
Evreus, John de, 69, 142.
—————— Walter de, 134
Ewias, Robert, Earl of, 21.
Eyton, Rev. R. W., 9n, 19, 67n.

Felileia, Ada de, 137.
Fenwick, Rev. J. E. A., 15, 59.
—————— T. Fitzroy, 59, 136n.
Feremon (Faremon) Robert, son of, 73, 77, 196.
—————— Leweric, brother of, 77, 160.
Field (Felda) Gilbert de, 70, 144.
———————————— Robert de, 153, 154.
Fitz Baderon, William of Monmouth, 62.
—— Harding, Robert of Berkeley, 9n.
—— Herbert, Herbert, 3n.
—— John, Pain, 7.
—————— Sibilla, wife of Pain, 7n.
Fitz John, Cecilie, daughter of Pain, 7.
Foliot, Gilbert, Bishop of Hereford, 11, 12.
————Hugh, do. do. 56.
Forda, Ada de la, 137.
Fosbroke, 2, 34, 35, 36, 89.
Fountains (Fontibus) William de, 5..
Fowle, William, 49.
Frene, Hugh, 83.
Fresel, James, constable of St. Briavell's Castle, 31, 51.
Frocester (Frouceftre) Abbot, 4.
Fryer, Richard of Hockerhill, 43n.
Fryor, Edward, 89n.

Fulco (of Chaxhill), Adam, son of, 63, 69, 75, 78, 114, 140, 141, 151, 152, 153, 154, 161, 168.
—— Durand, son of, 140, 152, 168.
—— Walter, son of, 140.
Fuller, Church History, 100, 101.

Gael, Samuel, 15, 59.
Gamages, William, 45.
Gardun, Addun, 31.
Garne, see Gerne.
Gaunt, Maurice de, 115.
Geoffry, son of Walfric, 16, 40.
—— son of Ralph, son of Geoffry, 155.
—— le Marchal, chaplain, 43.
—— le Mercer, 172.
—— le Bel, master, 78, 190, 191, 192, 193, 194, 195.
—— le Schereman, 172.
—— le Lorimer, 73, 196.
—— Cherebule, 172.
—— the parson, 128.
—— the smith, 172.
—— the reeve, 129.
—— 129.
—— the charcoal maker (Carbonarius), 138.
—— chaplain of Dimmoc, 158, 159.
—— Simon, nephew of G. chaplain of Dimmoc, 159.
Gerard, 128.
Geri (Gerhi), 143, 146, 147, 155, 156, 160.
Gerne (Garne), Hugh de, 45n, 72, 73, 75, 113, 115, 163, 168.
—— (Garne), Gerun, William, 33.
Gerneth, Hugh de, 190.
Gervasius, 188.
Giffard, Matilda, 36, 73n, 75, 115.
—— Helie, Helias, 74, 75, 79, 114, 115, 132.
—— Osbert, 115.
Gilbert, parson of Budicombe, 76, 191, 192, 194.
—— John, Bishop of Hereford, 84.
—— servant of Henry Kais, 149, 150, 151, 152, 153, 154.
—— son of Ralph, 73, 113.

Gilbert, son of Arnald, 147.
—— chaplain of St. Briavell's, 166.
Gloucester, Robert, Earl of, 6.
—— Milo de, 9n, 16n, 64n.
—— Alice de, 72, 174, 175.
—— Jordan de, 172.
—— Herbert de, 173.
—— Maurice, son of Durand de, 196.
Godchep, 128.
Godes, 129.
Godfrey, chaplain of Emnet, 78, 190, 191, 192, 193, 194, 195.
Godolphin, 100.
Gosintun, Rainald de, 136.
Granter, Robert, 131.
Gregory, the Sewer, 6n.
Grey, William de, 33
—— John de, of Retherselde, 117.
Greyndour, Robert, 44.
Gundeville, Hamelinus de, 195.
Gwilliam, Thomas, ap., 87.

H., Abbot of Gloucester, 75n, 158.
Hacheth, Walter, 128, 177.
Hageness, Henry de, 165.
—— Roger de, 165.
Hale, Robert de, 194, 195.
Harald, 128.
Hardy, Sir P. Duffus, 53n.
Harpetr, William de, 74, 114
—— Thomas, son of William de, 44, 114.
Hart, W. H., 4n, 7n, 74n, 87.
Hartshorne, A., 54n.
Hatheway, William, 42, 71, 165.
—— Nigel, son of William, 71, 165.
—— Sarra (Sarah), wife of Nigel, 165.
Hawere, 131.
Hayll, John of Borsley, 96.
Haylof, 45.
Heane, W. C., 89n.
Hearne, Thomas, 2n.
Heidun, Roger de, 73, 112, 165.
—— Reginald de, 113.
Helias, Reeve, of Gloucester, 156.

Helion (Heliun), William de, 78, 140, 141, 142, 148, 149, 163, 165, 167, 168, 169, 170.
Hendi, Walter, 74, 113.
Henneberge, Malle de, 177.
Henry I, King of England, 1, 5, 6, 7, 9n, 10n, 16n, 64n, 68n.
——— II, do., do., 2, 8, 9n, 10, 14, 17, 19, 20, 22, 23, 25, 26n, 29, 30, 36, 37, 38, 39, 40, 111.
——— III, do., do., 14, 22n, 23, 24, 25, 28, 29, 30, 31, 36, 37, 39, 40, 41, 42, 46, 50, 51, 56, 57n, 60, 63, 65n, 66n, 67n, 68, 69n, 70n, 78, 99, 112.
——— V, do., do., 44.
——— VI, do., do., 39.
——— VII, do., do., 39.
——— VIII, do., do., 43n, 46, 47, 48, 49n, 52, 119.
——— son of Odon, 73.
——— de Capella, 115.
——— rotarius, 177.
Herbert, son of Ernaldus, son of Cutelb, 77, 175.
——— Margaret, wife of Herbert, son of Ernaldus, 175.
Herderne, see Ardern.
Hereford, Milo Fitzwalter, Earl of, 1, 3, 4, 5, 6, 7, 9, 10, 11, 12, 19, 20, 35.
——— Sybill, wife of Milo, Earl of, 3, 5.
——— Roger, Earl of, son of Milo Fitzwalter, founder of Flaxley Abbey, 1, 2, 3, 4, 5, 7, 8, 9, 10, 11, 12, 16, 17, 18, 19, 20, 35, 40, 68n, 121.
——— Henry, son of Milo Fitzwalter, Earl of, 3, 11.
——— Walter, son of Milo Fitzwalter, Earl of, 3n, 11.
——— Mahel, or Michel, son of Milo F., Earl of, 3n.
——— William do., do., 3n.
——— William de, 133, 134.
Herleia, John de, 186, 187.
Hernicius, 174 175.
Hervicus, 172.
Hewlett, Henry, Q.C., 88.
Hexham, John of, 3.

Hingan, William, son of, 137, 138.
Hoc, Edward, 113.
Hooper, Bishop of Gloucester, 90.
——— Henry, 89n.
Hore, Walter le, 77, 175.
Hosate, Hugh, 61, 67, 68, 115, 192, 193.
——— Roger, 193.
Hubert, the clerk, 135.
Hucdredus, the clerk, 157.
Hugelin, Geoffry, 72, 166.
Hugh, le Petit, 16n, 37, 68, 136.
——— White (Albus), 157.
——— the tailor, 132.
——— de Mortuo Mari, 115.
——— Fal......, 129.
——— pauper, 177.
——— chaplain of Wunford, 192.
Hulla, Ralph de, 128.
Hulle, William de la, 42.
——— Hugh de la, 131.
——— Ralph de la, 176.
——— Philip of, 45n, 74, 113.
Humett, Richard de, constable, 17, 19.
Hyett, Robert, 86.
Hyla (Hylaria, Hela), 159, 160.
Humelmore, Henry of, 45, 74.

Innocent, Pope, 3n, 15, 79, 82.
Isabella, wife of Adam, son of Fulco, 140.
Ivigum, Robert de, 17.
Ivo, le Palmer (Paumer), 143, 154, 156, 160, 161.
——— Jordan, son of I., 154.

J. Archbishop of York, 117.
Job, Hugh, 173.
Jocelin, Bishop of Bath, 115.
——— Master, the clerk, 72, 174, 175.
Johanna, wife of Philip de Dunia, 69, 141.
——— wife of Hugh Chearke, 161.
——— daughter of John, 51.
John, King of England, 8, 14, 23, 24, 30, 40, 41n. 51, 53, 69, 71, 77n, 78.
——— chaplain of Gilbert Talbot, 137.

John, son of Geoffry, 30.
—— son of Aidanus, 76, 155.
—— son of Simon, 175, 187.
—— le Irmongere, 76, 155.
—— the smith, 137.
—— Abbot of Flaxley, 1509—84, 86.
—— le Blunt, 166.
—— son of Leweric, brother of Faremon, 77, 160.
—— the clerk, 150, 151.
—— the chaplain, 189.
Johns, Rev. C. A., Forest Trees of Britain, 26n, 29.
Jordan, son of Ralph, 53n, 76, 173, 176.
—— son of John, 75, 115.
—— brother of Adam of Blakeney, 68, 143.
—— brother of Roger, 147.
—— le Saluer, 156.
—— son of Adam the smith, 154.
—— son of Richard, son of Alfred, 161.
Jorge, John, 97.

Kainesham (Keinesham), William de, 193.
Kais (Keis) William, Vicar of Dimor, 75, 157, 158.
Kes, William, 151, 152.
—— (Kais), Henry, Reeve of Gloucester, 65, 151, 152, 153, 154.
—— Henry, 76, 77, 113, 149, 150, 156, 173, 196.
—— Henry, son of Henry, 113, 174.
—— Osmund, father of Henry, 173.
—— Osmund, son of Henry, 174, 175.
Kelneswombe, Helias, 150.
Kenepet, Osmund de, 131.
—— Gunnora, wife of O. de, 131.
Kerr, Russell, J., of the Haie, near Newnham, 37n.
Kes, see Kais.
Ketel, Edric, son of, 6n.
Ketelb, Arnald, 151
—— Herbert, son of Arnald, 151.
—— Ernisius, son of, 173.
Keteford, Walter, 157.
—— Arnald of, 158.
Kinardesle, Hugh de, constable of St. Briavell's Castle, 23.

Kingston, Sir William, 33, 36, 67n, 80, 87, 88, 89, 90, 96, 119, 120, 121.
—— Sir Anthony, 43n, 67n, 89, 90, 121.
—— Edmond, 43n.
—— Edward, 67n, 90n.
—— Anthony, 43n, 90n.
—— William, 43n.
Kingswood, Vido, Abbot of, 53.
Kinvet, see Knivet.
Knif Seftan, 37, 68, 136.
Knivet, Robert, 46, 146, 170.

Lacey, Edmund, Bishop of Hereford, 84.
Lacy, Hugh de, 7.
Lamb, Hugh, 128.
Lancaster, Lord Henry of, 97.
—— Henry, Duke of, 117.
Lane, Thomas, 49.
Lauda, Mauld de, 132.
Ledene, Herbert de, 150.
Ledentun, Roger de, 159.
—— Henry de, 159.
Lefredus, 128.
Lege, Hubert, 195.
Legge, 132.
Leie, Hubert de, 194.
Leinch (Lench), Roger de, 72n, 146.
—— Roger, son of Richard de, 160, 170.
—— Margaret, wife of Roger de, 170.
Leland, Itinerary, 2, 3, 4, 5n, 12.
Lench, Peter of, 31.
Leweric (Luveric) Reeve of Newcham, 78, 136.
Llewelyn, King of Wales, 55.
Littletuna, Geoffry de, 136.
Lob, Reginald, 173.
Long, Roger, 129, 177.
Longchamp (Longo ca(m)po) Geoffry de, 74, 114.
Longley, William, 49.
Longney, Robert, 43n.
Longo (Ca(m)po), see Longchamp.
Lorimer, Geoffry le, 73, 196.
London, 26n.
Lovestreng, Richard de, 191, 192.
Lucie, daughter of Milo, Earl of Hereford, 3n

Index to Names of Persons. 205

Lucius, Pope, 3n.
Luefred, John, 177.
Lupus, John, 144.
Lufeftreng, Richard, 193.
Luverich (Luveric), John, fon of 160.
────── 70, 143, 162, 169.
────── the reeve, 155.
Luverithus (Luveric), 144.
Luverfteng, Richard, 192.

Mabilia, 128.
────── the nun, 131.
Macecrer, William le, 156.
Macci, fee Mark.
Maclean, Sir John, 7n, 62n, 64n, 99.
Madan, Falconer, 85n.
Mael (Mahel), fon of Milo, Earl of Hereford, 3n.
────── 177.
Maigne d'Arnis, 24n.
Mainhaggere, Robert, 177.
Malcuvenant, Walter, 128.
Malet, Robert, 42.
Mallerp, Henry, 188.
Manaffer, Jew of Briftol, 66, 77n, 186, 188.
Manwood, Treatife on the Foreft Laws, 18n, 19n, 22n, 23n, 24n, 33n.
Map (Mapes), Walter, 20, 79, 135, 163.
Mara, William de la, 61, 63, 114, 195.
────── Bertram de la, 63, 79, 195.
────── Matthew of, 33.
Marasc', Godfrey, 188.
Margery, daughter of Milo, Earl of Hereford, 3n.
Margaret, wife of Roger de Pultun, 70, 144.
────── wife of Roger de Bofco, 163.
────── daughter of Geoffry, fon of William, 73, 123.
────── wife of Herbert, 77, 175.
Mark (Macci), reeve of Abergavenny, 134.
Marmiun, Richard, 133, 134.
────── Henry, 140.
Marfh (Marifco), William de, 133, 134.
Marfhall, William, 72, 136, 174, 175, 189.
────── John "Juvenis," 175.
────── Humfridus, 175.
2 D

Martel, William, 186, 187.
Martin, 67n.
Mafcall, Robert, Bifhop of Hereford, 84.
Matilda (Maud), Emprefs, 4, 6, 9, 10, 17, 20.
────── wife of Richard de Erlingham, 65.
────── daughter of Dru, 131.
Maus, Walter de, 61, 65. 149, 150, 151.
────── Robert de, 61, 65, 113, 149, 150, 151, 152, 153.
────── Salerna, wife of Robert de, 149, 150.
────── Johanna, daughter of Robert de, 150
────── Walter, heir of Robert de, 149, 150, 151, 152, 153.
Mayhew, Richard, Bifhop of Hereford, 84.
Mercer, Henry, 173.
Merri, Ralph de, 188.
Merton, Walter of, 33.
Mew, Walter le, 155.
Michael, Prieft of Blechedun, 137, 139.
────── clerk, 175.
────── chaplain, 165.
Michel, Aliter Mael qu. vide.
Middleton, J.H., Prof., 92, 93.
Mill, Richard of the, 163.
Millecrofte, Symon, 129.
Milo, brother of Hugh le Petit, 136.
Mineriis, William de, 16n, 61, 63, 134.
────── Henry de, 16n, 61, 63, 64, 78, 114, 135, 136, 139, 140, 141, 163, 166, 168, 169.
Minfterworth (Munftrewithe, Munfterword).
────── Manaffes de, 35.
────── Roger, fon of Manaffes de, 35.
────── (Munstrewithe), Roger de, 72n, 115.
────── William de, 72, 115, 157, 162, 163, 166, 167.
────── Walter, fon of William de, 72n, 115.
Mog, Godfrey, 53n, 76, 172, 173.
Molis, Nicholas of, 33.
Monaftery (Monafterio), William of the, of Dimmock, 77, 159.
Monmouth, John of, Conftable of St. Briavell's Caftle, 24, 26, 27, 29, 30, 40, 78, 108, 131.
────── Gilbert de, 61, 62, 80, 130, 133.
────── Berta, wife of Gilbert de, 61, 79, 133, 162, 170.

Monmouth, James de, 79, 133, 134.
——— Thomas de, 69, 142.
——— . . . de, 172.
——— Nicholas de, 172.
——— Gruinard de, 172.
Moraduo, 188.
More, William de la, 131.
——— Geoffry de la, 176.
——— Geoffry, in 129.
Morevilla, William de, 186, 188, 189.
Morker, Hugh, 159.
Mors, William, 96.
Mortimer (Mortuo Mari), Hugh de, 115.
Morton, Alan de, 189.
Mortuo Mari, see Mortimer.
Muchegros, Hamelin, 135.
Muchelgros, Richard de, 136.
Munftrewithe, see Minfterworth.
Munftre, Mabilia de, 176.
Muriel, 69n, 113.
Mufchet, Robert, 46, 61, 65, 130, 147, 148, 149, 166.
——— Helena, wife of Robert, 147, 148, 149.
——— Robert, fon of Robert, 147, 148, 149, 166.
——— Hugh, 131.
Mylling, Thomas Bifhop of Hereford, 84.

Nafh, Dr., Collectanea for Worcefterfhire, 32n.
Nafmith, James, 1.
Navarre, Queen of, 97.
Neirun, William, 196.
Nerber, Philip de, 188.
Nefta, daughter of Griffin ap Llewelin, 5.
Nevill, Hugh of, 28, 115.
Nevyll, Ralph de, 117.
Neweham, Ofmund of, 76, 154.
——— Alfred of, 172.
——— Luveric de, 137, 138, 143, 144, 145, 146, 147, 156, 166, 170.
——— Gerald de, 137, 138.
——— Hugh de, 173.
——— Simeon de, 173.
Newmarch, Bernard de, 3n, 5, 10n.
——— Sybill, daughter of Bernard de, 3n, 5, 10n.
Nexe, William, 70, 142.

Nexe, Arnald, fon-in-law of William, 142.
Niblett, J.D. Thos., of Hareffield Court, Gloucefter, 12n.
Nicholas, Hiftoric Peerage, 3n.
——— IV., Pope, Taxation of, 46, 48.
——— Abbot of Flaxley (1288), 82, 85.
——— the clerk, 135.
——— chaplain of Gloucefter, 158.
Nicholls, Foreft of Dean, 2, 22n, 29, 30, 35, 36, 90, 98n.
——— Perfonalities of Foreft of Dean, 40n, 45.
——— Collectanea Topographica et Genealogica, 15.
Normandy, Henry, Duke of, 9n, 15, 16, 17n, 39.
Norreis, William, 189.
North, Thomas, 49.
——— Roger, 129.
Nunant, Aleis de, 188.

Obeffune, 133, 134.
Odon, Henry, fon of, 73, 113.
Oilli, Countefs Margaret de, 70, 114.
Oliver, Lord Protector, 33.
Orleton, Adam de, Bifhop of Hereford, 83.
Ofbert the Reeve, 74, 114.
Ofmund, 172.
Ofmund, R., 73, 113.
Ofward, 190.

Page, Walter, 42.
——— Elys, 42.
Pain Fitz John, 7.
——— Sibilla, wife of, 7n.
——— Cecilie, daughter of, 7.
Parcho (Parc.), William de, 36, 65, 130, 153, 154.
Paris, Roger de, 77, 156, 174, 196.
Patot, William de, Sheriff, 51.
Pauncefot, Grimbald, 42.
Payto, fee Peyto.
Penrys, John of, 42.
——— Rofa, wife of John of, 42.
Pentecofte, clerk, 175.
Perceval, 67n.

Percy, Henry de, 117.
Peter, Mafter, 170.
Peyto (Payto), Richard, Abbot of Flaxley (1372), 83, 86.
—— Thomas, 83.
Phelpis (Philpis), Adam, 48.
Phelps, J. D., of Chevenage Houfe, Gloucefter, 98n.
Phillipps, Sir Thos., of Middlehill, Co. Warwick, 13, 15, 59, 60, 64n, 66n, 69n, 77n. 80, 128n, 129n, 130n, 136n, 171n, 176n.
Philip, the clerk, 132.
Pie, Thomas, 151, 152, 158.
Pichard, John, 68, 135.
—— William, fon of John, 135.
—— Milo, 136.
—— William, heir of Milo, 136.
Pickering, W., 12n.
Picot, William, 188, 189.
Poer, William, 136.
Polton, Thomas, Bifhop of Hereford, 84.
Pomfrey, William, 89n.
Ponte, Robert de, 187.
Pope, Mrs. Mary, of Flaxley, 12n.
Porterel, Walter, 172.
Pultun, Ralph de, 70, 144.
—— Roger, fon of Ralph de, 70, 144.
—— Roger de, 130.
—— Godwin de, 70, 144.
—— Margaret, wife of Roger de, 144.
—— Nicholas de, 144.

Rabbayne Elya de, 33.
Ragel, Walter de, 61, 66, 67, 190, 193.
—— Walter, fon of Walter de, 190.
—— Robert de, 61, 66, 67, 190.
Ralph, the goldfmith, 156.
—— the huntfman, 142, 163, 167.
—— fon of Nicholas, 30.
—— the Welfhman, 129, 160.
—— of Cirencefter, bifhop, 115.
—— brother of Adam, fon of Peter, 131.
—— fon of Eilwi, 142.
Ranewin, Richard fon of, 139, 163, 167.
—— Reginald, brother of Richard, fon of, 163.

Rawin, 167.
Ready, Robert, 98.
Redley (Rodleia), Moyes de, 71, 136, 142, 163, 165, 167.
—— Margaret, wife of M. de, 165.
—— Ralph de, 74, 113, 165.
—— Henry de, 165.
Reginald, Mafter, 141.
—— fon of Walter, 51.
—— chaplain of Effelefworde, 151.
Renewin, 167.
Rewys, Nicholas, 85.
Richard I., King of England, 25, 26n, 28, 30, 38, 39, 50, 77n, 111.
—— II., King of England, 39, 44.
—— III.,   ,,   14.
—— Abbot of Flaxley or Dene, 71, 72, 76, 77, 78, 85, 143, 154, 155, 156, 157, 158, 159, 160, 161, 175.
—— Dean of Flaxley, 78, 143.
—— Sub prior of Bordefley, 53.
—— Bifhop of Salifbury, 115.
—— Earl Marfhall, 55, 56, 57.
—— facriftan of St. Peter's Abbey, Gloucefter, 151.
—— draperius, the mercer, 73, 113, 151.
—— the fmith, 154, 176, 177.
—— the prieft, 147, 148, 149.
—— prieft of Chirchefdun, 69, 142.
—— the clerk, 136, 152.
—— le Rus, 156.
—— le Hagan, 134.
—— de capella, 137.
—— the chaplain, 174.
—— fon of Baderun, 140, 149.
—— fon of Jordan, 142, 152, 153, 154, 156, 173, 176.
—— fon of Ralph, 144.
—— fon of Lefredus, 128.
—— fon of William, 145, 161.
—— fon of Hugh the knight, 164.
—— fon of Alfred, 146, 147, 161, 166.
—— of Thornbury, clerk, 186, 187.
—— John, 134.
Ris, Edric, 114.
Rivall, Peter of, 33.

Index to Names of Persons.

Riveria, Roger de, 186, 187.
Robert, the chaplain, 76, 154.
—— prior of Monmouth, 133, 134.
—— the rich, 129.
—— de Ponte, 175.
—— reeve of Abergavenny, 134.
—— chaplain of Minsterworth, 141.
—— chaplain of Gloucester, 158.
—— son of Ralph, 133, 134.
—— son of Bertram, 146, 147.
—— juvenis, 186, 187.
Roberts, Rev. G., Vicar of Monmouth, 12n, 41n, 42n.
—— Cal. Gen., 41n, 42n.
—— Roches, William, 129.
—— Des, Bishop of Winchester, 55.
Rodley, John of, 32, 109.
Roger, le Venur, 160.
—— the knight, 135.
—— son of Manasse de Minsterworth, 35.
—— son of Ralph, 113.
—— son of Hugh, 137, 155, 173.
—— le forester, 129.
—— son of Andrew, 147, 159.
—— Roi, 129.
—— son of Richard, 147.
—— carpenter of Dimmock, 131.
—— the chaplain, 175.
—— physician of Gloucester, 133, 134.
—— prior of Llanthony, 75, 132.
—— de . . . 75, 115.
—— son of Robert, 147.
—— le Norreis, 177.
Rolues, John, 85.
Ruardean (Ruwordin), Lawrence de, 131.
———————— Elyas de, 131.
———————— Oderic, dux de, 131.
———————— William, priest of, 131.
Rudder, 1, 5n, 82n, 83n, 99.
Rudeleia (Rudele), Helias de, 162, 170.
Rudge, Archdeacon, 1, 34, 35, 90.
Ruffus, Arnald, 131.
—— Daniel, 186, 187.
Rufus, John, 114, 196.
——— Richard, 142, 152, 154, 156, 174, 196.
—— Richard, son of Richard, 142, 153, 154.

Ruk, John, 74.
—— Adam, 74.
Rupe, Thomas de, 175.
Russell, Ralph de, 188.
Ruwordin, see Ruardean.
Rya, William de, Abbot of Flaxley (1314), 83, 85, 97.
Rymers, Fœdera, 7, 52.

Sabyn, John, chaplain, 44.
Sale, Adam, 128.
Salewerpe, Randolph de, 163.
Salisbury, Philip de, 175.
Salt Marsh (Salso Marisco), Peter de, 74, 113.
Samford, Hugh de, 175.
Sancta Cruce, Robert de, 186, 188, 189.
———————— William, son of Robert de, 188, 189.
Scepeshesed, Henry 74, 114.
Sciptun, see Shipton.
Scrudelone, 173.
Seilard, William, 177.
Service, Edward, 89n.
Sevarus, Palmer, 161.
—— son of Bernard, 175.
Sharpe, Edmund, Architecture of the Cistercians, 91, 92n.
Shaw, John, 89n.
Shipton (Sciptun), Osbert de, 165.
Shirley, Evelyn P., Deer and Deer parks, 37n.
—— Rev. Walter, Royal Letters Hen. III., 56
Shloclenis, Robert de, 136.
Sidebire, Richard, the smith, of, 131.
Simeon, 156.
—— the reeve, 154, 160.
—— of Newenham, 173.
Simon, the clerk, 159.
—— nephew of Geoffry, chaplain of Dimmock, 159.
—— (Symon), the cobbler, 129.
—— le mercer, of Gloucester, 173.
Simonis Maid, 177.
Smith (Smyth), Agnes, 89, 121.
Smyths, Berkeley, MSS., 43n.
Snodhull, Thomas, 44.
Soppegrave, William de, 128.
Sortegrave, Wizaundus de, 177.

Sortegrave, Malle de, 177.
Speed, 89.
Spelman, Gloffary, 37n.
Spichfet, Thomas, 131.
Spofford, Thomas, Bifhop of Hereford, 84.
Spondre, Ralph, 177.
Sprot, Walter, of Ragel, 67, 114, 191, 192.
—— Isabella, wife of Walter of Ragel, 192.
—— Walter, fon of Walter Sprot, 67, 191.
—— Robert, brother of Walter S., of Ragel, 67, 190, 191.
—— Robert, fon of Walter S., 114, 191.
St. Antony, 35n.
St. Benedict, 20.
St. Bernard, 20.
Sl. Briavells, Alex. de, 131.
St. George, Alan de, 175,
St. John, William de, 115.
St. Leger (Leodegarius), Hugh de, 135.
St. Leodegarius, William de, 61, 65, 66, 113, 130, 136, 185, 186, 187, 188, 189, 190.
St. Matthew, London, Philip de, 174, 175.
St. Nicholas, Thomas of, 150.
St. Quintin, Herbert de, 68n.
St. Sepulcre, Walter of, 189.
St. Valery, Matilda de, 62n, 134.
Stanbury, John, Bifhop of Hereford, 84.
Stantun, William of, 132.
Staura, Leffric (Leuverie) de, 16, 18, 40.
—— William de, 143, 162, 170.
Stephen, King of England, 1, 6, 7, 9n, 20, 26n.
—— le Norreis, 133, 134.
—— parson of Wunford, 191, 192.
Stephanum, Robert de, 33.
Sterman, Luveric, fon of, 154.
Stevens, Supplement, 1, 52, 85, 86.
Stubbs, Gloffary, 39n, 45n, 56n, 77n.
Stutefcumba, Richard de, 175.
Surdus, Robert, 75, 114.
Swein, Robert, fon of, 150, 151.
Swinfield, Richard, Bifhop of Hereford, 10, 82, 83.

Taillur, Giliana, 177.
Tape, William, 129.

Talbot, Richard, 42.
—— Gilbert, 42n, 68, 131, 137.
—— Adeline, wife of Gilbert, 137.
Tanner, Bifhop, Notitia Monaftica, 1, 13, 44, 86, 100, 101.
—— William of Littledean, 49, 96.
Tewkefbury, Abbot A. of, 75n, 158.
—— Annals, 9.
Thalamo, William de, 128.
Thibertun, fee Tibberton.
Thingeworde, Robert, priest of, 150.
Tholi, Robert, 69, 78, 136, 142, 148, 149, 152, 153, 154, 156, 174, 176.
—— Thomas, 196.
Thomey, Lucarney of, 31.
Thurbnus, 159.
Thuvericus, 160.
Tibberton (Thibertun), Thudricus de, 133, 134.
Tintern, William, Abbot of, 53.
Toli, fee Tholi.
Tracy, William, 97.
Traveleg, Walter de, 134.
Trefnant, John de, Bifhop of Hereford, 84.
Treget, Baderon de, 187.
Trilleck, John de, Bifhop of Hereford, 83.
Tripel (Trupel), Geoffry, 68, 193.
Tukelega, fee Tukeley.
Tukeley Amis de, 75, 114, 150, 151.
Turc, William, 71, 164.
—— M. wife of William, 164.
Turpin, Robert, 177.
Turri Imbervo, Nicholas de, 33.
Tynte, Sir Halfwell, 67n.
—— Sir Charles Kemys, 67n.

Upton . . . . de, 172.
Uthred, the clerk, 16.
Uvenat, William, fon of, 150.

Vallis Dore, Abbot A. of, 75, 132.
Vido, Abbot of Kingswood, 53.

W., Bifhop of Hereford, 181.
Wace, the cook, 73, 113.
Wadham, George, 89n.

2 E

Walcot, Mackenzie, Englifh Minfters, 20.
Waldebof, William de, 134.
Waleran, Abbot of, Dene, 20n, 53, 71n, 76n, 85.
────── (Walerande, Waldrand), Robert, Cuftos, 31, 32, 33, 109.
────── William, 175.
Walefword, Arnald de, 150, 151.
────── Jocelin, fon of Arnald de, 150.
────── John, brother of, Arnald de, 150.
────── Jocelin de, 152.
────── Milo, brother of Jocelin, 152.
Walfric, 16, 40.
Walmore (Walemore), Henry of, 142, 167, 168.
────── William of, 163, 168.
Walter, Conftable of England, 5, 6n.
────── le Karl, 161.
────── the chamberlain, 175.
────── fon of Walter the brewer, 161.
────── fon of Wibert, 153, 154.
────── fon of Hugh, 158.
────── le Hore, 77, 175.
────── clerk of Aure, 78, 138.
────── the clerk, 135.
────── le charbuner, 129.
────── le Hunte, 129, 147, 148.
────── brother of Geoffry, 151.
────── brother of Adam, fon of Fulco, 140.
Waltun, William de, 172.
Ware, fee Were.
Warwick (Warrewic), William, Earl of, 70, 144.
Waryn, William, 44.
────── the faddler (fellarius), 73, 113.
Webb, Rev. John, 10n, 82n, 101n.
Wemyfs Colchefter, Maynard, 37.
Were (Ware), Thomas, Laft Abbot of Flaxley, 49n, 84, 86, 87, 88, 96, 120.
Wermecombe, Richard, 49.
Weftbury (Weftbirie, Weftburia), Richard of, 51, 171.
────── (Weftburia), Roger de, 78, 135, 140, 141, 142, 145, 149, 153, 154, 157, 163, 165, 167, 168, 169.
Wefton, Geoffry of, 97.
────── ....dus de, 172.
Wevereth, Alfred, 128.
Whitminfter (Albo Monafterio), Geoffry de, 135.

Wibert, Walter, fon of, 153.
Wich, Walter de, 77, 175.
────── Ofbern, fon of Walter de, 77, 175, 176.
Wike, Peter de, 145, 160.
Wilintune, Ralph of, 114.
Will, Eustace de, 132.
William, Abbot of Flaxley (1277), 81, 85.
────── do.   do.   (1426), 84, 86.
────── Abbot of Bordesley. 53, 148.
────── Bifhop of Winchefter, 117.
────── Bifhop of Hereford, 61, 78, 143.
────── Prior of Kingswood, 53.
────── the vintner, 172.
────── the hermit, 40n, 78, 143.
────── the clerk, fon of Alfred White, 151.
────── the clerk, 175.
────── fon of Robert, fon of Martin, 66, 185, 187, 188, 189.
────── Ingareta (Angareta), wife of William, fon of Robert, fon of Martin, 188, 189.
────── fon of Milo, 130, 146.
────── .... 166.
────── fon of Hernifius, 174, 175.
Wimund, 150, 154.
Winterbourne, Roger of, 114.
Wintle, Henry, 43n.
Wiper, fee Wither.
Wifham, Ralph of, 133, 134.
Wither, Hugh, 148, 149, 166.
────── Roger, 148, 149.
Withorn, Robert, 129, 176.
Wodecoc, fee Woodcock.
Wodeham, John de, 73, 113.
Wood, Anthony á, 89.
Woodcock, William, 138.
Wycombe, William de, 11, 12.
Wyniatt, Thomas, of Staunton, Glouc., 59, 60
Wynyet, John, of Dymmocke, 49.
Wyrall, George, of Bicknor Court, 34n.

Yate, H. G. Dobyns, 12n.
────── Walter, of Arlingham, 49.
Yllun, Richard, 150.

INDEX TO NAMES OF PLACES.

Abbenhall (Abbenhale, Abenhall), 26, 27, 42, 45, 64n, 108, 141.
Abbots Wood, 31, 32, 33, 109.
Abergavenny (Bergevenia), 6n.
Adfett (Adcette), hamlet of Weftbury-on-Severn, 120.
Alba Domo, co. Montgomery, 57.
Aldefword, 157.
Alefword, 71, 156.
Alinvecroft, 69n, 113.
Alinveplot, 69n, 113.
Aquitaine, 17.
Ardlond (Ardland, Erdlond, Hardlande), 32, 40, 42, 78, 109, 110.
Arlingham (Erlingham, Herlingham), 43, 47, 49, 64, 65, 75, 88, 115, 119, 146, 147.
Arlyngton, 120.
Afhton, 54.
Afton Rowant, co. Oxon., 86, 88n.
Aura, 8.
Auft Cliff, 2n.
Auftin Friars, Dutch Church of, 33n.
Axbridge (Axebrugg), 47.

Bachineffeld, 176.
Barkeley, 49.
Bath, 47.
Battledown Knoll, Charlton Kings, Chelt., 15, 59.
Becoltefegge, 115.
Berdun, 147, 159.
Berkeley, 2n, 43n.
Berwick-on-Tweed, 118.
Befpwike, Fifhery of, 36, 73n, 75, 115.
Beryntone, 5.
Birchingrove, 26n.
Blachedun (Blacaduna), 185, 187.

Blagdon, 67n.
Blaifdon (Blefdon, Bleyfdon, Blechefdun, Blechedun), 25n, 26n, 27, 43, 44, 48, 62, 88, 119, 120, 137.
Blecheden, fee Blaifdon.
Bleytyes bayllye, bailiwick in Foreft of Dean, 42.
Bollewere, fishery of, 36, 65, 153, 154.
Bordefley, Abbey of, 20, 53, 58, 108, 117, 118.
Borfley, 96, 120.
Bofbury, 82, 83.
Bofeley, 26, 27, 28, 44, 108.
Botloe, hundred of, 37, 45.
Brademede (Bradenmeda), 150.
Bradens Coke, 54.
Brechen, 61, 62.
Brecknock, 5, 6, 10.
Bredon, 21n.
Brimpffield (Brumeffeld), 74, 75, 114, 115.
Brimftons Yatt, 26n.
Briftol Caftle, 5.
—— 24, 67n, 186, 188.
Broadwell Down, 67n.
Brocrigge, 177.
Bromefberrow (Bromefberie), 12n, 42.
Bruerne (Briuwerna), Manor, 43, 51.
—— land in, 65, 74, 75, 113, 114, 150, 152, 153, 154.
Brumeffeld, fee Brimpffield.
Budicumbe, fee Butcombe.
Budifield, 74, 114, 115.
Bunewei, 140.
Butcombe, 67n, 68n, 76, 130, 194, 195.
Buveveie, croft called, 75, 114.

Calveleye, 97.
Camp Hill, near Littledean, 36.

Index to Names of Places.

Carlyon (Carleon-upon-Uske), 57.
Casteyerd, see Castiard.
Casthard,   do.
Castiard (Casteyerd, Casthard, Castpard), valley of, 16, 17, 18, 19, 21, 22n, 26, 27, 28, 38, 63, 64, 78, 108, 135, 138.
Castpard, see Castiard.
Charkefeld, 72n, 115.
Chekeshull (Cheakeshull), 73, 113, 140, 168.
Cheltenham (Cilteham), 8, 15.
Cheringa, 175.
Chestnuts, enclosure in the Forest of Dean, 26n.
Chevenage House, Glouc., 98n.
Chormayles, 129.
Cilteham, see Cheltenham.
Cinderford (Sinderford), 31n, 32, 109.
Cirencester Abbey, 89n, 99. 101.
Clarendon, 110.
Claxhill, 120.
Cleilega, 71, 163, 171.
Cleve, 120.
Climperwell (Clymperwell), 47, 49, 75, 88, 114, 115, 119, 120, 132.
Colford, 49.
Cotswold Hills, 21.
Courtrai, 33n.
Coventry, 100.
Cranham (Croneham), 74, 114.
Croneham, see Cranham.
Cubewordin (Cubeworde), 69, 140, 163.
Cumbefmedewe, 69, 167.
Cupleforerde, 145, 160.

Deans Hill, 25n.
Dene (Dean), Forest of, 2n, 3, 6, 8, 9, 10, 12, 16, 17, 19, 20, 21, 22, 23, 25, 26n, 30, 31, 33, 35n, 37n, 41, 42, 46, 48, 64n, 71n.
——— Castle of, 16, 18, 36, 68.
——— 25n, 46, 61, 70.
——— Abbey, see Flaxley.
——— Magna, 64n.
Denny, 120.
Devizes, Castle of, 55.

Dimmoc, see Dymmock.
Dore, Abbey, 21, 58, 75, 118.
Duddemed, 67, 191, 192.
Dumfronte, 112.
Dunye, fishery of, 35.
Dymmock (Dymoc, Dimoc), 8, 16, 18, 37, 42, 45, 47, 49, 50, 61, 75, 77, 88, 119, 120, 128, 157, 158, 159, 177.

Edland, 16, 29, 32n.
Eileshulle, 71, 163, 171.
Eilfifcroft, 70, 145, 162.
Eifnfeld, 71, 163, 171.
Eiffele, 72, 194.
Elneton, 43.
Elvyngton, 120.
Emneia, see Emnet.
Emnet, 67, 130, 191.
English, Bicknor (Byknore), 9n, 27n. 64n.
Erdlond, see Ardlond.
Erlingham, see Arlingham.
Ermegrave, 24.
Eshul, 71, 156, 157.
Evesham, 17, 19.
Ewyas (Ewias), 7, 21.

Feldedich, 115.
Feneftegate, 114.
Fifbechefegge, 115.
Flax Bourton, co. Somerset, 68n.
Flaxley (Flaxele, Flaxle, Flexeley, Flixlege, etc.), Abbey—references passim.
——— Grange in Littledean, 89n.
Forstal, 169.
Fountains Abbey, 91, 95.
Fowliatt (Fulhiate, Fowlyatt), 26, 27, 108
Framilode (Framulard), 26n.
Fulhiate, see Fowliatt.
Furnace Yard, Flaxley, 35.

Index to Names of Places. 213

Garden Cliff, Weftbury-on-Severn, 37.
Garne, 45.
Gavells Gate, 26n.
Gawlett (Gawl yatt, Gallyat), 26n, 27n.
Gawletts yatt, 26n.
Gerne, 72, 166.
Glefmere (Glefmers), 146, 159.
Gloucefter, 2n, 5, 6, 11, 12, 29, 31, 33, 41, 54, 55, 73, 77, 90, 99, 113, 120, 156, 172, 196.
Golden Vale, 21.
Goodrich (Goodrych), 48, 88, 119, 120.
—— Caftle, 131.
Gordrodaker, 115.
Grace Dieu, Monaftery of, 40n.
Graces, 87.
Grandis Acra, 146.
Guns Mills, 35n.

Habeal, 44, 45.
Habewoldefham, 74, 114.
Haie, The, near Newnham, 37n.
Hailes, fee Hayles.
Halpefcroft, fee Hulpefcroft.
Hamcroft, 72, 113, 167.
Hamme, 141.
Hanecombe, 36, 70n, 115.
Hangmans Hill, 27.
Hardlande, fee Ardlond.
Hareffield, Court, Glouc., 12n.
Hafpool, fifhery at, 11.
Hawerdine, Lordfhip of, 7.
Hay traps, place called, in Dymmock, 37n.
Hayles Abbey, 89n, 99.
Heilith, 73, 74, 113.
Hepenill, 172.
Hereford Caftle, 5, 7, 8.
—————— Haies of, 7, 37n.
—————— 12, 48, 54, 83, 85.
Herlingham, fee Arlingham.
Hethamftede manor, 11.
—————— chaplain of, 148, 159.
Hide, 70n, 113, 169.
Hinewere, fee Hynewere.
2 F

Hivetenon, 137.
Holemede, 73, 113.
Holle, 120.
Hope Parifh, 26, 27, 62, 108.
—— vill of, 62, 133.
—— mill of, 62, 80, 130, 133.
—— brook, 26, 27, 108.
—— woods, 26n.
—— fhard, 26n.
Howle, 48.
Hulpefcroft, 72, 113, 167.
Huntley, 44, 62.
Hurft, 44.
Hynewere (Hinewere), Fifhery of, 36, 41, 63, 114.

Irchenfeld, 52.

Jufty Path, 26n.

Kenecoftre, 172.
Kenepel, 177.
Keynfham, 49, 54, 55.
Kingberge, 72, 194, 195.
Kings Barton, 43.
Kingfwood Abbey, 53, 89n.
Koftrick (Courtrai), 33n.

Lamufardere, 97.
Lanultyt, 43, 51.
Ledebiri, 172.
Lege, 113.
Leicefter, 100.
Le Monken, 88, 119, 120.
Levepeley, 74, 114.
Ley, Leye, 26n, 44.
Lincoln, 6.
Linleg, 65, 147, 148.
Littledean, 26n, 27, 31, 36, 89n.

Littlemore, 69, 141.
Llanthony Priory, near Gloucester, 2n, 4, 5, 11, 12, 89n, 129, 132.
—— Abbey, co. Monmouth, 4, 5.
London, Tower of, 5, 55, 88.
—— diocese of, 11.
—— de Cheringa, 72, 174, 175.
—— 130, 174.
Longhope, 42, 43, 44.
Longlands, 71.
Luggewardine, Lordship of, 7.

Margan, 57.
Marlborough, 7n.
Micheldean, 26n, 62n, 71n, 89n.
Middichill, 13, 59.
Middleton, 72, 170.
Millfield, Flaxley, 35.
Minsterworth (Minstredwrd), 8, 120.
Monkhill, 27.
Monmouth, 2n, 41, 47, 54, 57.
Mynsterworthe, see Minsterworth.

Neath (Neth), 57.
Nemnet, 67n. 68n.
Newland (Nova Terra), 46, 49, 87, 88, 89n, 119, 120.
Newlond, see Newland.
Newerre (Nowere), 16, 18, 35.
Newnham (Newenham, Newneham, Newcham, Niweham), 2n, 16n, 34, 35, 37, 43, 48, 65, 68, 70, 72, 76, 77, 88, 119, 120, 136, 137, 138, 142, 145, 154, 155, 161, 166.
—— vill of, 8, 10.
Newnham's Pill, 25n.
Niwent, 177.
Northden, 40, 41.
Northampton, 100.
Northwode, 44, 113.
Northwood, 18, 37, 73, 120.
Nuneaton, 17n.

Oaklands, near Newnham, 31n.
Ombercrofte, 150.
Ope, see Hope.
Otleg (Otlege), 73, 113.
Oxford, 6n, 7, 85.

Painswick, 89.
Parva, Dene, 22n, 26, 49, 88, 96n, 108, 119, 120.
Penros, 54.
Pershore, 41.
Piresforlong, 153, 154.
Pirisfeld, 149.
Plymouth, 54.
Polton (Pultun), 48, 70n, 88, 113, 119, 120.
Poultons Hill, 25n.
Pudding Hill, 27.
Pulmede, 16, 18, 37, 64, 139.
Pulton, see Polton.

Quedgeley Court, 12n.

Rachelbury, 67, 190.
Rademoor, 41.
Ragel, 65, 114, 185, 186, 187, 188, 189.
Ragelbury (Regilbury), 66, 67, 190, 191, 193.
Ragiol, 67n.
Rareham, 26n.
Redlen, 8.
Redley (Redlege), 16, 18, 73, 74, 112, 113.
Regill (Regil), 67.
—— Manor of, 68n.
Reidley, 18, 35, 37.
Resmes, 149.
Reveneshokesfeld, 74, 114.
Rewarden, see Ruardean.
Rheims, 11.
Ridge Hill, Winford, co. Somerset, 67n
Rievaulx, 97.
Rinlega, 149.

Index to Names of Places. 215

Roan, 10n.
Rochellesbury (Rochelbury), 49, 88, 119, 120.
Rochester Castle, 5.
Rodley Manor, 25n, 45.
—— (Rodeleye), 35, 37. 44.
Rodmarton, 85.
Rome, 180.
Ross, 52.
—— Hayes of, 10, 37n.
—— Manor of, 10.
Roughway (Ruggerweye, Rugeweye, Rugweye), a road called, 32, 109.
Ruardean (Ruwarthin, Rewarden, Ruwordin), 40, 41, 88, 119, 120, 131.
Ruddekeshale, 68, 137.
Ruddle, 35.
Ruding, 69n, 71, 73, 113, 165.
Rugeweye, see Roughway.
Ruggemore, 24.
Rumsey, 76, 173.

Salisbury, 76, 173.
Seddestowe, 47.
Seilesseld, 159.
Severn River (Sabrina, Saverna), 2n, 8, 21, 36, 37, 41, 65, 70n, 73, 113, 114, 115, 196.
Seymour's Mill, 26n.
Shapridge, 27.
Side furlong (Sude furlong), 147, 159.
Sinderford, see Cinderford.
Sloo, hamlet in Arlingham, 43n.
Slymbrydge, 49.
Smalham, 74, 113.
Smallbrooke (Smalebroke), 32, 109.
Sodbury Hill, 21n.
Sollewell, 44.
Springwella, 149.
St. Albans, 6n.
St. Anthony's Well, 34, 35n, 36.
St. Augustines (Austines) Abbey at Bristol, 89n, 101.
St. Bernard's College in Oxford, 87n.
St. Briavell's Castle, 5n, 6, 8, 9, 10, 23, 24, 28, 30, 31, 40, 41, 51, 54, 55, 56, 86, 87, 88.

St. Briavell's forest, 25.
—— —— vill of, 44.
—— —— hundred of, 25n, 44.
—— —— hermitage of, 40n.
St. Dionysius, monks of, 70, 142.
St. Oswald's Priory, near Gloucester, 2n.
St. Peter's Abbey in Gloucester, 4, 5, 10, 40n, 70n, 87, 89n, 99, 101.
St. Sepulcres Hospital at Gloucester, 70n, 142.
Stangarst, 69n, 113.
Staunton, 49, 59.
Stielweie, 114, 115.
Stoke, 68n.
Stonhouse, 47.
Strata Florida, co. Cardigan, 57.
Sudeley (Suthleg), 31, 32, 109.
Sudefurlong, 159.
Sugwas, 83.
Sulley, 44.
Suthlege, see Sudeley.
Symond's Yat, 27n.

Tatemouncspslade, 114.
Tavistock, 100.
Taynton wood, 40n.
Tewkesbury, Abbey, 54, 89n, 99, 101.
Thame, 86, 88n.
Thetford Priory, 17n.
Thikegrove, 114.
Thirlestaine House, Cheltenham, 13, 15, 59, 136n.
Thornbury, 2n.
Tibberton, 62.
Tinbridge, 26n.
Tintern (Tyntharn) Abbey, 21, 48, 54, 55, 57, 92.
Torsthalle, 70, 162.
Tortworth, 26n.
Tribnell, 74, 113.
Trivele, forest of, 7.
Tuckelegn, see Tukeley.
Tukel, 114, 195.
Tukeley, 75n, 149.
Tunberhugge, 22n.
Tunbrug (Tymbrugg), 26. 27, 108.

Tureford, 54, 55.
Tymbrigge, see Tunbrug.

Ulnegate, 69, 113.

Vallis Dore, 75, 132.
Vincents Land, 18, 38.

Wadestok, 56.
Wadleie (Wodlege) 69, 113, 141, 163.
Wake Mill, 96.
Walden Abbey, 17n.
Wales, 2n, 55.
Wallmore (Walmore, Walemore, Walmoure), 18, 26n, 37, 46, 48, 65, 69, 72, 88, 115, 119, 120, 136, 147, 148, 163, 166.
Wallmoreshall, 69n, 113.
Walsebyre, see Welchbury.
Wastadene, 16, 18, 36.
Welchbury (Walsebery, Walsebyrie), 22n, 26, 27, 108.
Welipulle, 69, 163.

Wells, 47.
Westbury-on-Severn, 2n, 21n, 26n, 28, 35, 37, 43, 45, 48, 62, 72, 79, 85, 89n, 166.
Westmere (Westmers), 145, 146, 159, 160.
Westminster, 6n, 9n, 111, 115, 117, 120, 121.
Weston, 120.
Westwalle, 145, 160.
Wevelscomb, 101.
Whitelega, 71, 163, 171.
Wildemore, 113.
Wilton, Lordship of, 7.
Wincheombe Abbey, 89n, 99.
Windsor Castle, 62n.
Winford, 67n, 68n.
Witeleia, see Whitelega.
Wlnegate, see Ulnegate.
Wodecrofte, 114.
Wodelege, 113.
Wlstedeswelle, 114.
Wrplesfwei, 160.
Wrugehat, 75, 114.
Wudelond, 70, 162, 169.
Wye (Waye) River, 2n, 8.

INDEX TO SUBJECTS.

Abbenhall, fee Index of Places.
——— identified by Nicholls with "Habeal" in Hundred Rolls of Edw. I., 45.
Abbey of Flaxley, Church of, 25.
——— Abbots' Room in, 90, 91, 95.
——— Hofpice (Hofpitium), 73, 94; Cart. No. 96.
——— chapter house, fee Plates IV. and V., 92, 95.
——— cellarium or domus converforum, 94.
——— ground plan by Mr. J. H. Middleton, fee Plate VI., 94.
Abbots of Flaxley, 85.
Abbot Waleran, 20n, 53, 71n, 76n, 85.
——— Alan, 20n, 53, 65, 71n, 76, 85, 148.
——— Richard, 71, 72, 76, 77, 78, 85, 143, 154, 155, 156, 157, 158, 159, 160, 161.
——— William (1277), 81, 85.
——— Nicholas, 82, 85.
——— William de Rya, 83, 85, 97.
——— Richard Peyto, 83, 86.
——— William (1426), 84, 86.
——— Berkeley, 85, 86.
——— John, 84, 86.
——— William Beawdley, 84, 86, 87.
——— Thomas Were, 49n, 84, 86, 87, 88, 96, 120.
Abbots' Room at Flaxley Abbey, 90, 91, 95.
——— roof of, fee Plate III., 90.
Abbot's Wood, granted to Flaxley Abbey, 31, 32, 33.
Abergavenny, Caftle and Honour of, granted by Emprefs Maud to Earl Milo, 6n.
Annales Monaftici, Rolls Series, 14, 52, 54.
Affarts or Effarts, term explained in Manwood's "Foreft Laws, 18n, 22n.

2 G

Atkyns, Sir R., Hiftory of Glouceflerfhire, 11, 5, 24, 99
Attachments, Court of, 33n.

Baronage, Dugdale, 1n, 3, 5, 6, 7, 9, 10n.
Benedict, Saint, rule of, 20, 81, 82, 84.
Benedictine Order of Monks, 20.
Bernardines, a name fometimes given to Ciftercian monks, 20.
Bigland, Hiftory of Glouceflerfhire, 2, 21n, 28, 46 90 91, 92.
Bleytyefbayllyc, bailiwick in the Foreft of Dean, 42.
Books of Flaxley Monks, 60, 79, 80.
——— provifion for repair of, 62, 80, 133.
Bote, Houfe-bote, hay-bote, plow-bote, 24.
Botloe, hundred of, 37, 45n.
Bovey (Boeve), Mrs. Catherine, The "perverfe widow" of Sir Roger de Coverley, 33n, 34n.
Brecknock, Honour of, 6, 10n.
Browne Willis, "Mitred Abbeys," 52, 85, 86, 89n, 101
Bulls of Privilege, 61, 79, 81.
Burgh, Hubert de, infurrection of, 55,
——— men of Richard, Earl Marfhall, take refuge at Flaxley Abbey, 55, 56, 57.

Cableicium or Cablicia defined by Maigne D'Arnis, 24n.
Camden's "Golden Vale," 21.
Camden Society, publications, 10n, 20n, 21n, 82n
Cartæ Antiquæ, Calendar of Sir Jofeph Ayloffe, 14, 15n, 33, 38, 39.

Cartulary of Flaxley Abbey, 59.
———— original roll in Phillipps' Library at Middlehill, 59.
———— transcribed by late Sir Thomas Phillipps, and a portion privately printed by him, 59.
———— transcript copied by Mr. Fitzroy Fenwick, 59.
———— general contents of Cartulary, 61.
———— names of private benefactors, 61 to 73.
———— additional benefactors in confirmation charter of 11 Henry III., 73 to 75.
———— grants to Flaxley Abbey by ecclesiastics, 75.
———— grants by Abbot Alan on behalf of the Convent, 76.
———— grants by Abbot Richard, 76, 77.
———— agreement between Abbot Richard and William the Hermit, 78.
———— names of chief witnesses, 78.
———— Papal bulls of Privilege, 79.
———— catalogue of books, 79, 80.
———— text of Cartulary in extenso, 123 to 196.
Castiard Valley, meaning of name, 26n.
Catalogue of books in Flaxley Abbey Cartulary. 60, 79, 80.
Cellarium at Flaxley Abbey, 94.
Chantries near Flaxley, 89n.
Chapter House at Flaxley Abbey, 92, 95.
Charta de Foresta of 9 Hen. III., 22n.
Charter Rolls, Classified list of references to Flaxley Abbey, 105.
———— quoted, 8, 31n, 36n, 40n, 65n.
Chesnut Woods in Forest of Dean (Bosci castanearum), 26n, 28.
Chesnuts, Tithe of, in Forest of Dean, 16, 18.
———— name of forest enclosure, 26n.
———— timber, 26n, 29.
Cistercian, Flaxley a Cistercian Abbey, 20, 101.
———— rules for situation of Cistercian Abbeys, 21n.
———— Walter Map's description of Cistercian monasteries, 20.
———— Tintern, Dore and Flaxley, typical Cistercian Abbeys, 21.

Cistercian, Sharpe's Cistercian Architecture quoted, 91, 92n, 94, 95.
———— Persecution of Order by King John, 53.
Clare, Gilbert de, burial at Tewkesbury, 54, 55.
Clerical Subsidies, 52.
Close Rolls, classified list of references to Flaxley Abbey, 104, 105.
———— quoted, 23, 24, 25, 28, 29, 30, 31, 40, 41, 50n, 51, 55, 56, 57.
Coffin lids of stone discovered at Flaxley A.D. 1788, 92, 95.
Collectanea Glocestriensia quoted, 98n.
Collectanea Topographica et Genealogica, Nicholls, 15.
Collinson, History of Somersetshire, 67n, 68n.
Common of Pasture in Forest of Dean, 18, 22, 48
Confirmation charters, granted to Flaxley Abbey, 39, 40.
Corrody charged on Abbey at dissolution, 89.
Cowchers, great, Duchy of Lancaster Records, 9n.
Cox, History of Gloucestershire, 1.

Deanery of Forest of Dean, 12.
Dean, Abbey and Forest, see Dene.
Deer in Forest of Dean, 22n, 23, 41.
———————————— " fence month," 23.
———————————— Charta de Foresta, 9 Hen. III., 22n.
Deer and Deer Parks, by Evelyn P. Shirley, quoted, 37n.
Dene Abbey, see Flaxley Abbey.
———— Old Castle of, 16, 16n, 18.
Dene Forest, see Index of Places.
———— granted to Earl Milo by the Empress Maud, 6.
———— grant not recognised by Stephen, 9 and 9n.
———— reformed by Henry II., 8.
———— Flaxley Abbey founded within forest limits, 10, 16, 17, 19, 20.
———— grant to Flaxley Abbey of Castiard Valley, 16, 17.
———— meaning of name Castiard, 26n.
———— Placita de Foresta of 10 Edw. I., 22n.

Index to Subjects.

Dene Foreſt, grant of eaſements to Flaxley Abbey within the foreſt, 22, 23.
——— grants of wood and timber, 24 to 28.
——— tithes of cheſnuts from the foreſt, 28, 29.
——— grant of iron forge, 29.
——— grant of Abbots Wood, 31.
——— ſtationary forge, 34.
——— deanery of, 12.
——— perambulations, 25n, 46.
——— Roger Clifford, bailiff of, 30.
——— Robert Waleran, cuſtos of, 31.
——— William de Dene, "King's Foreſter, 16n, 37, 51, 61, 63, 64, 135, 138.
——— Alexander Bleyght, foreſter in fee, 41.
——— William Hatheway, keeper of, 42, 71n.
——— Grimbald Pauncefot, keeper of, 42.
——— Geoffry de Dangel, Juſtice of, 30.
——— Nicholls Hiſtory of, 2, 22n, 29, 30, 35, 36, 90, 98n.
Dignity of a Peer of the Realm, Lords' Report, 8, 50n.
Diſſolution of Glouceſterſhire Abbeys, 89n.
Domeſday Survey, 23n, 37n.
Domus Converſorum at Flaxley Abbey, 91, 94.
Duchy of Lancaſter Records quoted, 5n, 6n, 7n, 9, 9n, 10n, 14, 16n, 97, 98.
——— Regiſter of Royal Charters, 6n.
——— Great Cowchers, 9n.
Durham, Rites of, 93.

Earl, dignity of, 7.
Edward III., King, viſits Flaxley Abbey, 41, 53n.
——— ſuſpends Abbot of Flaxley, 57.
Engliſh Minſters, by Mackenzie Walcot, 20.
Eſtovers, meaning of term in foreſt law, 24.
Evelyn's "Silva," 26n.

Fence Month, term explained, 25.

Firewood, ſpecial grants to Abbey for, 25 to 28.
Fiſheries belonging to Flaxley Abbey.
——— Hynewere, 36, 41, 63, 114.
——— Bollewere, 36, 65, 153, 154.
——— Beſpwike, 36, 73n, 75, 115.
——— Dunye, 35.
——— Newerre or Nowere, 16, 18.
Fiſh ponds at Flaxley (ſtagna, vivaria et piſcariæ), 36, 71, 119, 157.
Flax Bourton, co. Somerſet, named from Flaxley in Glouceſterſhire, 68n.
Flaxley Abbey, otherwiſe called Dene Abbey, 1.
——— foundation of, 1 to 12.
——— date of foundation, 1, 2, 12.
——— founded by Roger, ſon of Milo Fitzwalter, Earl of Hereford, 1, 2, 4, 5.
——— to commemorate death of Earl Milo, 3, 4.
——— Chronicler's account of Earl Milo's death, 3, 4.
——— Biſhop of Hereford aſſiſts to build Flaxley Abbey, 2, 11, 12.
——— public records relating to, 13, 14, 15.
——— foundation charters, 15 to 20.
——— Flaxley a Ciſtercian Abbey, 20, 21.
——— ſaid to have been colonized from Bordeſley Abbey in Worceſterſhire, 20.
——— grant of common of paſture, 22, 23.
——— grants of wood and timber, 24, 25.
——— ſpecial grants for firewood, 25 to 28.
——— tithes of cheſnuts, 28, 29.
——— grant of an iron forge, 29.
——— grant of Abbots' woods, 31 to 33.
——— ſtationary forge at Flaxley, 34.
——— grants of fiſheries, 35.
——— miſcellaneous grants in charter of Henry II., 36.
——— protection Charter of Richard I., 38.
——— Royal confirmation charters, 38, 39.
——— other grants to Flaxley Abbey, 40.
——— viſits of Edward III. and ſpecial grant, 41, 116.
——— Inquiſitions and licences to aſſign land to the Abbey, 41 to 44.

Flaxley Abbey, Hundred Rolls of Edw. I., 44, 45.
— Taxation of Pope Nicholas, 46, 47.
— Valor Ecclefiafticus of Hen. VIII., 47 to 49.
— Flaxley Abbots, fummoned to Parliament, 50.
— Mifcellaneous references to the Abbey, 50 to 52.
— Vifitation of Ciftercian Abbeys in A.D. 1187, 52.
— Vifits of King John to the Abbey, 53, 54.
— Abbot attends burial of Gilbert de Clare at Tewkefbury A.D. 1230. 54, 55.
— men of Richard, Earl Marfhall, take refuge at Flaxley Abbey, A.D. 1233-34, 55 to 57.
— Abbot witneffes fettlement of difpute between Abbots of Margan and Carlyon, A.D. 1256, 57.
— Abbot fufpended for mifconduct A.D. 1335, 57, 58.
— Cartulary of the Abbey, 59 to 73 and 124 to 196.
— Confirmation charter of 11 Hen. III., 73 to 75.
— grants to Abbey by ecclefiaftics, 75 to 77.
— agreement with William the Hermit, 78.
— chief witneffes to deeds in Cartulary, 78, 79.
— Papal Bulls of Privilege, 79.
— Catalogue of books in Abbey Library, 79, 80.
— regifters of Bifhops of Hereford, 81 to 85.
— Berkeley Abbot, 85.
— lift of Abbots, 85, 86.
— printed ftate papers, 86 to 88.
— Abbey diffolved 4th Feb. 1536, 88.
— granted to Sir William Kingfton, 88, 89.
— granted to Sir Anthony Kingfton, 89, 90.

Flaxley Abbey, exifting monaftic remains, 90, 91.
— remains difcovered in 1788, 91 to 93.
— Mr. Middleton's paper on Flaxley Abbey, 93 to 95.
— original deeds of Thomas Were, laft Abbot, 96.
— Abbot's feal, 96 to 99.
— rank and ftatus of Abbots, 99 to 101.
Foreft laws, Manwood's Treatife quoted, 18n, 19n, 22n, 23n, 24n, 33n.
Foreft trees of Britain, by Rev. C. A. Johns, 26n, 29.
Forge, fee iron forge.
Fofbroke, Hiftory of Glouceflerfhire, 2, 34, 35, 36, 89.
Foundation charters of Flaxley Abbey, 15 to 20.
Frouceftre Abbot, MS. Chronicle quoted, 4.
Fuller's Church Hiftory quoted, 100, 101.
Furnace Yard, named from Flaxley iron furnace, 35.

Garden Cliff, Weftbury-on-Severn, 37.
Gefta Stephani quoted, 3, 4.
Gloucefter, Honour of, 6.
— Caftle, 5, 6, 29.
Glouceftershire, As fure as God is in, 101.
Glouceftershire, Hiftory of, Sir R. Atkyns, 1, 15, 24, 99.
— Rudder, 1, 5n, 82n, 83n, 99.
— Bigland, 2, 21n, 28, 46, 90, 91, 92.
— Rudge, 1, 34, 35, 90.
— Fofbroke, 2, 34, 35, 36, 89.
— Cox, 1.
Golden Vale, Camden's defcription of, 21.
Guns Mills near Flaxley, 35n.

Habeal Abbas de, Hundred Rolls of Edw. I., 44.

Index to Subjects.

Habeal, Abbas de, referred to in Nicholl's "Personalities of the Foreſt of Dean," 45.
—————— name not identified, 45.
—————— fuppofed by Nicholls to be identical with Abbenhall, 45.
Hawking, Eyries of Hawks referved to the King, 32n.
Hayes, 37, 7on.
Henry II., Charter to Roger, Earl of Hereford, 8.
Hereford, Earl of, Milo Fitzwalter, created by Empreſs Maud, 7.
—————— Roger, ſon of Milo, created by Henry II., 7.
—————— title diſcuffed in Lords' Report on the Dignity of a Peer, 8.
—————— Henry de Bohun, created by John, 8.
Hereford, Biſhops of, Robert de Betun, 4, 10, 11, 12.
—————— Gilbert Foliot, 11, 12.
—————— Hugh Foliot, 56.
—————— John le Bretun, 81n.
—————— Giles de Braofe, 62n.
—————— Thomas de Cantelupe, 15, 56, 76n, 79, 81, 82.
—————— Richard Swinfield, 10, 82, 83.
—————— Adam de Orleton, 83.
—————— Thomas Chorlton, 83.
—————— John de Trilleck, 83.
—————— Ludovic Charlton, 83.
—————— William Courteney, 83, 84.
—————— John Gilbert, 84.
—————— John Trefnant, 84.
—————— Robert Mafcall, 84.
—————— Edmund Lacy, 84.
—————— Thomas Polton, 84.
—————— Thomas Spofford, 84.
—————— Richard Beauchamp, 84.
—————— John Stanbury, 84.
—————— Thomas Mylling, 84.
—————— Richard Mayhew, 84.
—————— Charles Booth, 84.
Hereford, Caftle of, 7.
—————— haies of, 7.
Hermitage of Ardlond, 40, 143.
—————— in Taynton wood, 40n.

Hermitage at St. Briavell's, 40n.
—————— Rev. E. L. Cutts quoted, 40n.
Hokeday, 72n, 164, 168, 169, 170.
Honour of Brecknock, 6, 10n.
—————— of Glouceſter, 6.
—————— of Abergavenny, 6n.
—————— of Hugh de Lacy, 7.
Hooper, Biſhop, burnt at Glouceſter, 90.
Hoſpitium at Flaxley Abbey, 95.
Hundred Rolls of Hen. II. and Edw. I., 14, 44, 45.

Infangentheof, 39, 39n.
Inquiſitions poſt mortem, 14, 41, 42, 43, 44, 106.
—————— ad quod damnum, 14, 41, 42, 43, 44, 106.
Iron forge at Flaxley, 16, 18, 25n, 29.
—————— forgiæ errantes or itinerantes, 29, 30, 31.
Itinerary of Leland, 2, 2n, 5n.
—————— of King John, by Sir T. Duffus Hardy, 53, 54.
—————— of Henry II., by Rev. R. W. Eyton, 9n.

Jews, their perfidy noticed, 77, 154, 161, 176.
—— capitula de Judæis, A.D. 1194, 77n.
—— articles 10 and 11 of Magna Charter, 77n.
John King, viſits Flaxley Abbey, 53, 54.
—————— Charter to Henry de Bohun, 8.

Keynſham (Keyſhem) Abbey, 49, 54, 59.
King's Foreſter, title of William de Dene, 16n, 64.
Kingſton pedigree, paper by Mr. W. C. Heane, 89n.
Kingſton, Sir William, Conſtable of St. Briavell's Caſtle, 87.
—————— Sheriff of co. of Glouceſterſhire, 87.
—————— Conſtable of Tower of London, 88.
—————— firſt grantee of Flaxley Abbey at diſſolution, 88.
—————— died A.D. 1540, buried at Painwick, 89.
Kingſton, Sir Anthony, Provoſt Marſhall in 1549, 89.

Kingston, Sir Anthony, Commiffioner at Bifhop Hoopers execution, 89.
——— receives from the Crown a new patent for the Flaxley eftates, 89.

Letters and Papers, foreign and domeftic, Hen. VIII., 1519 to 1523, 86, 87.
Lives of the Saints, by Alban Butler, quoted, 35n.
Llanthony Priory near Gloucefter, fee Index of places.
——— founded by Earl Milo A.D. 1136, 4.
——— Earl Milo buried there, 5.
——— controverfy with St. Peter's Abbey, Gloucefter, 4, 5.
——— William de Wycombe, Prior, 11, 12.
——— relic of, at Flaxley, 12n.
——— "Some account of Llanthony Priory," by Rev. G. Roberts, Vicar of Monmouth, 12n.
Llanthony Abbey in Monmouthfhire, founded by Walter the Conftable, 5.
——— Walter the Conftable buried there, 5.
——— Robert de Betun, prior, 4.
Loudon's Arboretum, quoted, 26n.

Manor of Flaxley in Arlingham, 43n.
——— Bruerne, 43.
——— Rodley, 25n, 45.
——— Dimmoc, 45.
——— Habeal, 44.
——— Regil in Winford, co. Somerfet, 68n.
——— Rofs, 10.
Map (Mapes) Walter, De Nugis Curialibus, quoted, 20n.
——————— witneffes charters, No. 10 and 54 in the Cartulary, 79.
Materials for the Hiftory of Henry VII., quoted, 86.

Milo Fitzwalter, fon of Walter, Conftable of England, 5.
——————— councillor of Henry I., 5.
——————— married Sybill daughter of Bernard de Newmarch, 5.
——————— patron and founder of Llanthony Priory near Gloucefter, 4.
——————— received from Henry I. the Honour of Brecknock, etc., 6.
——————— received from Stephen the Honour of Gloucefter, with cuftody of Tower and Caftle there, 6.
——————— also Barony of Brecknock and all offices and lands poffeffed temp., Hen. I., 6.
——————— received from Empreſs Maud, St. Briavell's Caftle and Foreft of Dean, 6.
——————— created Earl of Hereford by Empreſs Maud, 7.
——————— received Caftle of Hereford, etc., 7.
——————— excommunicated by Bifhop of Hereford, 4.
——————— accidentally killed in Foreft of Dean while hunting, 3.
——————— account of death by John of Hexham and Gervafe of Dover, 3.
——————— date of death, Chriftmas Eve, A.D. 1143, 3.
——————— controverfy regarding his burial, 4, 5.
Mitred Abbey, term explained, 99 to 101.
——————— Flaxley, not a Mitred Abbey, 99.
——————— ftatement of Atkyns Rudder and others on this point, difcuffed 99, 100.
——————— Cowel, Godolphin and Fuller's "Church Hiftory" quoted, 100.
——————— Browne Willis' "Mitred Abbeys" 52, 85, 86, 89n, 101.
Monafticon Anglicanum, by Dugdale, 1, 13 17, 48n, 50, 67n.
Monkhill farm at Flaxley, 27.

Index to Subjects.

Neweham (Niweham) burning of, 72, 166;
———————— maladeria de, 145.
Newlond, lordship of, 87.
Notitia Monastica, by Bishop Tanner, 1, 13, 44, 86, 100, 101.

Oblata Rolls, 14, 51.
Observations on Iron Cinders by George Wyrall, 34n.
Old Castle of Dene, 16, 18, 36, 37.
Originalia Rolls, 14, 51.
Outfangthefe, 39, 39n.

Pannage, term explained, 23, 23n.
Parliament, writs of summons to Flaxley Abbots, temp. Ed. I., 50.
———————— number of Parliamentary Abbots, 100. 101.
Patent Rolls, 14, 35n, 36n, 41n, 43n, 44n, 58n, 119.
Perambulations of Forest of Dean, 25n, 46.
Pipe Roll, 14, 50, 51.
Placita de quo warranto, 14.
———— forestæ de Dene, of 10 Edw. I., 14, 22n, 26n.
Private benefactors of Flaxley Abbey, 61 to 73.
Protection Charter of Richard I., 38.
Public Record Office, List of references to Flaxley Abbey, 104, 105, 106.
Puche or Puchin, term explained, 36, 70n.
Purlieus in Forest of Dean, 46.
Purprestures, 22n.

Refectory at Flaxley Abbey, 91.
Regill in Nemnot parish co. Somerset, a cell to Flaxley Abbey, 67n.
Registers of Bishops of Hereford, 13, 81 to 84.
Richard, Earl Marshall's men take refuge at Flaxley Abbey, 55, 56, 57.
Richard I. grants protection charter to Flaxley Abbey, 38.

Richard I. grants the woods around the Abbey for firewood, 25 to 28.
Roberts, Rev. G., "Some account of Llanthony Priory," 12n.
———— Cal. Gen., 41n, 42n.
Roger Fitz Milo, son of Milo, Earl of Hereford, 2, 3, 7.
———————— married Cecilie, daughter of Pain Fitz John, 7.
———————— position of Roger at Earl Milo's death in 1143, 9n, 10, 19, 20.
———————— assumed title of Earl of Hereford, 9n.
———————— formally created Earl of Hereford by Henry II., 7, 8.
———————— founds and endows Flaxley Abbey within forest limits, 2, 10, 16, 18, 19, 20.
———————— benefactor of fee of Hereford, Abbey of St. Peters, Gloucester, and Monks of Brecknock, 10.
———————— forces William of Wycomb, Prior of Llanthony to resign, 11.
———————— became a monk of St. Peter's Monastery at Gloucester, 5n.
———————— died 1155, exact date unknown, 5n.
———————— buried in St. Peters at Gloucester, 5 and 5n.
Ross, hayes of, 10.
Royal Society of Literature, 60, 80.
Rudder, History of Gloucestershire, 1, 5n, 82n, 83n, 99.
Rudge, History of Gloucestershire, 1, 34, 35, 90.
Rymers Fœdera, 7, 53.

Sac, 39, 39.
Seal of Abbots of Flaxley, 96.
———— one original feal (A.D. 1534) of Thomas Were, last Abbot, preserved at Flaxley Abbey, 96.
———— one original feal attached to deed of 10 Ed. II. (A.D. 1316), Westminster Chapter House Records, P.R.O., 97.

Seal, one original feal attached to deed of 9 Ed. II., (A.D. 1315), Duchy of Lancaster Records, P.R.O., 97.
—— 2 Flaxley Seals in Doubleday collection of British Museum, 98.
Sheep cot, licenfe to keep in Ruwarthin and Northden, 40.
Soc, 39, 39n.
Sokemannus, 45.
Solda (Selda) Du Cange, 68n.
Somerfetfhire eftates of Abbey of Flaxley, 67n, 68n.
Stephen King, Royal Charters of, 6n.
—————— grants to Milo the Honour of Gloucefter, 6.
—————— capture of, in battle of Lincoln, 6.
St. Anthony's Well at Flaxley, 34, 36.
—————— fire, 35n.
St. Briavell's Caftle (fee Index of Places) granted to Earl Milo by Emprefs Maud, 6.
—————— refumed by Henry II., 8.
—————— conftables of, John of Monmouth, 24, 29, 30, 40, 78.
—————— Walter Afmoins, 30.
—————— Hugh de Kinardefle, 23.
—————— Hugh de Nevill, 28.
—————— James Frefel, 31, 51.
St. Peter's Abbey at Gloucefter, 4, 5, 10.
St. Sepulchre's Hofpital at Gloucefter, 70, 142.
Surrenden Collection of MSS. quoted, 5n.
Sufpenfion of Abbot of Flaxley A.D. 1335, 57, 58.
Swinfield, Bifhop's Roll, Abftract and Illuftrations of, by Rev. John Webb, 10n, 101n.

Taxation of Pope Nicholas A.D. 1292, 46.
Tewkefbury Annals, 3n, 9n, 54.
Theam, 39, 39n.
Tithes of Dymmock, 75.
Tol, 39, 39n.
Tortworth, celebrated chesnut tree, 26n.

Twyfden Collection, 3.

Valor Ecclefiafticus of Hen. VIII. A.D. 1534, 47 to 49, 67n.
Verderer (Viridarius), one who had charge of the vert and venifon, 24.

Walter the Conftable, 4.
—————— built Gloucefter Caftle on his own demefne lands, 4.
—————— built alfo caftles of Briftol, Rochefter, and Tower of London, 5.
—————— patron and founder of Llanthony Abbey in Wales, 5.
—————— became a Canon Regular of Llanthony Abbey, 5.
—————— died at Llanthony, buried in Chapter Houfe, 5.
Were, Thomas, laft Abbot of Flaxley, 86, 87, 88.
—————— turned out of the Abbey at the fuppreffion in A.D. 1536, 86.
—————— died at Afton Rowant, Oxon. A.D. 1546, 86.
—————— two original deeds at Flaxley Abbey, 96.
Weftbury, hundred of, 37.
Weftbury-on-Severn, Mr. Bainham of, 2.
—————— Walter Map, Incumbent of, 21n.
—————— Nicholas Rewys, Vicar of, 85.
Weftminfter Chapter Houfe Records, 14, 97. 98.
White Monks, a name given to Ciftercians, 2n, 20.
Writs of Summons to Parliament, 50.
Wycombe, William de, Prior of Llanthony, near Gloucefter, 11.
—————— biographer of, Robert de Betun, 11.

LIST OF SUBSCRIBERS.

LARGE PAPER COPIES (45).

No. 1. Crawley-Boevey, Sir Thos. H., Bart., Flaxley Abbey, Newnham, Glouc.
,, 2. Maclean, Sir John, F.S.A., Glafbury House, Richmond Hill, Clifton.
,, 3. James, Francis, Efq., Edgeworth Manor, Cirencefter.
,, 4. Fawn, James, 18, Queen's Road, Briftol.
,, 5. Guife, Sir William V., Bart., F.L.S., F.R.G.S., Elmore Court, Gloucefter.
,, 6. Heane, W. C., Efq., The Lawn, Cinderford, Gloucefter.
,, 7. Eaftwick, Capt. W., 12, Leinfter Gardens, Hyde Park, W.
,, 8. Church, A. H. Efq., Shelfey, Kew, Surrey.
,, 9. Stubbs, Mifs, Penyard Houfe, Wefton, Rofs, Herefordfhire.
,, 10. Baker, W. Proctor, Efq., Briflington, Briftol.
,, 11. Bruton, H. W., Efq., Bewick Houfe, Gloucefter.
,, 12. Crawley-Boevey, E. B., Efq., 7, Alexandra Terrace, Penzance.
,, 13. } Gibbs, H. Martin, Efq., Barrow Court, Flax-Bourton, Somerfet.
,, 14. }
,, 15. Adlam, William, Efq., The Manor Houfe, Chew Magna, Somerfet.
,, 16. Cooke, W. H., Efq., Q.C, 42, Wimpole Street, London.
,, 17. Jones, Rev. Canon C. J., Weftbury-on-Severn, Gloucefterfhire.
,, 18. Kerr, Ruffell J., Efq., The Haie, Newnham, Gloucefterfhire.
,, 19. Lothian, The Moft Hon. the Marquis of, Newbattle Abbey, Dalkeith, N.B.
,, 20. Gwinnett, W. H., Efq., Gordon Cottage, Cheltenham.
,, 21. Ducie, The Right Hon. the Earl of, P.C., F.R.S., Tortworth, Falfield, Gloucefterfhire.
,, 22. Rifley, Rev. W. C., Shalftone Rectory, Bucks.
,, 23. Crawley, Rev. H., Stowe, Weedon, Northamptonfhire.
,, 24. Dorington, Sir J. E., Bart., M.P., Lypiatt Park, Stroud.
,, 25. Thorp, Difney Launder, Efq., M.D., Lypiatt Lodge, Cheltenham.
,, 26. Dancey, Charles H., 6, Midland Road, Gloucefter.
,, 27. Mefham, Arthur (Major), Pontryffydd, Bodfari, Rhyl.
,, 28. Guife, Francis E., Efq., Dean Hall, Newnham, Gloucefter.
,, 29. Gibbs, Henry Hucks, Efq., Aldenham Houfe, Elftree, Herts.
,, 30. }
,, 31. } Gibbs, Mrs. William, Tynteffield near Briftol.
,, 32. }

List of Subscribers.

,, 33. Pickering, Mrs., 23, Queen's Gardens, Hyde Park, W.
,, 34. Daubeney, Gen. Sir H. C. B., G.C.B., Ofterley Lodge, Spring Grove, Ifleworth.
,, 35. Campbell, Sir James, Bart., Whitemead, Coleford, Gloucefter.
,, 36. Colchefter-Wemyfs, M. W., Efq., Adfett Court, Weftbury-on-Severn, Gloucefter.
,, 37. Cokayne, George E., Efq., F.S.A., Norroy King of Arms, College of Arms, London, E.C.
,, 38. Doggett, Edward G., Efq., 31, Richmond Terrace, Clifton, Briftol.
,, 39. } Oliver, Edmund, Efq., 19, Brechin Place, South Kenfington, S.W.
,, 40.
,, 41. Downing, W., Efq., Olton near Birmingham.
,, 42. Phayre, Lieut.-Gen. Sir R., K.C.B., 64, St. George's Square, Pimlico, S.W.
,, 43. Bute, The Moft Hon. the Marquis of, K.T., Cardiff Caftle, Cardiff.
,, 44. Fox, Francis F., Efq., Yate Houfe, Chipping Sodbury.
,, 45. Referved by the Author.

LIST OF SUBSCRIBERS.

SMALL PAPER COPIES (100).

Ackers, B., St. John, Esq., Huntley Manor near Gloucester.
Asher and Co., 13, Bedford Street, Covent Garden, W.C.
Baker, Mrs. Barwick, Hardwicke Court, Gloucester.
Bartleet, Rev. S. E., St. Mark's Vicarage, Gloucester.
Bazeley, Rev. W., Matson Rectory, Gloucester.
Birch, Mrs., Tyn-y Coed, Bettwys-y-Coed, North Wales.

Clark, G. T., Esq., F.S.A., Dowlais House, Dowlais.
Cokayne, G. E., Esq., F.S.A., College of Arms, London, E.C.
Cowburn, Major, T. B., Donnell Hill, Chepstow.
Crawley, W. S., Esq., Sea Bank, Liscard, Cheshire.
Crawley-Boevey, Sir Thos. H., Bart., Flaxley Abbey, Newnham, Gloucestershire.
Crawley-Boevey Dow., Lady, Flaxley Cottage, Newnham.
Crawley-Boevey, Rev. R. L., Flaxley Vicarage, Newnham.
Crawley-Boevey, Miss, Flaxley Cottage, Newnham.

Daubeny, Major Edward, Spring Grove, Isleworth.
Daubeny, William, Esq., Stratton House, Park Lane, Bath.
Daubeny, Rev. John, Winkfield Vicarage, near Windsor.
Deane, Rev. J. B., M.A., 20, Sion Hill, Bath.
Derham, Walter Esq., F.G.S., Henleaze Park, Westbury-on-Trym, Bristol.
Downing, W., Esq., Olton near Birmingham.

Fawn, James, Bookseller, 18, Queen's Road, Bristol.
Fenwick, T. Fitzroy, Esq., Thirlestane House, Cheltenham.
Flux, E. H., Esq., Cotswold, Bishopswood Road, Highgate, London, N
Fox, C. H., Esq., M.D., The Beeches, Brislington near Bristol.
Freeman, E. A., Esq., LL.D., Somerleaze, Wells, Somerset.
Fryer, K. H., Esq., late Maitland House, Gloucester.

Gibbs, H. Hucks, Esq., Aldenham House, Elstree, Herts.
Gibbs, Mrs. William, Tyntesfield near Bristol.
Godwin, J. G., Esq., 118, Grosvenor Road, London, S.W.
Gray, Henry, Bookseller, 25, Cathedral Yard, Manchester.

List of Subscribers.

Greenfield, Benjamin Wyatt, Esq., 4, Cranbury Terrace, Southampton.
Grist, W. C., Esq., Brookside, Chatford, Stroud.

Hale, C. B., Esq., Claremont House, Gloucester,
Hall, Rev. R., Saul, Stonehouse.
Hamilton, Mrs., 13, Ildersley Grove, Dulwich.
Hanby, Richard, Esq., Chetham's Library, Manchester.
Hardy, Rev. H. H., Micheldean Rectory, Gloucestershire.
Harrison, Robert Esq., London Library, 12, St. James Square, S.W.
Hatherton, Lady, Teddesley, Penbridge, Stafford.
Horner, J. F. F., Esq., Mells' Park, Frome, Somerset.
Howard, J. J., Esq., F.S.A., Dartmouth Row, Blackheath, Kent.
Hyett, F.A., Esq., Painswick House, Painswick, Stroud, Gloucester.

Lewis, W. T., Esq., The Murdy, Aberdare, South Wales.
Lindsay, W. A., Esq., Q.C., Portcullis Pursuivant of Arms, 17, Cromwell Road, South Kensington.
Lucy, W. C., Esq., F.G.S., Brookthorpe, Gloucester.
Lynam, C., Esq., Stoke-upon-Trent.

Norris, H. Esq., Swalcliffe Park, West Banbury, Oxon.

Oakeley, Rev., W. Bagnall, M.A., Newland, Coleford, Gloucester.
Overall, W. H., Esq., Corporation Library, Guildhall, London.

Page, Lieut.-Gen. George Hyde, 5, Tavistock Road, Westbourne Park, London, W.
Page, Miss, 16, Somerset Place, Bath.
Palin, Rev. E., Linton, Ross.
Percival, E. H., Esq., Kimsbury House, Gloucester.
Price, W. P. Esq., Tibberton Court, Gloucester.

Raitt, E. R. Esq., Broughtons, Newnham, Gloucester.

Sayer, J., Esq., Pett Place, Charing, Kent.
Sherard, Miss, M. E., Fairthorn, Parkstone, Dorset.
Sherborne, Rt. Hon. Lord, 2, St. James Place, London, S.W.
Simpson, J. J., Esq., Lynwood, Cotham Gardens, Bristol.
Skrine, Henry Duncan, Esq., Claverton Manor, Bath.
Somers, The Rt. Hon. Lord, Cliffords Mesne, Newent, Gloucester.
Sutton, C. W., Esq., Public Free Library, Manchester.

Trubner and Co., 57 and 59, Ludgate Hill, E.C.

Wagner, H. Esq., F.S.A., 13, Half Moon Street, London, W.
Wasbrough, H. Sydney, Esq., 7, Gloucester Row, Clifton.
Webb, E., Esq., Blaisdon Hall, Newnham, Glouc.
Wetherell, Mrs., Church House, St. Leonards-on-Sea.
Williams, J. A. A., Esq., Clan Benno, Carnarvon, North Wales.
Wintle, James, Esq., The Cottage, Newnham, Gloucester.

Yonge, Miss, Elderfield, Otterbourne, Winchester.

ERRATA ET ADDENDUM.

Page 26, Note line 10, for Michael read Michel.

" 32, Note 4, add the following words : " to powerful nobles and retainers of the King."

" 33, Note 3 line 3, for 1670 read 1570.

" 51, Line 13, for " x mare " read " x marc."

" 54, Line 3 from end, for " quierit " read " quievit."

" 56, Note 1 line 3, for " adarma " read " ad arma."

" 69, Line 13, for " father " read " brother."

" 87, Line 6, for " Hen. VII." read " Hen. VIII."

" 100, Line 4, for " Report " read " Repert."

" 108, Cart. Line 14, for " Rofeley " read " Bofeley."

" 124, Cart. 4, for " Dofe " read " Dore."

" 125, Cart. 41, for " Tremongere " read " Iremongere."

" 125, Note, for " feperate " read " feparate."

"NOTE.—While thefe fheets are paffing through the prefs my attention has been called to Mr. F. W. Maitland's valuable work, entitled 'Pleas of the Crown for the County of Gloucefter, A.D. 1221,' publifhed by Macmillan and Co. This work contains feveral references to the Flaxley monks in connection with the Crown pleas of the Foreft of Dean and the Hundred of Weftbury on Severn."

NOTE ON WALTER MAP, Conf. p. 79.

At page 79 the queſtion has been raiſed whether the Walter Map who appears as a witneſs in Cart. No. 10 and 54 of the Flaxley Cartulary can be identified with the well-known author of "De Nugis Curialium," and other works in proſe and verſe. A doubt was expreſſed whether this hypotheſis is conſiſtent with the date of Cart. No. 54, viz., A.D. 1195. According to Mr. Thomas Wright, who has edited for the Camden Society in 2 volumes the works of Walter Map, he was a great favourite of King Henry II., and was made Canon of the Churches of Saliſbury and of St. Paul's in London, precentor of Lincoln, incumbent of Weſtbury-on-Severn in Glouceſterſhire, with many other beneſices. He was finally appointed Archdeacon of Oxford; and according to Thomas of Walſingham this appointment was made in A.D. 1197.

Walter Map is believed to have died circ. 1210; and is ſaid to have held the Archdeaconry of Oxford and the parſonage of Weſtbury to the end of his life.

He was remarkable for his bitter hoſtility to the Ciſtercian Order of Monks. According to Giraldus de Barri, generally known as Giraldus Cambrenſis, who was an intimate friend of Walter Map, this hoſtile feeling originated in the encroachments of the Monks of "Newenham" on the rights and property of the Church of Weſtbury-on-Severn. On this ſubject ſome remarkable and very intereſting teſtimony is afforded by an extract from the "Speculum Eccleſiæ" of Giraldus de Barri, printed by Mr. Thomas Wright for the Camden Society. This extract ſtands as Appendix III. of Mr. Wright's Introduction to the poems attributed to Walter Mapes. The extract is headed "Further account of Walter Mapes from the Speculum Eccleſiæ of Giraldus," which work is the chief authority for the life of Walter Map. The extract in queſtion is taken from MS. Cotton, Tiberius B. XIII. fol. 62, r°, and was publiſhed in 1843.

It is perfectly clear from internal evidence that the whole extract relates to the Ciſtercian Monks of Flaxley or Dene, whoſe Monaſtery is deſcribed by Giraldus as ſtanding, "in limbo "foreſtæ de Dene non procul a Newenan, fundatum olim in loco ubi comes Herefordiæ Milo "ictu ſagittæ caſuali ad feram miſſæ perforatus letaliter fuit."

This paſſage ſeems to leave no doubt regarding the Monaſtery referred to by Giraldus. The pariſh of Weſtbury-on-Severn is diſtant about 2 miles from Flaxley Abbey; and it is clear from the Cartulary and foundation Charter that the Flaxley monks had large poſſeſſions in the pariſh of Weſtbury. The field, or meadow ſtill known as Pulmede, mentioned in the foundation charter, is ſituated in Weſtbury; and there are numerous references in the Flaxley Cartulary and Abbey records to Claxhill, Walmore, Boſeley and other hamlets of the ſame pariſh of Weſtbury-on-Severn. The whole extract ſhows that there was much ill-feeling between the Monks of Flaxley and Walter Map, Archdeacon of Oxford and Incumbent of Weftbury, on account of the alleged encroachments of the monks on the rights and property of the Church of Weftbury. Mr. Wright alludes in the introduction to Walter Map's Latin poems, publifhed 1843, to the encroachments of the monks of "Newenham," referred to by Giraldus; but he does not appear to have enquired who thefe monks of "Newenham" were, nor to have fixed the identity of the Monaftery referred to. In point of fact there was no religious houfe at Newenham or Newnham-on-Severn at all; and the reference of Giraldus to the fcene of Earl Milo's death in the Foreft of Dean clearly eftablifhes the identity of the Monaftery referred to. The Ciftercian Abbey of Flaxley or Dene was in fact the only religious foundation in that neighbourhood; and the Flaxley Cartulary fhows that the monks had feveral poffeffions in Newnham which adjoins Weftbury, and is diftant from Flaxley Abbey about three miles only.

If then we may affume on the grounds fhown that the interefting printed extract from the "Speculum Ecclefiæ" of Giraldus de Barri refers to the Ciftercian Monks of Flaxley, the query in the text feems to be fufficiently anfwered; and it may apparently now be accepted that the well known Walter Map, Incumbent of Weftbury, and Archdeacon of Oxford was a near neighbour and intimately acquainted with the Flaxley Monks, and was in all probability the fame Walter Map, who appears as a witnefs in Cart. No. 10 and 54.

The fact that the Ciftercian Monaftery of Flaxley or Dene apparently furnifhed to Walter Map and to Giraldus de Barri materials for their fatirical attacks on the order of White Monks is of fome importance; and the connection now difcovered will, perhaps, add increafed intereft both to the extract from Giraldus' "Speculum Ecclefiæ," printed for the Camden Society, and to the prefent notes on Flaxley Abbey.

Since the publication of the works of Walter Map (Mapes) by the Camden Society, thofe of Giraldus Cambrenfis, including the "Speculum Ecclefiæ," have been publifhed in the Rolls Series in feven volumes. The "Speculum Ecclefiæ" is contained in vol. iv, edited by Mr. J. S. Brewer, M.A., 1873. Distinctio III, cap. xiii, contains an account of the fecret drinking and gluttony of the Ciftercians, with fome amufing anecdotes of Henry II and the Monks of Dene, at p. 213. See alfo preface, p. 41. Cap. xiv contains an account of the witticifms of Walter Mapes againft the Ciftercians, relates that he was incumbent of Weftbury on Severn, and gives an amufing account of his relations with the Abbot and Monks of Dene. At page 201 of the fame volume, Flaxley Abbey (Flexleia) is again referred to in a difcreditable connection, a fifter of John of Monmouth having been compelled or induced by the Abbot to take the veil.

www.ingramcontent.com/pod-product-compliance
Lightning Source LLC
Chambersburg PA
CBHW021410230426
43666CB00006B/698